Assumptions About Human Nature

This book is dedicated to the memory of my mother.

Assumptions About Human Nature

IMPLICATIONS FOR RESEARCHERS AND PRACTITIONERS

Second Edition

Lawrence S. Wrightsman

SAGE PUBLICATIONS
The International Professional Publishers
Newbury Park   London   New Delhi

For information address:

 SAGE Publications, Inc.
2455 Teller Road
Newbury Park, California 91320

SAGE Publications Ltd.
6 Bonhill Street
London EC2A 4PU
United Kingdom

SAGE Publications India Pvt. Ltd.
M-32 Market
Greater Kailash I
New Delhi 110 048 India

Printed in the United States of America

Wrightsman, Lawrence S.
    Assumptions about human nature : implications for researchers and
practitioners / Lawrence S. Wrightsman. — 2nd ed.
        p.   cm.
    Includes bibliographical references and indexes.
    ISBN 0-8039-2774-6 (cl.).   — ISBN 0-8039-2775-4 (pb.)
    1. Attitude (Psychology) 2. Psychology. I. Title.
BF327.W75 1991
150—dc20   91-26209

Sage Production Editor: Astrid Virding

Contents

Preface

During such difficult times as these it is particularly important to explore our assumptions about human nature, since these assumptions underlie our reactions to specific events. The first edition of this book described a comprehensive program of research on the development of an instrument to measure our assumptions about people in general. Even though that edition is no longer in print, demand for information about the measurement of assumptions about human nature continues.

Counseling psychologists, in particular, have found that philosophies of human nature are especially useful as they seek to understand and assist their clients. Hence, this second edition has been prepared in order to achieve several goals: (1) to place the study of assumptions of human nature within the context of the ever-increasing cynicism in our society, (2) to report on the construction and validation of the Philosophies of Human Nature Scale, a measure of these assumptions, and (3) to review these concepts and measures from a social-psychological viewpoint while also considering the insights of other approaches, including philosophy, literature, and political science. Different chapters in the book deal with different recent issues in social-psychological research, such as the unidimensionality of attitudes, the relationship of attitudes to behavior, and the influence of social movements on beliefs.

Organization of the Book

Chapter 1 is a personal statement regarding the importance of studying assumptions about human nature. This chapter proposes that assumptions about people play a role in everyone's behavior, that psychology and sociology as scientific disciplines have promoted certain assumptions and have overlooked others, and that until recently these fields have neglected the study of assumptions about human nature held by everyone. The rest of this book is devoted to alleviating this neglect.

Chapter 2 reviews the historically predominant assumptions about human nature. It concludes by identifying four types of assumptions held by differing schools of psychology and by discussing the implications of these beliefs. Thus the chapter demonstrates that Western civilization has always speculated about human nature, although the particular assumptions have varied over time.

The theory behind the construct of "philosophies of human nature" is presented in Chapter 3, which places this construct within the network of current psychological thinking.

The measurement of philosophies of human nature is described in Chapter 4. Chapter 5 presents group differences on the scales devised to measure these philosophies, while Chapter 6 relates philosophies of human nature to other individual-differences variables.

An attitude measure is of less value if it cannot be shown to relate rather consistently to behavior, even after moderator variables are taken into account. In Chapter 7, the evidence for philosophies of human nature as an influence on behavior (including cardiac problems) is reviewed and placed within the recent controversy over the functional importance of attitudes.

Chapter 8 and Chapter 9 consider how assumptions about human nature develop, while Chapter 10 reviews attempts to change these assumptions. Chapter 11 looks toward novel approaches to the study of assumptions about human nature, focusing particularly on the assumptions held by members of communal groups.

The Appendices contain the items, scoring procedures, and factor analyses of the various scales developed in the research program.

Acknowledgments

The research program on philosophies of human nature began 30 years ago. Thus, chronologically at least, my acknowledgments should begin with the two children of Maureen and Bob Behrens, who in 1961 were a graduate-student couple at George Peabody College for Teachers. At that time, showing a state of noblesse oblige manifested only by young assistant professors, I associated not only with graduate students but also with their children. From the Behrens offspring I caught the measles, an indignity that not only humbled me, an adult, but also required that I remain in bed for two weeks.

It was during this period that boredom forced me to assess my professional development and, specifically, my research interests. In the three years since I had completed my graduate work, I had spent my available research time dabbling in various then-faddish social-psychological topics. I felt the need to concentrate on one issue and I sought one that also met some personal needs.

At that time I was trying to evaluate and coalesce my beliefs about human nature. Experiences as a newspaper reporter and college professor had shaken my earlier stance of unconditional trust. The social-psychological study of assumptions about human nature seemed not only overdue but potentially rewarding personally. Now, 30 years later, I can express satisfaction for the interest shown in my ideas by some psychologists, educators, and students.

In carrying out the research on philosophies of human nature reported in this book, I received grants-in-aid from George Peabody College, the Society for the Psychological Study of Social Issues, the University of Hawaii, and the University of Kansas. A Biomedical Sciences Support Grant financed many of the studies described in Chapter 7. Two long-term research grants to Stuart W. Cook from the National Institute of Mental Health and the U.S. Office of Education were instrumental in the development and validation of the measurement devices described n Chapter 4.

Completion of the research and writing that are new to this second edition was greatly facilitated by a sabbatical leave provided me by the University of Kansas during the 1990-1991 academic year. I wish to thank Dr. Del Brinkman, Vice Chancellor for Academic Affairs, and Dr. Edwin Martin, Chair of the Department of Psychology, for their support.

Over the years I have been blessed by my association with a number of graduate students whose efforts and insights have benefited this program of research; these include Carolyn W. Ashcraft, Jack A. Nottingham,

George W. Baxter, Norma Baker, John O'Connor, Robert Claxton, Lois C. Stack, Marilyn King, Barbara Hearn Jacobs, Carl E. Young, Carl M. Rogers, Jonatha Atyas, Leslie Wuescher, Maria Taranto, Louise Ward, Bill Wright, Bob Bruininks, William Lucker, David Catron, LaVeta Ligon, David McMillan, Heidi Steinitz, and Julie A. Weir. Also, undergraduates Clifford Uejio, David Mack, and Kelly Brusewitz contributed significantly to the research program. Over the years, at various times, colleagues Frank C. Noble, the late Barbara Wallston, John Harvey, Richard Gorsuch, J. R. Newbrough, Stuart Oskamp, and Jim O'Neil have been supportive when I needed such encouragement.

Once again, Terry Hendrix of Sage Publications deserves credit for urging me to put my ideas on paper and for easing the task of doing so. I wish to thank especially Katia Silva, who typed most of the chapters of this edition, and Bea Gray, who pitched in when I needed help.

—LAWRENCE S. WRIGHTSMAN

CHAPTER ONE

The Pervasiveness of Assumptions About Human Nature

I do not say it is good; I do not say it is bad; I say it is the way it is.

— TALLEYRAND

A recent book titled *The Cynical Americans* (D. L. Kanter & Mirvis, 1989) marshals logic, observation, and empiricism to argue that cynicism has become rampant in American life. The authors' survey, based on a representative sample of adults in the United States, concludes that 43% of these respondents fit the profile of the cynic, "who sees selfishness and fakery at the core of human nature" (D. L. Kanter & Mirvis, 1989, pp. 1-2). (For more detailed results of this survey, consult Boxes 1.1 and 1.2.)

Cynicism, at its foundation, reflects beliefs about human nature. The authors of *The Cynical Americans* propose that three factors act together to create this cynical outlook. First, the individual forms unrealistically high expectations of other people, as well as of himself or herself. These expectations generalize to expectations of institutions, like schools and the government, and of the future, including the future of one's children. Second, the individual experiences disappointment in him- or herself and in others, with concomitant feelings of frustration and failure. Third, the final result is disillusion, "the sense of being let down or letting oneself down, and more darkly, the sense of being deceived, betrayed, or used by others" (D. L. Kanter & Mirvis, 1989, p. 3).

Recent events serve as dry holes in this barren expanse of depressed environment. A U.S. president who runs on a platform of "Read my lips; no new taxes" changes his mind a year after the inauguration. Insider trading on Wall Street leads to a few well-publicized convictions, but also to some punishments that — in the eyes of many observers — fail to fit the crime. Television evangelists are exposed as paragons of hypocrisy, greed, and perverse sexuality. Widespread drug use seems uncontrollable.

1

Responses to Questions About Human Nature

D. L. Kanter and Mirvis (1989) administered the questions listed below to a representative sample of adults. The first figure under each choice of response is the percentage of adults who chose that response. The second figure is the percentage of University of Kansas freshmen who chose the response.

On some items the adults and the college freshmen do not differ in response. In response to the statement "Most people will tell a lie if they can gain by it," however, 84% of the college students agreed, whereas 60% of the adults did. Also, on the statement, "Most people are just out for themselves," 62% of the students agreed, compared to 46% of the adults.

The statements and responses were as follows:

Agree Strongly	Agree Slightly	Slightly Disagree	Strongly Disagree	

How much do you agree that . . . ?
Most people will tell a lie if they can gain by it.

| 29% | 31% | 27% | 13% | Adults |
| 35% | 49% | 14% | 3% | College freshmen |

People claim to have ethical standards regarding honesty and morality, but few stick to them when money is at stake.

| 25% | 37% | 27% | 11% | |
| 16% | 58% | 22% | 5% | |

People pretend to care more about one another than they really do.

| 23% | 35% | 28% | 14% | |
| 12% | 36% | 39% | 13% | |

It's pathetic to see an unselfish person in today's world because so many people take advantage of him or her.

| 30% | 23% | 20% | 26% | |
| 20% | 32% | 24% | 24% | |

Most people are just out for themselves.

| 19% | 27% | 35% | 19% | |
| 20% | 42% | 28% | 10% | |

Most people inwardly dislike putting themselves out to help other people.

| 14% | 32% | 34% | 20% | |
| 10% | 33% | 43% | 14% | |

Most people are not really honest by nature.

| 11% | 23% | 34% | 32% | |
| 7% | 26% | 49% | 18% | |

Gender Differences in Responses to Statements

The students' responses in Box 1.1 may be divided by gender, in an attempt to understand further the determinants of attitudes. The first figure under each response choice in this box is the percentage of freshman males; the second figure is the response rate of freshman females. Note that for every statement, men's responses are equally cynical or more cynical than women's; the percentage agreeing by statement is as follows: #1, Males, 82%, Females, 83%; #2, Males, 79%, Females, 65%; #3, Males, 54%, Females, 40%; #4, Males, 52%, Females, 51%; #5, Males, 69%, Females, 53%; #6, Males, 48%, Females, 36%; #7, Males, 38%, Females, 26%.

This gender difference, with regard to philosophies of human nature, is analyzed in Chapter 5.

Agree Strongly	Agree Slightly	Slightly Disagree	Strongly Disagree	

How much do you agree that . . . ?

College students

Most people will tell a lie if they can gain by it.

| 42% | 40% | 15% | 3% | Males |
| 25% | 58% | 14% | 3% | Females |

People claim to have ethical standards regarding honesty and morality, but few stick to them when money is at stake.

| 16% | 63% | 16% | 4% |
| 16% | 49% | 28% | 7% |

People pretend to care more about one another than they really do.

| 16% | 38% | 32% | 13% |
| 7% | 34% | 46% | 14% |

It's pathetic to see an unselfish person in today's world because so many people take advantage of him or her.

| 21% | 31% | 25% | 23% |
| 18% | 33% | 23% | 26% |

Most people are just out for themselves.

| 18% | 51% | 26% | 4% |
| 23% | 30% | 32% | 16% |

Most people inwardly dislike putting themselves out to help other people.

| 10% | 38% | 43% | 9% |
| 10% | 26% | 42% | 21% |

Most people are not really honest by nature.

| 9% | 29% | 47% | 15% |
| 5% | 21% | 51% | 23% |

These cynical reactions are manifested in attitudes and behaviors that, in themselves, threaten the fiber of society. Compared to the 1950s, trust in government has declined by 50% or more; similarly, more people than before believe that the mass media are biased in presenting the news (K. E. John, 1988). The United States has the lowest voter turnout (at 51%) of any industrialized nation. Apparently more people cheat on their income taxes than ever before. For the first time in recorded history, American adults anticipate that the standard of living to be experienced by their children will be worse than their own.

But feelings of disappointment and disillusion are associated not only with politicians and economic conditions. Increasingly we make such attributions about our neighbors, our colleagues, and even those less fortunate than ourselves. The obsequious panhandler with the outstretched palm receives a cold shoulder like never before. Gibbs (1988, p. 70) concludes that "what used to be for some a simple gesture with a noble motive has now become a complex calculation: Are the beggars what they say they are? Is the change going for coffee or whiskey? Would the money be better used elsewhere?" Similarly, the chairperson of the transit authority in New York City was quoted in 1990 as saying: "People who maybe a year ago would simply have walked away really snap back at panhandlers and homeless people who are acting aggressively" (quoted in Painton, 1990, p. 14). Such conclusions, if justified, are especially troubling for counseling psychologists, social workers, and other human-services delivery workers who work with individuals who report difficulties in relating to other people. An increase in cynicism in our society is a special problem for counseling psychologists, because—as we will show in this book—they possess especially favorable and optimistic beliefs about the nature of others.

Even though the content of our attributions may be changing, people have always found it necessary to label others in order to understand and explain the significant developments of our world. In furnishing such explanations we frequently rely upon "human nature." With a shrug of the shoulder, we may brush off more involved attempts at explaining human frailties by saying, "Why, everybody knows that's just human nature."

Such reactions are not surprising. Human nature is a pervasive concept; most of us use it to justify our own behavior as well as that of others. Our beliefs about human nature may influence everything from how we bargain with used-car dealers to whether we expect worldwide war to result from tension between nations in the Middle East or another remote part of the world.

Cynicism, based as it is upon attributions of selfishness and fakery to others, reflects a virulent assumption about human nature. But all such assumptions, whether pessimistic or Pollyannaish, can be adaptive as a means for self-preservation. For the cynic, to set one's sights lower when it comes to expectations about others, can reduce further disillusionment and avoid crushing unpredictability.

As noted earlier, in contrast to "the cynical Americans" described above, most counseling psychologists and others who work in mental health agencies have not "written off" human nature, nor have they come to accept hypocrisy and selfishness as among its central components. The very commitment to work with those who seek assistance reflects an assumption that people can change and achieve more positive attributes. When I have made presentations of research dealing with the measurement of assumptions about human nature, counseling psychologists have been among the most responsive members of the audience. My explanation for this consistent response is that dealing with "relatively normal" clients who are struggling to change makes more salient the dilemmas that we all have about the nature of human nature.

Psychologists, after all, are no different from the rest of us with respect to the formation and use of assumptions about human nature. In fact, Chapter 2 will show that the assumptions of psychologists are as varied and detailed as those of anybody else. Yet, as researchers, psychologists seem to have ignored their own assumptions. In fact, some of them have even castigated their own students for relying upon "human nature" as an explanation for behavior. If people do rely upon such assumptions, however, psychologists should study them. That is the position of this book.

Thus our purpose is to analyze assumptions about human nature, to measure them, and to determine what role they play in our everyday dealings with others and our psychological and physical adaptation.

American sociologist C. Wright Mills (1959) wrote: "It is the political task of the social scientist—as of any liberal educator—continually to translate personal troubles into public issues, and public issues into terms of their human meaning for a variety of individuals" (p. 187). The program of research described in this book was generated by a personal concern that I have tried to relate to a public issue. Possibly like some of the counseling psychologists referred to earlier, I have found that my beliefs about the trustworthiness of human nature are continually challenged. Individuals sometimes act in ways that betray trust (whether the topic of trust is a secret I have shared, or the loan of a favorite book, or the extension of a deadline upon receipt of a promise that it will be met).

My conception of human nature has been revised; not to one that says people are untrustworthy, but to one that recognizes a robust individual-differences component to human nature. My own struggle over the nature of human nature can be transmitted into a public issue for two reasons. First, many people who were brought up to believe that humankind is good, true, loving, and rational are now questioning those cherished beliefs. When we consider the seemingly unquenchable pollution of our environment, the increased acceptance of violence depicted in our mass media, the massive depersonalization in our way of life, and other lamentable developments including those mentioned earlier in this chapter, it is not surprising that such "personal concerns" affect many people. Second, and perhaps in conflict with the above, in many marvelous ways our society operates from an assumption that human beings can be trusted. A complex society, to operate efficiently, forces each of us to rely upon others to do some things for us. We expect postal carriers to deliver our letters without opening them, we expect physicians and counselors to keep the valued secrets that we have entrusted to them, and—as the jury showed in the trial of three Northwest Airlines crew members in August 1990—we expect airline pilots to be sober on the job. Recent events have shaken our trust. What will human life be like if we can no longer rely on each other?

Equally important as trustworthiness is an expectation that others can be caring and compassionate when the occasion demands it. The refusal to intervene by all 38 witnesses to Kitty Genovese's murder—though it happened 30 years ago—still serves to stimulate the question: Do people lack compassion? I grant that questions like these—questions about basic trustworthiness or altruism in human nature—could be labeled as either empirical or philosophical ones. Perhaps in the most sublime sense they are philosophical—not subject to empirical verification and beyond the pale of scientific psychology. William James, arguably America's greatest psychologist, later shifted his interest to philosophy and came to call psychology "that nasty little science." I have neither the motivation nor the intellectual resources to make a philosophical statement about the nature of human nature; I prefer to channel my "personal troubles" into the social-psychological study of attitudes about human nature, as reflected in the research program described in the subsequent chapters.

In doing so, and because in some ways this book is a very personal and subjective treatise, I should make explicit some assumptions of my own: (1) that people possess assumptions about human nature, (2) that these assumptions are pervasive and influential, (3) that they affect how we act in our everyday lives, and (4) that their substance and their effects are subject to investigation and measurement using social-science methodology. The validity of these assumptions will be scrutinized—and, I believe, supported—in subsequent chapters of this book.

Approaches to the Study of Assumptions About Human Nature

Throughout history theologians and social and political philosophers have speculated about human nature. Various "sovereign concepts," to use Allport's (1968) term, have been proposed as descriptions of the essential qualities of human nature; examples include "hedonism," "power," and "suggestibility." Certain qualities (such as rationality) have been emphasized during some eras of Western civilization and abandoned during others. Chapter 2 will present a framework for understanding those concepts that have waxed and waned throughout history.

Assumptions About Human Nature in Literature

It has been observed that fiction's most important activity is the study of human nature. If we look to postwar and contemporary literature for a reflection of basic concerns in our society, we find a profusion of themes dealing with the nature of humankind. For example, in the first two decades after the end of World War II, the novels that sequentially captured the attention of college youth were loaded with assumptions about human nature.

First, in *The Catcher in the Rye* by J. D. Salinger, published in 1951, Holden Caulfield despairs about the phoniness of the adult world. You may remember Holden as the 16-year-old misfit who had just been dismissed from his third prep school. His meanderings on his way home to New York City reveal a young man with a loving soul and a fantasy of playing with children in a field of rye and catching them before they fall. Holden wants to love all people indiscriminately, simply because they are human beings. As he says, even "a horse is human, for Godsake." But such a goal comes in conflict with his movement toward adulthood, for the adults he sees possess only a pretense of love for others. To Holden, the actions of adults reflect a lack of love, and therefore those actions inflict psychological injury on other persons. For example, there is the headmaster of one of Holden's schools, who seeks to charm all the "best" parents during their Sunday visits but totally ignores those who, in Holden's words, are "fat or corny-looking or something." Through the course of his travels, Holden is repulsed not so much by what people do to him as by what they do to one another (Wakefield, 1963).

It is interesting to speculate, as *Time* magazine did in one of its essays (Kanfer, 1972), about what the adult Holden Caulfield would be like. Would he have changed his contemptuous views of human nature? Would he be a middle-aged anarchist? Or would he have become an Establishment phony like his father? "Oh, not that!" you say. But you know that, according to Mark Twain, Huckleberry Finn ended as a "justice of the peace in a remote village in Montana, and . . . a good citizen and greatly respected."

Holden Caulfield could find genuine love only in children, who had not yet learned "the deadening rituals of pretense" (Wakefield, 1963, p. 199). But, in the only other novel to challenge *Catcher*'s popularity during the 1950s an entirely different set of moral assumptions about the nature of children emerges. *Lord of the Flies* (Golding, 1954) describes the experiences of a group of English schoolboys whose airplane has crash-landed on a deserted tropical island. No adults have survived. What happens to the boys without the benefit of adult supervision is the essence of the book—at least at the surface level. (A recent film version of the book was distributed in 1989.) But *Lord of the Flies* is a fable and can be analyzed at several levels of symbolism. At one level, the nature of Rousseau's "noble savage" is examined. The author, William Golding, admits that the violence of World War II caused him to revise severely his youthful conception that human nature was basically good and to shift to what might be described as a Calvinistic belief in our evil nature without the provision for the possibility of redemption (J. R. Baker, 1983). (Golding's own analysis of his feelings is described in Box 1.3.) He believed that the best thing for him to do was to trace the relationship between "man's diseased nature" and the "international mess" that man had gotten himself into (Golding, 1967, p. 86).

Perhaps you do not agree with Golding's scenario about the deterioration of a civilized life into blood and terror when traditional constraints are removed. Yet there is something in *Lord of the Flies* that has intrigued the younger generation; possibly it is the discovery of evil within themselves (Oldsey & Weintraub, 1965). Certainly a superficially similar book, *The Coral Island* (Ballantyne, 1927), did not so stimulate the interest of contemporary American youth. In *Coral Island* the same situation holds—a group of boys are abandoned on an isolated island. Even the names of major characters are the same (Ralph, Jack, and Simon-Peterkin). But

William Golding's View of Human Nature

Golding writes:

Before the Second World War, I believed in the perfectability of social man; that a correct structure of society would produce goodwill; and that therefore you could remove all social ills by a reorganization of society. It is possible that today I believe something of the same again; but after the war I did not because I was unable to. I had discovered what one man could do to another. I am not talking of one man killing another with a gun, or dropping a bomb on him, or blowing him up or torpedoing him. I am thinking of the vileness beyond all words that went on, year after year, in the totalitarian states. It is bad enough to say that so many Jews were exterminated in this way and that, so many people liquidated—lovely, elegant word—but there were things done during that period from which I still have to avert my mind lest I should be physically sick. They were not done by the head hunters of New Guinea, or by some primitive tribe in the Amazon. They were done, skillfully, coldly, by educated men, doctors, lawyers, by men with a tradition of civilization behind them, to beings of their own kind. (1967, p. 85)*

We should also note here that some critics (see Lapham, 1971; Tuchman, 1967) believe that the contemporary arts present a misleading, all-too-negative view of human nature. Tuchman claims that "writers who dislike their fellow man have taken over the literary world" (1967, p. 28). Lapham upbraids modern movies for always following the same theme: "that man is a weak and pitiable creature, that he stands no chance against the system" (1971, p. 106).

*From *The Hot Gates and Other Occasional Pieces,* by William Golding.

the outcome of *Coral Island* is drastically different. The boys master the difficult environment with ingenuity. Any evil that is present comes not from the boys but from the outside world. "The fierce pirates who invade the island are defeated by sheer moral force, and the tribe of cannibalistic savages is easily converted and reformed by the example of Christian conduct afforded them" (J. R. Baker, 1983, p. xiv). A comparison of *Coral Island* and *Lord of the Flies* presents us with two radically different pictures of human nature and its relationship to society—two hypotheses about what would happen if the usual laws and rules of society were to be removed. Which hypothesis is more accurate? Which best describes the behavior of human beings? Or does either?

Nonfictional Catch-22s

The irrationality of the military existence is not just a fictional phenomenon. Peter Tauber (1971, p. 97), in his diary of his eight weeks of basic training, recounts the following exchange:

"Tauber," whispers Drill Sergeant Wilson to me during closed-ranks inspection, "You're going to KP tonight, and do you know why?"

"Yes, drill sergeant," I reply.

"Why?" he asks, testing me.

"I don't know, drill sergeant," I answer.

"Why did you answer 'yes,' then?"

"Because you're not supposed to answer 'no,' drill sergeant," I reply truthfully.

"You lied when you said you knew why, didn't you?"

"Yes, drill sergeant."

"You're going to KP tonight for lying."

"Thank you, drill sergeant."

In the early 1960s, the ultimate modern "war novel," *Catch-22* (Heller, 1961), appeared. That book asked whether the world is rational and human nature is irrational, or vice versa. We can understand the author's beliefs about the irrationality of the situation if we know the meaning of the book's title. American airmen serving on bomber crews over Italy in World War II were required to fly 45 missions before they were furloughed for rest and relaxation. But, after they had flown 43 or 44 missions, the commander would raise the required number to 50. When they had flown 49, the magic number became 55. The situation is reminiscent of that of Sisyphus, the mythical king of Corinth who was condemned in Hell to roll a huge stone up a hill each day, only to find that it rolled back each night. An airman could escape the Sisyphean situation if he obtained a medical discharge because of insanity. But to get a medical discharge he had to apply for one, and to apply for a medical discharge—to attempt to escape from an irrational situation—is proof of one's sanity. That, says author Joseph Heller, is the catch—the system's way of preventing a rational person from escaping.

Science fiction also provides assumptions about human nature. For example, Robert Heinlein's (1961) *Stranger in a Strange Land*—which has sold almost five million copies—can be read as diverting science fiction, but its most important function is an iconoclastic one: It challenges contemporary systems of economics, religion, and marriage, and in place of them it substitutes a simple ethic of universal love. The book also recognizes that, until the world is converted to this ethic, steps may have to be taken to eliminate or "discorporate" those who oppose the philosophy. Hence, there emerges a theme that espouses both very positive and very negative views of human nature. Similarly, Hermann Hesse's novels, particularly *Steppenwolf* and *Demian,* attempt to integrate humanity's many-sidedness into a single being.

The world of science fiction offers a rich variety of conceptions of human nature, and, as Hillegas (1967) notes, "quality" science fiction always makes a significant comment about the human condition.[1] When fiction writers are unleashed from the restraints of today's world and start to fantasize about the nature of humankind in the future, their predictions can help us understand their assumptions about human nature—and our own assumptions as well. We should subject each book to the question: Is there anything in the nature of humans—as we see it—to prevent the emergence of a society as described in this book?

We should do this not only for sci-fi books but also for the multitude of utopian and anti-utopian works, because such books have served as means to expressing the civilized world's conceptions of an ideal society and of its goals for all of us (Manuel, 1966). We should ask "Is a *brave new world* possible?" "If established, would the microsociety described in *Walden Two* thrive and proliferate?"[2] and "Are the events described in *A Clockwork Orange* (Burgess, 1963) or in *1984* (Orwell, 1983) likely to happen?"

Certainly the most influential writer of utopian science fiction was H. G. Wells. His preoccupation with the nature of the future—both good and bad—is reflected in the work of his literary descendants—for example, in Aldous Huxley's (1932) *Brave New World,* Karel Capek's (1923) *R.U.R.,* and Evgenii Zamyatin's (1972) recently republished *We.* Wells began as a socialist visionary, whose *The Shape of Things to Come* described a rational utopia "founded on industrial might and technological progress" (Shayon, 1967, p. 50) and possessing a creative new type of human existence. But as Wells grew older and he saw his proposals for a utopian society rejected by "practical" politicians, he became pessimistic and bitter. His later novels, far from reflecting the clever ingenuity of his *The Time Machine* (Wells, 1971), were exceedingly pessimistic about humankind. For example, *The Island of Dr. Moreau* (Wells, 1981/1896) conveys an assumption that "civilization is only a thin disguise hiding the fact that man is essentially bestial in nature" (Hillegas, 1967, p. 36) and that human nature is a result of a cruel and arbitrary cosmic process. (In its sense of hopelessness and its use of a desert-island locale, *The Island of Dr. Moreau* foreshadowed Golding's *Lord of the Flies*.)

I do not propose here a detailed analysis of the change in Wells from someone possessing optimism and a belief in human willpower to a person who, in his last book, wrote, "The end of everything we call life is close at hand and cannot be evaded." But it should be noted that in all of his extensive writings about the future his then-current assumptions about human nature were made manifest. At a technical level, his predictions were accurate—for example, motor cars, space exploration, superhighways, the armored tank, and the atom bomb. His disillusionment with technological solutions to society's problems has more recently been reflected in Charles Reich's "Consciousness III" and Kurt Vonnegut's writing. The influence of Wells's novels has been immense.

But fiction of all types abounds with assumptions about human nature. Even comic strips do. The year 1990 saw the 20th anniversary of the syndication of *Doonesbury*. The strip's frequent message seems to resonate to the cynicism in our society surveyed by D. L. Kanter and Mirvis (1989), despite the apparent altruism and idealism of Garry Trudeau, its creator. Trudeau is quoted in a *Newsweek* cover story as saying "I'm really one of the last people who still believe in the perfectibility of man;" he spends one afternoon a week helping out at a center for the homeless (Alter, 1990).

As another comic [sic] example, we may quote from one of America's most familiar contemporary fictional characters: "I have an undying faith in human nature . . . I believe that people who want to change can do so, and I believe they should be given a chance to do so." That was spoken by Charlie Brown of *Peanuts* cartoon fame on the eve of one of his annual football place-kicking fiascoes. In the scene that follows, Lucy offers to hold the ball for a place kick, but—on the basis of past experience—Charlie distrusts her. Then he becomes convinced that Lucy has truly redeemed herself. Only when his foot is in the air does Charlie Brown realize that once again, at the last possible instant, Lucy has withdrawn the ball. As Charlie tumbles to the ground not only is his anatomy sorely abused but so is his "undying faith in human nature."

Moral Directives and Assumptions About Human Nature

Commentator Stefan Kanfer (1990) observes that in every decade some sage is designated to offer moral truisms that capture the public's attention. During the decade of the 1960s the advice of Kahlil Gibran (1923) in *The Prophet* experienced a revival. The year 1970 saw the publication of *The Greening of America* (Reich, 1970) (Consciousness III is now, however, a forgotten term from the seemingly distant past). The decade of the 1970s gave prominence to *Jonathan Livingston Seagull* (Bach, 1970). In the early 1980s Rabbi Harold S. Kushner (1981) consoled people *When Bad Things Happen to Good People.* As Kanfer notes, all these share a few simple rules that tell us how to be moral persons. What is considered to be moral is related to what people consider to be basic to human nature; these aphorisms focus on the discrepancy between the real and the ideal.

In the early 1990s, the recipe for moral rules was to be found in the Reverend Robert Fulghum's (1988) *All I Really Needed to Know I Learned in Kindergarten;* these included:

Share everything.

Play fair.

Put things back where you found them.

Wash your hands before you eat.

When you go out into the world, watch out for traffic, hold hands, and stick together.

Psychology's "Sanction for Selfishness"

Psychologists Michael A. Wallach and Lise Wallach (1983) have pointed out that the field of psychology communicates implicit assumptions of its own about the nature of human nature. What is the content of these assumptions?

They write: "A surprisingly broad and influential range of psychological theory turns out to legitimize selfishness . . . Our analysis suggests that the roots of psychology's ubiquitous sanction for selfishness lie in fundamental assumptions about motivation that almost all psychologists have come to take for granted" (pp. ix-x).

Recently, however, the well-regarded work of C. Daniel Batson (1990) has raised the question whether altruism, rather than selfishness, characterizes the human condition.

Assumptions About Human Nature in Everyday Life

It is not just in literature that human nature emerges as a fruitful theme. In everyday conversation references to human nature frequently serve as explanatory concepts. We often justify our decisions about an individual on the basis of our assumptions about human nature in general. Spend some time tabulating comments from office or cocktail-party conversations. You will note that statements such as "Most people will treat you fairly" or "Children need to be restrained every so often" pop up with remarkable frequency. For example, a psychology department held a series of discussions among faculty members and graduate students about due process for students. (In this context, "due process" involved such issues as "Do students have a right to see their files in the department chair's office?" and "Should they be present when they are screened for admission to doctoral candidacy?") The discussion proceeded in a spirit of good will but reflected clear differences between the students and the faculty members about just what was justifiable "due process." Finally, one of the younger faculty members emitted a magnificently typical response: "Students simply have to assume that faculty members are trustworthy." But is that assumption part of the ideology of seasoned graduate students?

References to human nature are also employed to explain the success or failure of political movements. Consider the comments of economist Andrew Tobias (1989, p. 39): "The thing about Communism is that it doesn't work. It tries to change human nature. This is its fundamental flaw. People are selfish. Give them an incentive to work, and they will. Give them a low-risk way to cheat on their taxes, and they will. We do, most of the time, what's in our own selfish best interest" (see also Box 1.5).

We develop such assumptions because the behavior of other people is a great influence upon our relative success in life. Whatever goals we may have, obstacles to their achievement result from other people as well as from ourselves and the physical environment. Hence, we seek to understand other people, to simplify them, and to make them appear to act in consistent ways. We also seek to develop substantive beliefs about people. Are they rational? Can they "stick by their guns" in the face of opposition? Does trying harder make any difference?

Psychology's Avoidance of the
Study of Assumptions About Human Nature

If we weigh the wealth of concerns about human nature in literature, in religion, in history, and—more importantly—in everyday life, at first glance it seems paradoxical that social psychology has largely avoided the scientific study of this topic. (Such avoidance does not mean that social psychology is free of assumptions itself; see Box 1.6.)

Several reasons for psychology's avoidance can be identified. First, psychologists recognize that laypersons frequently rely on "human nature" as an explanatory construct, but some psychologists see this reliance as an unjustifiable and tautological device. To explain a certain behavior by saying that "it is only human nature" is useless. So social psychologists, in spreading their gospel to the great unwashed—that is, in maintaining that there is no such thing as *the* human nature—have avoided examining the ways that the unwashed, as well as the relatively sanitized, continue to use "human nature" as an explanatory concept.

A second reason is that until rather recently psychologists have not emphasized extensive cross-cultural universalities in social behavior. The focus has been on one's own society, rather than on one's membership in the human species, as the primary explanation for much standard behavior. But unavoidable are certain cross-cultural universals such as the presence of a family structure, the meaning of certain gestures, the relationship between frustration and aggression, and the possible existence of an innate grammatical structure in infants. These even extend to shared motivations and interpersonal styles. In 1989 at the top of the nonfiction best seller list in Japan was a translation of *Lord Chesterfield and His Letters to His Sons* (see T. Scott, 1976). In order to achieve success, Chesterfield encourages his son to follow a strategy of manipulation through flattery (Berendt, 1990). He encourages his son to grovel at every turn. Why is this cynical book so popular in Japan? Perhaps, suggests Berendt, the Japanese "see specific similarities between present-day Japan and eighteenth-century England" (p. 30).

Third is the emphasis among research psychologists on experimental social psychology and narrow-range, more easily operationalized, concepts. Broad, "mushy" concepts have not been highly regarded in American social psychology during the last 40 years. Rather, social psychologists usually derive status among their peers by—if I may exaggerate—the extent to which they carry out highly intricate studies dealing with theory-generated variables in artificial laboratory situations. I was nurtured in this tradition at the center of "dust-bowl empiricism" (the University of Minnesota), where the unwritten rule was "If you can't manipulate it in the laboratory, don't bother studying it." Upward-mobile social psychologists experience great pressures to conform to such an orientation. For example, about three years after I received my PhD degree, I presented my first paper at an American Psychological Association convention. My topic was "philosophies of human nature." My major professor during my graduate work saw the listing on the program and confronted me: "How come you got interested in all this religious crap?" Even though assumptions about people—or, as I have called them, philosophies of human nature—can be studied within the rigorous frameworks of attitude measurement and experimental social psychology, many social psychologists still are reluctant to deal with such seemingly amorphous concepts. This aversion may stem from a disagreement about what social psychology's role *should* be.

I fear that one viewpoint and approach has come to dominate social psychology. This book is an attempt to redress the balance. When we consider the possible roles of social psychology, the classification by Shils (1961) and G. Winter (1966) of different functions of social science is helpful. They describe three approaches: the physical-science approach, the functional approach, and the voluntaristic approach. The physical-science approach assumes that we can understand human social behavior by explicating internal and external forces that can be analyzed and measured. The object of study is "out there," and the researcher has no responsibility other than to study it. For decades, social psychology has emulated the physical-science approach.

Functionalists see the goal of social science as the enhancement of self-understanding and social relationships, and, while they bear a greater "mission orientation" than do the adherents of the physical-science approach, the functionalists implicitly trust the wisdom of the evolutionary process and rationalize whatever happens as beneficial to humankind (G. Winter, 1966, p. 49). Functionalists also assume that their own scientific method and scientific judgments are enunciations of the truth.

In contrast, the voluntaristic approach defines the role of social science as one of criticism of our society from the outside. This approach takes for granted that the perspective of social science is not value free, and its adherents are less optimistic than are the functionalists that our society will turn out all right without intervention by pressure groups from outside the Establishment. Beyond this, the voluntarists are much less confident that the impact of social science on society is entirely good.

This book reflects something of each of these approaches. For example, it reflects the physical-science approach in that its conclusions are based upon the measurement of assumptions about human nature—measurement carried out in as objective a way as possible. Yet it shares the functionalist's orientation toward the study of concepts that make a difference in our behavior in the everyday world. It also shares the voluntarist's credo that traditional ways of doing things are not always the best, and that a scientist should stand on the outside and criticize if that approach is appropriate.

Changes in Social Psychology's Concern

In the decade of the 1960s, a gradual but growing concern on the part of some psychologists emerged that psychology's emulation of the more advanced sciences had caused it to avoid studying some of the more important aspects of social behavior. Gordon Allport gave the label "third wave" to the humanistic approach that supplemented the behavioristic and psychoanalytic approaches to the study of psychological processes. Nevitt Sanford proposed that new institutions "ought to encourage psychologists to study problems that people really worry about rather than only those problems formulated on the basis of reading the professional journals" (N. Sanford, 1965, p. 192). Sanford's behavior, in his directorship of the Wright Institute in Berkeley, CA (prior to his retirement), was consistent with his attitude. The Wright Institute has developed innovative doctoral training programs that combine the theoretical and research focus of social psychology with the service orientation of clinical psychology. These humanistic concerns began to emerge during the same decade remembered for campus activism, civil rights protests, and the civil-rights movement (Kohn, 1987).

Along with their search for new orientations and new topics of concern, some psychologists have expressed a growing belief that the assumptions about human nature required by a strictly "scientific" approach to human behavior communicate an image of humankind that is mechanistic, passive, and—most important—incomplete. Consider the words of one prominent behavior shaper:

> I would conceive of man clearly in the robot end of the continuum. That is, his behavior can be completely determined by outside stimuli. Even if man's behavior is determined by internal mediating events such as awareness, or

thinking, or anxiety, or insight, these events can be manipulated by outside
stimuli so that it is these stimuli which basically determine our behavior.
(Krasner, 1965, p. 22)

Along with the conception of the human as a robot, the behaviorists also
hold a view of humankind as malleable. For example, the late James V.
McConnell (personal communication, March 9, 1973) once said on a doc-
umentary television program that: "The time has come when, if you give
me any normal human being and six months, I can change his behavior
from what it is now to whatever you want it to be, if it's physically possible. I can turn him from a Christian to a Commie or vice versa."

Is this responsiveness to conditioning all there is to human nature?
Some psychologists, while recognizing the passive, malleable aspects,
prefer to accentuate another facet. In his presidential address to the American Psychological Association, cognitive psychologist George A. Miller
presented two contrasting conceptions of human nature offered by scientific psychology. One, reflected in the preceding quotations, emphasized
human nature as manipulatable—that is, through the judicious use of reinforcements human behavior can be modified to fit the goals of the controller. Miller evaluated the implications of this assumption as
"unfortunate, even threatening" (G. A. Miller, 1969, p. 67), because "it
has great appeal to the authoritarian mind . . . and our traditional competitive ideology based on principles of coercion, punishment, and retribution" (p. 67). The other conception, the one Miller opted for, is less clear;
even he admitted that (p. 67). However, it reflected assumptions of human
variability, of complexity, of the power of the will, and of receptivity to
positive incentives. Perhaps the most important and relevant part of
Miller's presidential address was his belief that psychology's greatest impact upon our world will stem from the image of humankind that it pro-
motes and its conceptions of what is humanly possible and humanly
desirable.

About the same time that G. A. Miller gave his address, sociologist
Alvin Gouldner (1970) explicated the assumptions about human nature
that were dominant in his field. Calling these "domain assumptions," he
wrote that such assumptions about humankind and society "might include,
for example, dispositions to believe that men are rational or irrational; that
society is precarious or fundamentally stable; that social problems will
correct themselves without planned intervention; that human behavior is
unpredictable; that man's true humanity resides in his feelings and senti-
ments" (Gouldner, 1970, p. 31). Like G. A. Miller, Gouldner saw his field

as shaped by the domain assumptions of its practitioners, and he reflected unhappiness about the assumptions held by the majority of his colleagues.

In the two decades since the publication of these views, it is hard to see any change in the status quo. Gouldner (1970) titled his book *The Coming Crisis of Western Sociology*; likewise, social psychology faced a crisis regarding its relevance in the early 1970s. But such crises are no longer topics of discussion. Certainly a diversity of roles is available for psychologists and other social scientists, including being advocates for the disenfranchised in our society. Behaviorism has become more cognitive. But the physical-science approach is still the predominant model. An article published in 1987 was even titled "Whatever Happened to Human Potential?" (Kohn, 1987).

Notes

1. Science-fiction writer Samuel R. Delany (cited in Jonas, 1972) takes to task the often unexamined assumptions of the typical science-fiction story—"that the universe is essentially a hospitable space, that one person can influence the course of history, that intelligence, even genius, works in an essentially linear way" (p. 46).

2. Communities designed on the basis of Skinner's (1948) plans in *Walden Two* are in operation now. Twin Oaks, in Virginia, is one (see Houriet [1971] or R. M. Kanter [1972] for a description.)

CHAPTER TWO

The Historical Background of Assumptions About Human Nature

Our youth today love luxury. They have bad manners, contempt for authority, disrespect for older people. Children nowadays are tyrants. They contradict their parents, gobble their food, and tyrannize their teachers.

—SOCRATES,
writing in the year 5 B.C.

As the above quotation shows, evaluations of others are nothing new. Conceptions of human nature can be traced back through all of recorded civilization. This chapter examines the sources of assumptions about human nature, going back even to the origins of philosophers' inquiries into the nature of matter. One of the goals of the chapter is to show how early inquiries into the nature of matter have contributed to present-day strategies for seeking an understanding of the nature of humankind. In doing so, the chapter offers a formulation of four domains that reflect the source material for theories of human nature: the individual, society, social process, and the environment. The chapter concludes with an analysis of the assumptions of human nature basic to four schools of thought in contemporary psychology: (1) Skinnerian behaviorism, (2) psychoanalysis, (3) humanistic psychology, and (4) George Kelly's personal-construct theory.

AUTHOR'S NOTE: The version of this chapter in the first edition of this book was authored by M. Leslie Wuescher and Lawrence S. Wrightsman.

From the Explanation of Nature to
the Explanation of Human Nature

For the ancient Greeks, questions about the nature of physical matter were of great concern. In attempting to explain the physical world around them, two Greek philosopher-scientists, Leucippus and Democritus, developed a landmark of early scientific thought, the atomistic theory. They proposed that matter was composed of solid, indivisible, moving particles that could not be seen, even though they existed everywhere and shared the same essential properties. While this explanation could not be tested empirically, it was not simply a metaphysical speculation. Instead, this analysis served as a model for the process of explanation itself. The atomistic theory implied that the behavior of matter is the result of a limited number of causes—specifically, such behavior is caused by the combination of particles, or atoms. Implicit in this explanation is the idea of an irreducible "essence" of matter, which somehow joins or interacts with other essences to form larger, more complex wholes. The idea of a limited, or finite, causality and the concept of irreducible essences, then, were basic to explanation. These remain central to the philosophical underpinnings of the scientific method today.

When Greek philosophers initiated their systematic speculations about *human* nature, not surprisingly they maintained their allegiance to these atomistic concepts. That is, they used the same logic of inquiry that was used to investigate physical matter; once more they began to search for irreducible essences.

To answer the basic question "What is human nature?" the Greeks looked to the irreducible qualities and attributes of humankind (see Box 2.1). These "essential properties" were seen as the causes for action. Again, the causal linkage between the essential quality and the action was more assumed than specific. The essential qualities, as before, were postulated, not based on an empirical approach.

The axioms that provided assumptions about human nature were not the province of the philosophers alone. During the lifetime of Plato and Aristotle, ordinary citizens also were conversant with the various theories of human nature examined so thoroughly in the writings of these two philosophers. It was, in truth, this commonplace, everyday use of concepts of human nature in discussing and analyzing local social and political issues that formed the foundation for Plato's *Republic* and led to the development of much of its subject matter (Sabine, 1961).

Box 2.1
Seven Theories of Human Nature

Leslie Stevenson (1987), a philosopher, has explicated the beliefs about human nature held by seven representative philosophical positions. Chapter 2 of this book concentrates on the development of the *process,* throughout Western civilization, of evolving a philosophy of human nature. Hence Stevenson's evaluation, summarized here, is helpful in understanding the *content* of landmark positions.

Plato
1. The human soul is indestructible, and it exists eternally before life and after death.
2. Within the mind are the elements of Appetite (or desire), Reason, and Spirit (or indignation or anger). Children show Spirit long before they display reasoning.
3. These are present in every person but to varying degrees. The ideal is a harmonious agreement among the three elements, with Reason in control.
4. There is such a thing as the truth about how we ought to live, and this truth can be known by the human intellect.
5. We are all social; each of us has many needs that we cannot supply for ourselves, so no one is self-sufficient.
6. Different individuals have different aptitudes and interests.

Christianity
1. God created humans to occupy a special position in the universe, to have dominion over the rest of creation.
2. The human race is unique in that it possesses something of the self-consciousness and ability to love freely that is characteristic of God.
3. But also, the human race is continuous with the rest of creation, made of the "dust from the ground."
4. There is life after death by resurrection.
5. The attainment of the true purpose of human life—love of God and living a life according to God's will—is available to all.

Karl Marx
1. Everything about individual persons is determined by the material conditions of their lives.
2. The real nature of humankind is the "totality of social relations," that is, our essential *social* nature. Whatever a person does is an inherent social act, which presumes the existence of a relationship with other people.
3. Even the ways in which we eat, sleep, copulate, and defecate are learned.
4. The kind of individual one is and what kind of things one does are determined by the kind of society in which one lives, or, "it is not the consciousness of men that determines their being, but, on the contrary, their social being determines their consciousness" (Marx, 1963, p. 67).
5. Humans are active, productive beings, distinguished from other animals by the fact that they produce their means of subsistence.

Sigmund Freud

1. Every mental event has preceding sufficient causes; that is, nothing that a person says or does is really haphazard or accidental.
2. Our consciousness, far from being perfectly "free" or "rational," is really determined by causes of which we are not aware. (In contrast to Marx, who saw the causes as social and economic in nature, Freud proposed they were individual and mental.)
3. The unconscious (our mental states of which we are unaware) is dynamic in nature, that is, it actively exerts pressures and influences on what a person says and does.
4. Three structural systems within the human personality—the id, the ego, and the superego—contain basic and often conflicting drives and desires.
5. Certain basic instincts or drives, such as a life instinct (Eros) and a death instinct (Thanatos), are the motive forces within mental states.
6. The experiences of infancy and early childhood are of crucial importance in the formation of adult character.

Jean-Paul Sartre and existentialism

1. In general, there is no such thing as "human nature," as our existence precedes our essence.
2. We have not been created for any purpose, neither by God nor by evolution nor by anything else. We simply exist, and then have to *decide* what to make of ourselves.
3. We are "condemned to be free;" there is no limit to our freedom except that we are not free to cease being free.
4. The concept of "nothingness" is used to make a conceptual connection between consciousness and freedom. To be conscious is to be free.
5. Every aspect of our mental lives is intentional, chosen, and our responsibility; if I am sad, it is only because I choose to make myself sad. Our emotions are ways in which we choose to react to the world.
6. Every moment requires a new or renewed choice.

B. F. Skinner

1. The empirical study of human *behavior* is the only way to arrive at a true theory of human nature.
2. Mental entities, such as desires, intentions, or postulated systems such as the id, are of no explanatory value in understanding human behavior.
3. People behave in lawful and determined ways in response to external conditions (i.e., environmental factors). That is, there is a finite set of environmental conditions (past or present) so that anyone to whom all those conditions apply will perform that behavior.

Konrad Lorenz

1. The human is an animal who has evolved from other animals; our behavior patterns are fundamentally similar to those of other animals.
2. Our behavior is subject to the same causal laws of nature as all animal behavior.
3. Like any other animal we have an innate drive to aggressive behavior toward our own species.
4. The excitedly aggressive nature of a crowd that has lost its rationality and moral inhibitions evolves from the communal defense response of our prehuman ancestors.

One of the major themes of Athenian intellectual life was reflected in the wide-ranging debate over what was human nature and what was human artifice. For example, Euripides wrote that "the honest man is nature's nobleman," and the sophist Antiphon argued that any distinction between a Greek and a barbarian was "unnatural." Diverse opinions about just what was natural and what was artificial or deviant proliferated in the literature of those times (Sabine, 1961, pp. 21-32). This is not a surprising development if we remember that, to the Greeks, any explanation had to distinguish between unchanging reality and a shifting transitory appearance, as well as differentiation between the essence of things and their nonessential qualities. Such a distinction between human nature on the one hand and human artifices on the other was a necessary product of the paradigm for explanation. If statements were offered that "everything is natural" or "everything is artifice," these would have destroyed the apparent utility of the human-nature paradigm.

It is true that social thinkers from various eras have taken these extreme positions. Yet, when either extreme position is advocated, we find that— as in Meyerson's 1930 atomistic theories—the search for natural "essences" does not stop. Even when the position is taken that everything human is artifice, some artifices are considered more natural or more usual than others. Equivalently, when the position is that everything is natural, some things are considered more natural than others. Not only is this evident in the doctrines of those theorists who advocate "natural laws"—we are thinking of Hobbes, Spinoza, or the Marquis de Sade— but it is also the case in those avowedly nonnormative, supposedly descriptive theories that search for underlying patterns or structures of human behavior.

The fact that people were using philosophies of human nature as explanations of the social world 2,500 years ago just as they still are today suggests that the idea of a basic human nature, like the idea of a basic physical nature, is an intrinsic part of our prevailing psychological schema of causal explanation. That is—to signal a recurring theme of this book—it is necessary for us to have before we respond to the physical world and to the others in it.

To summarize, then, a philosophy of human nature functions in at least two ways. First, in an epistemological sense, it is a paradigm that sets forth a causal explanation of social phenomena. Secondly, psychologically speaking, it is a set of social schemata that individuals use to help them understand their phenomenal world. Thus it is both a framework for a person's behavioral manipulations and instrumental dealings with his or

---

Box 2.2
The Issues to Be Faced in an Analysis of Philosophies of
Human Nature

1. What are the differing views of human nature?
2. How do these views explain behavior in interactions among people?
3. How do the behaviors explained and predicted by philosophies of human nature compare to the actual ongoing, observable ways in which people act?
4. What types of societies and institutions are to be inferred from these views of human nature?
5. How do these societies and institutions compare with existing social structures?
6. Which of the views of human nature are considered most nearly accurate?
7. Which behaviors are most congruent and which behaviors are least congruent with this view of human nature?
8. Just where is it possible to place societal and institutional constraints upon behavior, and how may these constraints be arranged to dampen or correct deviations and aberrations from human nature?
9. How can constraints be placed or removed in order to maximize the good in human nature?

---

her social world and a set of mental representations of that social world itself—representations upon which the person's cognitive symbolic operations are performed.

One way to look at how philosophies of human nature function is to examine how they have been used in the past. What have social thinkers from the time of Plato to the present tried to explain, symbolize, and clarify with their philosophies of human nature? Let us look first at the scope of those philosophies. In Box 2.2 are listed the nine issues derived from the most extended and well-developed statements of human nature. No theory can call itself comprehensive without seeking to confront each of these issues.

The Nature of Humankind and the Nature of Society

The scope of statements about human nature is broad, but this is not at all surprising. If we look at the intellectual history of Western thought—

with landmarks noted in Box 2.1—it becomes apparent that philosophies of human nature have been very closely tied to theories about the nature of society. One rarely finds one type of theory professed in isolation from the other type. This does not mean that philosophies of human nature and theories of the nature of society are one and the same. They are not.

Consider two sets of statements, each containing an assertion of a fact about society and an assertion of a fact about human nature:

> Society is X.
> Humankind, by nature, is X.
> Society is elitist.
> Humankind, by nature, is elitist.

Do both statements in each set use the attribute "X" or the attribute "elitists" to describe the same things? Consider these statements:

> Society is X; humankind, by nature, is not X.
> Society is elitist; humankind, by nature, is egalitarian.
> Society is egalitarian; humankind, by nature, is elitist.
> Society is dishonest; humankind, by nature, is honest.
> Society is honest; humankind, by nature, is dishonest.

Many social philosophers have made at least one of the above four distinctions. The debates between the followers of Hobbes and those of Rousseau or between the followers of Marx and those of Ayn Rand, for example, revolve largely around these distinctions (Wolcott, 1989). Saying that society is elitist is not the same as saying that human nature is elitist. Asserting that society is ethical or unethical is not the same as saying that human nature is ethical or unethical. Asserting that a society acts in a certain way is not the same as saying that humankind, by nature, acts in a certain way.

Although they are distinct and separate constructs, theories of human nature and theories of society are very closely tied together. These ties are not incidental. The bonds are clearly inferential and psychological. For example, if human nature is believed to be malleable, then it becomes the function of the government to mold people in socially desirable ways. But if, on the other hand, humankind is seen as endowed by nature with certain innate qualities, then it is the function of government to protect people's right to act in their individual ways (Weyant, 1971). It is also the function of government, then, to select out those individuals whose nature prevents them from being truly human.

Let us take a different kind of example. Some theorists claim that the achievement of a democratic form of government cannot be reached unless human nature is rational. For them, comparability must exist across social schemata—from the nature of people to the nature of society. The framers of the U.S. Constitution, however, saw it otherwise. While James Madison and the other authors of the Constitution assumed that people were motivated by self-interest (see *The Federalist Papers,* particularly No. X), they also advocated the method of counterpoise, that is, forming a representative legislative body in which factions representing conflicting special interests would effectively counterbalance one another (Lovejoy, 1961). Thus each faction would be unable to get a majority vote in favor of its special interest because all the other factions would oppose it, and thereby, Madison assumed, the "general good" would be realized.

Three Traditions as Sources of Philosophies of Human Nature

Our philosophies of human nature have developed around three great traditions of thought: the tradition of reason and nature, the tradition of will and artifice, and the tradition of the rational will (see, for example, Oakeshott's (1962) introduction to Hobbes's *Leviathan*).

THE TRADITION OF REASON AND NATURE

This tradition began with Greek thought and is still best represented by Plato's *Republic*. Humankind, in the tradition of reason and nature, is part of the natural order of things. The functioning of the universe is bound by natural laws, and human behavior—like any other part of the universe—is subject to these laws. Humans have the faculty of reason; through the skilled and proper exercise of that faculty, they can discover these natural laws. Moreover, this quality of reason holds sway over the drive to impulsive, excessive actions. These excesses are unnatural in humans, they are an imbalance in human nature, and they are correctable through the careful exercise of reason. Some people have a more careful, more insightful way of looking at things; therefore, they have a greater understanding both of the natural laws and of what is required in living a life that is in harmony with them. This reflectiveness is the mark of wisdom, and this insightful use of reason is the guide to all action. A proper use of reason cannot be taught and learned through experience alone—rather, it is developed by examining one's own experience in a probing, searching way. This was the goal of the French *philosophes* of the eighteenth century, who sought to understand humankind in order to promote human development (Weyant, 1971).

THE TRADITION OF WILL AND ARTIFICE

According to the tradition of will and artifice, humankind is governed not by reason but by passions and appetites. These are not under the domain of reason; rather, they are under the domain of a person's will—his or her impulses to act. In this tradition, it is unfettered, willful impulses that are natural in people. Humankind is a self-regarding, self-protecting, and self-fulfilling creature. In a society of such individuals, one does not appeal to another's reason but to his or her prudence. The guide to action is not reason before an impulsive act but the effect of the consequences following an impulsive act. Laws are generated not because they are reasonable but because society cannot prudently allocate force and power any other way. Without laws and without societal mechanisms for allocating force and power, there would be no systematic control of willful human impulses. Anarchy would reign. (The contrast in the views of Plato and Freud in Box 2.1 reflect these positions.)

Laws and rules of society are necessary to impose social order, but they are nothing but conventions—constructions of human artifice. There is nothing particularly hallowed or natural about them; they are merely more or less useful, more or less effective. Thracymacus and Hobbes are representative exponents of this tradition.

THE TRADITION OF RATIONAL WILL

This tradition houses such diverse theories as Hegel's idealism, Darwin's and Spencer's social evolutionism, Marx's materialism, and Burke's historicist conservatism. History, in this tradition, belongs not to the person of contemplation but to the person of action. The ideas and the passions of humans are exhibited in their institutions—the products of willful acts. Ideas and passions are realized and articulated only in their implementation, and only through action do the mind and will make themselves public and visible. A society's institutions are a natural, public, and visible product of the mind and will of its citizenry and are used by that citizenry as both a lens and a mirror to examine the product of their ideas and passions and to reflect those ideas and passions back to them more clearly. Human nature is reflected in the institutions and in the habitual patterns of action. Institutions are not products of human artifice designed to impose order upon humankind's actual impulses; rather, they are organic expressions of these impulses.

Through a progressive exhibiting of the products of the mind and will in a society, that society comes to understand better the consequences and implications of its collective ideas and passions. According to the approach of the rational will, society is then better able to redirect its actions in what can only be called a more rational way. Bad or unworkable ideas and passions are culled out as their negative attributes become more apparent, and they are replaced by other, ideally more workable ideas or passions. In this way, the society and its institutions evolve and progress. Humans are by nature evolutionary creatures. There is a split in the tradition over whether this evolutionary nature grounds forever in the imperfectibility of its past or holds out the prospect of perfectible future.

Several things should be noted from this brief description of the major traditions of philosophies of human nature. The basic relationship between theories of human nature and theories of society is again apparent. Furthermore, human nature is also explicitly considered both logically and psychologically antecedent to social structure and social theory in all three of these major systems of thought, despite their striking diversity, despite their different initial assumptions, and despite the different directions that the logical development of those assumptions take. These same points can be made with regard to any system of thought. The pattern still holds, for example, for Ayn Rand's egoism, neo-Hegelian idealism, or even Skinnerian hedonism. Moreover, we can compare "simple and sovereign" single-factor theories of human nature and society with multivariate, transactional, or infinitely complex theories of human nature and society, and we will still find that, in both, theories of human nature are logically and psychologically antecedent to the other theories within the same system of thought. The existential skepticism of Camus (in *The Rebel*, 1969) and the modern English skepticism of Oakeshott (*Rationalism in Politics and Other Essays*, 1962) are prime examples of complex systems of thought. Both vigorously attack single-factor theories of human nature, and both uphold the primacy of theories of human nature within their own multivariate theoretical framework.

How can this pervasive tie between philosophies of human nature and theories of society be explained? If we remember that these theories function as causal explanations and ask ourselves what they function to explain, some interesting notions arise. Theories of society function to explain social phenomena. Theories of human nature are the most basic causal root to which we have been able to extend our social explanations and, as such, function as a framework for social-theory building.

From the time of the Greeks up to the 19th century, when the empiricism of Hume and Comte and the secular evolutionary historicism of Burke, Hegel, Spencer, and Marx came to dominate social theory, Western social thought was characterized by a search for principles of natural law upon which an enduring ethical and social order could be based. From Plato and Aristotle to Hobbes, Rousseau, and Locke, social thinkers were engaged in the task of trying to formulate a science of the laws of human nature. Their confidence in reaching this goal was boundless; Locke wrote, for example, "Moral knowledge is as capable of real certainty as mathematics." As Allport's (1968) history of social psychology indicates, each formulation was built around a single conception of human nature.

The focus of inquiry changed with the advent, development, and integration of empiricism and evolutionary historicism. Theories began to concern themselves not with human nature per se but with the determinants of human nature. By the early 1900s, William Graham Sumner in sociology and John B. Watson in psychology were pushing these ideas to the extreme, and social-scientific determinism was taking a firm foothold in the 20th century.

Once we come to the view that there are empirical, causal determinants of human nature, then it would seem that human nature is no longer functioning as a final causal principle and it thereby becomes a useless construct that should wither and atrophy away. Many sociologists and psychologists take this position, as was implied in Chapter 1.

Yet, this is very much like asserting that because we have found subatomic particles the atomic theory is disproved. There is nothing wrong with the logic of the argument, but, if we consider Meyerson's (1930) analysis of the uses of atomic theories, we see very clearly that the validity of the argument rests on the assumption that atomic theory labels an entity rather than functions to assert a basic framework without which causal statements would be impossible. Similarly, if we accept the premise that theories of human nature function in much the same way as Meyerson's atomic theories, then it is far more accurate to view social and behavioral determinism as resting in assumptions of human nature than to see them as destroying all theories of human nature forever.

When we posit final causality with human nature itself rather than with determinants of human nature, we are imposing the most parsimonious solution to the problem of infinite regress in the social sciences. As the founder of behaviorism, John B. Watson's solution to the description of behaviors was to categorize and catalog all external determinants of those behaviors. Sociologists and cultural anthropologists, however, have found that, despite an orientation in which the uniqueness of any culture is assumed, it is still necessary to hypothesize universals applicable to all humankind in order to be able to analyze cultures in any systematic, scientific, cause-allocating way (Kroeber, 1955). And no less sympathetic a critic than B. F. Skinner (1938, pp. 10-11) has pointed out the severe problems of infinite regress that would follow from the implementation of Watson's program.

Domain of Social Schemata

What specific elements constitute a philosophy of human nature? It appears that a philosophy of human nature consists of at least four distinct classes of social schemata: schemata of society, of the individual, of social change and social process, and of the environment.

Within each of these distinct classes of schemata, several component subclasses may be listed. Box 2.3 is only an incomplete beginning at illustrating important subclasses, and Box 2.4 lists statements about human nature that reflect each classification. Regardless of whether one is interested in formulating a specific, sharply delimited theory of social humankind or in developing a broad general theory, the basic framework of that theory would be built from schemata similar to those we have outlined.

These domains contain mutually exclusive sets of propositions. To illustrate this, we can take an assertion about human nature, such as one of those in Box 2.4, and see how the meaning of that assertion shifts depending on whether we are considering it from the standpoint of the individual, the society, the environment, or social process.

For example, "Each person, by nature, desires to own and hold property" is a venerable assertion of human nature and one of the most closely analyzed and most frequently cited assumptions of human nature in the history of Western thought. Notice that the unit described in the proposition is the individual. In the sense that it asserts that all individuals, by

Box 2.3
Social Schemata and Their Subclasses

Society	Individual	Social Changes & Social Process	Environment
Leaders/elites	A human nature/no nature	External to the individual	Time of war/time of peace
Followers/masses	Altruism/selfishness	Internal to the individual	Time of hardship/time of plenty
Institutions, conventions/customs, traditions	Strength of will/rationality	View of progress	Urban/rural
Family/kinship	Trustworthy/untrustworthy	Individual to individual	
	Independent/dependent	Individual to group	
	Multiplexity/simplicity	Group to group	
	Variability/invariability		

Box 2.4
Examples of Statements
Reflecting Each Class of Social Schemata

Society
1. Morality is the product of legal and social sanctions, not something free-flowing from the individual.
2. Society is irrational and corrupting because it allows for great inequalities unconnected with differences in ability or merit.
3. True democracy is possible only in small societies.
4. All customs are reasonable—otherwise they would not be customs.

The Individual
1. Every person is basically out for himself or herself.
2. Human behavior is driven by irrational impulses.
3. Every person is the best judge of his or her own needs.
4. It is a biological fact that people have different capacities and abilities.

Social Change and Social Process
1. The rapid expansion of wealth by a few in a society is tied to the rapid creation of poverty in others.
2. People are like puppets pulled to and fro by social forces external to them—forces that they do not fully understand and over which they have little control.
3. The more people involved in making a decision, the worse that decision will be.
4. Some revolutionaries want to abolish all social hierarchies and thereby promote freedom; freedom, however, cannot be realized except through an elaborate hierarchical social script that allows for a great diversity of functions.

The Environment
1. Humankind's true behavior is most clearly seen in times of stress, danger, or warfare.
2. Human history is a function of human geography—of temperature, rainfall and soil, and topography.
3. The more crowded people become, the more vicious they become.
4. Where there is a scarcity of economic resources, human concern for others rapidly dissipates.

nature, desire to own and hold property, the statement is asserting that a specific universal attribute is found in all individuals. Nothing is asserted about the social organization of these individuals, and nothing is asserted about the social dynamics acting upon these individuals. Neither is there any inherent suggestion that economic scarcity or plentitude has any effect on this property-holding desire. The frame of reference of the proposition is an atomistic collectivity of individuals and as such asserts or implies nothing about society, social process, or environment influence.

Now suppose we change the proposition slightly to "In any and all societies, each person desires to own and hold property." The focus now is on humankind as part of a social organization, not as part of an atomistic collectivity of individuals. The logic of the proposition has shifted. In fact, we cannot stretch the logic of this new proposition to apply to a conception of the person as an atomistic individual entity. The proposition now asserts that we possess the desire for property within the organic structure of any society and does so as a component of that structure. This is a quite different view of humanity than the one we started with.

In contrast to our first proposition, the second proposition contains assertions about social process and environment. Society implies social process, and to talk about a universal occurrence found in any society is to explicitly recognize the geographical and environmental diversity of "societies." Yet no specific social process can be inferred from the proposition "In any and all societies, each person desire's to own and hold property." Neither can there be found any suggestion of specific environmental conditions affecting this desire for property.

If we tinker with our proposition once more and change it to "Each person's desire to own and hold property is the cornerstone of all social conflict," we clearly have a statement asserting something about social process. At first glance, it looks as if we also have a statement asserting something about society. Yet if we remember that society is generally conceived of as a structure, it becomes clear that "society" is implied in our proposition only in the sense that a structure must be established or postulated if a process is to be examined or postulated. This is in fact the very lesson handed down to us by the early Greek materialists. A structure of society is therefore implied by the proposition, but no specific structure of society can be inferred from it. The atomistic construct of the individual and the effect of environment are not implied in the proposition at all.

If we change our basic proposition to "In times of economic scarcity, each person desires to own and hold property to the point of hoarding," we have a proposition about a relationship between the desire for property and specific environmental factors. It is a universal tendency to respond to a specific situation that is noted. Neither society nor social process is implied in the statement. The social unit involved is again the individual, and, again, we have a statement that makes an assertion about an atomistic collectivity of individuals. Let us compare this proposition with our original proposition:

1. In time of economic scarcity, each person desires to own and hold property to the point of hoarding it.
2. Each person, by nature, desires to own and hold property.

Both, as we have said, are statements about atomistic collectivities of individuals. The first statement is an assertion about the universal effect of specific environmental conditions. The second is an assertion about a specific universal attribute of individuals. Nothing in the logic of the second statement implies the specific behavior under the specific environmental condition that we find in the first statement. Nothing in the logic of the first statement implies the universal attribute of individuals irrespective of environmental conditions that is asserted in the second. They are logically two mutually exclusive propositions. They come from different domains of social analysis.

With this model of the four domains contributing to beliefs about human nature, we can begin to look systematically at the various schemata that have been developed by different systems of thought. Hobbes and Plato, for example—each representing different traditions of thought—interpreted conflict and warfare quite differently. To Plato, war or conflict was an abrogation of reason and a gross temporary aberration from the natural laws governing human nature. For Hobbes, human nature was most clearly revealed in warfare and conflict, since these were precisely the situations that stripped away or temporarily suspended artificial conventions and codes of social conduct, allowing humankind's true nature to reveal itself.

Although these philosophers were conceivably able to agree on the factual question of the relative frequency of war and peace in the world, they could not agree on which is typical or atypical of the human condition, or on which is the natural environment for humanity. Both Hobbes and Plato anchor their theories within the domain of the individual. They anchor them, however, at opposite ends of the strength-of-will/rationality continuum (see Chapter 3). It is this dichotomy that is reflected in their views on war and conflict. The point at issue is not the vices and virtues of war and conflict at all; rather, it is whether each other is, by nature, a creature of will or of reason. Thus we may say that Plato and Hobbes constructed different schemata of the individual.

The task of specifying and measuring the salient components of each of these domains would be a monumental one. We have chosen to concentrate upon one domain, that of the individual. The remaining chapters of this book look systematically at the various schemata that may be encompassed with the domain of the individual: "Are people good?" "Are they thought of as agents or pawns?" "Are they each so unique that they are not subject to nomothetic laws?" But before considering the attributes of this domain in Chapter 3, we wish to indicate what ways contemporary social scientists rely upon this domain with regard to the implicit assumptions they make about human nature.

Assumptions About Human Nature in Contemporary Psychology

Contemporary psychologists don't talk much about human nature. In fact, Bannister (1970) claims that most psychologists "are unwilling to specify the subject matter of their discipline beyond the vague notion that it is 'man' " (p. 50). But every psychologist, in his or her daily professional activities, reflects an assumption about human nature. Does the psychotherapist believe that the instigation for change really lies within her clients, or does she believe that external forces must be brought to bear upon clients to change their behavior? Does the psychology instructor trust his students to do their own work; or, when they turn in term papers, does he suspect that the students have hired others to write them?

Psychologists involved in personnel selection have characteristically been guided by a set of assumptions that Max Freyd listed in 1923 (see also Guion, 1970). These are: (1) people have abilities; (2) people differ in any given ability; (3) these differences are relatively the same after training; (4) different tasks demand different abilities; and (5) abilities needed to perform a task are measurable. In fact, for good or ill, the research reported in this book reflects Freyd's set of assumptions about human nature.

Psychological researchers reflect assumptions about human nature in numerous ways. Doubtless one of the most widely discussed studies was Stanley Milgram's work in obedience (Milgram, 1963, 1965, 1974). (This study is described in Chapter 3.) Milgram has been strongly criticized for giving a human subject the task of administering increasingly

Box 2.5
Conceptions of Human Nature
Reflected by Influential Sociologists

Lester Ward (1841-1913)—believed that humans could modify, defeat, or hasten the processes of nature, particularly the blind evolutionary forces. He also believed that humankind developed from an antisocial and completely egoistic being to an altruistic one.

William Graham Sumner (1840-1910)—differed from Ward in his conception of the human response to evolution. He believed that human effort could not change either "social laws" or "physical laws." Sumner is responsible for the statement often used by racial segregationists that "stateways cannot change folkways," or "you can't legislate morality." Sumner also de-emphasized the rational side of human nature; he felt that people were simply a reflection of the cultural forces that played upon them. He saw life as a competition for survival.

Émile Durkheim (1858-1917)—proposed that the salient characteristic of human nature was its insatiability. People are creatures whose desires are unlimited; they are not satiated when their biological needs are fulfilled. Also, humankind is only fully human in and through society.

Max Weber (1864-1920)—possessed a conception of humankind radically different from the previously mentioned social theorists. To Weber, the essence of human behavior was the subjective meaning the person attaches to his or her behavior. Behavior is important to the degree that it reflects the values of the behaver.

Talcott Parsons (1902-)—Among these sociological theorists, Parsons has developed perhaps the most complex view of human creature. He proposes that:

1. All human actions are directed toward goals.
2. Human action is hence voluntaristic in the sense that the person possesses some freedom to choose between alternative actions.
3. Human behavior reflects both a cognitive orientation and a desire to gratify one's needs.
4. Order is brought to life through integration of common values.

Herbert Blumer (1905-)—A representative of the school of symbolic interactionism, Blumer explicitly recognizes that sociologists' views of humankind differ, depending upon their schools of thought. The human, to Blumer, is an organism that not only responds to others on a nonsymbolic level but also makes indications to others and interprets their indications. Humankind is an instigator as well as a responder.

(Michael J. Budde graciously provided the material for this box.)

severe electric shocks to another person. While the other person was not actually receiving any shocks, the experimental subject thought that he was, and most subjects reflected great degrees of discomfort and anguish as they continued their assigned task.

Milgram, in a sense, denied responsibility for the fact that many subjects continued to shock other individuals. Milgram assumed that subjects are free agents, that they are rational beings who have the power to act responsibly upon their environment. They may leave if they do not approve of the experiment. In contrast, many of Milgram's critics reflect a view that experimental subjects are, in a sense, captives of the experimenter, that the demand characteristics of the situation entrap them, and that they are no longer agents of their own free will. This conflict is a particularly beguiling one because the findings of Milgram's experiment generate, in most people, a pessimistic feeling about human nature.

Milgram's study has also been criticized on other grounds; Orne and Holland (1968), for example, claimed that subjects "saw through" the illusions of the experiment—that they were not really convinced that they were indeed hurting someone else. Milgram expressed a quite different assumption about the trusting nature of experimental subjects; he wrote: "I do not share the belief that people by and large are suspicious, distrustful, and given to outguessing scientific authorities; nor do I think that, among postal clerks, high-school teachers, salesmen, engineers, and laborers—our typical subjects—a great deal is known about psychological experiments" (Milgram, 1972, pp. 142-143). Here again, the researcher's assumption about an attribute of his subjects is intimately intertwined with his perspective on the nature and credibility of his research findings.

Beyond these examples we need to recognize that every psychological and sociological theory of human behavior rests upon fundamental assumptions about *what it is to be human,* and these assumptions influence the theory implicitly, even if their author does not state them or even recognize them (Holland, 1970). Abraham Maslow (1965) wrote:

> Every psychologist, however positivistic and antitheoretical he may claim to be, nevertheless has a full-blown philosophy of human nature hidden away within him. It is as if he guided himself by a half-known map, which he disavows and denies, and which is therefore immune to intrusion and correction by newly acquired knowledge. This unconscious map or theory guides his reactions far more than does his laboriously acquired experimental knowledge. (p. 23)

For example, the controversial nature of B. F. Skinner's *Beyond Freedom and Dignity* (1971) can be understood better if we examine its assumptions in contrast with those of other theoretical viewpoints. Likewise, Box 2.4 illustrates how the "giants" of sociological thinking have differed in their conceptions of human nature.

Our goal in this section is to bring out more clearly some of the assumptions that are the roots of four contemporary psychological approaches: (1) Skinnerian behaviorism, (2) psychoanalysis, (3) the humanistic-psychology movement, and (4) George Kelly's personal-construct theory. If an intelligent outsider approached a theorist from each of the schools of thought and asked "What is it like to be human?" each would give a remarkably different answer. Each approach reflects a different central concept in its theory of human nature. These concepts—"determinism," "innate aggressiveness," "growth," and "individuality"—will serve as guideposts for us (see Box 2.5).

Determinism refers to the assumption that human behavior has causes and, beyond this, that human "freedom" is illusory. In response to an outsider's question, B. F. Skinner (see Box 2.1) would have responded that humankind is not "free" in the traditional sense of the word. Rather, the human is an organism almost completely controlled by the puppet strings of social conditioning. A person's behavior is determined by his or her environment, even though it is an environment almost completely of the person's own making. Humankind has built this kind of a social environment; thus it induces persons to behave in certain ways—ways that people have labeled as "moral" or "immoral," "adaptive" or "maladaptive," and so on. To describe people as possessing "personalities" or "feelings" or "character traits" or "purposes" is unnecessary, for our behavior changes only when the consequences of our behavior change. There is no such thing as "mind" to be studied; a person's "mind does not change." Environments in which certain consequences are contingent upon our behavior are the factors that change that behavior; these environments, in Skinner's (1971) approach, take over the explanatory functions of "feelings," "states of mind," "intentions," and so on (p. 18). Interestingly enough for our purposes, while Skinner rejected such concepts as "attitudes," "values," "motives," and so forth as "prescientific," he recognized that almost everyone concerned with human affairs *assumes that such entities exist* (see Skinner, 1971, pp. 9-10).

In summary, Skinnerian behaviorism sees human nature as essentially a malleable substance that can be molded into either a good or a bad person. It sees human nature as neutral, and it claims to be free of evaluations and values. But we should not forget that behaviorism talks not only about the controlled but also about the controller. It recognizes that some people can control no one. The posing of such "internal" concepts as "aggressiveness" or "potential for growth" is considered by Skinnerian behaviorists to be superfluous, useless activity. Likewise, the concept of "individuality" is given little emphasis in Skinnerian explication of human nature. Differences in the reinforcement value of environments are recognized, however, as is the possibility that individuals will come to differ more and more as their past contingencies become more diverse.

The humanistic psychologist maintains a completely different picture. We quote at length from Carl Rogers's (1957) view:

> I do not discover man to be well characterized in his basic nature by such terms as fundamentally hostile, antisocial, destructive, evil.
>
> I do not discover man to be, in his basic nature, completely without a nature, a *tabula rasa* on which *anything* may be written, or malleable putty which can be shaped into *any* form.
>
> I do not discover man to be essentially a perfect being, sadly warped and corrupted by society.
>
> In my experience I have discovered man to have characteristics which seem inherent in his species, and the terms which have at different times seemed to me descriptive of these characteristics are such terms as positive, forward-moving, constructive, realistic, trustworthy.
>
> My experience is that he is a basically trustworthy member of the human species, whose deepest characteristics tend toward development, differentiation, cooperative relationships; whose life tends fundamentally to move from dependence to independence; whose impulses tend naturally to harmonize into a complex and changing pattern of self-regulation; whose total character is such as to tend to preserve and enhance himself and his species, and perhaps to move it toward its further evolution. (pp. 200-201)

Rollo May, while a humanist, also took a position quite critical to that of Carl Rogers. In what has been called a debate between the two (R. May, 1982; Rogers, 1982), May wrote:

> I propose the evil in our culture is also a reflection of evil in ourselves. . . . The culture is evil as well as good because we, the human beings who constitute it, are evil as well as good. . . . The issue of evil—or rather, the issue of not confronting evil has profound, and to my mind adverse, effects on humanistic psychology. (1982, pp. 12-13)

Abraham Maslow, like Rogers and R. May a developer of the humanistic movement in contemporary psychological theory, took a stance that emphasized humankind's positive qualities (B. G. Maslow, 1972).

But A. Maslow was more explicit than Rogers in bringing in the effect of environment. A. Maslow wrote:

> It is too simple to say "man is basically good" or "man is basically evil." These must be considered single-level statements and, therefore, obsolete against the new humanistic linguistics—that is, layers of meanings, levels of meanings.
>
> The correct way now would be to say "Man can become good (probably) and better and better, under a hierarchy of better and better conditions. But also it is very easy, even easier, for him to become bad or evil or sick, deprived of those fundamental 'conditions' or 'rights' " (B. G. Maslow, 1972, p. 88)

> The fact is that people are good, if only their fundamental wishes are satisfied, their wish for affection and security. (B. G. Maslow, 1972, p. 95)

> Every baby born is capable, in principle, of self-actualization. You should never give up on anyone, ever. Man has an instinctoid higher nature. It's possible to grow this or to stunt it. Society can do either. (B. G. Maslow, 1972, p. 133)

More than Rogers, Abraham Maslow reflects an awareness of the social schemata of *environment* and *society*. A deterministic framework is latent in Maslow's position, while it is denied by Rogers. The capacity for growth is the basic quality of human nature according to each of these representatives of the humanistic movement. While Rogers rejects the notion of innate aggressiveness, R. May and A. Maslow recognize that human aggression can occur if the environment conditions encourage it.

Rogers's theory had no explicit expression of individuality, despite the phenomenological and person-oriented credos of the humanistic movement.

The theory of psychoanalysis developed by Sigmund Freud offers a quite different response to the question "What is human nature really like?" Freud believed that the essence of human nature was a set of drives that society happened to find tolerable. Urges for immediate gratification of one's aggressive or sexual drives were, for Freud, basic to our nature, and society operated to curtail or rechannel these urges. Freud believed that most people had little understanding of the motives that truly energized their behavior; the motives they attributed to their own behavior were rationalizations or self-delusions that developed because the truth was too socially unacceptable to tolerate. While psychoanalysis might make a person more cognizant of his or her basic drives, it would not change basic nature.

Thus the Freudian position is a heavily deterministic one; not only do actions have causes, but the biological nature of the person also forces certain developments. For example, energy must be expended and many of its outlets are blocked from access because society considers them undesirable. Anxiety and repression become characteristic human ways of responding; this is inevitable as long as the individual submits to the conventions of society. Individuality is reflected only in the different reactions persons make to the constant demands of biological development and environmental circumstance.

Although Freud saw aggression as an inevitable expression of energy rather than as a calculated attempt to hurt others, his response to our question "What is it like to be human?" is the most pessimistic one.

The attribution of causes of human behavior to internal personalities is of course intolerable to the behavioristic model of human nature. Skinner (1971) wrote:

> Intelligent people no longer believe that men are possessed by demons (although the . . . daimonic has reappeared in the writings of psychotherapists). . . . A juvenile delinquent is said, for example, to be suffering from a destructive personality. . . . Psychoanalysts have identified three of these personalities—the ego, superego, and id—and interaction among them are said to be responsible for the behavior of the man in whom they dwell. (pp. 7-8)

In recent years there has been a cognitive revolution in psychology. Personal-construct theory established a basis for the cognitive approach (Jankowicz, 1987). This fourth school of psychological thought, George Kelly's personal-construct theory, is a response to both the psychoanalytic and behavioristic conceptions (Holland, 1970). Kelly (1955, 1963, 1970) proposed that we are essentially scientists in that we are constantly seeking an understanding of our world. To do this, each person develops a set of constructs that he or she refines and revises; these constructs serve as terms by which the person organizes and describes the world. Kelly (1955) wrote: "Man looks at his world through transparent patterns or templets which he creates and then attempts to fit over the realities of which the world is composed. . . . Let us give the name *constructs* to these patterns that are tried on for size. They are ways of construing the world" (pp. 8-9).

Thus like a scientist, each human being tries to choose constructs that will make his or her world understandable or predictable. Each person places his own interpretation on what he sees. While Skinner would propose that individuals strive for reinforcement and Freud might say that they seek to avoid anxiety, Kelly's view is that they are constantly trying to validate their construct systems (Oskamp, 1972). The dark predictability of human nature, as seen by Freud, is rejected by Kelly, who wrote that "a world jam-packed with lead pipe certainties, dictionary definitives, and doomsday finalities strikes me as a pretty gloomy place" (Maher, 1969, p. 7).

Kelly is equally critical of behaviorism, because he sees it as deterministic, manipulative, static, and pessimistic (Maher, 1969; see also Holland, 1970). Kelly also criticizes the humanistic and existential approaches, because, in his view, they are concerned exclusively with subjective experience, they portray the environment as a figment of people's imaginations, and they do not concede an external reality (Holland, 1970).

In fact, Kelly enjoyed noting that most of our theories in psychology fail to account for the behavior of those who devise and use them (Hinkle, 1970). Skinner claimed that people are not free, yet Skinner planned his own daily schedule. Freud, who believed that people were irrational, was convinced that through introspection he could understand his own dynamics. The unconditional acceptance advocated by Rogerian therapists acts as a reinforcing agent, thereby controlling the client's behavior. And even Kelly is not free of this taint. His attacks on other viewpoints (see Holland, 1970, pp. 116-118) reflect an ossified stereotyping of others.

Because personal-construct theory emphasizes that people are *responsible* for their construing and that their actions reflect their perceptions, Kelly objected to the deterministic aspects of behaviorism. (In turn, Skinner was most critical of the humanists and personal-construct theorists for their assumption of "autonomous" human nature. "What is being abolished [by a Skinnerian analysis] is autonomous man—the inner man, the homunculus, . . . the man defended by the literatures of freedom and dignity" [Skinner, 1971, p. 200].)

Kelly was critical of psychoanalysis because the human capacity to change—to revise constructs and resultant behaviors—is central to his view of humanness. And in personal-construct theory, Kelly assumed that there is a reality outside that can be studied, dealt with, and changed.

But the most important contribution of personal-construct theory to a conception of human nature is its emphasis on individual differences. As we have implied before, Kelly considers it quite presumptuous for many theorists to set up a series of constructs as explanations of the psychodynamics of every person. Instead, personal-construct theory proposes that every person develops a unique set of constructs by which he or she seeks to deal with the world. Kelly's (1970) "Individuality Corollary" states that "Persons differ from each other in their constructions of events" (p. 12). This idea of uniqueness has largely been ignored by the other approaches, yet it is a central part of our conceptualization, described in the next chapter.

Summary

Throughout Western civilization, assumptions about human nature have been developed and revised. The logic of inquiry used in the study of matter was employed by the early Greek philosophers to conceptualize human nature, and to a large degree this approach remains the most influential force in the study of human nature. That is, assumptions of determinism and other physical-science assumptions are the basis for contemporary behavioristic and psychoanalytic assumptions about human nature. The conceptions reflected in the humanistic-psychology movement and in personal-construct theory are in some ways shifts away from the predominant orientations (which heavily rely upon determinism and an analysis of irreducible essences), yet implicit assumptions of determinism remain.

CHAPTER THREE

Conceptualizing Philosophies of Human Nature

You can't treat a kid who grew up knife-fighting in Harlem the way you treat a blond, four-letter man from Christ Lake, Wisconsin. I don't want to fit all my players into one mold.

—AL McGUIRE,
while basketball coach
at Marquette University

Philosophies of human nature are attitudes about people in general—attitudes that emphasize the interpersonal qualities of people. They are expectancies that people possess certain qualities and will behave toward others in certain ways. While these attitudes may not be easily verbalized by the individuals who hold them, they seem to be learned early, held widely, and changed with difficulty. We all develop philosophies of human nature because other people play such a significant part in our environment that we must have some expectations about their behavior. Just as we question the performance of our car in preparation for a long cross-country trip, we speculate about the performance of people upon whom we rely and about the likelihood of their behaving in particular ways. F. H. Sanford (1961) wrote that "people constitute so significant a part of the world in which we live that we could not tolerate life if they were constantly surprising us" (p. 31). In fact, much of cognitive social psychology is concerned with how we make sense of our social world (Furnham, 1988).

For years and years, surveys have consistently revealed that inanimate things do not bother and irritate us so much as the behavior of other people does, particularly behavior that violates norms and hence is unexpected or unpredictable. The existentialist writer Sartre demonstrated the contribution of other people's behavior to our irritation in his play *No Exit* (1947). All three characters in the play have died and gone to Hell. All of them, having wondered what the afterlife would be like, are

---

Box 3.1
Philosophies of Human Nature—Basic Nature or Human Behavior After Socialization?

Philosophies of human nature reflect beliefs about what people are like after they have moved through a lengthy socialization process. The concept does not attempt to reflect beliefs about inherent or innate qualities. A person who has a negative philosophy of human nature might believe that people are born "good" but become corrupted through our society's socialization process. Judy Miles of the University of British Columbia (personal communication, October 1, 1971) developed a set of attitude statements to measure "basic human nature," or one's beliefs about innate qualities. (A sample item: "The young child is loving by nature.") Miles hypothesized that hippies would see basic human nature more favorably than other people would, even though both hippies and nonhippies might be similar in their philosophies of human nature. Both groups, however, had similar patterns of attitudes; both held somewhat more negative beliefs about basic human nature than about socialized humankind.

---

quite surprised to find themselves ensconced in a formal drawing room, luxuriously furnished—except that it lacks windows and mirrors. All their physical needs are met, but they cannot leave this room or even see out of it. Neither can they sleep, for their eyes cannot close. Conversation develops among the three, and with it come arguing and interpersonal bitterness. Finally, as the acrimony becomes prolonged, one of the characters articulates the theme of the play: "Hell is [living with] other people."

While the mass of humanity may not be hellish to all of us, people are important in our lives. We have to make certain assumptions about our fellows, just as scientists find it necessary to make assumptions about the universe with which they work. The assumption of finite causation in science (Underwood, 1957) postulates that each event in the natural world has only a limited number of causes; similarly, we attribute the behavior of others to a limited number of factors (situational characteristics, personality, motives, pressures, luck, chance, and so on), and we assume that behavior of others is not completely capricious and random. In line with this, Heider (1958) states that, "by referring transient and variable behavior and events to relatively unchanging underlying conditions" (p. 79), we may achieve some order and predictability in our world (Bar-Tal & Greenberg, 1973).

The *implicit personality theories* that most of us develop reflect an assumption of finite causality in our everyday interpersonal behavior. Implicit personality theories (Bruner & Tagiuri, 1954; Cronbach, 1955; Wegner & Vallacher, 1977) are reflected in sets of traits, attributes, and behaviors that a person believes to be associated in people in general. If a person is stubborn, other people may also expect him or perceive him to be stingy, because most people have their own expectations that these two traits are associated. (In actuality, we do not know if stubborn people are any more stingy than anyone else.) These beliefs are "implicit" because people infer such associations from their spontaneous descriptions of and expectations about particular groups; they do not state them as formal theories. Box 3.2 describes Furnham's (1988) distinctions between formal, scientific theories and the theories that laypersons develop and use as they seek to understand human nature.

Similarly, the concept of balanced states of cognitions (Heider, 1958) may be useful in understanding the sources of philosophies of human nature. Heider theorizes that, in triads composed of two people and an object, a state of balance will develop so that "the relations among the entities fit together harmoniously" (p. 201). For example, if John likes Stephen and if John likes heavy metal music, he will expect Stephen to like heavy metal too. Beyond this, balance theory says that we expect good people to act fairly and to receive just treatment for their acts. To assume that injustice occurs in the world is so threatening to us that we often deny it through clever stratagems. To many well-meaning citizens of Nazi Germany, the imprisonment of seemingly innocent Jews in concentration camps might have seemed "unfair" upon initial consideration, but most Germans became persuaded—even convinced—that the Jews were indeed guilty of serious crimes (Bettelheim, 1943). Later in this chapter, examples of the assumption of a "just world" (Lerner, 1980) will be documented.

A plant manager's ways of motivating workers may also reflect his or her assumptions about what is just treatment for them. Douglas McGregor (1960) observed and analyzed two theories of motivation prevalent in industry, each reflecting a vastly different set of assumptions about human nature. Theory X—the traditional view—pictures the average worker as someone who dislikes work and avoids it as much as possible. According to Theory X, workers must be coerced into work and they will avoid responsibility as much as they can. In contrast to this picture, McGregor's

Box 3.2

Lay Persons' Theories Versus Scientific Theories

In a provocative and wide-ranging book, Adrian Furnham (1988) has analyzed the lay theories and scientific theories that are used to explain human behavior. Based on the work of Valentine (1982), eight criteria are identified that distinguish between a scientific theory and a lay person's explanation of behavior:

1. Explicitness and formality: "Lay theories are often implicit rather than explicit, with tacit, non-specified assumptions or axioms. On the other hand, some (but by no means all) scientific theories are *formal* in the sense that they are set in a logically internally consistent manner" (Furnham, 1988, p. 3).

2. Coherent and consistent: Lay theories can be ambiguous, incoherent, and internally inconsistent; that is, people can hold two beliefs at the same time that are incompatible or contradictory; to the consternation of the consistency theorists, they may not even be troubled by the incompatibility. Scientific theories, in contrast, seek to be both coherent and consistent.

3. Verification versus falsification: Furnham writes: "Although not universally accepted, many epistemologists accept Popper's principle of falsification as the criterion of science. On the other hand, the layman often asks for verification rather than falsification" (1988, p. 4). That is, the principle of falsifiability states that a theory must have the capacity to be disproved and holds until it is disproved.

4. Cause and consequence: Lay theories often confuse correlation with cause; scientific theories attempt to distinguish between those relationships in which one agent can be identified as the cause of another and those in which other factors may play a role.

5. Content versus process: Furnham (1988) notes: "Many academic theories are process rather than content oriented whereas the opposite is frequently true of lay theories. Consider theories of human nature; academic theories of the etiology of personality and individual differences are frequently concerned with processes whereby people differ from one another on various dimensions—intellectual or cognitive reactions, emotional responses, and so on. Most lay theories, on the other hand, are content oriented in the sense that they are primarily descriptive of types or categories" (p. 5).

6. Internal (individualistic) versus external (situational): Lay people give less emphasis to situational causes of behavior and locate the causes of behavior within the individual.

7. General versus specific: This is a dimension for which disagreement exists between experts, but Furnham observes that agreement seems to be present on the point that lay theories are not as concerned with generalizing to abstract theoretical principles.

8. Strong versus weak: Strong theories, according to Eysenck (1960), are based on numerous accurate observations made by many different people. Predictions are straightforward and precise; the phenomena in question are relatively clear-cut and ambiguous. Weak theories do not possess these qualities.

Theory Y—the integrative view—portrays the worker as a self-directed and self-controlled person who not only accepts responsibility but also seeks it out. Theory Y ascribes characteristics of imagination and creativity to the worker. Industrial managers often employ one of these theories in their management procedures, because predicting the behavior of the worker is of great importance to them.

How Do Philosophies of Human Nature Develop?

We have proposed that philosophies of human nature may be considered as the belief component of attitudes. Like all attitudes, they are learned. Although we have adequate conceptions of how general social attitudes develop, we know little about the development of attitudes toward human nature (Furnham, 1988). F. H. Sanford (1961) many years ago stated that "there is in existence no scientific literature bearing directly on the ways we learn our theories of people nor on the precision with which we predict their behavior or our own" (p. 32); the statement is still mostly true. If we assume, however, that philosophies of human nature develop as other social attitudes do, the sources of their development seem to be subject to classification. For example, Sarbin, Taft and Bailey (1960) have listed four major sources: induction or experience; construction or inference and deductions from observations; analogy or extrapolation from a specific encounter; and authority or acceptance of ideas from others, the media, and so on (cited in Furnham, 1988, p. 8). Based on the above, we propose the following specific sources: (1) observation of behavior of others; (2) opinions expressed by others and training received from others; (3) constant retesting in real life of one's philosophies; and (4) one's own personality. Illustrations of these sources follow.

OBSERVATION OF BEHAVIOR OF OTHERS

Most people agree that a child learns basic values and attitudes toward specific objects as a result of his or her environment. Other people are a major part of that environment, and children's attitudes are dependent upon their observation of the behavior of others. If a child sees that his or her mother is helpful, reassuring, and likable, he or she may assume— until shown otherwise—that this is the type of behavior to expect from others. It seems likely that the mother's caretaker behaviors exert a great influence on the development of the child's philosophy of human nature—greater, in fact, than even her extensive exposure to the child would suggest. We may hypothesize that children's philosophies of human nature are related to the styles of behavior exhibited by their mothers. (Tests of this hypothesis will be evaluated in Chapter 8.)

Although a mother normally influences her child more than any other person does, she is not the only significant agent. The child constantly has the opportunity to observe the behavior of others—his or her father, siblings, teachers, and playmates. As A. L. Baldwin (1955) stated, the development of attitudes is partly a process of discovering characteristics of other people. Thus if the child concludes that these other people are basically untrustworthy, unhelpful, and abusive, his or her conception of human nature will probably develop into a negative one. Of course, in real life such things are not so straightforward. Probably every person whom the child observes possesses some qualities worth emulating and some not-so-worthy qualities, and it is difficult to specify which aspects will have the greatest influence on the child's assumptions about human nature.

OPINIONS EXPRESSED BY OTHERS
AND TRAINING RECEIVED FROM OTHERS

Children seem to resemble malleable clay in their ability to be altered by others. (But perhaps that is *our* assumption about human nature!) They internalize the attitudes and behaviors of others and adopt them for their own. They learn by listening to their parents and other prestige figures who seemingly possess the truth. In fact, they learn so much that for any parent the phenomenon of latent learning in children is a very viable one. Our most unwise or intemperate observations seem to be the ones that our children remember and throw back at us.

Adults' attitudes toward people are readily expressed in many different ways and their evaluations of people are easily conveyed to children. If parents are suspicious and distrustful, they are likely to demonstrate this distrust to their children directly and they are certain to demonstrate it indirectly. The child, always looking for a model, may accept such beliefs and adhere to them. This is especially true in the case of attitudes toward human nature, for the older child is constantly grasping for answers to the vital question "What are people really like?" Assuming that the child will accept his or her parents' attitudes in this area as he or she does in other areas (Newcomb & Svelha, 1937), we may hypothesize a relationship between the philosophies of parents and those of their offspring (Chapter 8 reports on tests of this hypothesis).

Although adults often unintentionally convey their attitudes to children, on many occasions they are more deliberate in their influences. Some child-rearing techniques, for example, seem to play a role in the development of a child's personality. Although early studies relating specific child-rearing practices to children's emerging personalities seemed inconclusive (Orlansky, 1949), the general social climate of the home appears to influence the development of certain traits in children. Radke (1946) found that nursery school children raised in more restrictive and autocratic home environments were less aggressive, less popular, and less competitive than were children raised in more democratic environments. J. P. Anderson (1940) reported that junior high school pupils who were brought up in warm, affectionate families with little in the way of adult dominance were mature, poised, cheerful, cooperative, obedient, and responsible.

It is more difficult to find studies demonstrating the specific influence of home environment upon the child's assumptions about human nature. We believe some research is relevant, however. Watson (1957) studied children aged 5 through 12, all of whom had been brought up in "good, loving homes." Those children who had been strictly disciplined by their parents showed more hostility toward others, whereas children with permissive parents expressed more positive feelings toward others. These differences were consistent at various ages but since Watson's subjects were chosen from extremely strict and extremely permissive families we cannot be sure that the relationship would apply in more typical home environments. Of greater concern here is the applicability of this finding to attitudes toward human nature. In Watson's study, hostility and friendliness to others were determined by responses to the pictures on the Thematic Apperception Test and to the inkblots on the Rorschach Diagnostic Test, by free play with dolls, and by figure-drawing responses. We cannot assume that children who "express" hostility to others in these projective-test responses will also respond to inventory and open-ended measures with a view that human nature is hostile and unfriendly. The question is of more than just methodological significance, however, and gives rise to a hypothesis that a positive relationship exists between expressions of hostility on projective measures and indications of negativism in inventory and open-ended measures of philosophies of human nature.

The evidence regarding a relationship between inventory and projective measures of the same concept is, of course, incredibly extensive and mercilessly contradictory. For a fascinating example of how the two types of instruments can present an entirely different picture of the same person, see Davids and Silverman (1960). We will consider this in Chapter 4 when we review types of measurements.

Daniel Levinson's early work with an inventory of traditional family ideologies has some bearing on the relationship between child-rearing disciplines and children's attitudes. Levinson and Huffman (1953) constructed a 40-item scale measuring the autocratic-democratic dimension of family relationships. The following aspects were seen as parts of a "traditional," or authoritarian, family ideology: conventionalism, authoritarian submission, exaggerated masculinity and femininity, extreme emphasis on discipline, and moralistic rejection of impulsive behavior. On the other hand, persons favoring the democratic orientation preferred to "decentralize authority within the family, to seek greater equality in husband-wife and parent-child relationships, and to maximize individual self-determination" (Levinson & Huffman, 1953, p. 101). Levinson and Huffman presented evidence that adherence to the traditional family ideology is related to a high degree of authoritarianism as measured by scores on the California F scale. This is hardly surprising since the two groups of statements have a similar clichéd ring to them and, in fact, have one statement in common (Item 58 on the T.F.I.—Traditional Family Ideology—scale). But since a negative view of human nature seems to be one aspect of the authoritarian syndrome and since authoritarianism seems to be a basic part of this traditional family ideology, the theory behind the development of philosophies would predict that traditional family ideology, authoritarianism, and negativistic views of human nature are all related to some extent. (Results bearing on these expectations are presented in Chapters 4 and 6.)

CONSTANT RETESTING IN REAL LIFE OF ONE'S PHILOSOPHIES

As children grow older, their attitudes change. School-age children come into contact with more people. Television viewing also generates an onslaught of impressions about people who, to the child, appear to be real. The child learns that people are different and that although a concept of "human nature" may still be serviceable it cannot be applied with equal utility to everyone. Blake and Dennis (1943) have shown, in their study of the development of the stereotype of African-American, that as children grow older they begin to differentiate. The older child sees things less certainly as "all good" or "all bad" and uses extreme categories less frequently. Part of the reason for these changes is that children are constantly testing their ideas against everyday experiences. A girl may remember that one teacher gave her a lift to school but that another lied to her. Older children's conceptions of human nature attain a richness and complexity that they lacked before. While the substantive qualities of the child's beliefs may not change as he or she grows older, the child's realization of the complexity and variability present in human nature should grow. The relationship between age differences and philosophies of human nature is reviewed in Chapters 5 and 8.

ONE'S OWN PERSONALITY

The human personality is always working in conjunction with the environment—reacting to it, modifying it. Just as our personalities, motivations, expectancies, and needs influence our perceptions of ambiguous stimuli, they also color our perceptions of people, including ourselves. Is our self-perception related to our perception of the mass of people around us?

The concept of self-acceptance is a cornerstone in the personality theory of Carl Rogers (1949). Self-acceptance is often a goal in counseling. Rogers felt that people who are self-accepting are accepting of others. In our framework, then, Rogers was saying that persons are more likely to have favorable philosophies of human nature if their own personalities are what they desire them to be. A person with undesirable attitudes regarding himself or herself is likely to be rejected by others, thus giving truth to latent ideas about the basic perversity of human nature.

Such assumptions generated a great deal of empirical work 30 to 40 years ago. McCandless (1961), reviewing this body of work, concluded that "the majority of studies of this subject indicate a clear and significant relation between acceptance of self and acceptance of others" (p. 196). At least 10 studies (E. M. Berger, 1951; Bossom & Maslow, 1957; V. J. Crandall & Bellugi, 1954; Fey, 1955; Levanway, 1955; McIntyre, 1952; Omwake, 1954; Phillips, 1951; Wylie, 1957; Zuckerman, Baer, & Monashkin, 1956) confirmed the hypothesis and led to a generalization that, to quote McCandless (1961), "the self-accepting person sees the world as a friendlier and more benign place than the self-rejecting individual" (p. 196). However, as Wylie pointed out in her comprehensive review (1961), some of the correlations obtained in these studies may have been inflated because of common response formats. A tendency toward acquiescence or, conversely, a response set that is generally critical could lead to the appearance of strong relationships where they do not exist. Omwake's (1954) study, comparing structurally different measures of self-acceptance and acceptance of others, came to such a conclusion. However, although two studies (Zelen, 1954; Zimmer, 1956) failed to confirm the relationship, it seems highly probable that self-accepting individuals view human nature in a more favorable light than self-rejecting persons do. We test this hypothesis with more recent and relevant procedures further in Chapter 6.

In this section, we have attempted to describe some of the factors leading to the development of specific philosophies of human nature. But we have almost ignored the kinds of philosophies that people express, having been content to make off-handed references to traits that might fit their way into someone's philosophy of human nature. A description of the kinds and variety of philosophies of human nature follows in the next section.

What Kinds of Philosophies of Human Nature Are Held?

As Chapter 1 pointed out, we frequently stumble across expressions of philosophies of human nature. We hear them in everyday conversation, and the mass media abound with them. The expressions in Box 3.3 give some indication of the richness and intricate development of our beliefs.

Most people are not so articulate, or not so introspective, about their feelings as the editor and the novelist quoted in Box 3.3. But we propose that each person makes certain assumptions about the expected behavior of others. (Thank goodness, not all of us make the same ones!) Of course, we develop attitudes toward those specific individuals with whom we have extended contact, but these are not philosophies of human nature. Rather, a philosophy of human nature is the residue that remains after we remove those attitudes that are accounted for by such cues as our familiarity with a person and our knowledge of the person's behavior. Our attitudes toward others are most clearly revealed in our dealings with strangers—particularly in our dealings with nondescript or bland strangers who do not display such cues as dirty fingernails, hand-tailored clothes, pro-life buttons, or other signs that influence our expectations. For, in our reactions to such strangers, we have no specific data from past

---

Box 3.3
A Random Collection of Outlooks on Human Nature

1. The editor of a prize-winning newspaper (Peter, 1961) states the philosophy that he has developed as a result of 20 years of dealing with the newspaper-reading public: "I'll concede my outlook is cynical. People, by and large, aren't capable of objective thinking" (p. 8).
2. A survey of businessmen (Baumhart, 1961) reveals general pessimism about the ethical behavior of their fellows. A majority of the 1,500 businessperson-respondents believed that "businessmen would violate a code of ethics whenever they thought they could escape detection" (p. 19). The case histories presented in Heilbroner's *In the Name of Profit* (1972) reflect instances of such violations of ethics.
3. A successful novelist, James Gould Cozzens, describes the philosophy that permeates his work: "I think a person can be at the same time officious and devoted, self-important and self-sacrificing, insensitive and sympathetic. Indeed, I think that is exactly what most people are most of the time" (personal letter quoted in Bracher, 1959, pp. 68-69).

---

encounters. We have virtually nothing to go on but our assumptions about how people in general behave. These assumptions constitute a philosophy of human nature.

Our philosophies of human nature are thus revealed in the ways in which we predict and interpret the ambiguous behavior of others. Do we expect the worst or the best? Do we reserve judgment or do we have a ready explanation for every behavior? Do we tend to evaluate every action or to treat actions more impassively? Obviously, we cannot be completely factual and objective in our orientation toward others—the material dealing with our needs for predictability, the development of our attitudes in childhood, and our constant retesting of them should indicate that. But some of us are more evaluative than others. Hence, individuals may differ in the extent to which they are ready to ascribe expected behaviors to others. In fact, the possibility of such differences is a basic part of the theory of philosophies of human nature. Some people are reticent to prejudge their peers, while others are "sure" that certain behaviors occur because of certain motives. People may be quick to judge for several reasons. Their training, their jobs, or their environments may require them to make snap judgments about others. Their feelings of inadequacy in coping with others may cause them to make hasty—and often inaccurate—judgments. Thus people vary not only in the philosophies they hold but also in the reticence with which they express them.

Approaches to Conceptualizing Philosophies of Human Nature

We have maintained that it is easy to identify expressions of philosophies of human nature. A great problem remains, however, in conceptualizing them. How can we structure philosophies of human nature? We may find some help in the ways in which personality theorists approach the question of the structure of personality. For example, Maddi's (1976) text on the psychology of personality presents a useful frame of reference for the study of assumptions of human nature as reflected in divergent personality theories. Maddi divides personality theories into three models and separately considers the parts of the theories dealing with the common, inherent nature, or "core of personality."

More general approaches have been through such conceptualizations as personality styles, personality types, responses to specific situations, and personality traits. This section illustrates how each of these conceptualizations might be used in the study of philosophies of human nature.

PERSONALITY STYLES

Stagner (1961) has stated that the concept of personality style (or personal style) refers "to the fact that, entirely aside from specific precepts or specific responses, the person may show a characteristic pattern of perceiving or of responding" (p. 137). (The studies of George S. Klein [1951] and of Witkin, Lewis, Machover, Meissner, & Wapner [1954], emphasizing the characteristic ways in which we deal with our environment, have contributed significantly to this view.) People may be described, then, by their idiosyncratic processes of perceiving and responding. In fact, Stagner (1961) points out that "the individual may develop a characteristic style not only in his gestures, or in his way of acting out an emotion, but in the manner of relating to his environment and to other people" (p. 151). This "manner of relating . . . to other people" reflects a stylistic component of a philosophy of human nature.

How can the "personality-style" approach be applied to the conceptualization of philosophies of human nature? Theories emphasizing the operation of a particular ethic are perhaps the best examples. The German sociologist Max Weber used the word *ethic* to designate a person's character or ideals of character (LaPiere, 1959). A person's prevalent ethic would seem to determine his or her style of responding and his or her expectations about how others would or should respond.

Weber believed that the predominant style of life should reflect the "Protestant Ethic." Human nature was seen as independent and self-reliant. People were strongly motivated and responsible for their own welfare. They possessed the vibrant feeling of control over their own welfare and the belief that, through thrift, hard work, and competitive struggle, they could raise their position in life. The Protestant Ethic was a variation of the Spartan view of durable humankind "modulated by the humanitarian idea of the inherent dignity and integrity of the individual" (LaPiere, 1959, p. 15). It was the dominant philosophy of human nature in that "Century of Hope," the 19th century, that seems so far away from our own time. Political theory in the last century also conceptualized the human as a rational being, "one who, if but given the opportunity, would be stable, self-impelled, responsive to rational considerations" (Nisbett, 1961, p. 64).

To no one's surprise, the view of later writers is that the Protestant Ethic and the rationalist assumption in political theory are passing from the American scene. In a book whose significance is often overlooked, La Piere (1959) described the predominant style of human behavior in America as the "Freudian Ethic," while Whyte (1957) chose to label a similar conception the "Social Ethic."

Weber (1930) implied that the Protestant Ethic was a conception of the *desirable* way of responding, but more recent analysts seem to use the term *prevalent ethic* to mean the *accepted* way of responding.

LaPiere (1959) bemoaned the development of what he called the "Freudian Ethic." The term is derived from Sigmund Freud's views on human nature. As we indicated in Chapter 2, it is apparent that Freud had little faith in people; he once wrote: "In the depths of my heart, I can't help being convinced that my dear fellowmen, with few exceptions, are worthless" (quoted in E. L. Freud, 1960). D. E. Walker (1956) traced Freud's view that people are "destructive, antisocial, and anticultural" (S. Freud, 1949, pp. 110-111) back to St. Augustine, but, unlike the saint, Freud made no provision for humankind's return to a position of esteem. LaPiere (1959) feels that this conception of human nature has come to dominate our present-day society. He described the Freudian Ethic as follows:

The rise of Freudian doctrine as the prevailing concept of the nature of man is at once a measure of the decline of the Protestant Ethic and a denial of the idea that man is a creature of reason. In the Freudian concept, man is not born free with the right to pursue life, liberty and happiness; he is shackled by biological urges that can never be freely expressed and that set him in constant and grievous conflict with his society . . . Freud does not say, in the theological manner, that man fell from Grace and must therefore suffer in this life. But he does come to much the same concept of man: that man is by nature (or at least by virtue of the inevitable conflict between man's nature and society) a weak and irresolute creature without the stamina to endure the stresses and strains of living, and who cannot therefore hope to enjoy life on this earth. (LaPiere, 1959, p. 60)

Why has this view of human nature developed? LaPiere felt that, as a consequence of Freud's frequent exposure to the neurotic side of the human continuum, he came to assume these hopeless, helpless people to be representative of humankind in general. But was this really Freud's view of people? If people were "worthless," why did he spend so much time trying to restitute them? Carl Rogers (1957), whose views of human nature are in opposition to the Freudian Ethic, felt that Freud continued to exaggerate the focus on the "evil" feelings of humankind in an effort to communicate its irrationality and "evil" urges to the people of his Victorian era. Rogers believed that Freud's view could not have continued in this pattern; "Freud's own experience with his patients must have shown him that, once these 'evil' feelings were known, accepted, and understood by the individual, he could be trusted to be a normally self-controlled, socialized person" (Rogers, 1957, p. 202). If we accept Erich Fromm's (1959) analysis of Freud's personality, however, we find confirmation for the previous hypothesis of a relationship between maladjustment and negative philosophies of human nature. Fromm's analysis is a devastating one; he describes Freud as rigid, cold, and authoritarian, and he does so with such intensity that he destroys our perception of Freud as warm, egalitarian, accepting, loving, and possessing other qualities often attributed to psychotherapists.

LaPiere (1959) saw the Freudian Ethic as the dominant philosophy of humankind in America, encroaching upon society and altering it in the direction of permissive homes, progressive schools, emphasis on adjustment over achievement, and leniency toward criminals. It is reflected in many comments about contemporary occurrences. Consider, for example, the reactions to the Central Park "wilding" incident in which a young woman jogger was raped, assaulted, and left for dead. Some commentators explained the behavior of the attackers by concentrating on the limitations in their environment. Thus they were excused for their deplorable acts. In some ways, Whyte's (1957) analysis of American philosophies of human nature is similar to that of LaPiere. Both saw a decline in the Protestant Ethic, and both decried this decline. Whyte appears a little more realistic with regard to what kind of a basic style to expect in contemporary life; he recognized the complexities of modern society and the resultant need for reliance upon others. Whyte described what he calls the "Social Ethic" as follows:

> By Social Ethic I mean that contemporary body of thought which makes morally legitimate the pressures of society against the individual. Its major propositions are three: a belief in the group as a source of creativity; a belief in "belongingness" as the ultimate need of the individual; and a belief in the application of science to achieve the belongingness. . . . Man exists as a unit of society. Of himself, he is isolated, meaningless; only as he collaborates with others does he become worthwhile, for by sublimating himself in the group, he helps produce a whole that is greater than the sum of its parts. (Whyte, 1957, pp. 7-8)

To Whyte, the contemporary person is motivated by social considerations. He or she is not oriented toward achieving so much as toward being accepted. Rewards accrue not from hard work but from the ability to work with and through one's fellows. David Riesman's view (1955) of a prevalent other-directed orientation in our society is similar. Both of these philosophies of human nature are milder than the one proposed by LaPiere (1959). Although both Whyte and Riesman revealed the regret with which they described the American scene, they were able to trace reasons for the change in the American character.

Twenty years ago a new conception suddenly surfaced. Although no longer mentioned anymore, Consciousness III, as it was called, is experiencing a resurgence in the 1990s under other labels. Charles Reich's (1970) analysis of what he called Consciousness III reflected a historical development. To Reich, "consciousness" was not just a set of opinions, items of information, or values but a total configuration that makes up an individual's whole perception of reality—or world view. New levels of consciousness are developed to meet the particular needs of society. One hundred fifty years ago, humankind was idealized as rugged individualists, competitive and able to improve themselves. This "Consciousness I" meshed well with the orientation of an expanding, self-aggrandizing country with a wealth of land and relatively few people to develop it. In the 1930s, a new consciousness was necessary because the needs of the country were different. Reich's "Consciousness II" resembles Riesman's theory of the "other-directed man" and Whyte's Social Ethic; in Consciousness II, humankind was group-oriented, progressive—even liberal—but people worked within a system to achieve change. In the *Greening of America,* Reich (1970) looked with dismay at the life that the technological development and bureaucratic superstructure of Consciousness II bequeathed us. A new consciousness, he predicted, was evolving—a Consciousness III that desired a return to nature and naturalness, a rejection of technology and competitiveness, a renewing and freeing of humankind, and a creation of a more human community. While Reich did not see most Americans as then achieving Consciousness III, he saw the movement toward this level of consciousness operating as a nonviolent revolution that would inundate the United States. Recent concerns to achieve a "green revolution," to avoid further pell-mell destruction of the physical environment, and a concern with preservation of natural resources are congruent with Consciousness III.

PERSONALITY TYPES

A type-theory approach to personality description maintains that people can be classified into two or more categories. Stagner (1961) stated that

> a type approach to personality will be defensible if we can demonstrate (1) that certain rules hold for personalities falling into one type and are simply inapplicable to persons belonging to another type; or, (2) what amounts to the same thing, that differences in quality or pattern, not reducible to dimensional scales, can be identified as distinctive of each type. (p. 264)

A classic example of a type theory in psychology is Jung's theory of extroversion and introversion.

An application of the type-theory approach to philosophies of human nature is the Calvinistic doctrine that divides people into those who are saved and those who are damned. This view qualifies as a type-theory approach because people in the two groups are clearly distinguishable and because a qualitative difference exists between the types (that is, only the believer is favored by God).

In a lighter vein, but relevant, is boxer Muhammad Ali's theory. Invited by the graduating seniors to speak at Harvard University's commencement ceremonies about the time that he was at the height of his success, Ali expressed his theory about people, which was built around four types. These were the walnut, "hard on the outside, but soft on the inside"; the prune, "soft on the outside but hard on the inside"; the pomegranate, "hard on the inside and outside"; and the grape, "soft on the inside and the outside." He also stated that of all the fruits in the bowl, the grape is the most attractive. He said that he usually lets the public see only his "walnut" personality, but confessed to being more of a "grape" (Wrightsman, 1977).

Another type theory of personality that is relevant to philosophies of human nature is that of Spranger (1928). Spranger viewed each person as motivated primarily by one of six values: the "theoretical" (or quest for truth), the "aesthetic" (or love of beauty), the "religious" (or the seeking after the Cosmos), the "economic" (or an orientation toward the practical), the "social" (or desire to help others), or the "political" (or quest for power). Allport, Vernon, and Lindzey (1960) have used this framework in their measure of values. Similarly, Charles Morris (1956) attempted to classify people according to their preferences for 13 "ways of life."

Other attempts by psychologists to classify people in ways that reflect their basic natures are those by Havighurst and Taba (1949) and by Peck and Havighurst (1960). Havighurst and Taba classified adolescents into "basic personality types": the "self-directive person," the "defiant person," the "maladjusted person," and so on. Peck and Havighurst related developmental periods to certain "character types": the "amoral," the "expedient," the "conforming," the "irrational-conscientious," and the "rational-altruistic." However, as Stagner (1961, p. 265) points out, these can be viewed as extremes of some attribute rather than as true types. In contrast, Box 3.4 reflects an anthropological approach to typing basic human values in different cultures.

Generally, American psychologists have found type theories to be unsatisfactory, since psychology on this side of the Atlantic emphasizes the variety of aspects of personality and the normal distribution of people along a continuum of personality. A conceptualization of philosophies of human nature similar to a type theory would probably also be unsatisfactory. Although some individuals may be content with a simple pronouncement that "some people are good and some are evil," most of us probably want to view human nature as more dimensionalized and complex than that.

Box 3.4

Kluckhohn's Classification of Basic Value Orientations

Florence R. Kluckhohn, an anthropologist, has made the assumption that there is a limited number of basic human questions for which all people at all times and in all places must find answers: (1) "What is the dominant modality of the relationship of man to other men?"; (2) "What is the significant time dimension?"; (3) "What is the valued personality type?"; (4) "What is man's relationship to nature?"; (5) "What are the innate predispositions of man?"

To each of these five basic questions, Kluckhohn (1953) suggested three possible answers.

Question	Possible Answers		
	Familiaristic	Collateral	Individualistic
Modality of relationship among men			
Time dimension	Past	Present	Future
Valued personality type	Being	Being-in-becoming	Doing
Man's relationship to nature	Man subjugated	Man equal to nature	Man over nature
Innate predispositions	Evil (mutable or immutable)	Neither good nor bad (mutable or immutable)	Good (mutable or immutable)

RESPONSES TO SPECIFIC SITUATIONS

The third approach is quite different from the first two. Advocates of the specific-response approach to personality description feel that each response that a person makes should be viewed separately. According to this approach, each situation is unique and so one's response to it will also be unique. There may be little consistency in a person's responses from one situation to another, and type and trait approaches fail to do enough justice to the unique aspects of every event and every person.

If we relate this approach to a conceptualization of philosophies of human nature, we will be concerned with the reactions of people to particular events. Hence, we should not try to extract general descriptions of human nature; instead, we should draw conclusions about human nature in particular situations. It is difficult to find a philosophy of human nature that carries this flavor, although there are points of view that emphasize actual "how-to-do-it" behaviors rather than underlying attributes. In *The Prince,* for example, Machiavelli (1952) gave prescriptions for dealing with the problems of court. He wrote: "men are so simple and so ready to obey present necessities that one who deceives will always find those who allow themselves to be deceived" (p. 92). Machiavelli advocated specific activities to control specific quirks of character.

An approach that focuses on particular responses to particular situations has a virtue in the clarity of its communication value. That is, if we try to determine people's philosophies of human nature by asking them how most people would act in a particular situation (such as when confronted with the problem of whether to declare $1,500 of cash income on their income-tax form), we may assume that they are responding to essentially the same stimulus. Knowing how people feel about behavior in specific situations, however, is not enough; we must be able to generalize those attitudes to other situations. The trait approach, which makes such generalizations, will be examined next.

PERSONALITY TRAITS

A personality trait is a relatively enduring aspect of personality that underlies a variety of behaviors in a variety of situations. Stagner (1961, p. 156) defined it as "a consistent feature of personality which has some emotional or ideational content, in opposition to the term 'style,' which is relatively pure process without any reference, either external or internal."

Box 3.5
The "Big Five" of Personality Traits

Literally thousands of words in the English language describe personality or human behavior. But is there a taxonomy that combines these specific descriptions in a simplified way (O. P. John, 1990)? During the last decade, researchers on the psychology of personality have come to general agreement that five terms may adequately summarize the important descriptive characteristics of personality. The "big five" factors are the following:

1. Surgency (or Extraversion vs. Introversion)
2. Agreeableness
3. Conscientiousness (or Work Orientation or Superego Strength)
4. Emotional Stability (contrasted with Neuroticism)
5. Intellect/Openness to Experience (or Flexibility vs. Rebelliousness)

A trait, then, is covert, but it is implicit in many types of behaviors. It is of necessity generalizable.

For several decades, followers of the trait approach generally assumed that there were from 10 to 20 basic factors with which we can describe personality. In the last 5 years, however, consensus has emerged regarding "the Big Five" traits (see Box 3.5 for an elaboration). The trait approach is actually a compromise between the detailed nature of a specific-response approach and the lack of refinement in a type-theory approach. We find that philosophies of human nature, or their fragments, are frequently expressed through traits, for when people describe people with a list of nouns or adjectives they are using a trait approach. For example, Carl Rogers's expression of his philosophy about human nature, presented in Chapter 2, reflects a trait description.

For many people, a trait approach would be a comfortable means of expressing a philosophy of human nature. They might describe others as "selfish" or "trustworthy" or "friendly" or "immoral." These descriptions qualify as traits, for they are characteristics that underlie behavior and apply in a variety of situations. Other people might express their philosophies of human nature through reference to specific behaviors or to specific responses in particular situations. They may describe people by saying that "they cheat on their income tax" or that they "usually will tell you the truth whether it hurts or not."

In the last two decades, the stability and consistency of traits over time have been vigorously questioned (see Mischel, 1968). As Mischel acknowledged, however, people assume that traits operate over a variety of situations and use them as explanations of human behavior. What people are actually like and how they are perceived by others are two separate issues and we will assume, as Schneider (1971) does, that people in general perceive in trait terms. But what traits do they use? We consider that question in the next section.

In our conceptualization of philosophies of human nature, we have chosen to use a modified trait approach. Rather than a general evaluative dimension or a typology, we sought more specific dimensions of views of human nature. To aid us in identifying these dimensions we asked college students to write essays on "What Is the Nature of Human Nature?" and then we tabulated the terms used. We also considered and analyzed the writings of philosophers, theologians, and observers of society, both past and present. Certain dimensions emerged with consistency, although our procedure in selecting them was admittedly a subjective one.

The resulting conceptualization of philosophies of human nature includes four substantive dimensions and two further dimensions that cut across the first four and deal with beliefs about individual differences in human nature. In a sense, these beliefs about individual differences constitute a separate part of one's philosophy of human nature. Two persons, for example, may possess extremely favorable beliefs about the substantive characteristics of humankind, but they may have divergent beliefs about the degree of individual differences present in human nature. The one who believes that all people are trustworthy and that all people are alike may be less likely to seek information about another person before interacting with that person. In contrast, the person who believes that each of us is different, even though all people are basically trustworthy, may behave differently in various interpersonal situations.

With these considerations in mind, we will describe each dimension along with its relevance to contemporary thinking and research.

Six Dimensions of Philosophies of Human Nature

The first dimension of a personal philosophy of human nature is *trustworthiness versus untrustworthiness,* or the extent to which one believes that people are basically trustworthy, moral, and responsible as opposed to believing that people are untrustworthy, immoral, and irresponsible. As we will see in more detail in Chapter 8, Erik Erikson (1950, 1959, 1964) has postulated that the first conflict in an infant's psychological development is whether to trust or mistrust his or her mother. Edith Weigert (1962), a psychoanalyst, wrote that every human being is a creature who must experience trust: "Before the child develops any thinking or verbal expression of his emotions, he learns to trust, since he experiences without consciousness that his needs for survival, growth, and development fit into his parents' needs to give gratification and protection in mutually adaptive, tender cooperation" (p. 7).

But is humankind basically trustworthy? We have already quoted Carl Rogers's vigorous affirmation. But certain philosophical viewpoints note the sinful nature of people, and Albert Outler, a contemporary theologian, has criticized Rogers for considering only one side of human nature.

The second dimension of philosophies of human nature, *strength of will and rationality versus external control and irrationality,* is the extent to which one believes that people have control over their own lives and understand the motives behind their behavior. The core of the American value system has traditionally been characterized by a belief in the effectiveness of willpower and motivation. The self-help movement, from Mary Baker Eddy to Dale Carnegie to Norman Vincent Peale, has long been a strong force in amateur American philosophy. Yet the opposite view has had its adherents. St. Paul believed that willpower was not enough: "I can will what is right, but I cannot do it." (One is reminded in this context of Adlai Stevenson's quip—that, as for evangelists, he found St. Paul appealing and Dr. Peale appalling.)

More recently, some psychologists and social commentators have emphasized hardiness, defined as a set of beliefs about the world and oneself (Fischman, 1987). Emphasized by Suzanne C. Ouellette Kobasa (1979), hardiness is a form of self-help that focuses on developing a sense of control over your life.

But our contemporary society, with its heavy emphasis on technology, also evokes pessimism: With a growing number of skilled jobs and increasing emphasis on aptitude-test results for personnel selection and academic admission, there appears to be less and less room for sheer motivation or willpower as a determinant of success.

We can even argue that the government, by sponsoring lotteries, has contributed to the diminution of beliefs in success through hard work. As George Will (1989) notes,

Aggressive government marketing of gambling gives a legitimizing imprimatur to the pursuit of wealth without work. By blurring the distinction between well-earned and "ill-gotten" gains—a distinction blurred enough by Michael Milken, LBO's and other phenomena—government-run gambling repudiates an idea once important to this republic's sense of virtue. The idea is that citizens are distinguished more by the moral worth of the way they make money than by how much money they make. . . . The more people believe in the importance of luck, chance, randomness, fate, the less they believe in the importance of stern values such as industriousness, thrift, deferral of gratification, diligence, studiousness. (p. 78)

This second dimension of the philosophies of human nature also includes beliefs about rationality and irrationality. Rationality here means that one's ego is in control and that cognitions dominate over emotions. Yet there seems to be a growing belief among psychologists (Carl Rogers to the contrary) that people are not basically rational—that they are easily controlled and manipulated. Behavior therapists have viewed people as "being at the robot end of the continuum" (Krasner, 1965); and even Freud's views reemerged 30 years after his death in the posthumous publication of a book about Woodrow Wilson (S. Freud & Bullitt, 1967) that communicated Freud's assumptions about the irrational, emotional determinants of behavior. In this book, President Wilson's virtues were portrayed as weaknesses and his visions as the fruits of compulsion; his idealization of the League of Nations was interpreted by Freud and Bullitt as evidence of a passive, feminine relationship between Wilson and his father (L. F. Brown, 1967). According to Freud, subconscious factors are the major influence on decisions, even at the highest levels of international affairs. Indeed, freedom may be a vanishing orientation, and the rationalist wonders whether there remains any place in our world for the rational decisions of free persons. In a fascinating study, Charlotte Doyle (1965, 1966) showed that experimental psychologists believe more strongly in determinism than do members of any other academic group, whereas physical and biological scientists tend toward the opposite end of the continuum (see also E. L. Walker, 1970). Experimental psychologists are also reported to believe that freedom is illusory, whereas physical scientists accept freedom as a reality rather than as a word relating an absence of the knowledge of causes.

Yet if we return to the person on the street, we find that he or she believes that life is rational and that one's outcomes in the world are sensible and justified. In Melvin Lerner's (1966) words, "there is an appropriate fit between what [people] do and what happens to them" (p. 3).

People cannot believe that they live in a "world governed by a schedule of random reinforcements." This belief in justice—or that people get what they deserve—leads to some perverse findings. Lichtman (cited by Lerner, 1966) exposed ninth-grade students to a tape recording in which a number of people talked about a boy named Bill Johnson. The students learned that Bill had had an automobile accident that stemmed from a blowout in a front tire of a used car that he had recently purchased. As a result of this accident, Bill was hospitalized and suffered two weeks of intense pain. He even faced the possibility that he would be left with a permanent limp. *All* the subjects were led to believe that Bill had been warned about the tires when he bought the car. Half of the subjects were told that Bill later bought new tires and that it was one of these tires that blew out, while the other subjects were told that he had not bought new tires. Couched within the ruse were questions concerning how responsible Bill was for the accident and how attractive Bill appeared to be to these subjects. For which group would you expect Bill to be less attractive? Here's the surprise: Bill was judged to be *less* attractive when it was established that he *had replaced* the defective tires with new ones prior to the blowout. To be sure, he was described as less responsible for his suffering, but, most important, he was also described as a less desirable person (Lerner, 1966, p. 6). The students apparently concluded that there must have been something else very wrong with Bill or he wouldn't have suffered this misfortune.

You might be tempted to explain this irrationality in the pursuit of justice as simply the product of ninth-grade minds. But Lerner (1970, 1971; Lerner & Simmons, 1966) has found similar results with college undergraduates. And others have reached the same finding with other populations of subjects. Lerner (1974) reviewed the generalizability of studies that find a derogation of an "innocent" victim. For example, high school students show effects similar to those found by Lerner (Piliavin, Hardyck, & Vadum, 1967; Simons & Piliavin, 1972), as do housewives from a low-socioeconomic area of Canada (Johnson & Dickinson, 1971, cited in Lerner, 1974). MacDonald (1971a) presented his subjects with the report of a stabbing. The more innocent they thought the victim to be, the less attractive they considered him to be. Likewise, Lincoln and Levinger's (1972) subjects denigrated an African-American man who was the innocent victim of a policeman's attack, but only if the subjects were not able to make a public complaint about the injustice.

After a series of intriguing experiments, Lerner concludes that "anyone (who is) suffering is most likely to arouse people's dislike if he conveys the impression that he was a noble victim. And finally the victim who allows people to believe that he brought his suffering upon himself will be best liked!" (Lerner, 1966, p. 9). People believe you deserve what you get, and if what you get is bad, you must be bad.

Rubin and Peplau (1973, 1975) have developed a scale to measure "beliefs in a just world" and have related the responses of draft-age males to the degree of sympathy they have with their fellows who got "unlucky" draft-lottery numbers.

Thus an assumption of justice operates among many of us. This assumption derives from our need to believe that the rewards and punishments we receive in life will be just and the ones that we deserve (Lerner, 1974). Hearing that someone else is not getting what he or she deserves threatens our assumption that *we* will be appropriately rewarded for our own efforts. Here again, we see the relationship between self-concepts and our conceptions of others.

For those who believe that success comes from effort and self-deprivation (the Protestant Ethic), people who live in poverty are objects of scorn (MacDonald, 1971a); those who are at "the bottom of the barrel" are there because "they deserve to be" (Lerner & Elkinton, 1970).

Thus the "just-world" approach relies on the assumption that when one's belief in justice is threatened, the result is an attempt to restore justice (Lerner & Simmons, 1966). Lerner and Miller (1978) proposed that as an event becomes more important to the person, "his or her concerns with justice will become more salient, as will the need to explain apparent injustices" (Weir, 1990, p. 32). As Weir (1990) notes in a review of the theory, a prediction that the character of a victim will be devalued by observers in order to restore justice in the minds of those observers led to initial research confirmation, but failure to replicate later.

Furthermore, when only attributional dependent measures are cited as support for the theory, a circular argument occurs. Weir observes: "If subjects do assign responsibility to a victim, then this is support for the theory, but if subjects do not see a victim as deserving her fate, then proponents of the theory can, and do, argue that this instance is not relevant to the theory, because no threat has occurred" (1990, p. 34).

Another meaning of *rational* exists when applied to conceptions of human nature. Many of us assume that we are "rational" in the sense of being logical and clear-headed when making a decision. We may object to an idea that our thinking is flawed or that desires may interfere with our reasoning (Dawes, 1988).

A great deal of psychological research challenges the assumption that people are rational, as defined in the above paragraph. Here are some examples:

1. Imagine that the United States is preparing for an outbreak of an unusual Asian disease that is expected to kill 600 people. Two different interventions to combat the disease have been proposed. If Program A is adopted, 200 people will be saved. If Program B is adopted, there is a 1/3rd probability that 600 people will be saved and a 2/3rds probability that no people will be saved. Which programs do you favor?

Tversky and Kahneman (1974, 1983) reported that 72% of college students chose Program A. But a second group of subjects was presented with two different choices:

If Program C is adopted, 400 people will die.

If Program D is adopted, there is a 1/3rd probability that nobody will die and a 2/3rds probability that 600 will die.

Only 22% chose Program C, even though it is identical in outcome to Program A. As Dawes (1988) notes, this is irrational, because a criterion of rationality is that choice is made on the basis of the consequences of behavior. Such "framing effects" are particularly strong in life-or-death decisions such as the above.

2. Nisbett and Wilson (1977) asked people to indicate their preference from an array of merchandise (for example, dresses and stockings). The items were always arranged in a single row facing the subject. No matter where particular items were placed, the people tended to choose the item at the far right (Dawes, 1988).

3. Marcus (1986) surveyed a national sample of 1,669 high-school seniors. They were asked the same questions at three different times: 1965 (the year they graduated), 1973, and 1982. Also, in the last survey, they were asked how they had responded to each scale in 1973, a decade before. As Dawes (1988) summarizes, "with the exception of the ratings on the overall liberal-conservative scale, the subjects' recall of their 1973 attitudes in 1982 was more closely related to their rated attitudes *in 1982* than to the attitudes they had *actually* expressed in 1973" (p. 107). A bias occurs in retrospection.

The third dimension of philosophies of human nature is *altruism versus selfishness,* or the extent to which one believes that people are basically unselfish and sincerely interested in others rather than selfish and unconcerned about others. Again, both theories and research on this issue are conflicting. The Golden Rule is a guide for behavior in our society, and no doubt some people adhere to it. But perhaps it is a rule that is honored more in the breach than in the observance. Edward Hoagland (1969) suggests that we usually reduce the Golden Rule to a sort of Silver Rule: We do unto others "just about what we think they would do to us if they had the opportunity" (p. 38). And some people do not advocate the Golden Rule at all. For example, George Bernard Shaw instructed us: "Do not do unto others what you would like done unto you—their tastes may be different" (quoted in Erikson, 1964).

Conceptions of this dimension cut across academic disciplines. Thomas Sowell (1987), an economic historian, recently published a book in which he divided people according to differing views of human nature: the "constrained vision" and the "unconstrained vision." The underlying differences center around self-interest and perfectibility. The person with a constrained vision (he cites Adam Smith, Oliver Wendell Holmes, and Alexander Hamilton as examples) views people as basing all their acts on self-interest and possessing a very limited ability to affect their surroundings.

People with unconstrained vision—such as John Stuart Mill, Thomas Jefferson, and Ramsey Clark—see people as perfectible; they possess "a moral vision of human intentions." Furthermore, they are viewed as being guided by reason and always able to improve things. Sowell (1987) proposes that the two types differ in their attitudes toward a variety of issues—ways to prevent war, the function of government in improving life, the value of youth versus age, and others (Friedrich, 1987).

Well-publicized incidents in which persons seeking help were ignored by many passersby have caused some Americans to reevaluate their belief that altruism is characteristic of human nature. A case in point is the murder of Kitty Genovese, who was repeatedly stabbed by an assailant as she returned home in Kew Gardens, NY, in 1963. She continuously screamed for help during the attack. Thirty-eight persons admitted witnessing the event, but not a single one came out of his or her apartment to help—even after the assailant left the girl to die. No one even called the police. They later told reporters that they did not want to get involved. This incident deservedly received much publicity, and it has been frequently interpreted as an indication of the growing apathy and indifference to human distress that result from the impersonal complexities of modern life (Wainwright, 1964). But it also generated a useful research program by Darley and Latané (1968a, 1968b; Latané & Darley, 1968, 1970a, 1970b; Latané, Nida, & Wilson, 1981), who found that one reason why each person failed to act was the awareness that a large number of other people were also watching. A diffusion of responsibility occurs when a large number of observers, separated and unable to communicate with one another, are witnesses to an emergency. Each assumes that someone else is responding.

Subsequent research by Latané and Rodin (1969) dealt with responses to the victim of a fall. Their findings show the difficulty in making a general statement about the degree of altruism present in human nature. For example, if the observers of the accident were strangers to one another, they were less likely to aid the victim than if they were acquaintances. Other situational factors are also important. If a person has just observed another person perform a helpful act, he or she is more likely to act as a Good Samaritan (Bryan, 1970; Bryan & Test, 1967). Demographic differences also appear to be important in determining willingness to help. People in urban areas are less likely to help than are those from smaller towns or rural areas (Clark & Word, 1971; Milgram, 1970).

The fourth dimension of philosophies of human nature is *independence versus conformity to group pressures,* or the extent to which one believes that a person can maintain his or her convictions in the face of pressures to conform coming from a group, from society in general, or from some authority figure. Indeed, the middle of the 20th century in the United States has sometimes been called the age of conformity. We have already mentioned William H. Whyte, Jr.'s criticism, in *The Organization Man* (1957), of the emergence of the business leader who possesses more ability to "get along" than creativity or integrity. Stanley Milgram's (1963, 1965) work on obedience also elicits a pessimistic view of human nature.

Milgram hired men from the community to participate in what appeared to them to be a learning experiment. Each man's job was to help a second subject, seated in an adjoining room, to learn a list of associations. Whenever the second subject—who was actually an accomplice—made an error, the real subject was instructed by the experimenter to give him an electric shock. With each mistake—and of course, the accomplice had been instructed to make frequent errors—the intensity of the electric shock was increased by 15 volts. The level soon reached 300 volts, and at that point the accomplice pounded on the wall of the room in which he was bound to an electric chair. The subject could hear the pounding. Milgram's basic research question was "How many subjects would continue to obey the experimenter in the face of this reaction—that is, how many would continue to administer shocks of ever-increasing intensity even after hearing the pounding—and after the subsequent failure of the learner to answer?" Before answering this question, we should point out that Milgram had asked psychologists, psychiatrists, and Yale undergraduates what proportion of the subjects would continue administering shocks to the end of the shock series (450 volts) when confronted with these reactions. In effect, this was a measure of their beliefs about human nature in a specific situation. All respondents predicted that only an insignificant minority would go to the end of the shock series. The estimate ranged from 0% to 3%; that is, the most pessimistic member of the group predicted that, of 100 persons, 3 would continue through to the most potent shock available on the shock generator. Yet among Milgram's 40 subjects, 26, or 65%, administered the final 450-volt shock. They did so despite their manifestations of great tension and anguish, including stuttering, groaning, lip biting, nervous laughter, and even one convulsive seizure. But despite such qualms most of the men responded to the requirements of their "job."

Although we have serious questions about the ethics and propriety of such an experimental manipulation, we believe that Milgram's research has generated provocative and disturbing evidence about the dominant need to obey and to conform to the demands of an authority figure.

The fifth dimension that deals with beliefs about individual differences is *complexity versus simplicity,* or the extent to which one believes that people are complicated and hard to understand rather than simple and easy to understand. Most psychologists appear to be in agreement that a goal of psychological training is the development of a stronger belief in human complexity. Seward Hiltner (1962) has written that "there seems now to be a greater consensus among psychologists about their view of man than in any previous time in our century, and this view includes more factors of greater complexity" (p. 246). Yet there is little theorizing on the subject, with the exception of George Kelly's role-construct theory (1955, 1963) and the work of Harvey, Hunt, and Schroder (1961) on four levels of conceptual systems. A few rudimentary studies have been done to show that there are individual differences in beliefs about the complexity of human behavior. Gordon Allport (1958, 1966) did a small investigation showing that, when asked to list the "essential characteristics" of some friend, 90% of the "judges" employed between 3 and 10 trait names, the average being 7.2. But the difference between 3 and 10, we submit, is a large difference in complexity.

Building from the concept of cognitive complexity, Crockett (1965) counted the number of concepts used by subjects when asked to describe each of several people they knew. To measure the complexity of integration of descriptive concepts, Schroder, Driver, and Streufert (1967) had subjects write open-ended protocols. In scoring these protocols, Schroder and his colleagues defined a low level of complexity as the use of a single fixed procedure or rule, no consideration of alternative suggestions, and demonstration of a high degree of certainty. High levels of complexity were indicated by such phenomena as comparison of alternative views, a more relativistic stance, and the presence of sophisticated causal theorizing.

Psychologists' interest in complexity got a second wind as a result of the development of attribution theory in the 1970s. For example, Kelley (1972, 1973) distinguished between two causal schemata: the *multiple necessary causal schema* assumes that a number of causes are necessary for a given behavior to occur, while the *multiple sufficient causal schema* assumes that a single cause is enough to produce a given effect. These two conceptions clearly differ in their assumptions about complexity.

But a question remained: Is it the nature of people to readily make causal inferences from a single example (Read, 1983) or can naive perceivers produce relatively complex and sophisticated explanations of human behavior (Fletcher, 1983)?

Both the above conclusions received support in the empirical literature. One way to reconcile the conflicting conclusions was to propose that some people possess a more complex attributional schema than do others, a position consistent with our decision to include beliefs about complexity as a part of philosophies of human nature.

Fletcher, Danilovics, Fernandez, Peterson, and Reeder (1986) proposed *attributional complexity* as an individual-differences concept that would be applied to clarify previous contradictory findings. They postulated seven attributional constructs in defining attributional complexity:

1. Higher levels of intrinsic motivation to explain and understand human behavior
2. Preference for complex rather than simple explanations
3. The tendency to think about the underlying processes involved in causal attribution
4. Awareness of the extent to which people's behavior is a function of interaction with others
5. Tendency to infer abstract or causally complex internal attributions
6. Tendency to infer abstract, contemporary, external causal attributions
7. Tendency to infer external causes operating from the past

The factor structure of the scale items designed to measure these qualities indicate that they do hang together, supporting the validity of the concept of attributional complexity.

Fletcher and colleagues write: "The critical theoretical point here is that attributionally complex people are capable of using either complex or simple schemata in generating causal attributions; conversely, attributionally simple folk are permanently restricted to the more primitive forms of causal schemata" (Fletcher et al., 1986, p. 883).

The sixth dimension is *similarity versus variability,* or the extent to which one believes that people differ in their basic natures. Again, most psychologists (clinicians, at least) would argue that it is desirable to believe that people are different and that each person is unique. Yet with the exception of Gordon Allport (1961, 1962), who has consistently urged us to recognize the uniqueness of individuals, most personality theorists have taken the easy way out and have been content to imply that most people are basically alike.

Relationship to Other Concepts

Over the last 25 years other concepts relevant to assumptions about people have been developed and used. These include Christie's (1970) "Machiavellianism" and Rotter's (1966) "locus of control" and "interpersonal trust." This section describes each and speculates about its relationship to philosophies of human nature.

Machiavellianism is characteristic of the person who manipulates others through guile, deceit, and opportunism (Christie & Geis, 1970; Geis, 1978). It reflects not only a cluster of attitudes about human nature but also a zest for dominating and controlling others. The cluster of attitudes at the center of Machiavellianism is, of course, negative—even cynical—for these attitudes reflect Machiavelli's advice to rulers about how best to control their citizenry. But there is more to the construct than the possession of cynical attitudes alone. To measure Machiavellianism, Christie and Geis composed three types of attitude statements:

1. Statements that advocated the use of manipulative interpersonal tactics (for example, "Never tell anyone the real reason you did something unless it is useful to do so").

2. Statements that expressed an unfavorable view of human nature (for example, "The biggest difference between most criminals and other people is that criminals are stupid enough to get caught").

3. Statements that dealt with abstract or generalized morality (for example, "People suffering from incurable diseases should have the choice of being put painlessly to death").

Christie and Geis (1970) developed fewer statements reflecting the third category because, in following Machiavelli's writings closely, they found less concern with abstractions and ethical judgments than with pragmatic advice.

Since unfavorable beliefs about human nature are a major component of Machiavellianism, highly Machiavellian persons should possess negative philosophies of human nature. Chapter 6 reports correlations between measures of these constructs.

The concept of *locus of control* was originally developed by Rotter (1966) and defined as an indication of attitudes about one's self; it makes a distinction between beliefs that rewards are contingent upon one's own actions *(internal control)* and beliefs that rewards are the result of forces independent of one's own actions *(external control)*. The latter includes both the actions of others and simple fate or chance. Rotter and most other researchers have viewed the Internal-External Control (I-E) concept as unidimensional in nature; that is, there usually has been no distinction between the belief that these forces are applicable in one's own life situation and the belief that they operate in the society at large. The measurement of the construct contains items that reflect both perspectives (Lefcourt, 1991). For example, a forced-choice pair of statements from the I-E Control scale that reflects the *people in general* orientation is "Many of the unhappy things in people's lives are partly due to bad luck" versus "People's misfortune result from the mistakes they make." A forced-choice pair of statements reflecting a *personal* orientation is "Many times I feel that I have little influence over the things that happen to me" versus "It is impossible for me to believe that chance or luck plays an important role in my life."

Although the factor analyses reported by Rotter (1966) supported his assumption of unidimensionality in the I-E Control scale, several subsequent studies call for distinctions, particularly when the concept is applied to the responses of members of minority groups or of the educationally and economically disadvantaged (Abramowitz, 1973; Coleman et al.,

1966; B. E. Collins, 1974; V. C. Crandall, Katkovsky, & Crandall, 1965; Gurin, Gurin, Lao, & Beattie, 1969; Hersch & Scheibe, 1967).

In their inquiry into the attitudes of African-American students, P. Gurin et al. (1969) factor analyzed a pool of items, including those phrased in the self-other forced-choice format, and found different results for items phrased in the first person than for items that referred to people in general. G. Gurin (1968) has also found this pattern in his studies of participants in job-training programs. In G. Gurin's studies, African-American and white trainees did not differ on responses to statements concerning people in general. There were, however, clear racial differences in responses to statements regarding the sense of control in one's own life ("personal efficacy"); African-American trainees reported a lower sense of control than their white cohorts did. G. Gurin and his staff concluded that African-Americans and other disadvantaged groups may adopt the general beliefs of our society regarding the power of internal control and the Protestant Ethic, but they find these beliefs inapplicable in their own life situations.

The research of P. Gurin et al. (1969) indicates that it is the personal-efficacy aspect rather than the society-at-large aspect that operates in African-Americans' motivation and performance. Subjects who have a high sense of personal control express higher expectancies of success and more self-confidence about academic and job performance and "aspire to jobs that are more prestigeful, demanding, and realistic in terms of their own abilities and interest" (p. 43). However, while African-American subjects may believe that people in general exert control over their lives, this belief is not related to expectations of personal success, self-confidence about performance, and other such variables. P. Gurin et al. (1969) summarize as follows:

> We find that the two control measures, the personal and ideological, work in opposite ways. Students who are strongly internal in the personal sense have higher achievement-test scores, achieve higher grades in college, and perform better on an anagrams task which was included in the instruments administered in the study. In contrast, students who are strongly internal in the sense of believing that internal forces are the major determinants of success in the culture at large (ideological) perform *less* well than the more externally-oriented students. Given that these opposing results from the two types of control measures cancel each other, the total Rotter score understandably bears no relationship to these performance indicators. (pp. 33-34)

All this shows the need for a series of studies of the relationship between the internal-external locus-of-control construct and philosophies of human nature, using different types of samples for each comparison (Hamsher, Geller, & Rotter, 1968; Stack, 1978). It is expected that the relationship is stronger for some groups than others. Chapter 6, which describes relationships between pairs of individual-differences measure, will present some relevant findings.

Interpersonal trust, a construct also advanced by Rotter (1967, 1971), is defined as "a person's generalized expectancy that the promises of other individuals or of groups with regard to future behavior can be relied upon" (Hochreich & Rotter, 1970, p. 211). Rotter notes that an extensive number of our everyday decisions—"buying gasoline, paying taxes, going to the dentist, flying to a convention" (Rotter, 1971, p. 443)—involve trusting someone else. In a complex society, we are forced to rely upon others—to move us, to produce our food, to doctor us.

Thus although interpersonal trust and trustworthiness seem to overlap to some degree, there are differences between the two concepts (Wrightsman, 1991). Interpersonal trust deals with the credibility of specific people, groups, or institutions regarding specific actions—actions that have an influence upon the respondent. "Can I believe what I read in the papers?" "Will my friend pick me up when he said he would?" Trustworthiness deals with beliefs about people and about actions that may or may not directly affect the respondent. "Would most people cheat on their income tax if they thought they could get away with it?" The two concepts are probing the same theoretical field, but each draws out a somewhat different aspect of that field. The empirical relationships between measures of the two constructs are reported in Chapter 6.

More recent scales designed to measure trust (Johnson-George & Swap, 1982; Rempel & Holmes, 1986; Rempel, Holmes, & Zanna, 1985) focus on trust in close relationships rather than trust in people in general or in institutions.

However, a recently publicized scale (Unger, 1990), the Attitudes about Reality Scale (AAR), deals with higher order values and personal epistemologies and hence would seem to be of interest to those who wish to understand philosophies of human nature. The Attitudes about Reality Scale examines the way people perceive the relationship between subjective and external reality. The two poles of the relevant continuum are labeled "positivist" and "constructionist" (Unger, Draper, & Pendergrass, 1986). To quote Unger's description of this distinction:

A positivistic world view is structured around belief in the legitimacy of both external reality and external authority. People who score as positivistic . . . tend to believe that their own values and those of their source of authority are universally true; favor the socio-political status quo; and prefer determinist and biological explanations to social and relativistic ones when they examine most social issues. . . . People who score as constructionist tend to see external reality as historically and situationally determined; accept individual efforts to change society as legitimate, and prefer social explanations to biological ones. (1990, p. 2)

Thus Unger's (1990) concept has some overlap with the approach of Furnham, Johnson, and Rawles (1985), who distinguished between people's beliefs in heredity or in environment as determinants of specific aspects of human nature.

Summary

This chapter has defined philosophies of human nature as attitudes about people in general—attitudes that emphasize interpersonal behavior. Philosophies of human nature are learned, just as attitudes are. Primary sources of learning seem to be the behavior and attitudes of the person's parents, the environment in which he or she grows up, deliberate programs (such as religious education) aimed at developing attitudes, and the person's own personality.

In conceptualizing philosophies of human nature, we considered it important not only to include a classification of substantive beliefs but also to recognize the role of beliefs about individual differences. These include beliefs about the simplicity versus complexity of human nature (Are people simple and easy to understand or complicated and hard to understand?) and beliefs about similarity versus variability (Are individuals similar to one another, or is each group unique?). In addition, four substantive dimensions were proposed: (1) trustworthiness versus untrustworthiness, (2) strength of will and rationality versus external control and irrationality, (3) altruism versus selfishness, and (4) independence versus conformity to group pressures. These substantive dimensions seem to be unrelated to the individual-differences dimensions.

Other constructs dealing with assumptions about human nature—Machiavellianism, locus of control, and interpersonal trust—were described and their proposed relationships to philosophies of human nature were evaluated.

CHAPTER FOUR

Measurement of Philosophies of Human Nature

Anything that exists, exists in some quantity. If it exists in some quantity, it can be measured.

—E. L. THORNDIKE

Once the theoretical dimensions of philosophies of human nature had been conceptualized, the next step was the construction of instruments to measure these dimensions. This chapter describes the procedures developed for the measurement of philosophies of human nature; it contains the most technically detailed material in the book. Those readers interested in substantive findings may wish to move on to Chapter 5.

Likert-Scale Construction

Since each of the six components of philosophies of human nature (see Chapter 3) was assumed to be bipolar in nature, we decided to construct Likert-type attitude scales for each. Likert-type scales, also called summated-rating scales, measure the extent of positive or negative evaluations of attitude objects. We prepared 20 statements for each dimension, using as sources writings of philosophers and social scientists, essays of college students on the topic of human nature, and expressions of assumptions about human nature found in the mass media.

The formation and selection of this pool of statements was, of course, critically important; no final, revised, purified scale could succeed if the initial pool of items was weak. The process of selecting items, although thorough, was hampered because there was no classification of situations from which to select representative statements. For example, the dimensions of trustworthiness of human nature has been defined as the extent to which people are seen as moral, honest, and reliable—but moral in *what*?

Box 4.1
What Are the Limits of Trustworthiness?

Does each of the following situations have anything to do with trustworthiness or untrustworthiness?

1. A businessman avoids paying for a daily long-distance call by using a code to tell his wife what commuter train he'll come home on. He dials home from a Manhattan phone booth, lets the phone ring twice, and hangs up. Then he dials again. If he lets the phone ring only once, it means he'll be on the 5:09; twice, the 5:34; three times, the 6:05.
2. Sam, the machinist, sometimes takes a rejected piece off the scrap pile. On his home workbench, he polishes it into an attractive bookend, flowerpot, or whatever his imagination suggests. The company used to sell that scrap, but nowadays a hauler has to be paid to take it away.
3. Eddie just got a job as clerk in a supermarket. It's inventory time, and Eddie's count of the canned goods is three cases short of what it should be. Actually, another clerk stole the three cases, but Eddie doesn't know that. To avoid making any fuss, Eddie quietly writes down the number that should be there, instead of his own count.
4. Four of the saleswomen in a department store know that a fifth saleswoman is stealing merchandise. They think it's deplorable but don't tell on her.

There are many diverse activities and relationships in which a person can be trustworthy or untrustworthy—with money, with secrets, with responsibilities to perform, with someone else's wife or husband. In a very thorough and self-disciplined way, an employee of the Committee to Re-Elect the President carries out his assigned duties to bug the Democratic party headquarters—although he knows his actions are illegal. The butcher who owns a small meat market always resists the temptation to cheat on his income tax but routinely overweighs the meat that he sells to his customers. Are such people untrustworthy? The situations presented in Box 4.1 reflect the multitude of behaviors for which a dimension of trustworthiness versus untrustworthiness may or may not be relevant. For those who set forth to measure beliefs about trustworthiness, this problem will remain unsolvable until situations in which people can be considered trustworthy or untrustworthy are classified. We selected statements for the Trustworthiness scale that tapped attitudes about a variety of situations, including monetary activities, cheating on exams, and tasks that involve individual responsibility.

Half of the original 20 statements for each substantive component conveyed a favorable view of human nature and half an unfavorable view. For the Complexity subscale, half of the statements implied that human beings were simple and easy to understand, whereas the other half implied that they were complex and incomprehensible. In a similar manner, half of the statements measuring variability expressed a belief in the basic similarity of individuals and in people's lack of change over time, whereas the other half conveyed a belief in basic interindividual differences and in people's capacity for change over time. Thus if an acquiescent-response set were operating, its presence would not contribute to a high positive score on the subscale. When there is a balanced number of positively scored and negatively scored statements, a person who responds in a completely acquiescent, or "yea-saying," manner receives a neutral score.

The 120 original statements were administered to 177 undergraduates at three colleges (two in the South and one in the Midwest). These subjects were asked to respond to each statement by using a 6-point scale of agreement and disagreement. No opportunity for a neutral or "cannot-say" choice was provided; the six options were "strongly agree" (+3), "moderately agree" (+2), "slightly agree" (+1), "slightly disagree" (-1), "moderately disagree" (-2), and "strongly disagree" (-3). A separate item analysis was performed for each school; the summated scores on the entire set of items for that component were used as the criterion. Responses by the upper 25% of the group were compared with responses by the middle 50% and by the lowest 25% of the group. An analysis of each item was then prepared. Table 4.1 reports the responses to Item 88, which states: "Most people are basically honest." The table indicates that, at School W, the highest 25% of the sample on the Trustworthiness scale averaged a response of 1.0 (slightly agree) on this item, whereas the middle 50% averaged -0.2 (neutral) and the lowest 25% averaged -2.0 (moderately disagree). The difference between the highest and lowest quarters of the sample was 3.0 points out of a possible 6 points—a very good separation between these groups and a statistically significant difference. Item 88 has a relatively good balance; the upper 25% showed mild agreement with the statement, while the lowest 25% showed disagreement. The item popularity was also good, with an average near 0.00, or absolute neutrality.

(The term *item popularity* refers to the average degree of agreement or disagreement with an item statement. For example, on our 6-point scale, an item popularity of +2.03 would indicate that the average response for

TABLE 4.1 An Example of the Item-Analysis Results

Item 88.   Scale T+.   Statement: "Most people are basically honest."

School	N	Upper 25%	Middle 25%	Lowest 25%	Difference Top-vs.- Lowest 25%	Statistically Significant?	Good Balance	Right Order?
		Average Response						
W	42	1.0	-0.2	-2.0	3.0	Yes	Yes	Yes
P	80	1.8	1.1	-0.3	2.1	Yes	Yes	Yes
B	55	1.9	0.9	0.4	1.5	Yes	Partly	Yes

the item was close to "moderately agree." An average item popularity of 0.00 is desirable on a Likert scale because it shows that the typical respondent has neither endorsed nor rejected the statement. Of course, a good dispersion of responses for each statement is also necessary.)

The order of the three groups was the expected one—that is, the middle 50% of the sample had an average score that was between those of the two extreme quarters. The item analyses of many earlier scales have ignored this middle 50% of their respondents and hence had no way of showing that linearity existed. We included this middle group in all item analyses of the Philosophies of Human Nature (PHN) Scale. Table 4.1 indicates that, in Schools P and B, a good dispersion in average response existed among respondent groups. Although the sheer difference between the averages for the top and bottom quarters was not so great as at School W, in both cases it was at least 1.5 points and was statistically significant. School B's responses were a bit one-sided—that is, even the most negative 25% on overall trustworthiness averaged a slight agreement (0.4) with the statement. Had only School B been used in the selection of items, this statement would not have been so impressive a choice. Yet the use of respondents from three different colleges shows that different samples produce different average popularities for the same item. In this case, when the three samples are combined, the average response approaches neutrality, as desired, and the variability in responses is extensive, which is also desirable. Developing a scale that discriminates well among subjects at all points along a belief continuum requires a rectangular distribution of scores (W. A. Scott, 1968)—that is, an even distribution across score values (for example, five subjects scoring +3, five scoring +2, five scoring +1, and so on). Thus the score distribution can be manipulated by selecting items that differ in item popularity (Humphreys, 1956).

TABLE 4.2 Characteristics of the Subscales of the Philosophies of Human Nature Scale[a]

The Philosophies of Human Nature Scale is a Likert-type scale that measures a person's beliefs about human nature. Each subscale is composed of 14 statements (items). Subjects indicate their agreement or disagreement with each item by circling a number from +3 to -3.

The Six Subscales Are:	*Range*
1. Trustworthiness versus untrustworthiness + = belief that people are trustworthy, moral, and responsible - = belief that people are untrustworthy, immoral, and irresponsible	+42 to -42
2. Strength of will and rationality versus lack of willpower and irrationality + = belief that people can control their outcomes and that they understand themselves - = belief that people lack self-determination and are irrational	+42 to -42
3. Altruism versus selfishness + = belief that people are altruistic, unselfish, and sincerely interested in others - = belief that people are selfish and self-centered	+42 to -42
4. Independence versus conformity to group pressures + = belief that people are able to maintain their beliefs in the face of group pressures to the contrary - = belief that people give in to pressures of group and society	+42 to -42
5. Complexity versus simplicity + = belief that people are complex, complicated, and hard to understand - = belief that people are simple and easy to understand	+42 to -42
6. Variability versus similarity + = belief that individuals are different from one another in personality and interests, and that a person can change over time - = belief that people are similar in interests and that they do not change over time	+42 to -42

a. The first four subscales (T, S, A, and I) can be summed to give a positive-negative score (range +168 to -168), indicating a person's general positive or negative beliefs about substantive characteristics of human nature.

The last two subscales (C and V) can be summed to give a multiplexity score (range +84 to -84), indicating a person's beliefs about the extent of individual differences in human nature.

Of the original 120 items, the 96 that showed the largest group differences were included in a more purified draft of the scale. This version was administered to 100 undergraduates and 160 graduate students at two Southern colleges, and a second item analysis was performed. Five items did not survive this analysis because of their nonsignificant discriminatory power. These inadequate items and seven others of limited discriminatory power were removed, leaving 84 items for the final form of the Philosophies of Human Nature Scale. Of the 14 items on each subscale, half were worded positively and half negatively, in order to neutralize the

TABLE 4.3 Split-Half (Odd-Even) Reliability Coefficients for the Six Subscales of the Philosophies of Human Nature Scale (*N*s = 50)

Subscale	Undergraduate Men	Undergraduate Women	Graduate Men	Graduate Women
Trustworthiness	.87	.84	.75	.51
Strength of Will and Rationality	.64	.75	.51	.40
Altruism	.91	.81	.60	.62
Independence	.73	.92	.46	.60
Complexity	.76	.60	.64	.48
Variability	.61	.74	.78	.66

Note: All correlations are significantly different from zero at the .01 level.

influence of an acquiescent-response set. Characteristics of the subscales are described in Table 4.2. The 84-item scale, with the items in the sequence in which they usually appear, may be found in Appendix A. In Appendix B, the items are grouped by subscale, and their popularities as well as their correlations with their respective subscales are given.

Reliability of the Likert Scale

The 84-item scale was administered to previously untested groups of 100 undergraduates and of 100 graduate students to determine its reliability. Within each sample, 50 subjects were male and 50 were female. The split-half reliability of each subscale was computed to determine if the subscales were internally consistent. That is, each subscale was divided into two sets of seven items, individual subjects' scores for each half were calculated, these half-scores were then correlated, and the Spearman-Brown Prophecy Formula was applied to determine the reliability for each full-length subscale. The split-half reliability coefficients for each subscale are presented in Table 4.3; those for the male and female undergraduate samples are of generally acceptable magnitude. All are more than .60, and 9 of the 12 are more than .70. The reliability coefficients for the graduate students are from .40 to .78; this finding reflects the great homogeneity of attitudes in the graduate-student sample.

A follow-up reliability study was done by John O'Connor (1971), who used 480 male cadets at the Air Force Academy as subjects. These men were selected randomly from among those freshman cadets who were

taking introductory psychology. Cronbach's measure of reliability, coefficient alpha (W. A. Scott, 1960), was computed for each subscale,
with the following results: Trustworthiness, .78; Strength of Will and
Rationality, .63; Altruism, .80; Independence, .77; Complexity, .69;
and Variability, .68. These are similar in value to the split-half
reliabilities for the previous sample of male undergraduates. Of the
four substantive subscales, the Strength of Will and Rationality subscale rather consistently lacks the inter-item agreement present in the
other subscales. This distinction will again become apparent when the
item-factor analysis is discussed. The overarching conclusion, however,
is that the subscales possess acceptable degrees of internal consistency.

Thirty-five subjects from the original sample of 100 undergraduates
were retested three months later to determine test-retest stability. (These
subjects were not chosen randomly from the original pool of 100; they
were students in psychology classes and were easily available. Their initial scores did not differ significantly from the rest of the 100 original
subjects, however.) All of the subscales except Complexity produced good
test-retest stability (that is, more than .70). The subscale test-retest stability coefficients were as follows: Trustworthiness, .74; Strength of Will
and Rationality, .75; Altruism, .83; Independence, .75; Complexity, .52;
and Variability, .84. When the scores from the substantive subscales were
summed to give a positive-negative score, the stability coefficient was
.90. The stability of the multiplexity score, obtained by summing Complexity and Variability, was .86.

Degree of long-term stability was studied by George Baxter (1968),
who readministered the PHN scale to college students at the end of their
first or second year in college. (All had originally taken the scale during
their freshman-orientation week.) Table 4.4 reports Baxter's findings. For
the 8-month interval, the general picture is one of moderate stability; 11
of the 12 subscale stability coefficients are between .38 and .68. However,
the Strength of Will and Rationality stability coefficient for the men is
only .10. On the other subscales, the stability shown by the men is similar
to that shown by the women, although the number of men is much smaller
(39 versus 152). As expected, the 20-month stability coefficients are usually lower than their 8-month counterparts; however, they remain in the
moderate-relationship category, ranging from .26 to .70.

(The retested samples did not include all of the originally tested subjects. The shrinkages are as follows: women, 8-month interval, 189 originally, 152 retested; women, 20-month interval, 261 originally, 112
retested; men, 8-month interval, 56 originally, 39 retested; men, 20-month

TABLE 4.4 Long-Term Test-Retest Reliability of PHN Subscales

| | 8-Month Interval | | 20-Month Interval | |
| | Women | Men | Women | Men |
Subscale	r	r	r	r
Trustworthiness	.65*	.65*	.38*	.59*
Strength of Will and Rationality	.38*	.10	.45*	.41*
Altruism	.55*	.58*	.38*	.60*
Independence	.60*	.68*	.31*	.41*
Complexity	.53*	.42*	.57*	.26
Variability	.51*	.65*	.32*	.53*
Positive-Negative	.67*	.68*	.38*	.70*
Multiplexity	.58*	.58*	.52*	.42*

Note: *N*s are as follows: women, 8-month interval, 152; women, 20-month interval, 112; men, 8-month interval, 39; men, 20-month interval, 31.
*Significantly different from zero at .05 level or better.

interval, 84 originally, 31 retested. To see if the retested subjects were a nonrepresentative sample, Baxter (1968) compared mean scores on the first testing for retested subjects with first-test means for all subjects. For the women, only 1 of the 12 subscale differences [six subscales and two retest groups] was greater than 1.00 point, and none of the differences was statistically significant. It is quite clear that the retested women did not differ in original scores from the initial pool. For the men, of the 12 subscale differences, the largest [on Altruism] was 3.86 points [the mean for the original sample was – 4.80, and the mean for the retested sample was – 0.94]. This difference approached statistical significance [$p < .10$]. Six other differences were greater than 1.00 point, but they were not in a consistent direction. The retested men did not seem to be an especially unrepresentative sample of the original population.)

An evaluation of Baxter's findings is challenging, for we have little information about the comparative stabilities of other attitude scales when subjects are retested after such intervals. As a comparison, the test-retest stabilities for the American College Testing Program Examination (ACT) may be useful. The ACT test is designed to be a measure of scholastic abilities. When the ACT test was administered to 63 graduating high school seniors and readministered two years later, the subtest reliabilities were as follows: English, .73; mathematics, .77; social studies, .67; natural sciences, .70; and composite, .84 (from American College Testing Program, 1965).

We are not sure what an ideal coefficient would be for such an interval (Harris, 1963). Clearly in the ensuing 20 months each person had experiences, good or bad, that could have changed his or her score, and the subscales should be sensitive to those changes. Thus we would not want reliabilities approaching +1.00, but we would want and expect some degree of consistency. When two measures are compared, a correlation coefficient of .45 indicates that approximately 20% of the variance in one measure is accounted for by the other; this value is typical of the 20-month-interval values. We may safely conclude that the long-term consistency of the PHN subscales is within acceptable limits.

To gain some information on the long-term reliability of attitude scales, Wrightsman, Wrightsman, and Cook (1964) retested 75 female undergraduates on a battery of scales. The time intervals between testings were not the same for all subjects; they ranged from 2 to 10 months, the average being 166 days. The test-retest reliabilities were as follows: Chein's Anti-Police Attitudes Scale, .66; Christie's F Scale, .73; Machiavellianism Scale, .68; Christie's Anomie Scale, .60; and Komorita's School Segregation Scale, .82.

Relationship of PHN Subscales to One Another

We have hypothesized that the four substantive components of philosophies of human nature share a common evaluative orientation, but that each component possesses enough specificity to justify the use of its subscale as a separate measure. Do the data verify this expectation?

Several intercorrelations of the subscales, based on tests involving relatively large numbers of subjects, are reported in Table 4.5. The last of these in Table 4.5 was collected on a sample of 516 freshmen in September 1990. The results for different samples measured across a 25-year period are quite consistent. In each sample there are moderate to high positive relationships among the Trustworthiness, Altruism, and Independence subscales, usually between .60 and .70. But the correlations between each of these subscales and the remaining substantive subscale, Strength of Will and Rationality, are always lower—usually in .20s or .30s. So the general evaluative thread that was hypothesized to run through the substantive dimensions does bind three of the four together, but it leaves the fourth more loosely connected.

Turning to relationships between Complexity and Variability, we find that all five samples show a modest positive relationship between the two

TABLE 4.5 Intercorrelations of PHN Subscales

Subscale	Strength of Will and Rationality	Altruism	Independence	Complexity	Variability
Trustworthiness	.35**	.69**	.64**	-.20**	-.04
	.41**	.66**	.62**	-.05	-.07
	.37**	.71**	.65**	-.04	-.04
	.24*	.68**	.42**	-.06	-.07
	.17	.67**	.44**	-.01	-.09
	.27**	.63**	.56**	-.03	-.18**
Strength of Will and Rationality		.39**	.30**	-.26**	-.12
		.31**	.44**	-.13*	-.01
		.34**	.39**	.04	-.01
		.21*	.28*	.08	-.08
		.32**	.44**	-.13	.06
		.24**	.35**	-.07	.15**
Altruism			.61**	-.21**	-.10
			.65**	-.11	-.10
			.64**	-.10	-.08
			.54**	-.13	-.15
			.47**	-.19	-.00
			.57**	-.16**	-.10*
Independence				-.16**	-.04
				.02	-.04
				-.03	.01
				-.06	-.03
				-.15	.09
				-.05	-.05
Complexity					.40**
					.30**
					.32**
					.40**
					.30**
					.23**

Note: Correlations for each pair were based on the following samples: (1) 333 undergraduates—153 men and 180 women—at six colleges (Wrightsman, 1964a); (2) 352 freshman men, Air Force Academy (O'Connor, 1971); (3) 61 freshman women, George Peabody College for Teachers, 1965 freshman orientation (unpublished data); (4) 84 freshman men, George Peabody College for Teachers,1965 freshman orientation (unpublished data); (5) 71 freshman women, George Peabody College for Teachers, volunteer sample (Hearn, 1972); (6) 534 freshmen of both genders, University of Kansas, 1990.
*Significantly different from zero at .05 level
**Significantly different from zero at .01 level

individual-differences subscales, with correlations ranging from .30 to .40. Although we expected this relationship to be higher, it is statistically significant and high enough to give some support to a theory that there is a separable "individual differences" component. Additional support comes from the fact that these two subscales have consistently low correlations with the four substantive subscales. While different from zero, none is greater than .26; in fact, 28 of the 48 are less than .10. There is essentially no relationship between people's opinions about the general goodness or wickedness of human nature and their opinions about the complexity and variability of individuals. In the most general sense, two domains of attitudes are necessary to describe any person's philosophy of human nature; both substantive evaluative beliefs and beliefs about individual differences must be represented.

Factor Analyses of PHN-Scale Items

Further evidence for the relationship of the subscales with one another can be derived from an involved statistical procedure called *factor analysis*. A factor analysis surveys all the correlations among many different tests, and extracts what is common to all possible relationships. These commonalities are called *factors*; they are hypothetical entities that serve to label the common variance among different entities.

A factor analysis is thus a complex set of statistical procedures that identifies items or tests that intercorrelate and cluster together. Just because a test constructor *claims* that all the items on the same scale measure the same thing is no proof that they do. Factor analysis can be used to evaluate this claim of commonality of items empirically. Additionally, factor analyses can be used as a way of item refinement or of identifying items that are not contributing to a hypothesized factor (Wiggins, 1973).

Two types of factor analysis were done: first, a factor analysis of the PHN scale in a battery along with other scales, and second a factor analysis of items from the PHN scale alone.

SCALE FACTOR ANALYSES

The relationship of philosophies of human nature to other measures of attitudes toward people is detailed in Chapter 6. Perhaps, at this point, it is sufficient to note that when the PHN scale is included in a heteroge-

TABLE 4.6 Sources of Subjects for Nottingham et al. Item Factor Analysis

School	Description	Men	Women
George Peabody College for Teachers	Private teachers' college, Nashville, TN	20	52
Belmont College	Southern Baptist college, Nashville, TN	48	41
University of North Carolina	State university, Chapel Hill, NC	50	50
Central Michigan University	State college, Mt. Pleasant, MI	44	62
Wheaton College (IL)	Private college promoting a Fundamentalistic orientation	33	62
Carson-Newman College	Southern Baptist college, Jefferson City, TN	36	64
Kentucky-Southern College	Southern Baptist college, Louisville, KY	29	15
Western Maryland College	Private liberal-arts college in Westminster, MD, with 90% of its students from the Northeast	47	54
	TOTAL	307	400

neous battery of instruments, the analysis generates a factor labeled Attitudes Toward People that includes the Machiavellianism Scale, various measures of anomie, the Faith-in-People Scale, and a social-desirability scale. Two separate factor analyses (S. W. Cook & Wrightsman, 1967; Wrightsman & Cook, 1965) found that the PHN positive-negative score and the substantive-subscale scores load heavily on this factor—that is, these subscales contribute to the determination and naming of this factor. Beyond these results, a later study designed to factor analyze only the scales that load heavily on this ATP (attitudes toward people) factor found that on the only meaningful factor that emerged the PHN positive-negative score had a higher loading than any other measure (Simon, 1972).

ITEM FACTOR ANALYSES

Three item factor analyses were completed using five different samples. Nottingham, Gorsuch, and Wrightsman (1970) analyzed the responses of 400 women and 307 men, recruited from eight colleges and universities that differed in size, location, function, and type of students. These schools are described in Table 4.6. It should be noted that although all subjects were college students, the variety of schools and the resultant diversity of subjects' backgrounds were greater than those of the usual sample of factor-analysis subjects. All subjects were tested within a 13-month period. Testing conditions were not rigorously standardized from one school to another, but in most cases the testing was done in introductory psychology classes. The students were always told that the testing was for research purposes and that they were not to use their names. Since gender differences are often present on the subscales (see Chapter 5), male and female groups were factored separately.

The following technical procedures were used in this factor analysis: For each sample, the product-moment correlations for all pairs of items were calculated. Principal components were then extracted. To determine the most appropriate number of factors, Nottingham et al. (1970) examined each sample's latent roots by the scree test (Cattell, 1966); this analysis suggested that approximately 10 to 12 factors were needed (in contrast to the 6 dimensions originally proposed). As a further check on the necessary number of factors, 10, 11, 12, and 13 factors were rotated to the varimax criterion. By searching each consecutive varimax solution for the number of loadings greater than an absolute value of .40, Nottingham et al. found that only 10 factors for the women and 12 factors for the men warranted the title of common factors. These were rotated to oblique simple structure by the promax procedure (Hendrickson & White, 1964). The correlations among factors proved too small to warrant a second-order analysis.

A second item factor analysis was done by O'Connor (1971) using 352 Air Force Academy freshmen. Although the procedures were different the results were essentially the same, and we shall report the results of both studies at the same time.

O'Connor's procedure was a cluster analysis, a procedure developed by Tryon and Bailey (1965, 1966, 1970), technically called the "BC TRY computer system of cluster and factor authorities." Like Nottingham et al.'s procedure, it first determines the product-moment correlations between all possible pairs of the 84 items. But then communality estimates are made by the highest absolute correlation in the diagonal, and the dimensionality of the solution is determined by a cumulative-communality-exhaustion criterion of .92. Thus the BC TRY cluster-analysis procedure is completed when 92% of the variance is accounted for.

O'Connor (1971) randomly divided his sample into two groups for separate factor analyses. The results were so similar that the two groups were pooled together, and all items were then correlated with each subject's factor scores. For example, each group produced eight factors, seven of which were the same. The other two factors were specific for each group.

In the BC TRY program, the pivot variable is selected by the variance of R-squared method, while the key variables are selected by the mutual-colinearity method. In the expanded cluster structure (oblique), variables are cumulatively assigned to a cluster by their highest oblique-factor coefficients.

In regard to the loading of specific items on similar factors, the results for the two studies were very much alike, although they were not always what the test constructor had anticipated. First of all, items from the Trustworthiness and Altruism subscales did not load on "theoretically pure" factors; instead, they crossed label lines. Consider, for example, O'Connor's (1970) first factor reproduced in Table 4.7. O'Connor has chosen to call this factor Beliefs That People Are Conventionally Good, because (1) the factor is composed entirely of items with favorable content, (2) the statements reflect the middle-class morality of America, and (3) the statements come not from only one subscale but from all four substantive subscales. (Seven of the 12 are from the Altruism subscale, however.)

Table 4.7 shows that this factor is remarkably similar to the third factor that emerged in both the male and female samples of Nottingham et al.'s (1970) study. As the table illustrates, of O'Connor's 12 highest items, 9 loaded on Nottingham's Factor 3 for both men and women. The remaining 3 in each sample load on Nottingham et al.'s Factor 7, which correlates approximately .50 with Factor 3.

Tables 4.7 through 4.13, which present the obtained factors and list the items loading on each, also include information about mean score, standard deviation, homogeneity ratio, and Cronbach coefficient-alpha reliability. The homogeneity rations of .19 to .43 for the factored scales are within acceptable limits (W. A. Scott, 1968).

If the positively scored items from the Altruism subscale and to a lesser extent those from the other substantive scales load together, what happens to the negatively scored items? A substantial number of them—*and to an impressive degree the same ones*—appear on O'Connor's Factor 7 and Nottingham et al.'s Factor 1 (for both men and women). Note Table 4.8. Both investigators chose to call this factor Cynicism, because it is composed entirely of negatively scored statements that not only are critical of human nature but also portray people as double-dealing, hypocrisy-ridden, or self-deluding. Of the 10 highest items on O'Connor's factor, 7 are among the highest-loading 10 in Nottingham's male sample and 6 are in

TABLE 4.7 O'Connor's First Factor—Beliefs That People Are Conventionally Good

Factor Loading O'Connor	Nottingham				
Factor 1	Men Factor 3	Women Factor 3	Original Scale	Item No.	Item Statement
.71	.70	.73	A+	16	Most people will act as "Good Samaritans" if given the opportunity.
.68	.56	.74	A+	22	"Do unto others as you would have them do unto you" is a motto most people follow.
.65	.66	.57 Female #7*	A+	10	Most people do not hesitate to go out of their way to help someone in trouble.
.64	.42	.52	I+	81	Most people will speak out for what they believe in.
.63	.51	.68	A+	28	The typical person is sincerely concerned about the problems of others.
.61	.35	.67	A+	4	Most people try to apply the Golden Rule even in today's complex society.
.59	.40	.57	I+	45	Most people have the courage of their convictions.
.56	.50 Male #7*	.57 Female #7*	S+	67	In a local or national election, most people select a candidate rationally and logically.
.55	.51	.51	T+	14	People usually tell the truth, even when they know they would be better off by lying.
.55	.59 Male #7*	.44	I+	63	The average person will stick to his opinion if he thinks he is right, even if others disagree.
.53	.50 Male #7*	.37 Female #7*	A+	57	It is achievement, rather than popularity with others, that gets you ahead nowadays.
.51	.56	.44	A+	40	Most people would stop and help a person whose car is disabled.

Note: Mean score = +0.06; SD = 7.32; homogeneity ratio = .30; Cronbach coefficient-alpha reliability = .85 (based on O'Connor's sample).
*Male and Female Factors 3 and 7 correlated +.50.

TABLE 4.8 Cynicism Factor

Factor Loading					
O'Connor	Nottingham				
Factor 7	Men Factor 1	Women Factor 1	Original Scale	Item No.	Item Statement
.64	.65	.65	T-	68	Most people would tell a lie if they could gain by it.
.62	.39	.56	T-	44	People claim they have ethical standards regarding honesty and morality, but few people stick to them when the chips are down.
.60	.65	.60	T-	56	If most people could get into a movie without paying and be sure they were not seen, they would do it.
.58	.51	.51	T-	74	Most people would cheat on their income tax if they had a chance.
.57	.36	.36	A-	58	It's pathetic to see an unselfish person in today's world because so many people take advantage of him.
.56	NR	.44	A-	70	Most people inwardly dislike putting themselves out to help other people.
.54	NR	.46	I-	21	The typical student will cheat on a test when everybody else does, even though he has a set of ethical standards.
.54	.37	.56	A-	64	People pretend to care more about one another than they really do.
.51	.51	.39	A-	46	The average person is conceited.
.52	.56	.61	T-	62	Most people are not really honest for a desirable reason; they're afraid of getting caught.

Note: Mean score = -0.10; SD = 6.40; homogeneity ratio = .24; Cronbach coefficient-alpha reliability = .77 (based on Cronbach's sample).
NR—Not reported

95

the female sample's top 10. There is one item on which there is a gender difference of possible interest. Item 82 ("People are usually out for their own good") has a loading of .82 on the women's factor but is absent from the factors for the men in both the Nottingham and the O'Connor samples. Does this statement have a particular tone of sexual exploitation for women?

At this point, the bulk of the Altruism items (11 of 14) and 6 of the Trustworthiness items have been accounted for by two factors that group themselves not by theoretical similarity but by direction of wording and content. Are these factors related to each other? Since items of one factor are worded so that a high score indicates a belief that people are good and items of the other are worded to express cynical beliefs, we would expect a negative correlation between the two factors. The results are as follows:

r, O'Connor Factor 1 and Factor 7	=	−.61
r, Nottingham et al. Factor 1 and Factor 3 for men	=	−.27
r, Nottingham et al. Factor 1 and Factor 3 for women	=	−.33

Although all three samples have the expected negative relationship, only one is significant. The absence of consistent solid relationships causes us to question our original assumption that beliefs about human nature could best be conceptualized along such bipolar theoretical dimensions as altruism, independence, and so forth. Is another framework possible?

The third factor analysis (Wrightsman, Weir, & Brusewitz, 1991) was completed 20 years after the previous two. A total of 273 males and 261 females at the University of Kansas completed the PHN scale, and a principal-components analysis and a varimax rotation were completed, as in the first factor analysis. Results are exceedingly consistent with the two previous analyses. For example, the first factor extracted was composed of only negatively scored items, almost all from the Trustworthiness (T), Altruism (A), and Independence (I) subscales. Of the 21 possible negatively scored items from these subscales, 17 loaded above .40 on this factor. Only one item from another subscale (#13, a C-item) did. We labeled this factor Negative View of Human Nature. *Every one of the 10 Cynicism factor items on Table 4.8 loaded above .40 on this factor,* truly remarkable consistency over two decades.

The second factor in the 1991 factor analysis was composed of 17 items, all positively scored and mostly from these same subscales (4 from T, 5 from A, and 6 from I). Two items were from the Strength of Will and Rationality subscale. Of the 12 items from Table 4.7, the Beliefs

TABLE 4.9 Internal-Locus-of-Control Factor

Factor Loading					
O'Connor	*Nottingham*				
	Men	*Women*	*Original*		
Factor 4	*Factor 2*	*Factor 2*	*Scale*	*Item No.*	*Item Statement*
.76	.71	.70	S+	73	Most persons have a lot of control over what happens to them in life.
.72	.53	.64	S+	61	The average person is largely the master of his own fate.
-.39	-.58	-.55	S-	19	There's little a person can do to alter his fate in life.
-.38	-.67	-.76	S-	25	Most people have little influence over the things that happen to them.
-.35	-.57	-.54	S-	7	Our success in life is pretty much determined by forces outside our own control.

Note: Mean score = +1.77; SD = 5.85; homogeneity ratio = .43; Cronbach coefficient-alpha reliability = .46 (based on O'Connor's , 1971, sample).

that People Are Conventionally Good factor, 10 loaded above .40 on the second factor in the third factor analysis, and the other two loaded above .30. We labeled the second factor from this new factor analysis as Positive View of Human Nature because, with 17 items loading above .40, it is more comprehensive than the factor in Table 4.7.

A consistent pattern in this most recent factor analysis is the emergence of factors that are more general and more congruent with the theoretically derived subscales than was the case of the two previous factor analyses. Factor 3 is an example. As Table 4.9 indicates, the previous factor analyses both generated an Internal Locus of Control factor. While the items were all from the same subscales, they were limited in number (only 5) and specific in content. In the most recent factor analysis, Factor 3 had 9 items load above .40 and 10 above .30, with 6 of the 10 from the Strength of Will and Rationality subscale. We called this factor Strength of Will. The items from other subscales that loaded on this factor (#60, #78, and #84, C-items; and #15, an I-item) reflect the outcomes of motivation, also.

In the new factor analysis, Factor 4 was composed of 12 of the 14 Variability subscale items, all with loadings above .30. It was similar to but broader in coverage than Factor 5 in Table 4.10. Factor 5 had 6 items, all from the Complexity subscale, load above .40; it overlapped almost perfectly with the factor in Table 4.12. Likewise, the sixth factor to emerge

TABLE 4.10 Variability Factor

Factor Loading O'Connor	Nottingham				
	Men	Women	Original		
Factor 5	Factor 5	Factor 5	Scale	Item No.	Item Statement
.79	.58	.53	V+	23	People are quite different in their basic interests.
.77	.52	.64	V+	29	People are pretty different from one another in "what makes them tick."
.68	NR	.35	V+	41	People are unpredictable in how they'll act from one situation to another.
NR	NR	-.60	V-	47	People are pretty much alike in their basic interests.
NR	NR	-.41	V-	53	People are basically similar in their personalities.
NR	NR	-.46	V-	59	If you have a good idea about how several people will react to a certain situation, you can expect most other people to react the same way.
NR	NR	-.60	V-	83	When you get right down to it, people are quite alike in their emotional makeup.

Note: Mean = -0.27; SD = 2.79; homogeneity ratio = .34; Cronbach coefficient-alpha reliability = .62 (based on O'Connor's , 1971, sample).
NR—Not reported

in the new factor analysis, which we called Accuracy in First Impressions, had 4 of the 5 items from Factor 6 in Table 4.13.

The eigenvalues for the first six factors in the most recent factor analysis ranged from 8.04 for Factor 1 to 2.16 for Factor 6. The cumulative percentage of the variance accounted for by these factors was 32.3%.

We feel confident in concluding that the factor structure of the Philosophies of Human Nature Scale is remarkably stable over samples and over a 20-year period.

TABLE 4.11 Similarity Factor

O'Connor Factor 6	Nottingham Men Factor 11	Nottingham Women Factor 8	Original Scale	Item No.	Item Statement
.71	.46	.40	V–	59	If you have a good idea about how several people will react to a certain situation, you can expect most people to react the same way.
.69	.64	.41	V–	53	People are basically similar in their personalities.
.65	NR	.35	C–	42	Give me a few facts about a person, and I'll have a good idea of whether I'll like him or not.
NR	.73	See Table 4.10	V–	47	People are pretty much alike in their basic interests.
.40[a]	.60	.36	V–	83	When you get right down to it, people are quite alike in their emotional makeup.
NR	–.58	See Table 4.10	V+	23	People are quite different in their basic interests.
NR	NR	.64	V–	65	Most people are consistent from situation to situation in the way they react to things.
NR	NR	.60	V–	77	If I can see how a person reacts to one situation, I have a good idea of how he will react to other situations.
NR	NR	–.47	V+	41	People are unpredictable in how they'll act from one situation to another.
NR	NR	.41	SWR+	67	In a local or national election, most people select a candidate rationally and logically.

Note: Mean = -0.90; SD = 1.74; homogeneity ratio = .19; Cronbach coefficient-alpha reliability = .54 (based on O'Connor's , 1971, sample).
a. O'Connor did not list Item 83 in this factor because it loaded above .50 on more than one factor.
NR—Not reported

Application of Kerlinger's Construct of Criterial Referents

Because great emphasis was placed upon the evaluative quality of a PHN attitude, it was perhaps natural to conceptualize each PHN component as a

TABLE 4.12 Complexity Factor

Factor Loading O'Connor	Nottingham		Original		
	Men	Women			
Factor 2	Factor 4	Factor 4	Scale	Item No.	Item Statement
.82	.69	.57	C+	84	People are so complex that it is hard to know what "makes them tick."
.81	.58	.66	C+	78	People are too complex to ever be understood fully.
.67	.55	.63	C+	60	I think you can never really understand the feelings of other people.
.57	NR	.43	C+	54	Some people are too complicated for me to figure out.
NR	.54	NR	V+	41	People are unpredictable in how they'll act from one situation to another.
.52	.40	NR	C	+66	You can't accurately describe a person in just a few words.

Note: Mean = 1.12; *SD* = 4.30; homogeneity ratio = .33; Cronbach coefficient-alpha reliability = .71
(based on O'Connor's, 1971, sample).
NR—Not reported

TABLE 4.13 First-Impressions Factor

Factor Loading O'Connor	Nottingham		Original		
	Men	Women			
Factor 3	Factor 6	Factor 6	Scale	Item No.	Item Statement
.74	.75	.72	C-	6	I find that my first impression of a person is usually correct.
.69	.41	.47	C-	24	I think I get a good idea of a person's basic nature after a brief conversation with him.
-.66	-.76	-.70	C+	48	I find that my first impressions of people are frequently wrong.
.60	NR	NR	C-	30	If I could ask a person three questions about himself (assuming that he would answer them honestly), I would know a great deal about him.
.53	NR	.25	C-	18	It's not hard to understand what really is important to a person.

Note: Mean = +0.02; *SD* = 3.90; homogeneity ratio = .26; Cronbach coefficient-alpha reliability = .63
(based on O'Connor's, 1971, sample).
NR—Not reported

continuum ranging from an extremely favorable position toward the attitude content to an extremely unfavorable one. This conceptualization of attitudes as generally bipolar in nature has been predominant ever since G. W. Allport's 1935 review of attitude research. Whether the attitude object is Madonna, gay rights, or flag-burning, the bipolar-continuum approach claims that a person's attitude can be placed at some point along a single continuum from "good" to "bad," "like" to "dislike," or "favorable" to "unfavorable." But this assumption has been questioned in other quarters, too. Kerlinger (1958, 1961, 1967a, 1967b) hypothesized that the nature of social attitudes "is not basically bipolar; it is . . . dualistic" (1967b, p. 112). If we conceptualize an attitude as a bipolar continuum, we would expect that a politically liberal position and a conservative one would be at opposite ends of this solitary continuum. But the liberal is not necessarily the opposite of the conservative; rather, each may have an attitude system that is relatively independent of the other. Kerlinger's position would posit not one continuum but two (or more) points of reference that are unrelated to each other.

In developing his position, Kerlinger (1967b, p. 110) employed the concept of a *referent*—that is, any object or construct of psychological importance to the subject. Bipolarity occurs when the referents that act as standards for one set of individuals—"criterial" referents, in Kerlinger's words—are used as negative standards by another set of individuals. For example, bipolarity would exist if, for conservatives, the issue of a ban on pornography were "criterial" (that is, if this issue was basic and if such censorship was attractive to conservatives) and if liberals also "cued in" on this issue but had a reaction to the banning of pornography that was the opposite of the conservative reaction. Of course, there still are some issues on which liberals advocate one position and conservatives, the other. But on many issues liberalism and conservatism are not shunted to opposite ends of a single continuum. The issue of invasion of privacy is an example. The right to privacy is not an issue for which we can put liberals at one end of a continuum and conservatives at the other; instead, the issue is criterial for both groups—that is, both advocate the same referents.

A specific and trivial attitude may usually be conceptualized as a bipolar continuum. For example, a person's attitude toward butter-pecan ice cream may be favorable, neutral, or unfavorable, and that reaction may be all there is to the attitude. But there is some evidence that certain attitude domains may be better viewed through the concept of *criterial referents* than through the concept of *bipolar continua*. For example, Kerlinger (1967a) measured attitudes toward a progressive philosophy of education

and a traditional philosophy of education, two attitude objects that most
of us might expect to be polar opposites. (For instance, we might expect
an adherent of student-centered teaching to reject a traditional approach
that emphasizes the "three Rs.") Instead, two dimensions emerge, one
with a traditional philosophy of education as a criterial referent (favoring
such objects as subject matter and discipline) and the other with a progressive philosophy of education as a criterial referent (favoring such objects
as social development and individualized instruction). The important
finding is that those two dimensions are essentially unrelated—that is, a
person's favorable attitude toward progressive education is independent
of his or her attitude toward traditional education.

Kerlinger's conclusion that most attitudes are not bipolar was criticized
by Zdep and Marco (1969) because Kerlinger's evidence was limited to
attitudes about philosophies of education. The results of the PHN factor
analysis, however, show that a criterial-referents approach may be applied
fruitfully to other attitude domains. By this we mean that a person may
agree that most people are conventionally good and yet subscribe to cynical beliefs about them. We do not know what thought processes are involved here. Does the subject perceive an inconsistency in his or her
responses? Is one set of beliefs more content oriented? Does the cynicism
reflect a personality style? It would be useful to interview persons with
high scores on both factors to determine if they perceive any inconsisten-
cies themselves.

Example of Agreement
Between "Theoretical" and Factorial Scales

Continuing our comparison of the results of the three item factor analyses, we find cases of agreement between the results of these analyses and
the original theoretical dimensions of philosophies of human nature. For
example, the second factor to emerge for both the men and women tested
by Nottingham et al. (1970) is composed entirely of items from the
Strength of Will and Rationality subscale. This is O'Connor's (1971) Factor 4 (see Table 4.9). The same five items load highest in all three samples.
Because these statements reflect beliefs about the locus of the determinants of one's outcome in life rather than beliefs about willpower per se,
the factor has been labeled an Internal Locus of Control factor. It should
be noted that none of the rationality items are included. The factor is
broader in the most recent sample, however.

The Variability subscale also appears as a separate factor in all three samples. It is Factor 5 for O'Connor's group and for Nottingham's female subjects and Factor 11 for Nottingham's male subjects (see Table 4.10). All seven items listed in Table 4.10 are from the original Variability subscale; yet only two of these items share high loadings in all three samples. The highest loading items seem to be tapping beliefs about basic human differences, so the factor has been labeled Variability. The recent analysis confirms this conclusion.

Items from the Variability subscale, however, also contribute to another factor (see Table 4.11). Some of the items that loaded on the previous Variability factor for Nottingham's female subjects load on this factor for one or both male groups (that is, Items 47, 53, 59, and 83). Eight of the 10 items on this factor are from the Variability subscale, but there is not much consistency from one sample to another on what items (or how many items load above .40). Only two items—both originally Variability subscale—load consistently, and their content is the source for the label Similarity for the factor.

The fate of the original items from the Complexity subscale resembles the fate of the Variability items. In the O'Connor analysis, 10 of the 14 items appear on either Factor 2 or Factor 3. With the exception of one Variability item, no other subscales have items that load above .50 on these factors. Factor 2, described in Table 4.12, is composed entirely of positively scored items that share a feeling of complexity about people— almost an expression of the futility of trying to understand people. Each of Nottingham's samples show great overlap in item coverage with O'Connor's sample on this factor.

The tendency for directionality of content to influence factor results is again apparent in O'Connor's Factor 3 (Nottingham's Factor 6), as five of the six items share a negatively scored direction. All are from the Complexity subscale. Because of their content, this factor has been labeled First Impressions (see Table 4.13). The correlation between O'Connor's Factor 2 and Factor 3 is only -.208, indicating that different sets of items from the original Complexity subscale really represent two quite independent pools of content.

The only subscale still unaccounted for is Independence. In none of the factor analyses did a separate factor emerge for Independence, and only four Independence items surface in O'Connor's first seven factors; the outcome is similar for the women in Nottingham's sample. For the men in his sample, Factor 7 includes four Independence items (Items 45, 57, 63, and 81) as its highest loaders, but most of the rest of the items draw from

TABLE 4.14 Correlations of Original Subscales with Factors

| | O'Connor | | Nottingham | | | |
| | | | Men | | Women | |
Original Subscale	Factor No.	r	Factor No.	r	Factor No.	r
Trustworthiness	7	-.749	1	-.484	1	-.644
	1	.789				
Strength of Will	4	.617	2	.608	2	.719
and Rationality	1	.396				
Altruism	1	.856	3	.583	3	.565
	7	-.723				
Independence	1	.706	7	.582	1	-.542
	7	-.714			7	
Complexity	2	.748	4	.490	4	.454
	3	-.715	6	-.480		
			8	-.463		
Variability	5	.723	11	-.716	5	.684
	6	-.620			8	-.516

Note: Includes all correlations above .40, plus several lower correlations of particular interest.

other substantive scales. In the most recent analysis, items from the Independence subscale play a stronger role; three load on Factor 1 (Items 9, 21, and 33) and six on Factor 2 (Items 81, 45, 57, 63, 75, and 51). Yet it is clear that the Independence scale is the weakest in terms of factorial purity, even though its split-half reliability is within the normal limits.

How well do the empirically derived factors correlate with the original subscales? Here we can assess the statistical purity of the original subscales. In O'Connor's sample, the factors correlate moderately well with all the subscales—even the Independence subscale. In that sample, five of the hypothesized six dimensions were confirmed, using a criterion index of a correlation of .70 or better between the original subscale and the factor. (A correlation of .70 was used because it accounts for approximately half of the variance.) The weakest dimension, Strength of Will and Rationality, correlates only .62 with O'Connor's Factor 4. Correlations between subscales and factors in Nottingham et al.'s samples produce relationships of generally modest size. The indication is that most of the original subscales reflect a desirable degree of statistical purity and homogeneity.

The splitting of subscales into two separate factors, usually on the basis of direction of content, is again revealed in Table 4.14. Particularly likely to divide in such a manner are the subscales for Trustworthiness-plus-Altruism, Complexity, and Variability.

What are we to make of all these factor-analysis results? Several conclusions and recommendations seem justified:

1. The original subscales and the empirically derived factors generally correlate with each other adequately enough to defend the continued use of the original subscales. The one subscale for which this is not the case, Strength of Will and Rationality, is apparently composed of too heterogeneous a set of items. In the future, the empirically derived factor scale Internal Locus of Control (see Table 4.9) should be substituted.

2. The Trustworthiness and Altruism subscales are so similar that they should be considered as parts of the same construct. Although their positively scored items and negatively scored items load on different factors, the two subscales are functionally equivalent. When the original scales are used, the number of items can be reduced by deleting one of these two subscales.

3. Although the summing together of the four substantive subscales to get an overall positive-negative score is a generally defensible process, it is not recommended because of the ways that the items cluster into different factors on the basis of the direction of content.

4. A one-dimension conceptualization of complexity seems inadequate. It is better conceptualized as composed of two independent aspects—one, a feeling of the futility of trying to understand people, and the other, a set of beliefs regarding the importance of first impressions in judging people.

Since large amounts of data have been collected and analyzed using the original subscales, subsequent chapters of this book will report findings and make conclusions based on these subscales. We suggest, however, that future research use a shortened form of the PHN scale with six empirically derived subscales of 5 to 12 items each. (These are reproduced in Appendix C.) Each of these is factorially pure except Scale E, which includes items from both the Similarity and Variability factors. The 45 items should be shuffled so that no 2 items from the same scale appear sequentially.

Do these factor-pure scales predict external criteria better than the original subscales do? The answer is a complex one, if research on the effectiveness of *personality scales* constructed by different strategies is any guide. For example, when Hase and Goldberg (1967) used four different strategies (factor analysis, a rational procedure similar to the one used here, a "theoretical" strategy, and a contrasted-groups method similar to the Minnesota Multiphasic Personality Inventory construction) their initial conclusion was that the four methods of scale construction were equally effective in predicting 13 external criteria. For each, the initial multiple-correlation coefficient was between .48 and .51, and for each, the cross-validated multiple-correlation coefficient was between .25 and .28. But when Goldberg (1972) completed a comprehensive reanalysis of these data, an intriguing strategy-by-criterion interaction emerged (Wiggins, 1973). These interactions are too complex to report here, except to use them as an indication of the difficulty of establishing any overall conclusion that factor-derived scales are any more effective than are those that are first theoretically derived and then item-analyzed.

Other Instruments for Measuring Philosophies of Human Nature

In addition to the Likert-scale measure, we have constructed two other devices for measuring philosophies of human nature. One is a set of bipolar-rating scales and the other a series of paragraphs describing ambiguous situations about which subjects are asked to write their explanation or interpretation of what has happened.

BIPOLAR RATINGS

The bipolar-rating measure used the popular semantic-differential technique (Osgood, Suci, & Tannenbaum, 1957). Subjects are presented with a concept—in this case, "people in general, as they are today"—at the top of a sheet of paper. They are then instructed to rate this concept on a series of bipolar scales, each arranged on a 7-point continuum. An example would be:

         Good _____ Bad

Seventeen bipolar scales that seemed related to the six PHN dimensions were used. Specifically, by dimension, they were:

Trustworthiness: completely good versus completely bad
                     religious versus unreligious
                     honest versus dishonest
                     trustworthy versus untrustworthy
                     trusting others versus distrusting others (suspicious)

Altruism: selfish versus unselfish
                     peace-loving versus warlike
                     self-centered versus thoughtful of others

Strength of Will
and Rationality: able to understand themselves versus unable to
                 understand themselves

Independence: brave versus cowardly
                 do what others say is right versus do what they want
                 to do

Complexity: simple versus complex
                 silly versus serious
                 deep versus shallow

Variability: same as other people versus different from one
                 another
                 predictable from time to time versus unpredictable
                 from one time to another

Responses on each of the bipolar scales were given scores from 1 to 7. To obtain the scores for a particular PHN dimension we summed and averaged responses on all the adjective pairs representing that dimension. A study by Marilyn King (1971) related these scores to the same subjects' PHN scores on the Likert-scale version.

The Likert form and the bipolar-rating form of the PHN were administered to 65 students in educational psychology and social psychology classes at George Peabody College for Teachers. For 61 of the students, both measures were obtained during the fall semester of 1971. For the remaining four students, the Likert-scale version of the PHN had been administered previously as part of the annual freshman testing battery. For the total group of subjects, King intercorrelated scores on both forms of the PHN, using the 16 scores of each subject as elements.

The bipolar-rating version of the PHN was constructed so that low scores on each subscale should correspond to high scores on the subscales of the Likert regular form. That is, a score of 1 on the Trustworthy-Untrustworthy scale means that the subject rated people in general as trustworthy. A score of 7 implies a rating of untrustworthy. On the Likert-scale version, however, a negative score indicates a belief in untrustworthiness, and a positive score implies a favorable belief.

In general, the correlations between scores on the two forms of the test were high and in the expected negative direction (low scores on the semantic-differential form corresponded to high scores on the Likert-scale form and vice versa). For example, the Trustworthiness subscales of the two forms were correlated -.60. For the Strength of Will and Rationality

TABLE 4.15 Correlations Between Likert-Scale and Open-Ended Measures of PHN (N = 273)

Open-Ended Measure	Trust-worthiness	Strength of Will & Rationality	Altruism	Independence	Complexity	Variabilty	Positive-Negative	Multiplexity
				Likert-Scale Measure				
Trustworthiness	.466**	.251**	.412**	.385**	.036	-.088	.475**	-.026
Strength of Will and Rationality	.146*	.111	.090	.138*	-.070	-.003	.153*	-.051
Altruism	.342**	.194**	.398**	.357**	-.027	.057	.410**	.013
Independence	.165**	.203**	.210**	.304**	-.131*	.007	.274**	-.082
Positive-Negative	.467**	.316**	.470**	.487**	-.055	.007	.547**	-.033
Multiplexity	.152*	.099	.129*	.185**	.004	.079	.177**	.048

Note: Correlations reflecting two measures of the same variable are in boxes.
*Significantly different from zero at .05 level.
**Significantly different from zero at .01 level.

subscales, the correlation was -.44; for Altruism, -.56; for Independence, -.57; and for a general positive-negative score (which was derived from scores on the previous four subscales), -.48. All these correlations were significantly different from zero at the .001 level. However, correlations between the two forms for Complexity and Variability were low and nonsignificant (r = .02 and r = -.21, respectively), and the correlations between the two forms of the multiplexity score (which was derived from these two subscales) were also low and nonsignificant (r = .04).

In summary, the results generated by the bipolar-rating form are quite consistent with those of the Likert-scale form in the case of the four substantive dimensions. The individual-difference dimensions do not appear to be as amenable to measurement by a rating-scale procedure.

SITUATIONS TEST

The Behavior Insight Test, reprinted in Appendix D, is an open-ended measure of philosophies of human nature that poses everyday situations and requires the respondent to interpret them or predict their outcome. Each of the 17 situations deals with one of the substantive dimensions of philosophies of human nature. (The specific allocations are as follows: Trustworthiness, Items 1, 4, 6, 7, 9; Strength of Will and Rationality, Items 2, 8, 11; Altruism, Items 12, 13, 14, 15; and Independence, Items 3, 5, 10, 16, 17.) Responses to the question following each situation were scored and summed so that each respondent obtained a score on each of the four substantive dimensions. An indication of the respondent's reliance on concepts of complexity and variability in his or her answers was gleaned by tabulating the number of times the subject used such expressions as "probably" or "most people" or "maybe," or any responses that reflected a recognition of the possibility of several interpretations.

To determine relationships between scores from the situations measure and the Likert-scale version of the PHN, S. W. Cook and Wrightsman (1967) administered measures to 273 female undergraduates within a heterogeneous battery of personality, ability, and attitude tests. The subjects, who were paid, came from five different colleges in the Nashville area.

The correlations are reported in Table 4.15. The Trustworthiness measures from the two formats showed a moderate relationship (.47), as did those for Altruism (.40). The two Independence measures correlated somewhat lower (.30). Although all three of these correlations are significantly different from zero, they account for relatively little common variance—from 9% to 21%. Even the correlation of the two summed positive-negative measures (.55) produces only 30% in common variance. Furthermore, the open-ended measure of Strength of Will and of multiplexity produced no significant relationships with their Likert-scale counterparts. Further work and refinement are necessary before an open-ended measure of philosophies of human nature may be used with confidence.

We may apply D. T. Campbell and Fiske's (1959) multitrait, multimethod analysis to the data in Table 4.15. D. T. Campbell and Fiske were concerned first of all with the convergent validity of measure—that is, two different methods that measure the same trait (or attitude, in our case) should agree with each other. We have noted that most of the correlations along the diagonal in Table 4.15 are significantly different from zero—one of D. T. Campbell and Fiske's criteria—but they are not of large magnitude—the other criterion for convergent validity. D. T. Campbell and Fiske also propose that such validity correlations (that is, two different methods that measure the same attitude) ought to be higher than heterotrait heteromethod correlations. This is the case in Table 4.15; for example, the two methods of measuring Trustworthiness correlate .47, which is higher than the trust-open-end-versus-altruism-Likert correlation (.41) or the trust-Likert-versus-altruism-open-end correlation (.34). But the Likert measure of Trustworthiness and Altrusm correlate .65, higher than the .47 for two methods of measuring Trustworthiness. This last finding violates D. T. Campbell and Fiske's third criterion, that a variable will "correlate higher with an independent effort to measure the same trait [or attitude] than with measures designed to get at different traits [or attitudes] which happen to employ the same method" (D. T. Campbell & Fiske, 1959, p. 83). Although D. T. Campbell and Fiske acknowledge the difficulty of achieving this criterion, such comments are of little solace to us when we recognize that two attitude-scale measures of "different" attitudes correlate higher than two measures of the same attitude. Here we see the importance of the second type of validity analyzed by D. T. Campbell and Fiske—discriminant validity. They note that methods can be invalidated if they are designed to measure different variables and yet correlate highly with one another. In a sense, the correlations discussed here simply recapitulate the findings of the item-factor analyses—that the Altruism and Trustworthiness subscales function in such similar ways that they would be considered as measuring the same construct.

Summary

Three ways of measuring philosophies of human nature have been described in this chapter. Much more confidence, however, is placed in the Likert-scale approach than in the use of bipolar ratings or of a situations test, which presents subjects with paragraphs describing ambiguous situations and asks them to interpret what is happening in each. The Likert scales were subjected to two item analyses, which resulted in an 84-item Philosophies of Human Nature Scale, with 14 items for each of the six subscales. The split-half and test-retest reliabilities of the subscales are adequate for group comparisons.

Intercorrelations of the subscales indicated that, as hypothesized, responses to the individual-differences subscales (Complexity and Variability) bore no relationship to responses to the substantive subscales. Thus two kinds of attitudes are needed to describe a person's philosophy of human nature.

Three factor analyses of the items were done to determine if the factor structure resembled the hypothesized structure of the dimensions. In some ways it did, but in other ways it did not. On the basis of these analyses, we concluded that the Trustworthiness and Altruism subscales are so similar in content that they could be combined. It also appears that Strength of Will and Rationality may be thought of as a Locus of Control factor. Complexity, as a construct, appears to be composed of two independent aspects: a feeling component—that it is futile to try to understand people—plus a belief component that centers on the importance of first impressions in judging people.

A suggested short form of the PHN scale, based on the factor analyses, is reproduced in Appendix C.

The tendency for positively scored items from a scale to cluster on one factor while negatively scored items from the same scale cluster on another was consistent in three factor analyses across several decades. Kerlinger's (1967b) concept of criterial referents was employed in the interpretation of these findings.

CHAPTER FIVE

Group Differences

I shall never cease to be amazed by those persons who, in the name of equal opportunity, advocate undifferentiated treatment of all persons—men and women, black and white, old and young—with little or no regard apparently for the greater social good to be served by treating people as individuals rather than as undifferentiated and undistinguishable members of the human race.

—MARVIN D. DUNNETTE

A police officer working a beat in the East Los Angeles ghetto is likely to possess beliefs about human nature that are extremely different from those of an elementary school teacher in Grosse Point, MI. A freshman at a state university and a member of the board of trustees at the same school are likely to attribute different characteristics to people in general, as are an army private and his or her commanding officer. If philosophies of human nature play an important role in structuring our dealings with other people, we should find meaningful group differences in responses to the PHN scale. For example, we expect gender, religious background, and occupation to influence people's philosophies of human nature. This chapter reports and interprets these and other group differences. But first, we will consider scores obtained from a heterogeneous sample of college students on the PHN scale. Their average scores will provide a baseline with which to compare more specific groups.

PHN Scores of a Heterogeneous Sample of College Students

During the standardization of the PHN scale, the scale was administered to 1,072 students (473 males and 599 females) in 12 colleges and universities across the United States. These schools differed not only in location but also in size, in function, and, in fact, in almost any manner imaginable. There were state universities, small liberal-arts colleges, church-related

112

schools, a predominantly African-American school, and a teacher-training institution. A tabulation of the student responses permits a statement of what—at least at that time—was a representative set of scores for college students. Table 5.1 presents the mean scores.

On three of the four substantive subscales, the mean scores are near a neutral point. That is, the average student-respondent sees human nature as neither trustworthy nor untrustworthy (mean = 1.35, with a possible range of +42 to -42); as neither altruistic nor selfish (mean = -2.38, with the same range as for trustworthiness); and as neither independent nor conforming (mean = -1.41). These respondents tend to see people as possessing strength of will and rationality (mean = 7.40). The mean on this subscale, however, is still within the neutral range; a score of +7 on a 14-item scale indicates that the average response was halfway between 0 (neutral) and +1 (slightly agree).

The standard deviation (*SD*) in Table 5.1 reflects the amount of dispersion in responses to each subscale. For the four substantive subscales, standard deviations range from 10.20 to 12.99 points, indicating that, in a given set of respondents, some people will approximate or even achieve the most extreme scores possible (+42 and -42). Inspection of actual scores shows that this is true. Scores such as -39 or +42 do occur, indicating that, within one group of subjects, there is extreme diversity in beliefs about the substantive aspects of human nature.

Compared with the rather neutral average scores on the substantive subscales, the average scores on the two individual-differences subscales (Complexity and Variability) are more extreme. The mean of 11.41 on the Complexity subscale indicates that the average student-respondent believes that human nature is complex rather than simple and easy to understand. Similarly, the mean score of 15.83 on the Variability subscale suggests a belief that people tend to be different rather than alike. These two averages are not surprising when we consider that social-science instructors have constantly told these students that people are different and unique.

Although Complexity and Variability produce higher average scores than the substantive subscales, their standard deviations (11.30 and 10.14, respectively) indicate that by no means do all college respondents see human nature as hard to understand and variable. The actual scores on these two subscales show about as much dispersion as do the scores on the substantive subscales.

The two summated scores give the following results: positive-negative score (summation of the substantive subscales), mean of 4.98, *SD* of 37.16;

TABLE 5.1 Means and Standard Deviations for a Heterogeneous College Undergraduate Population on the PHN Scales

PHN Subscale	Mean	Standard Deviation
Trustworthiness	1.35	12.99
Strength of Will and Rationality	7.40	10.20
Altruism	-2.38	12.80
Independence	-1.41	11.48
Complexity	11.41	11.30
Variability	15.83	10.14
Positive-Negative Score (Summation of T, S, A, & I)	4.98	37.16
Multiplexity (Summation of C & V)	27.18	17.55

Note: Based upon scores of 1,072 undergraduates (473 males and 599 females) at 12 colleges and universities. These students were tested under similar conditions in 1962 and 1963.
   Possible range of scores: for each subscale (first six listed above), +42 to –42; for positive-negative
summated scores, +168 to –168; for multiplexity, +84 to –84.

and multiplexity (summation of complexity and variability), mean of
27.18, SD of 17.55. The positive-negative score indicates that the average
respondent sees human nature as neither good nor bad; a mean of 4.98,
when considered against the possible range of +168 to –168, is certainly
a neutral score. The standard deviation of 37.16 for this score indicates
that, in a typical sample of respondents, we may expect scores of approximately +115 to 105 (based on a definition of the limits as ±3 standard
deviations from the mean). Inspection of actual scores indicates that these
limits are close to the most extreme scores that do occur. Occasionally, a
score as high as +140 or +145 occurs, but, at the other extreme, scores of
less than –110 are rare.

   Administration of the scale in the early 1990s (Wrightsman, Weir, &
Brusewitz, 1991) to a group of 534 freshmen at the University of Kansas
produced subscale mean scores sometimes consistent and sometimes at
variance with the 1962-1963 means. For example, the mean on Trustworthiness for the new sample was –2.70, compared to +1.35 for the combined samples almost 30 years before. Altruism showed a very similar
shift toward negative attitudes, from –0.49 to –2.38. The shift for Independence was somewhat less, from +0.23 to –1.41. On the other hand, the new
mean for Strength of Will and Rationality was very similar to the previous
one (+7.32 versus +7.40).

On the two individual-differences subscales, the new group was less positive than the previous samples (only +1.75 on Complexity versus the previous +11.41, and only +11.55 on Variability versus the previous +15.83).

Interpretation of the causes of such shifts is fraught with danger, because the comparison not only is across almost 30 years, but is of different schools with different types of student bodies. In keeping with the claim of *The Cynical Americans* (D. L. Kanter & Mirvis, 1989) book, however, it is interesting to note that the shifts in trustworthiness and altruism are in a negative direction.

Group Differences and Construct Validity

The validity, or accuracy, of a measure is its most important characteristic. How can we show that the PHN scale accurately measures assumptions about human nature? This question may be answered in several ways. For example, Chapter 7 will describe the relationship of PHN scores to behavior, giving evidence for the relationship of the PHN measure to an external criterion. The "construct validity" of the scale can be assessed in a different manner—that is, by determining if groups that according to the underlying theory should differ actually do differ in score. For example, because boys and girls are socialized differently in our society and because child-rearing practices are thought to be important determinants of the philosophies of human nature held by adults, we would expect men and women to differ in average PHN score. If such differences occur, they offer evidence that the scale possesses construct validity. In the subsequent sections of this chapter we present several types of group differences that give evidence for the construct validity of the PHN subscales.

Gender Differences

In heterogeneous samples (that is, samples that are not restricted by occupation or other value-related factors), men's philosophies of human nature seem to be less favorable and less oriented toward individual differences than are women's. Evidence of gender differences is presented in Table 5.2. The subjects for this study were undergraduates in psychology courses at seven colleges differing in type, location, and year of testing. Women consistently reported a more positive view of human nature than

TABLE 5.2 Mean Scores for Men and Women at Seven Colleges for Each of the PHN Subscales

Sex	N	Trust-worthiness	Altruism	Independence	Strength of Will & Rationality	Complexity	Vari-ability
			Wheaton College (IL)				
Men	33	-9.0	-12.6	-8.3	2.4	14.2*	18.7
Women	62	-6.9	-9.1	-6.4	2.1	18.6*	18.3
Total	95	-7.6	-10.4	-7.0	2.2	17.1	18.4
			Central Michigan University (MI)				
Men	44	-0.1*	-4.9*	-4.8*	6.5	12.3	15.2*
Women	62	5.1*	0.9*	-0.1*	7.4	15.1	20.7*
Total	106	2.9	-1.5	-2.0	7.0	14.5	18.5
			David Lipscomb College (TN)				
Men	20	-5.1*	-9.2*	-4.7	7.5*	7.2	13.3
Women	23	4.6*	3.6*	-0.9	15.9*	10.3	13.2
Total	43	0.1	-2.4	-2.7	12.0	8.9	13.3
			Belmont College (TN)				
Men	48	-0.2	-9.2*	0.1	9.6	8.3	16.8
Women	41	3.0	-3.1*	0.0	9.9	11.9	15.4
Total	89	1.3	-6.3	0.0	9.8	10.0	16.2
			Kentucky Southern College (KY)				
Men	31	1.3*	-3.9*	-1.3*	5.2*	12.6	16.8
Women	30	8.9*	3.6*	4.3*	10.9*	10.3	16.6
Total	61	5.1	-0.2	1.5	8.1	11.5	16.7
			Western Maryland College (MD)				
Men	47	3.6*	-3.8*	-4.1	5.3	12.7	17.4
Women	59	10.6*	4.5*	-0.4	8.3	12.8	16.2
Total	106	7.5	0.8	-2.0	7.0	12.8	16.7
			University of Kansas (KS)				
Men	273	-3.4*	-1.9*	-1.0*	6.8	3.6*	12.0
Women	261	-1.9*	1.0*	1.7*	7.9	-0.3*	11.1
Total	534	-2.7	-0.5	0.2	7.3	1.7	11.55

Note: On the first four dimensions, positive scores indicate favorable views of human nature; on the fifth dimension, a positive score indicates complexity; on the sixth dimension, a positive score indicates variability.
*Mean scores for males and females significantly different at .05 level or greater (by t tests).

men did. As the Table 5.2 illustrates, in only 2 of 28 comparisons based on the four substantive dimensions was the men's average score more favorable than the women's, and in these two comparisons the differences were not statistically significant.

Do women also believe human nature to be more complex and variable than do men? Table 5.2 indicates that the women's average Complexity score is higher than the men's average for five of the seven schools, but

TABLE 5.3 Gender Differences on PHN Subscales in Freshman Classes at Peabody College

Freshmen of	Sex	N	Trust-worthy	Altruism	Indepen-dence.	Strength of Will & Rationality	Com-plexity	Vari-ablity
1962	Men	63	8.38	1.54*	2.95	13.21	7.06	15.87
	Women	250	9.80	5.10*	4.30	15.30	8.80	16.20
1965	Men	84	3.98	-4.80*	0.17	9.86	4.90	14.36
	Women	261	6.93	-0.46*	2.36	12.52	6.88	17.47
1966	Men	56	-0.43*	-7.95*	-2.05	8.55	5.59	15.41
	Women	189	3.57*	-3.16*	-0.26	12.27	6.48	16.46
1967	Men	54	0.50	-3.37	-2.00	9.22	6.39	16.31
	Women	170	4.38	-1.54	-0.11	10.11	8.8	17.88
1968	Men	50	-5.38*	-11.58*	-4.66	8.30	5.48	16.02
	Women	165	0.41*	-3.91*	-1.17	9.08	9.17	16.99
1969	Men	70	-4.80*	-11.17*	-5.37*	4.66	6.13	15.27
	Women	175	1.86*	-1.46*	-0.11*	9.33	7.90	18.23
1970	Men	50	-4.10*	-8.30*	-5.06*	6.76	8.84	15.70
	Women	231	2.00*	-1.72*	0.18*	9.22	7.87	17.14
1971	Men	47	-3.34	-10.08*	-4.36	8.93	9.21	14.47
	Women	202	0.50	-3.19*	-2.13	9.09	9.24	18.39

Note: Gender difference significantly different at .05 level or greater.

only for one is the difference large enough to be statistically significant. Gender differences on the Variability subscale are less clear-cut. Although women at one college had a significantly higher mean score, at the other six schools the men had nonsignificantly higher mean scores.

Gender differences in the same direction on the PHN scale have also been found among graduate students (M. S. Winter, 1969), social workers (Dretz & Dretz, 1969), and the entire freshman class at Oklahoma State University (Bayless, 1971).

Further evidence of gender differences is also found in the PHN scores for freshman classes at Peabody College, tested between 1962-1971 (see Table 5.3). In each of the eight freshman classes, the women's scores were more positive for Trustworthiness, Altruism, Independence, and Strength of Will and Rationality than were the men's scores, and, in 12 of these 32 comparisons, the differences were statistically significant. In seven of the eight entering classes, women had higher Complexity scores than men did. On the Variability subscale, the women in each of the eight classes scored higher than did the men. Similar gender differences were obtained in a study by Cox (1972). He tested a representative sample of

762 students at a community college and found that women's scores on the four substantive subscales were significantly more positive than men's scores. Although differences on the Variability subscale and on the Complexity subscale were not statistically significant, they indicated that women also scored higher than men did in those areas.

All of these findings confirm our expectations and give some evidence for the construct validity of the PHN subscales. Even at age 2, girls show more interest in other persons than boys do. In addition, women's responses on measure of prejudice and other social attitudes typically indicate a more favorable attitude toward human nature than do men's responses; women also choose a greater number of socially desirable answers than men do (V. C. Crandall, Crandall, & Katkovsky, 1965). On the Thematic Apperception Test, women show stronger needs for affiliation than do men (N. Sanford, Adkins, Miller, & Cobb, 1943). Thus women may be more alert to individual differences in the responsiveness of others and hence may be more likely to believe that people are different and individualized.

There are several possible reasons why women believe people to be more trustworthy, more rational, more altruistic, and more independent from group pressures than do their male classmates. One hypothesis has been that women were more removed from many of the unpleasant aspects of human nature than were men; for example, police officers, divorce lawyers, and probation officers traditionally were more likely to be men. But gender differences in attitudes toward human nature occur prior to entry into an occupation. Perhaps the socialization process trains women to assume the best or to think well of others. Certainly girls do not participate in the physically aggressive activities of boys, and competitiveness is a value that is not so firmly encouraged for girls as for boys. Women's heightened social-desirability score and PHN scores may stem from their greater interconnectedness with others; they may report good things about people in general so that all people will like them.

Women's greater tendency to see human nature as complex fits with the different role orientations of the two genders. Traditionally, the man has been object-oriented—he struggled all day long with a drill press at a factory or plowed the fields and harvested crops. The woman's job was to raise the young, care for the home, and prepare for her husband's return. The clichéd picture portrays the wife waiting on the doorstep at the end of the day, searching for her husband and trying to read the expression on his face to find out if he had had a good day or a bad one. If this kind of behavior were still modal in American society, it would not be surprising that women score higher than men do on complexity. It is not, however; today, men deal with objects less and people more, and so many women are in the work force that gender differences in person-versus-object orientation are greatly lessened.

Gender differences in social sensitivity can also be demonstrated—that is, women are better than men at simulating the personality patterns characteristic of other people (Kimber, 1947; Noll, 1951). In summary, as Tyler (1965) concludes, a statement that "females are more personal than males in their orientation to life seems clearly warranted" (p. 269). Recent research (Fletcher et al., 1986) indicates that women also make more complex attributions of human behavior than do men.

Racial Differences

A great deal of justification exists for a hypothesis that African-Americans possess negative attitudes about human nature. For example, in *The Fire Next Time* (1963), writer James Baldwin described how he was trained to react to whites. When growing up in New York City, he once gave up his seat on the subway to a white woman. An African-American man, a minister, drew young James aside and told him that never, under any circumstances, should he rise and give his seat to a white woman. After all, white men never did that for black women (J. Baldwin, 1963, p. 58).

An African-American man writes about the mistrust between whites and blacks:

> My 40-year journey through life has revealed to me that more often than not, I need only be in the presence of a white woman and she will begin clutching her pocketbook. . . . I rarely enjoy what is properly called the public trust of whites. That is to say, the white person on the street who does not know me from Adam or Eve is much more likely to judge me negatively on account of my skin color. (Thomas, 1990, p. A15)

Is the mistrust reciprocated?

The *New York Times* recently completed a telephone survey; columnist William Raspberry (1990) summarizes the findings:

> Three out of four black New Yorkers believe that it is true, or at least *possibly* true, that black politicians have been targeted by the government; 60 percent of blacks believe that it is true, or may be true, that the government is part of a conspiracy to put drugs into black neighborhoods; and 29 percent of blacks

TABLE 5.4 PHN Scores of Students at Predominantly African-American Colleges

School	Sex	N	Trust-worthy	Altruism	Indepen-dence	Strength of Will & Rationality	Com-plexity	Vari-ablity
Fisk	Men	39	-5.69	-1.46	-3.23	+7.31	+13.23	+14.69
University	Women	44	-3.66	-1.48	+0.02	+7.50	+9.98	+14.66
	Total	83	-4.62	-1.47	-1.51	+7.41	+11.51	+14.67
Tennessee	Men	30	-6.80	-3.50	+1.60	+4.00	-1.65	+12.30
State	Women	42	-2.97	+1.25	+2.81	+7.81	+2.75	+13.28
University	Total	72	-5.10	-1.39	+2.14	+5.69	+0.30	+12.82

credit the notion that AIDS has been engineered to destroy blacks. (Whites believe that the charges are "almost certainly not true" by margins ranging from 57 percent in the case of black politicians, to 75 percent in regard to drugs, to 91 percent for AIDS.) (p. 28)

Table 5.4 presents mean scores for students at two predominantly African-American institutions, Fisk University and Tennessee State University. Although they are located in the same city, the two colleges are quite different. Fisk University is a private school that draws middle-class students from all over the United States. Its orientation is toward scholarship in the liberal arts and sciences. It offers a variety of artistic and cultural experiences and participates in a student-exchange program with several other prestigious liberal-arts colleges. Tennessee State is a state university and land-grant institution. It was originally racially segregated and still enrolls very few whites. Few of its students go to graduate school, for the curricular emphasis is on applied, quasi-professional careers. Students identify with the school primarily because of Tennessee State's renowned athletic teams.

The difference between the two student bodies is aptly verified in their mean scores on the Complexity subscale (see Table 5.4). We previously suggested that this could be interpreted as a measure of sophistication. The means for Complexity at Fisk are quite high, indicating previous contact with people of varying backgrounds and a mature open-mindedness about the possibility of understanding them. The men's Complexity mean is the fourth highest of 22 schools in the norm tables prepared by Wrightsman and Satterfield (1967). The Tennessee State Complexity means are quite low relative to other college samples. The men's average is even slightly negative (-1.65), indicating no general recognition of the complexity present in people. The Variability scores are more within the normal range, however.

Yet consistencies do exist in the responses of the two samples; the most important is a shared distrust in human nature. The two schools are unusual in that, in each, the mean Trustworthiness score is more negative than is the mean score for Altruism or Independence. From these data, we may generalize that the most unusual aspect of African-Americans' philosophies of human nature is the strong component of distrust. This racial difference is consistent with an earlier finding by Pierce-Jones, Reid, and King (1959) that white and black adolescents differed in their orientations toward society. Likewise, Davis (1971), who administered the PHN scale to 490 teachers in 31 elementary schools in Houston, TX, reports that the mean positive-negative score for the one school with an all-black faculty was 2.22, whereas the mean score for all schools was 31.11, a difference of almost one standard deviation.

But what does this distrust mean? When African-Americans answer PHN statements about "most people," are they thinking of blacks, whites, or both? A study by Warren Johnson (1969) has provided an answer to this question. Using African-American and white high school seniors in Columbia, TN, as subjects, he administered four different forms of the PHN scale to different groups of subjects. One group completed the usual form; another received a form on which "most Negroes and whites" was substituted for "most people." The statements read "most blacks" on the third group's form and "most whites" on the fourth group's form. Results indicated that each racial group saw itself as distinctly more positive on the substantive scale than it saw "most people." Similarly, when answering statements about "most whites," African-American subjects indicated *even more negative* attitudes than when they responded "most Negroes and whites." (Likewise, white respondents demonstrated their most negative attitudes when the stem was "most blacks.") Clearly, when black subjects in a small Southern town respond to statements about "most people," they are thinking mainly of whites, and their distrust is primarily distrust of whites. Whether this conclusion could also be applied to the responses of adult African-Americans in a large city such as Detroit or Washington, D.C., remains to be determined.

A conclusion of Johnson's study is that members of a particular segment of society have more favorable beliefs about their own group than about people in general. Wilkinson and Hood (1973) reached the same conclusion when he asked college students to complete either the usual Likert scale or one in which the word *student* was substituted for the word *people*

TABLE 5.5 PHN Differences Between Black and White Trainees

PHN Subscale	Blacks Trainees (N = 121)		White Trainees (N = 92)		t Value for Mean Diffs.	p Value (Two-Tailed)
	Mean	SD	Mean	SD		
Trustworthiness	−8.30	11.24	−4.77	12.40	2.17	<.02
Strength of Will and Rationality	+10.90	9.33	+12.56	10.88	1.19	NS
Altruism	−2.82	11.95	−4.10	14.20	.71	NS
Independence	+4.01	9.16	+3.75	11.93	.18	NS
Complexity	+4.76	12.43	+4.81	9.73	.02	NS
Variability	+10.49	11.43	−12.19	12.48	1.03	NS

Source: Adapted from Claxton, 1971.
Note: NS—Not significant.

wherever it appeared in the scale. The subjects, students at High Point College in North Carolina, rated students significantly more favorably on each of the substantive scales. For example, the mean on the regular form was −5.41, whereas on the "students" format it was 7.81 (p of difference < .001). On Strength of Will and Rationality, the mean increased from 7.19 to 13.27. The shifts on Altruism and Independence were 15 and 11 points, respectively. Respondents made no distinction between "people in general" and "students" in regard to Complexity (mean of 8.22 and 9.19, respectively); in regard to Variability, "students" elicited stronger beliefs (mean of 18.16) than did "people in general" (mean of 12.41), but the difference was not statistically significant.

Further evidence that it is the trusting aspect of philosophies of human nature that most differentiate African-Americans from whites comes from a study by Claxton (1971) of participants in a manpower retraining program. These men, 121 blacks and 92 whites, were unskilled workers who were receiving training as electrical workers, auto mechanics, cooks, and so on. Their age range was from 17 to 72, with a mean of 24.5 years. Mean scores for the two racial groups are presented in Table 5.5. Only in regard to Trustworthiness is there a significant difference, with African-Americans more negative than whites.

A comparison of black and white social-work trainees, however, produced differences on more subscales. Dretz and Dretz (1969) tested 37 white and 15 nonwhite graduate students in social work who were preparing for a summer internship. (Of the 15 nonwhites, 12 were black and the other 3 were Orientals.) The mean scores are reported in Table 5.6. Dretz

TABLE 5.6 Mean PHN Subscale Differences Between White and Nonwhite Social-Work Trainees

Subscale	Whites (N = 37)	Nonwhites (N = 15)	Difference in Mean
Trustworthiness	11.37	2.33	9.04
Strength of Will and Rationality	8.94	2.80	6.14
Altruism	6.16	-4.06	10.22
Independence	1.94	-4.13	6.07
Complexity	10.91	3.46	7.45
Variability	11.29	11.46	-0.17
Positive-Negative	28.43	-3.60	34.03
Multiplexity	23.16	14.93	8.23

Source: Adapted from Dretz & Dretz, 1969.

and Dretz were interested in changes in PHN score resulting from a summer internship (see Chapter 9) and did not test the significance of the difference on the pre-internship measures. Table 5.6 indicates differences of 6 or more points on all the subscales except Variability, with scores for the whites always higher. The differences on Trustworthiness and Altruism are greater than 9 points, and it is likely that these differences are significant.

The hypothesis of racial differences in philosophies of human nature is well confirmed. Consistent differences in trust of human nature are found between blacks and whites, whether the groups compared are middle class or lower class, college students or adults, unskilled laborers or professional workers. There is also a tendency for lower-class African-Americans to view human nature as less complex and less difficult to understand, but this is probably a class-determined rather than racially determined response.

Age Differences

Do older people have more cynical beliefs about human nature? Or with increasing age, does an increase in tolerance of human foibles emerge? Support for a hypothesis of age differences in assumptions about human nature comes from research on the Machiavellianism Scale. Christie (1970) included 20 questions from two forms of the

Machiavellianism Scale in a survey administered by the National Opinion Research Center in the spring of 1963. A total of 1,482 respondents, representative of noninstitutionalized adults in the United States, completed the items. Compared with the mean score for the response of 1,782 students in 14 different colleges collected in the fall of 1964, the mean score for the adult sample was significantly less Machiavellian. Within the adult sample, the older respondents also had significantly less Machiavellian attitudes than did the younger adults (Christie & Geis, 1968).

No representative sample of the general adult population has been tested with the PHN scale, so there are no hard data regarding age differences on that instrument. Chapter 1, however, reported a comparison of college freshmen with D. L. Kanter and Mirvis's (1989) adult sample on 6 items from the PHN scale; when differences occurred, the college students were more cynical. Furthermore, there are four PHN studies that do find consistent age differences although they do not use representative samples. R. L. Anderson (1969) compared students at Central Washington State College with adults from the same local area who were members of the Democratic or Republican party. Both sets of adults were more positive than the college students on the Trustworthiness, Altruism, and Independence subscales. Of course, the adults and college students differed in regard to many variables other than age, and we have no way of knowing if age per se contributed to the difference.

Another study with limitations regarding age-based conclusions but with interesting results is Hamrick's (1970) comparison of PHN responses of trustees, administrators, faculty members, and undergraduate students at Wake Forest University. All 36 trustees were asked to complete the scale anonymously; 21, or 58%, complied. Of the 21 college administrators who were contacted, 12 (57%) completed the scale. Hamrick drew a one-third sample of the faculty (67 of 200), and 34 complied. For student respondents, she randomly chose 70 students per class; of these 280, 96 (or 34%) completed the scale. Not only did a smaller percentage of the students participate, but their scores were also significantly less positive on Trustworthiness ($p < .001$ for trustees versus students, $p < .01$ for faculty versus students), on Independence and on Strength of Will and Rationality ($p < .01$ for both comparisons), and on Altruism ($p < .02$ for trustee versus students; $p < .05$ for administrators versus students). Had a higher percentage of the students been tested, the student means might have been even more different from those of the trustees. Here again, it is fallacious to attribute the differences to age. The category "trustee of Wake Forest

TABLE 5.7 Comparisons of Mean PHN Group for Different Groups at Two Colleges

	Trustees	Counselors	Administrators		Faculty		Undergraduate Students	
	WFU	*BCC*	*WFU*	*BCC*	*WFU*	*BCC*	*WFU*	*BCC*
Trustworthiness	14.48	19.20	8.00	13.04	9.38	9.29	2.36	-1.85
Strength of Will and Rationality	11.66	16.70	7.75	14.64	3.20	7.70	9.67	8.00
Altruism	5.90	7.40	6.50	7.12	1.59	0.91	-2.61	-5.60
Independence	8.57	8.10	2.50	3.16	-0.91	-0.95	-0.29	-1.16
Complexity	13.00	8.40	11.00	5.96	12.38	11.97	14.80	6.60
Variability	14.80	13.70	8.58	10.00	13.53	16.34	14.86	
Positive-Negative	40.61	51.40	24.75	37.96	13.26	16.95	9.13	-0.16
Multiplexity	27.80	22.10	19.58	15.96	25.91	25.49	31.14	21.42

Note: WFU = Wake Forest University, data from Hamrick (1970). BCC = Broward Community College, data from Cox (1972). *N*s: WFU trustees = 21; BCC counselors = 10; administrators, WFU = 12, BCC = 25; Faculty, WFU = 34, BCC = 167; undergraduates, WFU = 96 (random sample from each class), BCC = 762 (sample of 4,000 full-time students).

University" is a rather restricted sample, as all trustees must be residents of North Carolina and members of the Southern Baptist Church.

A similar study by Cox (1972), however, comparing PHN scores of students, faculty, counselors, and administrators at a two-year college, showed the same sorts of differences—that is, the students were the most negative. Cox carefully chose his samples, and if potential subjects failed to fill out the questionnaire after his first contact with them, he contacted them two more times to urge them to do so. Therefore, he received impressive degrees of cooperation from his groups. All 10 counselors and all 25 administrators at Broward Community College completed the scale; of 209 full-time faculty members, 167 (or 80%) completed the scale. Cox also tested 762 of the 4,000 full-time students. (He also planned to include a trustees group, but since only three of the five trustees completed the scale, Cox decided not to include them.)

Table 5.7 presents the mean scores for the groups tested by Hamrick and by Cox. In both schools, the students were the most negative group on the Trustworthiness, Altruism, and Independence subscales. (The striking similarity in PHN scores of the two faculty samples in Table 5.7 is worth noting.) In Cox's study, significant differences between groups occurred for each subscale and for the two summed scores; the p values for the analysis of variance F ratios for these ranged from .05 on Independence and Variability to .001 on four measures. Using the Scheffé test of differences in pairs of groups, Cox found that students differed significantly from faculty members on these three scores plus the Complexity score.

Additional evidence on age differences comes from studies that take a particular group and relate the PHN scores and ages of individual group members. For example, graduate students in several social-service areas (clinical psychology, rehabilitation counseling, school counseling, special education, speech pathology, and social work) plus graduate students from two other departments (English and chemistry) were subjects in a study by M. S. Winter (1969). There was a slight but significant positive correlation ($r = .15$) between positive-negative summated scores and age, indicating that among members of this group older students had somewhat more positive attitudes.

A comparison of older and younger psychotherapists by Eugene P. May (1971), however, indicated contradictory differences. The 79 psychotherapists, all males, were members or fellows of APA Division 29 (Division of Psychotherapy); they were divided into an older group ($N = 44$), all aged 46 or more, and a younger one ($N = 35$, all aged 45 or less). On each of the substantive subscales, the older psychotherapists had less favorable attitudes, and on two of these subscales as well as on the positive-negative summated score the difference was statistically significant ($p < .01$ for Independence, $p < .05$ for Altruism and positive-negative). On the other hand, older therapists had significantly higher scores on Complexity ($p < .05$).

In comparing older and younger faculty members of a community college (with age 44 as the dividing point), Cox (1972) found that the older group had higher scores on Strength of Will and Rationality, Complexity, and multiplexity.

Because of the absence of representative samples that permit genuine age comparisons, we cannot say with confidence that older adults have more favorable beliefs about human nature than do younger adults. It does appear that college-student samples possess less favorable beliefs than do the older adult samples that have been tested. Further evidence for age differences is presented in Chapters 8 and 9.

Political-Party Differences and Voting Preferences

No clear-cut relationships have appeared between political-party preference and PHN scores. In the study described in the previous section, R. L. Anderson (1969) randomly selected 120 adults from the Republican and Democratic party membership lists in Kittitas County, WA. Neither the summed scores nor any of the subscale scores distinguished between members of the two parties. But level of political involvement was related to PHN score across party lines. That is, politically involved individuals in both parties had significantly stronger beliefs in Complexity and Variability than did members of the same party who were not so involved. However, involved party members' beliefs in Independence and Strength of Will and Rationality and their positive-negative scores were significantly less positive than were those of other party members.

Nottingham (1968) compared two groups of students on the Vanderbilt University campus. From all the student organizations, Nottingham selected the two groups that, on issues including civil rights, student activism, and the Vietnam War, seemed to be the most liberal and the most conservative. After administering the PHN scales to 12 members of the liberal group and 13 members of the conservative group, Nottingham found that there were no significant differences in mean scores. But the variances on the subscales in the liberal sample were significantly larger than those in the conservative sample, suggesting that the liberal group may be more tolerant of deviations within the overall framework of the organization. In general, the liberal and the conservative subjects appeared to have beliefs about the substantive qualities of human nature that were significantly more negative than the beliefs of the college-student population at Vanderbilt.

In a national comparison of students favoring Lyndon Johnson and those favoring Barry Goldwater in the 1964 presidential election, Wrightsman (1965) found no significant PHN-subscale differences between the two groups. Students who preferred neither candidate, however, had significantly higher Complexity scores.

Box 5.1 summarizes a recent study that uses philosophies of human nature to assist in understanding voters' conceptions of ideal presidential candidates.

Occupational-Group Differences

Choice of an occupation reflects one's values, attitudes, and self-concept, as well as education, skills, and training. It is hypothesized that strong differences in philosophies of human nature exist in dissimilar occupational groups. The PHN subscales have been administered to more than 20 occupational groups, and a selection of the findings is reported here.

Guidance counselors, for example, have extremely favorable beliefs about human nature. Table 5.8 reports mean scores for four different groups of guidance counselors who, at the time of the testing, were participants in NDEA-sponsored guidance-and-counseling institutes at seven Southern colleges (Ligon, 1970; Mason, 1966; Wrightsman, Richard, & Noble, 1966). The means for the substantive subscales for all four groups reflect a positive attitude as great as that of any group ever tested. As a group, guidance counselors believe that people in general are extremely trustworthy, rational, altruistic, and independent of group pressures. Rousseve (1969) has called upon counselors and counselor educators to appraise their own convictions about human nature; these studies indicate that when counselors do so, they judge human nature to be essentially positive. Kayloe (1976), in such a study, found social work students to have more favorable views of human nature than students in three other major fields.

Eugene May (1971) has compared the philosophies of human nature of counselors and practicing psychotherapists. Specifically, the subjects

---

Box 5.1
Appraisals of Political Candidates and Assumptions About Human Nature

Political scientists (for example, Kinder, 1986, and A. Miller, Wattenberg, & Malanchuk, 1986) have demonstrated that voters evaluate the personalities of presidential candidates. A recent study (Sullivan, Aldrich, Borgida, & Rahn, 1990) carried this idea a step further by hypothesizing that voters' philosophies of human nature might provide "a normative baseline against which candidates can be measured" (p. 464). Using a sample of 1,509 voting-age adults surveyed by the Gallup Organization, they asked respondents to rate "most people" as well as each of the 1984 U.S. presidential candidates, Ronald Reagan and Walter Mondale. Rather than using PHN scale items, they asked their subjects to rate these on three of the dimensions: Unselfish or Selfish, Trustworthy or Untrustworthy, and Able to Control What Happens to Them or At the Mercy of Things Beyond Their Control. Thus they created a "human nature" profile for each respondent and compared the respondents' image of each candidate with this profile.

In general, the two candidates were seen as similar to "most people," but Reagan was seen as more in control than most people and than Mondale. The responses to the Trustworthy questions found that people saw Reagan to be more trustworthy than Mondale but significantly less so than their impressions of people in general.

With regard to the Selfish-Unselfish dimension, more than 40% of the respondents thought that Mondale was less selfish than most people, while only 25% thought he was more selfish. In contrast, one third saw Reagan as more selfish than "most people," one third saw him as less selfish, and one third thought he was just as selfish or unselfish as most people. Thus Mondale had a significantly higher score on fairness.

The data are interpreted to conclude that most voters want their president to be as trustworthy, altruistic, and in control as possible. The correlations between the extent to which perceptions of each candidate exceeded the respondents' expectations of "most people" and the difference scores between the two candidates were .77, .56, and .43 on Trustworthy, Unselfish, and Control. Such a conclusion is consistent with Kinder's (1986) conclusion that people compare candidates to their conception of the ideal president.

---

were 21 male counselor-trainees enrolled in the counseling-psychology program at the University of Illinois and 79 male therapists, members or

TABLE 5.8 Mean Scores of Guidance Counselors on the PHN

Subscale	1963 Summer Inst. Participants (N = 26)	1964 Summer Inst. Participants (N = 29)	Mason's Participants in NDEA Institutes in Guid. & Couns. (N = 72)	Ligon's Participants in NDEA Elem. School Guidance Inst. (N = 16)
Trustworthiness	14.85	17.62	8.89	12.50
Strength of Will and Rationality	9.12	9.24	9.06	12.13
Altruism	10.42	12.69	6.60	7.81
Independence	−0.23	6.52	3.61	5.31
Complexity	10.04	12.97	Not given	7.94
Variability	11.35	10.48	Not given	7.63
Positive-Negative	34.16	45.72	28.21	37.75
Multiplexity	21.39	23.10	Not given	15.57

fellows of APA Division 29. The mean scores and standard deviations for these two groups are reported in Table 5.9. The PHN scores of the counselors in training are more favorable than those of the psychotherapists, but the difference is statistically significant only on the Strength of Will and Rationality subscale ($p < .05$).

TABLE 5.9 Comparisons of Mean PHN Scores of Male Counselors and Psychotherapists

Subscale	Counselors (N = 21) Mean	SD	Psychotherapists (N = 79) Mean	SD
Trustworthiness	6.90	9.86	3.78	12.66
Strength of Will and Rationality	10.76	9.86	4.35	11.39
Altruism	1.00	10.03	0.63	10.67
Independence	0.42	11.43	−2.16	10.32
Complexity	8.00	12.46	7.82	11.20
Variability	10.61	9.18	10.01	10.37
Positive-Negative	18.61	30.49	7.21	38.52
Multiplexity	18.61	19.14	17.70	15.83

Source: Adapted from E. P. May, 1971.

TABLE 5.10 Means for Trainees in Clinical Psychology, Counseling Psychology, and Vocational Rehabilitation

Subscale	Clinical Psych. Students (N = 66)		Counseling Psych. Students (N = 31)		Vocational Rehab. Students (N = 45)	
	Mean	SD	Mean	SD	Mean	SD
Trustworthiness	5.42	11.55	7.45	10.15	9.33	12.21
Strength of Will and Rationality	11.60	9.73	10.68	9.91	10.64	10.14
Altruism	1.50	11.64	3.61	10.63	4.22	13.72
Independence	0.45	11.84	2.06	12.08	1.98	9.66
Complexity	8.79	11.04	12.58	10.35	10.78	9.21
Variability	10.88	8.71	10.84	8.59	15.98	10.27

National samples of graduate students in counseling psychology, clinical psychology, and vocational rehabilitation were compared on the PHN scales by Dole, Nottingham, and Wrightsman (1969). All three groups tended to have slightly favorable beliefs about trustworthiness, favorable beliefs about strength of will and rationality, and neutral beliefs about altruism and independence. All groups endorsed beliefs in complexity and variability. Dole et al. (1969) concluded that trainees in these three

TABLE 5.11 Mean PHN Scores for Graduate Students in Different Areas of Psychology at University of Hawaii

Subscale	Clinical and Counseling Students (N = 14)		Social, Devel., & Industrial Psych. Students (N = 25)		Experimental Psych. Students (N = 11)	
	Mean	SD	Mean	SD	Mean	SD
Trustworthiness	6.07	11.91	7.76	13.27	-3.09	10.81
Strength of Will and Rationality	12.29	8.23	12.84	11.13	9.00	12.66
Altruism	-1.14	14.13	2.40	13.88	-9.64	10.96
Independence	-0.64	12.97	0.44	14.20	-4.00	9.56
Complexity	11.86	10.50	10.92	10.70	14.00	7.82
Variability	11.21	11.44	12.36	8.82	10.27	13.87
Positive-Negative	16.57	41.59	23.44	46.28	-7.73	36.02
Multiplexity	23.07	18.18	23.28	15.67	24.27	17.82

TABLE 5.12 PHN Scores of U.S. Marine Corps Recruits ($N = 95$)

Subscale	Mean	SD
Trustworthiness	-1.70	9.49
Strength of Will and Rationality	8.08	9.93
Altruism	-5.41	9.43
Independence	1.34	9.05
Complexity	1.83	10.95
Variability	8.46	9.69
Positive-Negative	2.27	25.77
Multiplexity	10.27	17.24

mental-health subspecialties do share a common goal in regard to their beliefs about human nature. (Means are reproduced in Table 5.10.)

Experimental psychologists in training do not share these beliefs, however. Table 5.11 indicates that doctoral students in experimental psychology at the University of Hawaii possess beliefs about trustworthiness and altruism that are significantly more negative than the beliefs of students in clinical-counseling psychology or in social, developmental, or industrial psychology.

As an example of a quite different occupational group, U.S. Marine Corps recruits on Okinawa, on their way to combat in Vietnam, were tested by W. E. Collins and Wrightsman (1966). Most of these men were 19 or 20 years of age, and few of them had completed high school. Their mean scores are detailed on Table 5.12. The resultant pattern is a simplistic view of human nature as selfish and untrustworthy yet capable of self-improvement. The low score on Complexity combined with the peak of Strength of Will and Rationality indicates an unsophisticated view of human nature.

Thus there is ample evidence that the PHN differences from one occupational group to another are large and consistent with other things that we know about these groups.

Religious Differences

Persons who have been immersed in a fundamentalistic religious orientation—particularly those whose religious training is internalized—should reflect such training in their beliefs about human nature. Several

TABLE 5.13 PHN Scores of Roman Catholic Nuns (*N* = 30)

Subscale	Mean	SD
Trustworthiness	17.73	10.05
Strength of Will and Rationality	17.17	8.42
Altruism	13.97	9.05
Independence	6.17	11.12
Complexity	16.60	9.41
Variability	8.97	8.05
Positive-Negative	55.04	38.64
Multiplexity	25.57	17.46

Source: Adapted from Gardiner, 1972, Table 1, p. 369.

religious groups have been tested, permitting tests of a hypothesis of religious differences.

Wheaton College (Illinois) is a religiously oriented college that attracts bright, religiously sophisticated students who have been brought up in the strict fundamentalist tradition to which the school subscribes. The Wheaton College catalog, in a doctrinal statement of faith, says, "We believe . . . that human beings are born with a sinful nature, and, in the case of all those who reach moral responsibility, become sinners in thought, word, and deed" (Ashcraft, 1964, pp. 7-8). As Table 5.2 indicates, the responses of Wheaton students to the PHN reflect this credo. Scores on the four substantive dimensions are 1 to 1½ standard deviations below those of students at other schools. Wheaton students reflect the assumptions of their religious background. (Yet they possess exceedingly high scores in Complexity and Variability, indicating high degrees of sophistication about people.) Ligon (1963) has also shown that college students with a fundamentalistic religious background hold less favorable views of human nature than do students with humanistic religious attitudes.

Yet a background in a fundamentalist religious atmosphere is not always integrated into a functional philosophy of human nature. For example, students at such colleges as David Lipscomb, which is a Church of Christ school and draws 99% of its student population from that denomination, must have sat in church pews on countless Sundays and listened to their pastors fulminate about the sinfulness of man. Yet their scores (see Table 5.2), although not positive, do not reach the depths of negativeness that the scores of the Wheaton students do.

Harry W. Gardiner (1972) administered the PHN scale to 20 Roman Catholic nuns who were attending summer-school courses at a private liberal-arts college in Minnesota. Their ages ranged from 22 to 50 (mean of 37.10). The means and standard deviations are reported in Table 5.13. This group presents a different profile from any other, because of the Trustworthiness mean that is higher than the Strength of Will and Rationality mean. Beliefs about altruism are also exceedingly favorable. Standard deviations are quite similar to those of other groups, indicating that a shift in a more favorable direction has occurred throughout the group.

Evidence for relationships with religious orientations and practices came from a study by Lupfer and Wald (1984) that sampled the attitudes of 359 adults in Memphis, TN. People who adhered to orthodox Christian tenets, who made a habit of private devotions, and who were active in their churches saw human nature as more altruistic and trustworthy, but less rational and complex.

Volunteers for a Crisis-Call Center

Another self-selected sample of some interest is a group of persons who volunteered to serve as trainees at a crisis-call center. By their actions they appear to be reflecting a belief that people with difficulties can be helped through the communication of concern and therapeutic assistance. Stack (1972b) administered the PHN scale to 53 male and 99 female volunteers at the Nashville crisis-call center. The men, as a group, were significantly younger than the women (means of 34.5 and 41.6 years; $F = 3.84$, $p < .001$). Average educational level was above the national average in that only 8% of the males and 19% of the females had had no education beyond high school. Approximately one fifth of the volunteers were college graduates, and half of the men and a quarter of the women had done graduate work. Marital status of both genders was similar, with 57% of the males and 63% of the females married at the time of the testing. Thirty-three percent of the men were single, 8% were divorced, and 2% were widowers, whereas 21% of the women were single, 10% were divorced, and 6% were widows. Mean scores for the trainees are reported in Table 5.14 which indicates that, on the Trustworthiness and Strength of Will and Rationality subscales, both groups showed positive conceptions of human nature. Indeed, Trustworthiness scores that are as high as Strength of Will and Rationality scores are quite unusual. But these scores do confirm our

TABLE 5.14 PHN Scores for Crisis-Call Center Volunteers

PHN Subscale	Men (N = 53)		Women (N = 99)		Total (N = 152)	
	Mean	SD	Mean	SD	Mean	SD
Trustworthiness	7.23	14.70	10.77	11.85	9.53	12.98
Strength of Will and Rationality	8.83	9.24	10.45	8.80	9.89	8.96
Altruism	0.66	13.36	6.70	11.82	4.59	12.67
Independence	2.06	11.45	3.45	11.61	2.97	11.54
Complexity	10.55	11.67	7.03	13.07	8.26	12.67
Variability	15.45	9.84	14.08	9.92	14.56	9.88
Positive-Negative	18.92	40.07	31.39	32.94	27.05	35.95
Multiplexity	26.00	16.19	21.11	17.70	22.82	17.29

Source: Adapted from Stack, 1972b, Table 2, p. 4.

expectations about the specific ways in which crisis-center volunteers would differ from other types of samples.

The other noteworthy finding in Table 5.14 is the high Variability mean of 15.45 for the men; it is higher than the mean for any other adult male group tested. Of the 14 Variability items on the PHN, at least 5 may be interpreted as reflecting beliefs in the varied situational effects upon a person's behavior rather than as reflecting beliefs in variation among individuals. We may speculate that a belief in the situational effects upon an individual's behavior may characterize persons who volunteer to help others in crisis situations. As Stack (1972b) suggests, the volunteers might be more likely than other people to treat callers as individuals reacting to a stressful situation, the alleviation of which would allow the caller to change to fit a changed situation. It is not clear whether such a speculation can be extended to the female sample of volunteers, for the mean Variability score of 14.08 is lower than that of the college students and student nurses reported in the norms (Wrightsman & Satterfield, 1967) but slightly higher than the means of the two most comparable all-female samples: two groups of public school teachers.

Juvenile Offenders

Two studies have shown that juvenile offenders possess a profile of PHN scores unlike that of any other group. Richard, Mates, and Whitten

TABLE 5.15 Comparisons of Juvenile Offenders and Nonoffenders on PHN Scales

	Delinquent Groups			
PHN Subscale	Tennessee Females (N = 51)	Florida Females (N = 51)	British Columbia Males (N = 40)	Control Group of Nondelinquents Males (N = 40)
Trustworthiness	-4.57	-6.37	-6.65	2.98
Strength of Will and Rationality	7.94	9.00	3.68	8.32
Altruism	-4.20	-5.00	-7.48	-7.93
Independence	4.67	0.33	8.95	-1.90
Complexity	0.00	0.14	4.93	8.90
Variability	9.10	9.71	12.68	15.15
Positive-Negative	3.84	-2.03	-1.53	1.47
Multiplexity	9.10	9.85	17.65	24.05

Note: Data for female groups from Richard, Mates, & Whitten, 1967; for males from Allan, Hunter & Lum, 1971.

(1967) administered the PHN scale to two groups of girls between the ages of 12 and 18 who were confined to state correctional schools—one group in Florida (N = 51) and one group in Tennessee (N = 51). No subject was allowed to complete the scale unless she could read and understand the statements. The girls were confined primarily for running away from home, habitual truancy from school, and violation of parole. A few girls had been convicted of more serious crimes, such as shoplifting, larceny, forgery, and prostitution.

Similarly, Allan, Hunter, and Lum (1971) tested 40 male juvenile delinquents from a municipal juvenile-detention home in Vancouver, British Columbia. All these boys, aged 12 to 18, had been convicted of crimes and the majority of them were incarcerated because of the seriousness of their crimes or the high degree of deprivation in their home environments. Of the 42 so classified, 40 were able to read, understand, and complete the PHN scales.

Allan, Hunter, and Lum also tested a control group of noninstitutionalized boys of the same ages and family backgrounds; these boys were chosen from schools in Vancouver.

The results for the delinquent groups show a pattern that is different from the patterns of other groups (see Table 5.15). All three delinquent groups show the expected negative beliefs on the Trustworthiness and Altruism subscales. On Strength of Will and Rationality, the two female groups show a positive peak that is characteristic of unsophisticated groups of subjects. The scores on Complexity are quite low for all three delinquent groups, reflecting a lack of concern for understanding people. On the Independence subscale, the pattern for the delinquent groups differs from that of other underprivileged groups. In such groups, the Independence score is usually negative—perhaps an average of –4 or –5. In all three juvenile offender groups, however, it is positive; the males have an average of 8.95 and the Tennessee females, 4.67. On Independence ($p <$ .001), Trustworthiness ($p < .01$), and Strength of Will and Rationality ($p < .05$), the boys' mean score differs significantly from that of the control group of noninstitutionalized boys. The heightened Independence scores of the juvenile delinquents may reflect a projection of their own strivings for independence and their deviations from the norms of society. Reviews of characteristics of socially maladjusted boys (Conger & Miller, 1966; Martin & Fitzpatrick, 1964) indicate that they value impulsivity, reactivity, independence, and self-gratification. Surveys of the responses of delinquent girls indicate that those who acted out their hostilities were more independent, callous, and impatient than were well-adjusted girls (Myers, Borgatta, & Jones, 1965).

Summary

It was hypothesized that group differences exist on the PHN scale. Specific hypotheses were confirmed for almost every comparison studied. For example, it was found that:

1. Women possess more favorable beliefs about human nature than men do; they also tend to see human nature as more complex and variable than men do.

2. Racial differences are in line with expectations. African-Americans see human nature as less trustworthy than whites do. Further research indicates that, when blacks respond to statements about "most people," they are thinking of whites. Lower-class blacks view human nature as less complex, but this response seems to be class-related rather than racially determined.

3. Age differences have not been adequately studied, but several studies are consistent in finding that college students have less favorable beliefs about human nature than do older adults.

4. Occupational differences are consistent with the values and orientation of each occupation.

CHAPTER SIX

Relationship of Philosophies of Human
Nature to Attitude, Personality, and Aptitude Variables

If a man has a strong faith, he can indulge in the luxury of skepticism.

—FREDERICH WILHELM NIETZSCHE

Each day, near Torrington, CT, a farmer named Edmund Dean would leave a box of money, including both coins and bills, at his roadside vegetable stand. The box provided change for customers who bought eggs, vegetables, and syrups when Dean was not around. The farmer had been doing business this way for 25 years before someone emptied the money box. But Dean replenished the box with more money, and his faith was maintained. "I trust people," he said.

Farther west, on Highway 50 near Lawrenceburg, IN, a newspaper editor used to place $10 in a "borrowing box" every night. Instructions would tell people that they could treat the money as a loan. Gene McCann had been given $2,000 by an anonymous philanthropist who wanted to assess people's honesty. McCann claimed that the donor was confident that the borrowing-box fund would be self-perpetuating—that is, that those who took out some money would replace it.

Was the donor's assumption verified? In the first 90 days, $900 was placed in the box and "loaned"; only $3.10 was returned.

In these two examples, provided two decades ago by Fales and Seder (1973), the farmer and the anonymous donor demonstrated a belief that people can be trusted. A basic thesis of this book is that beliefs such as these are coherently organized and that together they form a central core of each person's orientation toward the world. Knowing the farmer's and donor's beliefs in trustworthiness, we should be able to predict their attitudes toward other variables. But can the cohesiveness of such core constructs be demonstrated? Do different variables that measure various "attitudes toward people" hang together? This chapter explores these pos-

138

sibilities. It also evaluates the relationship of philosophies of human nature to other attitudes, personality variables, and aptitudes. In doing so,
we will provide further evidence for the construct validity of the concept
"philosophies of human nature."

Is There a Construct of "Attitudes Toward People?"

To answer this question, Wrightsman and Cook (1965; S. W. Cook &
Wrightsman, 1967) carried out factor analyses of two heterogeneous test
batteries with several goals in mind: (1) to determine if a general factor of
"attitudes toward people" exists, (2) to see if such a factor is generalizable
across groups of subjects and across methods of factor analysis, and (3) to
identify the place of the PHN scale in such a factor.

Before reporting the results of these analyses, we should explain why
the test batteries were developed. In the spring of 1961, S. W. Cook and
Wrightsman began administering to small groups of college women a test
battery that took about 12 to 15 hours to complete. The subjects were paid
volunteers from five colleges and universities in Nashville, TN. Although
the test battery was described to subjects as test-development projects, its
true purpose was to identify possible subjects for an attitude-change project that Cook was conducting. His project dealt with the effect of invol-
untary contact with an African-American person upon the antiblack
attitudes held by extremely prejudiced white people (S. W. Cook, 1970).

The subjects for the initial factor analysis were 177 female undergraduates. All were white, under age 25, and residents of Southern or border
states, and all were tested between May 1961 and November 1962.

In this analysis, product-moment correlations for 73 variables from 30
tests were computed, and a centroid extraction and a varimax rotation
were employed.

Eleven factors emerged from this initial factor analysis. Table 6.1 lists
those of present interest to us. Each factor is listed in order of its extraction, along with the variables (tests or subtests) that have a loading of .35
or more on that factor. For each factor, variables above the dotted line
have their highest loading on that factor—thus they contribute largely to
the labeling and interpretation of that factor. Variables listed below the
dotted line have higher loadings on another factor or factors. It is important to remember that, although the statistical analysis is objective and
straightforward, the naming of factors must be done by humans and hence
may be subjective and biased.

TABLE 6.1 Results of the First Factor Analysis

Variable	Loading
Factor 5: Positive Attitudes Toward People	
Cornell Anomie Scale	-.7019
Chein's Anomie Scale	-.5810
Rosenberg's Faith-in-People Scale	.5666
Christie's Machiavellianism Scale	-.5185
Suspicion Subscale on Buss-Durkee Hostility Inventory	-.5067
Wrightsman's Behavior Insight Test	.4001
Liverant's External Locus of Control Scale	-.3988
Chein's Anti-Police Attitudes	-.3664
. . . .	
Extent of Stereotyping of Negro	-.4523
Christie's Anomie Scale	-.3892
Factor 7: Tolerance for Unpleasantness	
Low Need for Social Approval on Behavior Interpretation Inventory (BII)	.6441
Low Need to Escape Present Unpleasantness on BII	-.5434
Number of "I Like" Responses on Welsh Figure Preference Test	-.4183
Factor 8: Negativism About Self	
Discrepancy Between Self and Ideal Self	.4127
Wc on Schutz's FIRO-B	.3654
Chein's Personal Optimism	-.3629
. . . .	
Rehfisch Rigidity	.3804
Guilt Subscale on Buss-Durkee Hostility Inventory	.3516
Taylor MAS	.4571

Source: Adapted from Wrightsman & Cook, 1965.
Note: Variables above the dotted line have their highest loading on that factor.

Factor 5 in Table 6.1 we have labeled an Attitudes Toward People factor. The scales that loaded negatively on this factor tap several attitudes: feelings of personal futility and helplessness (anomie scales and External Locus of Control Scale), beliefs that people may be manipulated through threats, flattery, and deceit (Machiavellianism Scale), hostile attitudes toward police (Anti-Police Attitudes Scale), and expressions of suspicion of others (Suspicion subscale on the Buss-Durkee Hostility Inventory). Variables loading positively on the factor are from Rosenberg's Faith-in-People Scale and the Behavior Insight Test—an open-ended measure of philosophies of human nature described in Chapter 4. (When the testing was begun a Likert-scale version of the PHN had not yet been developed.)

Thus Factor 5 appears to be a definitive accumulation of variables that share a concern with attitudes toward people. For example, an aspect of anomie and alienation is a belief that other people are uninterested and unsympathetic. Similarly, the Machiavellianism Scale communicates a cynical belief about others, and the other measures, as denoted by their titles, show a concern with the nature of others. S. W. Cook and Wrightsman (1967) later discovered that this Attitudes Toward People factor was very helpful in determining which of the prejudiced subjects had changed after working with a black; these findings are reported in Chapter 7.

To see if this factor was robust enough to emerge even with different subjects and statistical procedures, S. W. Cook and Wrightsman used a second test battery, again about 12-15 hours in length, to test a new sample of white female undergraduates. Many of the instruments used in the first battery were included, but certain tests that had not loaded heavily on any factor were replaced with more promising instruments.

Subjects for the second battery were 101 female undergraduates from the same schools as the first subjects. They were tested between December 1963 and May 1965. As far as can be determined, they came from the same backgrounds as did the first group; comparison of means and variances between groups indicates a general similarity, although the later group appears to be somewhat less antiblack on the prejudice measures. Of course, just like the first group, the second group cannot be considered a representative sample of women from the five colleges, since the group members voluntarily responded to an advertisement seeking test-takers.

The scores from the second group were also factor analyzed. The method of factor analysis used on the second battery was the cluster-analysis procedure developed by Tryon and Bailey (1965, 1966, 1970). The steps in this analysis were as follows: A correlation matrix was computed, "maximally colinear dimension-defining clusters" were then selected and orthogonal factor coefficients computed, and finally, the "direct solution" was made so as to describe the oblique structure of the dimension-defining clusters. Eleven factors again emerged, and Table 6.2 presents those that are relevant to our discussion.

Factor 4 is labeled Negative Attitudes Toward People because the scales that load positively on it are the Machiavellianism, External Locus of Control, Manifest Hostility, and Political Cynicism scales and the two anomie scales. The scales that negatively load on this factor measure favorable beliefs about human nature (PHN positive-negative score and Faith-in-People Scale) or social desirability. Thus the scales defining Factor 4 are quite similar to those defining Factor 5 in the first factor analysis. The direction of each of the loadings has been reversed, but that, of course, is of no importance.

TABLE 6.2 Results of the Second Factor Analysis

Variable	Loading
Factor 4: Negative Attitudes Toward People	
Positive-Negative Score on Philosophies of Human Nature	-.7493
Chein's Anomie Scale	.7309
Rosenberg's Faith-in-People Scale	-.7209
Machiavellianism	.7195
Cornell Anomie Scale	.6489
Edwards' Social Desirability Scale	-.5774
Siegel's Manifest Hostility Scale	.5483
External Locus of Control	.5433
Political Cynicism	.5282
MMPI K-Scale	-.5090
Personal Optimism	.3630
Anti-Police Attitudes	.3542
Couch and Keniston's Overall Agreement Score	.3521
Manifest Anxiety Scale	.3479
Suspicion Subscale on Buss-Durkee Hostility Inventory	.3469
Factor 5: Belief That Human Nature Is Complex	
Complexity Score on Philosophies of Human Nature Scale	.7316
Multiplexity Score on Philosophies of Human Nature Scale	.7015

Source: Adapted from S. W. Cook & Wrightsman, 1967.

Factor 5 in the second analysis appears to be a specific factor reflecting beliefs that human nature is simple or that it is complex. It is not similar to any factors in the first analysis; in fact, the measures contributing to this factor were not included in the first battery.

Otherwise, a remarkable similarity exists in the outcomes of the two factor analyses, despite their use of somewhat different test batteries, different subjects, and different methods of analysis. Not only did both analyses result in 11 factors, but the first 5 factors in the two analyses were also quite similar. In both cases, a separate Antiblack Attitude factor emerged, as did an Aptitude factor and a factor of Attitudes Toward People. In addition the two different methods of specifically assessing philosophies of human nature—the open-ended situations test and the Likert scale—loaded on similar factors in the two separate analyses. Each is related to the same assortment of attitudes, including measures of alienation and anomie, hostility, and a manipulative orientation toward others. Table 6.3 reflects the coherence of these intercorrelations, based on the PHN positive-negative summated score. Subscale correlations with Machiavellianism were as follows: Trustworthiness, -.673; Strength of

TABLE 6.3 Intercorrelation Between Variables Loading on Attitudes Toward People Factors

	Anomie-Chein	Faith-in-People	Machiavellianism	Cornell Anomie	Manifest Hostility	External Locus of Control
Positive-Negative on Behavior Insight Test or PHN Scale	(1) -.246 (2) -.489	.211 .640	-.386 -.659	-.224 -.432	-.304 -.411	-.185 -.343
Anomie-Chein		(1) -.427 (2) -.524	.318 .543	.486 .585	.353 .453	.234 .468
Faith-in-People Scale (Rosenberg)			(1) -.441 (2) -.555	-.526 -.450	-.387 -.424	-.302 -.249
Machiavellianism Scale				(1) .506 (2) .464	.600 .548	.432 .318
Cornell Anomie Scale					(1) .422 (2) .522	.453 .562
Manifest Hostility Scale						(1) .390 (2) .386

Source: Adapted from S. W. Cook & Wrightsman, 1967.
Note: The first correlation refers to the results of the first test battery; the second refers to the results of the second test battery. In row 1, the open-ended measure of philosophies of human nature was used; in row 2, the Likert scale was used. $Ns = 177$ for first battery and 101 for second.

Will and Rationality, -.383; Altruism, -.574; Independence, -.470; Complexity, -.082; Variability, .086. It has been pointed out (for example, by Hunter, Gerbing, & Boster, 1982) that Machiavellianism, as measured by the scale, reflects several components (see Chapter 3). A factor analysis by Hunter et al. generated four different factors, labeled Flattery, Rejection of the Belief That People Are Moral, Rejection of Honesty, and a Belief That People Are Vicious and Untrustworthy. If these separate factors were correlated with the PHN scale, the above correlation coefficients might be even higher.

Further evidence for an emerging factor of attitudes toward people comes from studies by Earl Carlson (1966) and by Gottlieb Simon (1970, 1972). Carlson was concerned with two aspects of attitudes toward people—faith in the basic goodness of people and the extent to which we are seen as able to control our own fate. With Raphael Hanson, Carlson first set forth to see how many identifiable, independent dimensions result from judgments about people in general. A 50-item questionnaire was constructed and administered to 180 students at California State University, Long Beach. The items were then factor analyzed and five discernible factors emerged. Four of these factors conceived of people as basically honest or dishonest, altruistic or selfish, industrious or lazy, and reasonable or unreasonable in making decisions. (Carlson grouped these together, since each reflected a general evaluative aspect.) A fifth factor dealt with the extent to which people were seen as having control over their fates in life.

At this point, Carlson (1966) became aware of the work on the PHN scale and incorporated items from the PHN, along with some of his previous items, into a second factor analysis. Thus a 100-item battery that reflected 10 a priori scales was administered to a second group of subjects, and the scores were, as you may have expected, factor analyzed. The scales having a high evaluative factor in common did not separate. Instead, a clear, general Faith in People factor emerged, trailed by a second factor dealing with "control." Smaller factors, which saw humankind as complex or simple, as independent or conforming, and as adaptable or rigid, also emerged.

Carlson then investigated relationships between the newly constructed questionnaire on "concepts of man" and attitudes on a range of social and political issues. The resultant measure of "concepts of man" consisted of 72 items on 10 subscales. Each item was judged on a 4-point scale, with both ends of each scale defined fully, in the following example.

| Almost every person would work hard in life if he were rewarded for it. | Many people would not work hard even if they were rewarded well for it. |

To measure beliefs about control, Carlson used an 8-item subscale from the concepts-of-man ratings and Rotter's Internal-External Control Scale. All of these measures were related to attitudes toward major political and social issues. Faith in people was found to correlate positively with liberal attitudes on such issues as medical care, relations with Communist countries, civil liberties, and federal aid for education. Beliefs in high degrees of control were related to conservative positions on these issues. As Carlson (1966) indicates, the conservative position is also characterized by a belief in personal responsibility for one's destiny.

Further evidence for a vigorous Attitudes Toward People factor emerged from Gottlieb Simon's dissertation (1972). Simon composed a battery of nine scales expected to load on this factor. He also included Christie's version of the F scale as a negative marker variable. The nine tests were the PHN, Chein's Anomie and Anti-Police scales, the Suspicion subscale from the Buss-Durkee Hostility Inventory, Rosenberg's Faith-in-People Scale, Rotter's Internal-External Control Scale, Christie's Anomie and Machiavellianism scales, and the Political Cynicism Scale by Agger, Goldstein, and Pearl. This battery was completed by 172 introductory-psychology students (83 females and 89 males) at New York University— at some distance geographically or ideologically from the previously analyzed Tennessee and California students. Simon used the BMD03M factor analysis procedure (Dixon, 1965) to obtain an orthogonal, unrotated solution. Estimates of communality were obtained from squared multiple correlation coefficients, and the scores of men and women were analyzed separately. Six factors fully accounted for the common variance for both men and women, but only the first factor in each analysis met the criterion for a necessary, reliable, and meaningful factor (Kaiser, 1960).

On the basis of the emergence of a strong first factor, Simon (1972) concluded: "Both qualitative and quantitative considerations indicate the identity of this overarching factor and ATP (attitudes toward people)" (p. 316). For example, all the scales that loaded on S. W. Cook and Wrightsman's Attitudes Toward People factor also loaded on Simon's first factor; the Christie F scale of authoritarianism did not load on this ATP factor, either in the previous studies or in Simon's studies. The PHN scale had the highest loading in both of Simon's analyses as well as in the Cook-Wrightsman analysis (.85, .76, and .75, respectively). Quantitative evidence for the similarity of Simon's first factor to S. W. Cook and Wrightsman's ATP factor is given by two measures of factorial invariance—the root mean square and the coefficient of congruence. If two factors match each other perfectly, their coefficient of congruence will be 1.0; in the present comparison, coefficient-of-congruence values ranged from .96 to .99. The root mean square, equal to zero when the matching is perfect, yielded values ranging from .10 to .17. Although there is no adequate significance test for these and their interpretation requires caution, we share Simon's (1972) conclusion that a factor of Attitudes Toward People is "a reliable factor, invariant across sex, regional, and investigator differences" (p. 316).

This conclusion is especially significant because studies of *other* aspects of attitudes toward people have not always found correlations between measures. For example, Lasater and Ramirez (1970) found low relationships between measures of helplessness: Rotter's I-E scale, Srole's Anomie Scale, Zimmer's Powerlessness Scale, and an adaptation of a measure of powerlessness used by Ransford. Neal and Rettig (1967) concluded that if certain types of factor analysis are used, "alienation" emerges as a multidimensional construct. MacDonald (1971b) reported a mixed bag of correlations among various measures of internal-external locus of control.

Relationships of PHN to Other Attitudes

We have shown that a core construct of "attitudes toward people" exists and that the PHN scale is a robust measure of this construct. But how broad are the relationships between measures of attitudes toward people and other individual differences measures? How extensive or narrow is the ATP construct? Does it include values and ideologies? This section uses the PHN scale as an index of attitudes toward people and reports on explorations that have found positive relationships between PHN measures and other attitudes. In relating the PHN to other measures of individual differences, we can, in Christie's words, "subjectively triangulate its location in a hypothetical space composed of previous findings" (1970, p. 35).

INTERPRETATIONS OF MOTIVES
BEHIND OUR GOVERNMENT'S POLICIES

The actions of our government in its dealings with other nations are constantly in the news. Therefore, most Americans have at least a general notion of our country's policies or actions in such noteworthy events as the latest conflict in the Persian Gulf, the crisis in the Soviet economy, or the possibility of "global warming." But people are often in strong disagreement about the motives behind these governmental actions. We propose that a reason for this difference is that each person's basic orientation toward the actions of others may color his or her interpretations of governmental actions. One salient dimension that seems useful in categorizing the varying interpretations of our government's motives is, for want of a better name, the "tender-minded" versus "tough-minded" dimension—a dimension that reflects the extent to which moral considerations are superimposed upon interpretations of policy decisions. Persons who are "tender-minded" in their interpretations are basically idealists. They see our country as ethical and unselfish. In contrast, extremely "tough-minded" individuals are coldly realistic. To them, our government is basically selfish and power-oriented, and our leaders are little influenced by moral principles. For example, did President Bush send U.S. troops to Saudi Arabia to protect that country from a possible invasion by Iraq, or did he send them in order to maintain the flow of oil to the United States?

Admittedly, the above characterizations are extremes, and most people would probably fall somewhere between them. The dimension, however, does seem to be a vital one, as well as one that is worthy of research. Thus a scale was constructed (Wrightsman, 1964d) to measure this dimension, and subjects' scores on the scale were related to their attitudes toward people. It was hypothesized that tough-minded persons would possess Machiavellian and cynical views of people, whereas those who were more tender-minded in their interpretations of governmental motives would have favorable views of human nature with regard to such traits as trustworthiness, altruism, independence, and strength of will.

In constructing the scale, Wrightsman chose 16 government policies, actions, and beliefs that were relevant to U.S. foreign policy at that time. For each, two varying interpretations of the reason behind the policy were prepared, one "tender-minded" and the other "tough-minded." Subjects were instructed "to decide which reason *you think* is nearer to the real reason for the government's policy." Each time a "tender-minded" response was chosen, one point was scored. The scale was administered to

200 students at three colleges for the purposes of an item analysis. Responses to each item were tabulated for the members of each group, and a 2 × 3 chi-square test of independence was performed on the total score. Appendix E contains the scale statements and results of the item analysis. (For contemporary use, certain statements need to be revised, replaced, or discarded because they are no longer timely.)

In brief, this item analysis indicated that 6 of the original 16 items failed to discriminate significantly among the high, medium, and low groups. The remaining 10 items constitute the Interpretations of Government Policy Scale (IGPS). For men, the mean score on the 10 items was 3.96 (SD = 2.04); for women, the mean score was 4.53 (SD = 2.14). The mean for men is somewhat more "tough-minded," although not significantly so (t = 1.86; p > .05). As indicated by the standard deviations, the scale produces a wide spread of scores for both genders.

It was hypothesized that the IGPS would be related to attitudinal measures that deal with one's view of human nature and its ramifications. For example, the IGPS was expected to correlate negatively with the Machiavellianism Scale. The correlations for four groups were all in the expected direction; specific correlations were as follows: 62 Wheaton (IL) women, -.36; 33 Wheaton men, -.58; 100 Peabody women, -.46; 30 Peabody men, -.37 (all were significantly different from zero at .01 level). Highly Machiavellian persons, in selecting tough-minded interpretations of the motives behind government policy, generalize their "winning-is-what-counts" attitude to the relationship among nations.

The IGPS was also expected to correlate negatively with the Political Cynicism Scale. Again all correlations—this time for eight groups—were in the expected direction; for example, 62 Wheaton women, -.20; 33 Wheaton men, -.43 (significant at the .01 level); 100 Peabody women, -.30 (significant at the .01 level); 30 Peabody men, -.15; 62 Central Michigan women, -.30 (significant at the .01 level); 44 Central Michigan men, -.17; 41 Belmont women, -.06; and 48 Belmont men, -.10. Only in three groups is the relationship high enough to be significantly different from zero; hence, a conservative conclusion is that the hypothesized relationship between tough-minded interpretation and political cynicism is only partly confirmed.

On the PHN scale, tender-minded subjects were expected to have views of human nature that were more favorable than were those of their tough-minded counterparts. The correlations for eight groups are as follows: 62 Wheaton women, .41; 33 Wheaton men, .36; 100 Peabody women, .57; 30 Peabody men, .53; and 62 Central Michigan women, .38 (all significant at the .01 level) and 44 Central Michigan men, .16; 41 Belmont women, .06; and 48 Belmont men, .22. Once more, all correlations are in the hypothesized direction; that is, tender-minded interpreters of government motives are more likely to see people as trustworthy, altruistic, rational, and independent. Thus the hypothesis is confirmed. In general, it may be concluded that the construct "attitudes toward people" also encompasses interpretations of the reasons underlying our governmental policies, reflecting perhaps the respondents' tendency to "personalize" the actions of larger institutions. This is especially important when we consider Rotter's (1967) Interpersonal Trust Scale, because many of the items on this scale deal with the reliability of institutions rather than individuals.

Yet the correlations between scales were not so high in some groups as in others. There apparently was a difference among groups with regard to degree of structuring of beliefs and attitudes. Some campuses may have contained more sophisticated and knowledgeable respondents, whose attitudes toward people and interpretations of governmental policies went hand-in-hand. At Belmont College the relationships were only tenuous. Perhaps students at that school had not read about government issues so extensively as had other subjects. Carlson (1966), in the study described earlier in this chapter, found what may be a similar kind of distinction between groups of his subjects. Comparing college-student respondents (a "sophisticated" group) with their parents (a "less sophisticated" group), Carlson related attitudes toward people in general, attitudes toward social issues, and attitudes toward specific political figures and groups. For example, although the correlation between attitudes toward Ronald Reagan and attitudes toward Martin Luther King was -.73 in the sophisticated group, it was .20 for the unsophisticated group. The correlation in attitudes toward Hubert Humphrey (at that time a symbol of liberalism) and the John Birch Society was -.60 in the sophisticated group and -.03 for the unsophisticated group. As Carlson (1966) indicates, "These results reflect this basic fact that the patterning is quite different for those who know what's going on and those who don't" (p. 3). Carlson's conclusion is verified by studies of other attitude domains (such as those by Converse, 1964; Gamson & Modigliani, 1966; and McClosky, Hoffman, & O'Hara, 1960) that have found that attitudes are more consistent, both within and across domains, in that part of the population that is well informed on the issues.

But why do people differ in their perceptions of the reasons for specific governmental actions? Possibly, interpretations of behavior in such an ambiguous area as this one stem from what we believe should be the rationale for governmental actions. Thus the tender-minded person believes that national and international behavior, just like individual behavior, should emerge from a well-developed body of moral principles. The tough-minded individual, however, who may or may not advocate moral principles in his/her own life, certainly believes that they should have no influence in determining actions in international affairs.

It is fascinating that justifications for each of these positions can be found in the writings of recent American social and political philosophers. Hans J. Morgenthau (1951), an exponent of the realistic or tough-minded position, chastised his fellow Americans for believing that some sort of universal moral values can justify the means and ends of foreign policy. He was aware of the danger of identifying one's own cause with that of morality in the abstract, and he preferred the idea of "national interest" as a foundation for national policy (Russell, 1990). Similarly, Arthur Schlesinger, Jr. (1971), cautioned that personal principles of morality may not be applicable in international relations.

In contrast, American theologian Reinhold Niebuhr (1953) attempted to justify international morality. He believed that individuals and nations cannot follow their interests without claiming to do so in obedience to some general scheme of values. All nations justify their actions in terms of their morality, he believed, although at times it is an unconsciously false self-justification.

Both these philosophical positions seem to have their correlative positions in the extremes of the IGPS, although these extremes are perversions of Schlesinger's and Morgenthau's, and Niebuhr's views. Research is needed to determine whether such orientations are also related to attitudes about the desirability of disarmament, possibilities of nuclear war, and the necessity for civil-defense measures, as well as to basic values such as those measured by the Allport-Vernon-Lindzey Study of Values. A master's thesis by Heidi Steinitz (1987) gives some general support to an expectation that beliefs about the likelihood of nuclear war, liberal-conservatives attitudes, and locus of control scores are all related to each other.

ATTITUDES TOWARD DESEGREGATION

Do attitudes toward people influence attitudes toward desegregation? In the early 1960s, Koepper (1966) classified Southern teachers into groups according to their race and the status of their school (segregated or

TABLE 6.4 Relationships Between External-Internal Locus of Control Scale and PHN Scale in Three Samples

PHN-Scale Correlate	*152 Freshman Women*	*39 Freshman Men*	*273 Undergraduate Women*
Trustworthiness	-.332**	-.359*	-.233**
Strength of Will			
and Rationality	-.355**	-.352*	-.434**
Altruism	-.382**	-.276	-.274**
Independence	-.312**	-.258	-.217**
Complexity	.065	.061	.123
Variability	-.004	.157	.066
Positive-Negative			
Summated Score	-.425**	-.394*	-.345*
Multiplexity	.040	.125	.122

Note: Locus of control scale is scored so that a high score indicates external locus of control. Samples: 152 women and 39 men from 1966 Peabody freshman class and 273 undergraduate women from the Cook-Wrightsman test-development study.
*Significantly different from zero at .05 level.
**Significantly different from zero at .01 level.

desegregated) and of their classroom (segregated or desegregated). In most groupings, there was significant positive correlation between the teacher's positive-negative score on the PHN scale and the extent of his or her willingness to teach in a desegregated school. Attitudes toward people are thus related to the respondents' positions on one of the most salient of social issues in contemporary American life; beliefs about human nature are used in adopting a position on racial desegregation.

LOCUS OF CONTROL

Scores on Rotter's External-Internal Control Scale (Rotter, 1966) have been correlated with scores on the PHN scales for three samples of undergraduates. Table 6.4 presents the results, which are consistent in showing that persons who believe that the locus of control resides outside themselves have negative scores on the substantive qualities of philosophies of human nature. In theory, the Strength of Will and Rationality dimension should be most highly related to Locus of Control, but there is only a slight tendency for this to be the case. In only the third sample is the correlation with Strength of Will (-.43) much higher than the correlation with Trustworthiness (-.23) or with Altruism (-.27).

Nonsignificant Relationships with Attitude Measures

In order to understand more thoroughly the nature of the construct "philosophies of human nature," we need to know what measures it does *not* correlate with. Thus we can gain awareness of its limits; sometimes these limits are surprisingly restricted. This section details attitude constructs that *do not* appear to be related to philosophies of human nature.

AUTHORITARIANISM

As Simon's (1970) study indicated, Christie's revised version of the California F Scale has no significant relationship to measures contributing to attitudes toward people. Likewise, a study (S. W. Cook & Wrightsman, 1967) that tested a heterogeneous group of women from five colleges found that the PHN positive-negative scale showed low correlations with the original California F scale (-.18) as well as with the Christie revision (r = -.12). This is surprising, as (1) the F scale has the reputation of correlating with almost everything and (2) one of the nine theorized components of the authoritarian personality is a set of cynical beliefs about human nature. Yet it appears accurate to conclude that measures of attitudes toward people are unrelated to degree of authoritarianism. Christie (1970) reports that nine studies relating the Machiavellianism Scale to the California F Scale had correlations of .04 to -.15; none of these was significant. Perhaps there is no relationship because, as Christie puts it, the highly authoritarian person believes that "people are no damn good, but they *ought* to be" (Christie, 1970, p. 38).

ATTITUDES TOWARD APPROPRIATE FEMININE ROLES

Hearn (1972) noted that feminine sex roles involve cognitions or beliefs about women. She hypothesized that women's attitudes toward their gender roles would be related to other attitudes that they held. For example, advocacy of a nontraditional role for women was expected to be related to beliefs in the variability and complexity of human nature.

To test these and other relationships, Hearn administered the Attitudes Toward Feminism Belief Patterns Scale (Kirkpatrick, 1936) to 71 freshman women at Peabody College. They completed the test in their dormitories about three weeks after they had completed a freshman-orientation test battery that included the PHN scale. Although Kirkpatrick's scale was developed more than 50 years ago, it covers topics that are surprisingly contemporary: equal rights for women in business and the profession, educational opportunities for women, women's appropriate civic involvement, marriage and family life, a single standard of morality for men and women, and stereotypes about women's emotions and personalities. The freshman women's responses to the Kirkpatrick Scale had enough spread for relationships with PHN multiplexity measures to emerge if they did exist. Yet they did not emerge. Correlations were as follows: with Complexity, .08; with Variability, .03; with multiplexity, .07. Thus women's favorable attitudes toward nontraditional roles for their sex are unrelated to their beliefs about the degree of individual differences in human nature. (Correlations with the PHN substantive scales were also in the range of −.06 to +.08.)

CONSCIOUSNESS LEVELS

Although no longer a currently-used concept, 20 years ago almost every literate person was at least somewhat familiar with Charles Reich's typology of three "consciousness levels" in *The Greening of America* (1970). As Reich used the term, a person's *consciousness level* reflects his or her entire constellation of attitudes and opinions—a world view. Reich proposed that American society had passed from one level to another, as different societal needs demanded different world views and life styles. Consciousness I was appropriate for a frontier America of 100 years ago, because it reflected a valuing of individualism and self-reliance. Because it proposed that one could achieve through hard work and competition with others, Consciousness I necessarily saw people as mean, competitive, and selfish. But by the 1930s, Consciousness II began to emerge; it emphasized rationality and competence. According to Consciousness II, persons are judged by their usefulness to society and by their willingness to operate out of a specific niche in the organizational structure. Value was placed on technology, management, and planning for the future. But in our contemporary times—filled with pollution, "labor-saving devices," and energy crises—technology has developed to a point at which it has become a Frankensteinian monster, controlling us—even hamstringing us— instead of operating as our servant. More recent times have demanded the emergence of a new life-style, Consciousness III, which according to Reich is best characterized by self-liberation. A Consciousness-III person seeks to discover his or her own role in society and the unique qualities of each individual. Additionally, the Consciousness-III person is oriented toward the development of internal resources rather than of technological or artificial ones.

It should be clear that central to Reich's thesis was an assertion that each consciousness level makes different assumptions about human nature (N. Baker, 1972). Reich, without so naming it, employed the PHN concept in his writing. For example:

> the Consciousness I belief [is] that human nature is "bad," that men have always been stupid or vicious, that nothing is to be expected of "popular taste" or mass man. Closely connected to this is the Consciousness I idea that all men are "free," and they are morally responsible for what they make of themselves or fail to make of themselves. (Reich, 1970, p. 285)

The following is Reich's description of the Consciousness-II orientation:

> Behind a facade of optimism, Consciousness II has a profoundly pessimistic view of man. It sees man in Hobbesian terms; human beings are by nature aggressive, competitive, power-seeking; uncivilized man is a jungle beast. . . . Consciousness II is deeply cynical about human motives and good intentions, and it doubts that man can be much improved. It is this philosophy that helps to explain the great emphasis on society and institutions; these are designed to do the best possible job of administering the doubtful and deficient raw material that is human nature. (Reich, 1970, pp. 66-67)

Consciousness III's philosophy of human nature was not so clearly spelled out, but it assumed that each person possesses absolute worth, even while it sharply criticized society in general. For example, "Consciousness III postulates the absolute worth of every human being—every self. Consciousness III does not believe in the antagonistic or competitive doctrine of life" (Reich, 1970, p. 226). At this level, the dimension of variability also was highlighted; Reich wrote, "Consciousness III refuses to evaluate people by general standards; it refuses to classify people, or analyze them. Each person has his own individuality, not to be compared to that of someone else" (pp. 226-227).

The attitude-measurer savors—even salivates at—the opportunity to operationalize Reich's rather loose conceptions. For example, N. Baker (1972) constructed two measures of Reich's three consciousness levels—a set of Likert-type attitude statements and a descriptive paragraph for each level. These were administered to 70 Peabody freshman women in May 1971, and the scores were correlated with the PHN subscales that had been given them eight months earlier.

TABLE 6.5 Correlations of PHN Subscales with Measures of Reich's Consciousness Levels

PHN Subscale	Consciousness I		Consciousness II		Consciousness III	
	Baker's Sample	Hearn's Sample	Baker's Sample	Hearn's Sample	Baker's Sample	Hearn's Sample
Trustworthiness	.07	.06	.01	.06	-.18	-.16
Strength of Will and Rationality	-.06	-.06	-.19	-.12	-.26*	-.00
Altruism	-.02	.04	-.10	-.02	-.08	-.01
Independence	-.09	-.04	-.20	-.05	-.26*	.00
Complexity	.00	-.13	-.11	-.15	-.19	-.09
Variability	-.02	-.13	-.17	-.20	-.16	-.07
Positive-Negative	.07	.01	-.08	-.04	-.24*	.05
Multiplexity	.02	-.17	-.16	-.22	-.18	-.10

Source: Adapted from Baker, 1972, and Hearn, 1972.
Note: Ns: Baker's = 70; Hearn's = 71.
*p = .05

155

The following fall, Hearn (1972) administered the PHN and N. Baker's consciousness scales to freshmen during orientation week. Table 6.5 reproduces the results of N. Baker's and Hearn's analyses. Despite the assumptions proposed for each consciousness level, neither substantive beliefs nor multiplexity orientations predict a person's consciousness scores. We find this a surprising and inexplicable finding. Although Reich's ideas were often hard to convert into Likert-type attitude statements, an investigation of responses to specific statements as correlates of PHN score still produced little relationship. World views and assumptions about people were two essentially unrelated attitude domains, according to the results of this study.

RELIGIOUS ATTITUDES

Kawamura and Wrightsman (1969) sought to determine the place of philosophies of human nature in the factor structure of religious attitudes and related constructs. Forty-seven variables were derived from a 3-hour battery administered to 104 introductory-psychology students at University of Hawaii. Of these, 19 were measures of religious attitudes and 28 were measures of values, attitudes, or personality. A principal axes factor analysis yielded 11 factors that were subjected to a varimax solution. There were two religiosity factors, one general (Factor I) and one personal (Factor IX). The second factor to emerge included all the measures of attitudes toward people (PHN, Political Cynicism, Faith-in-People, and Machiavellianism scales). Thus religious attitudes and beliefs about human nature were independent of one another in this rather heterogeneous sample of college students.

All the Christian denominations were represented in the Kawamura-Wrightsman study. One Jew and 19 Buddhist also participated. In a rather different study of religious attitudes, Maddock and Kenny (1972) report more trusting subjects to possess more intrinsic religious orientations.

In summary, it appears that the construct "philosophies of human nature" is internally cohesive but at the same time independent of certain other attitude domains. It appears unrelated to authoritarianism, to religious attitudes, to attitudes toward women's roles, and to consciousness level as defined in *The Greening of America* (Reich, 1970). Such zero-order relationships are a mixed blessing, if they are a blessing at all. We interpret them to reflect the purity of the measurement; the results also permit us to reject false hypotheses that the PHN scales are simply a new way of measuring religious orientations or authoritarianism. Yet, zero-order findings always suggest an alternative hypothesis—that is, that poor measuring instruments may be their cause. The strong relationships in the predicted direction between PHN and such measures as Machiavellianism, anomie, and locus of control would seem to serve as adequate refutations of such a hypothesis.

Relationships with Personality Characteristics

In introducing his review of the relationships of Machiavellianism to personality variables, Christie (1970) expressed an expectation that "there should be little or no relationship between Machiavellian orientations and measures of psychopathology" (1970, p. 42). But some relationships between the Machiavellianism measures and personality measures began to appear. What should be made of these? Christie sought to demonstrate that the apparent relationship between Machiavellianism and personality was often there only because of a third variable. For example, the correlations between Machiavellianism and the Taylor Manifest Anxiety Scale (MAS) in four medical-school student samples ranged from .38 to .42, a finding inconsistent with Christie's expectation that Machiavellianism is unrelated to psychopathology. So Christie introduced the concept of social desirability as a possible common factor in Machiavellian and Taylor MAS scores. A forced-choice version of the Machiavellianism Scale, supposedly eliminating social desirability, was correlated with the MAS scores of eight more classes of medical students. The resulting correlations were from -.01 to .21 and none was statistically significant.

However, when the obtained correlation between Machiavellianism and another measure is significant and in line with Christie's expectations, the role of social desirability was not considered. For example, Christie (1970, p. 42) reports a correlation between Machiavellianism IV and PHN Trustworthiness. No mention of social desirability was made here, even though both measures were probably loaded with it. (Since both Machiavellianism IV and the PHN are Likert scales, method similarity may also contaminate the correlation.)

Thus if social desirability is used to explain away one relationship, its effects should be partialed out in all relationships under scrutiny (Paulhus, 1991). We prefer, however, to ignore social desirability, for in our opinion it is not a very useful concept. The social desirability of a statement is indicated by the percentage of respondents who would like to say that that statement is true of themselves. According to the theory, test-takers to varying degrees respond to attitude statements in terms of social desirability. But instead, to varying degrees they respond in terms of personal desirability—that is, in terms of what they individually judge as desirable. The personal desirability of a statement may or may not be consonant with its social desirability; the fact that 75% of a certain group of people would like to be known as punctual does not mean that every individual wants to be described as a punctual person. Thus introducing procedures to control for social desirability is a rather ineffective procedure.

But beyond this, is social desirability something that needs to be controlled for? We are not so sure that the traditional conception of social desirability—as something extraneous to the construct to be measured—is appropriate for the construct of "philosophies of human nature." (We recognize that there are occasions—such as taking an attitude scale as part of an employment interview—in which downright faking occurs. This is not what we are referring to here.) *Wanting to say that people are good* may be a valid part of a person's philosophy of human nature; it may be the element that distinguishes those with positive scores from those with negative scores on the PHN. We grant that such a claim cannot be proven, but we also believe that it cannot be proven that social-desirability elements can be separated out from other elements of a response to an attitude scale. Thus in reviewing relationships of personality variables and the PHN we will simply "tell it like it is," without incorporating social desirability as an explanation.

REPRESSION VERSUS SENSITIZATION

Byrne (1961; Byrne, Barry, & Nelson, 1963) developed the Repression-Sensitization (R-S) dimension as a way of reflecting two rather disparate means of defensive expression. Repressers tend to use avoiding mechanisms such as denial and regression; in contrast, sensitizers tend to use approach-oriented mechanisms such as intellectualization and obsessions (Bell & Byrne, 1978). Duke and Wrightsman (1968) correlated the PHN and Byrne's R-S scale, using as subjects 150 men and 45 women in an introductory-psychology class at a state university. The results are presented in Table 6.6; high R-S scores indicate sensitization. Male sensitizers consistently saw human nature as more negative than did repressers, while no significant relationship existed in males between the R-S dimension and multiplexity scores.

TABLE 6.6 Correlations Between PHN Subscales and the Repression-Sensitization (R-S) Scale

PHN Subscale	Men (N = 150)		Women (N = 45)	
	r	p	r	p
Trustworthiness	-.33	.001	-.10	NS
Strength of Will				
and Rationality	-.31	.001	-.30	.05
Altruism	-.34	.001	-.04	NS
Independence	-.21	.01	-.32	.05
Complexity	.04	NS	.17	NS
Variability	.02	NS	-.21	NS
Positive-Negative	-.38	.001	-.25	.05
Multiplexity	.04	NS	-.02	NS

Source: Adapted from Duke & Wrightsman, 1968, Table 2, p. 237.

The women presented a somewhat more complicated picture. They were not so consistent as the men in regard to the relationship between R-S and PHN substantive scales. Female sensitizers tended to see others as having less strength of will and less independence (as did the men), but they did not show a significant relationship between the repression-sensitization dimension and their perception of altruism and trustworthiness (unlike the men).

The tendency for sensitizers to have a more negative view of human nature is compatible with previous research findings, as sensitizers characteristically have been found to focus on the more negative or unpleasant aspects of their own experience. They more strongly tend to recall failures and material associated with shock (Lazarus & Longo, 1953), to recall uncompleted tasks in threatening situations (Eriksen, 1952), to respond more quickly to aggressive stimulus words on a word-association test (Eriksen & Lazarus, 1952), to admit to inadequacy (Wiener, Carpenter, & Carpenter, 1956), and to respond to sexually arousing stimuli with anxiety (Byrne & Sheffield, 1965). On the other hand, repressers not only hold more positive views of human nature but also tend to remember successes better than failures (Eriksen, 1952), to forget anxiety-arousing projective-test pictures (Perloe, 1960), to express less sexuality and hostility on a sentence-completion task (Lazarus, Eriksen, & Fonda, 1951), and to give fewer TAT scores that reflect aggressive themes (Eriksen, 1951).

The absence of a relationship between the R-S dimension and the Variability subscale suggest that, although repressers deny humankind's

undesirable qualities, they do not attempt to simplify human nature any
more than sensitizers do.

SELF-CONCEPT

The congruence between a person's perceived self and his or her ideal
self has been proposed as a reflection of the person's degree of adjustment
(A. H. Maslow & Mittelman, 1941; Rogers, 1949), and one of the outcomes of client-centered counseling is a greater degree of congruence between these two measures (Butler & Haigh, 1954). Chapter 3 reviewed a
multitude of studies that found relationships between attitudes toward self
and attitudes toward others. Additionally, A. H. Maslow (1962), in his
investigation of more fully functioning individuals, reported that such
people are more congruent in regard to both values and self-perceptions
and are more accepting of others—that is, they are less tolerant of the
complexities of others.

Several studies have related PHN scores to various measures of self-
concept. Using bipolar-rating scales of perceived self and ideal self,
Wrightsman (1964a) found a correlation of -.65 between self/ideal-self
discrepancy and positive-negative summated score (N = 100, p < .001),
indicating that persons with positive attitudes possess smaller self/ideal-
self discrepancies. A study of 30 police officers (Prytula, Champagne,
Grigsby, & Soltys, 1972) reported that the more emotionally mature officers saw people as more complex and more trustworthy; in addition, officers with more positive attitudes toward their job had more favorable
philosophies of human nature. Silva (1972) administered the Interpersonal Check List (LaForge & Suczek, 1955) to 30 undergraduates who had
previously completed the PHN. On the Interpersonal Check List, discrepancy scores were computed by subtracting Level V (description of self)
from Level II (description of ideal self) for each of the eight subscales and
then summing the scores to produce one discrepancy score for each subject. Then, on the basis of these scores, Silva divided the subjects into two
groups. On three of the PHN substantive subscales, the highly congruent
subjects had attitudes that were more favorable than those of the less congruent subjects, but the mean differences were small except for Altruism.
On that subscale, the highly congruent mean was -1.67, the less congruent
mean was -11.00, and the t value for the difference was 2.15, significant
at the .05 level.

Another aspect of the self-concept is its openness. In his book *The Transparent Self* (1964), Jourard contrasted the willingness to disclose the self openly with the need to protect the self by keeping personal attitudes and feelings secret from others. Jourard developed a self-disclosure scale that consisted of 10 topics in each of six areas, including money, one's body, work (or studies), and personality. The subject indicated how much he or she has discussed each of the 60 topics with four different people— his or her mother, father, male friend, and female friend. Ashcraft (1967) related PHN scores to self-disclosure responses of 73 white female sophomores and 37 black female sophomores at two different colleges. Contrary to expectations, there was little tendency for the more self-disclosing subjects to be more trusting of others. Although there was a correlation of .368 between Trustworthiness and amount disclosed to a female friend, the correlations for the other three target persons were .026, -.060, and -.110. Subsequent unpublished research that correlated these measures confirms the absence of a significant relationship; in fact, the correlations between Trustworthiness and disclosure to target persons were mostly negative. It may be that people who disclose abnormally large amounts of intimate information do so partially to test the trustworthiness of others; the self-discloser may be able to confirm or disconfirm his or her own doubts about others by observing how they use the intimate information he or she has revealed to them.

Relationship with Aptitude and Ability

Philosophies of human nature are not expected to be related to measures of intelligence, aptitude, or scholastic ability, and the evidence we have indicates that in samples of undergraduates the resultant correlations are quite low. If we move from a specific IQ-test score to a broader, subjective criterion of "achievement" or "ability," however, we may expect relationships to emerge, particularly when the "criterion" stems from the ratings given the subject by another person.

The inspiration for such a hypothesis was a finding reported by Hunt (1963) in a study of personality variables and achievement in seminaries. Hunt included the PHN scale in a long battery of instruments given to ministerial students at two seminaries. Scores on each instrument in the battery were related to two faculty ratings that served as criteria of student success. Three or more of the faculty members at each seminary classified each student into one of five categories ranging from "best" to "poorest."

One faculty rating was done on the basis of the student's present overall seminary achievement level (including classroom work, participation in student activities, and extracurricular seminary activities), whereas the second was done on the basis of "the student's promise of future effectiveness as a minister in the field" (Hunt, 1963, p. 7).

There were several surprising findings. At one of the schools, Perkins School of Theology at Southern Methodist University, significant negative correlations emerged between the substantive scales on the PHN and the ability and achievement measures. (At this time, before the Graduate Record Examination (GRE) test became popular, the major measure used to predict graduate-school aptitude was the Miller Analogies Test [MAT].) For example, the Trustworthiness subscale of the PHN correlated -.35 (significant at $p < .05$ or greater) with the Miller Analogies Test score, -.30 with grade-point average (GPA), -.28 with the first faculty rating, and -.35 (significant at $p < .05$ or greater) with the second faculty rating. Altruism on the PHN scale correlated -.44 (significant at $p < .05$ or greater) with the Miller Analogies Test score (significant at $p < .05$ or greater), -.40 with GPA, and -.18 and -.41 (significant at $p < .05$ or greater) with the faculty ratings.

Thus students who believed that people in general were untrustworthy and selfish had higher ability scores, higher grade-point averages, and higher ratings of effectiveness. This went contrary to a notion that a set of positive beliefs about human nature facilitates effectiveness. Logan Wright (1964), however, has clarified the acceptance of the logic of this relationship in the seminary students by indicating that, in contemporary theology, there is a point of view that emphasizes a more balanced view of human nature than does the Rogerian "man-is-positive" view that has heavily influenced contemporary psychotherapy. Thinking negatively about human nature is more congruent with the Zeitgeist for ministers than it is for psychotherapists.

A further surprise came when the PHN and the Miller Analogies Test (MAT) scores were compared as predictors of academic success. In summary, the results at Perkins are summarized in the top portion of Table 6.7. The PHN measures are as highly related to academic success measures as is the MAT score. In the case of the evaluation of future effectiveness, PHN measures are significant whereas the MAT score is not.

Can it be that attitude has more influence than aptitude upon performance in ministerial school? The results appear to say so. There are two qualifying factors, however:

TABLE 6.7 Correlations for Measures for Ministerial Students

| | *Perkins Seminary Students* | | |
	GPA	*Faculty Rating I*	*Faculty Rating II*
Miller Analogies Test Score	.38*	.20	.29
Trustworthiness on PHN	−.30	−.28	−.35*
Altruism on PHN	−.41*	−.18	−.41*
	Brite Seminary Students		
	GPA	*Faculty Rating I*	*Faculty Rating II*
Otis Mental Ability Test	.31*	.24	.26
Trustworthiness on PHN	.04	−.00	.01
Altruism on PHN	.03	−.04	−.06

Note: *Significantly different from zero at .05 level.

1. The group may have been selected on the basis of MAT scores, thus reducing the distribution within the selected group. It is unlikely that this was the case, however, although selection was indirectly based upon mental ability, in the sense that previous GPA was utilized.

2. At Brite Seminary, the attitude scores did not do a better job of predicting than did the aptitude measure. There, the Otis Mental Ability test was used instead of the MAT. These results are also shown in Table 6.7.

Despite these qualifications, the idea that an attitude measure could do as a good a job of predicting as the MAT does deserves further study, particularly because of the universal reliance upon the Graduate Record Examination (GRE) and MAT as selection devices in determining admission to graduate programs. (This statement and many others in this chapter assume that validity is linear; that is, if some of a trait is good and if more of it is better, then still more of it must be better yet [Guion, 1970]. Perhaps someone should examine this assumption that the highest scoring students *are* the most able.)

We decided to repeat Hunt's (1963) study, using as subjects the graduate students in the psychology departments at the University of Hawaii and at George Peabody College.

In March 1966, in the Department of Psychology at the University of Hawaii, there were 65 active graduate students for whom a Miller Analogies Test or Graduate Record Examination score was available. Each of these students was asked to complete the Philosophies of Human Nature Scale. Although the student was required to put his or her name on the answer sheet, confidentiality was promised. Fifty-two of the 65 students completed the scale.

Each of the 14 department faculty members was asked to rate each of these 52 students in terms of "his future effectiveness as a psychologist when he reaches his maximum achievement as an active psychologist in the field." A space was provided for indicating that the professor did not know the student well enough to rate. Faculty members were not asked to identify themselves by name, although some did. Eleven of the 14 returned the rating forms (although one failed to do one page).

The rating behavior is of some interest in itself. One faculty member rated 15 of the 52 as "excellent" and 11 as "not adequate," thus showing a wide range of opinions. Another faculty member rated none as "excellent," 2 as "good," 14 as "adequate," and 4 as "not adequate," perhaps displaying a critical-response set.

Despite differences in rater sets, the ratings appear to have interjudge reliability. Only two of the students were not used in the study because they elicited widespread ratings. One of these received two "excellent" ratings and one "not adequate." The other received three ratings, one "adequate" and two "excellent." One student was not used because of receiving only two ratings. Other students were rated by from 4 to 11 faculty members, and usually all the ratings for a particular student were in only two adjacent categories.

Ratings were assigned the following point values: excellent, 4; good, 3; adequate, 2; not adequate, 1. For each student, an average rating was computed. Actual averages ranged from one possible extreme (4.0) to the other (1.0), and the average of these ratings was approximately 2.3.

Faculty ratings were correlated with the Philosophies of Human Nature Scale, the Miller Analogies Test, and the Graduate Record Examination verbal (V) and quantitative (Q) scores; these are reported in Table 6.8. All the correlations are low; none is significantly different from .00. They are, however, in the expected direction (except for GRE-Q); that is, the attitude correlations are negative, as was the case with the ministerial students. It is interesting that the attitude correlations are higher than the aptitude ones, although the difference is too small to be considered significant.

There also appears to be a slight tendency for those students who see people as untrustworthy and lacking in willpower to receive better faculty ratings. This finding is in the same direction as the finding for ministerial students, even though the extent of the relationship is less. In fact, any greater relationship would have been surprising when one considers that,

TABLE 6.8 Correlations for Graduate Students in Psychology at University of Hawaii

Measure	N of Students	Product-Moment Correlation
PHN-General Positive-Negative	47	−.196
PHN-Trustworthiness	47	−.213
PHN-Strength of Will and Rationality	47	−.208
PHN-Multiplexity	47	+.146
MAT	37	+.141
GRE-Verbal	42	+.106
GRE-Quantitative	42	−.004

on the average, experimental-psychology students and clinical-counseling students differ significantly in their PHN scores. Yet this sample includes both experimental psychology and clinical psychology students, with some students in each field receiving good faculty ratings and some in each field receiving bad ratings.

The correlation of .15 between PHN-multiplexity scores and faculty ratings is in the expected direction (but is ever so slight). Students who see human nature as complex and variable receive more favorable ratings.

The correlations between faculty ratings and aptitude scores are disappointing. Some possible reasons for this low relationship are:

1. Faculty ratings are invalid.
2. The aptitude measures are invalid.
3. There is an increase in aptitude for each new yearly crop of graduate students, but faculty ratings do not discriminate against the "older" student.

Reason 1 does not *seem* to be the case. There does seem to be interjudge reliability, and faculty judgments are often the most important variable in labeling a graduate student's effectiveness. Reason 2 may be correct for this homogeneous sample. It may be that a certain level of aptitude is required for success in graduate school, and beyond that other factors influence effectiveness more. Reason 3 is a possibility, although we doubt that it could have much of an effect.

At any rate, it appears that an increase in the cut-off point on aptitude scores would have eliminated some of the most promising students at Hawaii, as assessed by faculty ratings.

The procedures for the Peabody study were similar to those at Hawaii. All of the active graduate students in psychology in the spring of 1966, as well as those graduate students entering in the fall of 1966, were asked to complete the PHN, and a total of 107 out of 130 did so. In May 1967 each of the 22 departmental faculty members was asked to rate each student in terms of his or her future effectiveness as a psychologist. Each student was rated as "excellent," "good," "adequate," or "not adequate," and a space was included to indicate that the faculty member did not know the student well enough to rate him or her. As at Hawaii, these faculty ratings were anonymous. Seventeen of the 22 faculty members completed the rating forms.

Of the 107 students, 60 had taken both the PHN and the GRE. These 60 were divided into two groups. The first group included 26 students, all of whom entered the doctoral program in September 1966. Some had master's degrees from other schools; some did not. These students, to varying extents, participated in the first-year core program—a set of eight courses, passing of which sufficed for passing the written preliminary exams. All of these students also participated in a research apprenticeship for which they received a grade.

The advantage of pooling these students together as a separate group lies in the fact that they all entered at the same time, had been at the school the same length of time when rated by the faculty (9 months), and to a large degree had taken the same courses. Thus it was possible to compute a grade-point average at the end of the first year for each student and to compare the students on this measure.

The other group (N = 34) was a more heterogeneous group. It was composed of doctoral and master's-level students active in the spring of 1966 plus nondoctoral aspirants who entered in the fall of 1966. GPAs were not computed for these students, but each did have—in addition to her or his faculty ratings—scores on the PHN, the GRE, and the MAT.

Let us look at the results for the 26 first-year doctoral students. Correlations with average faculty ratings of future effectiveness are included in the first column in Table 6.9. None of these correlations was significantly different from zero. The attitude correlations, however, were higher than the aptitude correlations, as was the case in the previous studies. The surprising finding was that the direction of the PHN faculty rating correlations was opposite that in the Hawaii sample. The correlation between faculty ratings and GPA in this sample was a disappointing .40 (p < .05). Correlations of GPA with the aptitude and attitude measures are presented in the remaining column in Table 6.9. None of these is significantly different from zero. By looking at Table 6.9 we can see that the aptitude measures correlate better with GPA than with faculty ratings, whereas the

TABLE 6.9 Correlations for 26 First-Year Doctoral Students in Psychology

	Rating on "Future Effectiveness" by Faculty	First Year Grade Point Average
GRE-Verbal	−.016	−.125
GRE-Quantitative	+.198	+.272
PHN-Positive-Negative	+.257	+.082
PHN-Trustworthiness	+.309	+.068
PHN-Multiplexity	−.096	−.147

attitude measures correlate better with faculty ratings than with GPA. The finding makes sense, as it is saying that attitude contributes more to a subjective and broader criterion (faculty rating) than a narrower and more objective one (grade-point average).

Let us turn to the results for the other group of Peabody students. Correlations with faculty ratings are in Table 6.10. In this sample, two measures—both attitudes—are significantly related to faculty ratings. The aptitude measures are not. Once again, the attitude indicator appears to be a better predictor than does the aptitude measure. The previous qualification still applies, however; students are selected partially on the basis of aptitude scores, and hence the range is reduced.

It is asking too much to ask the predictor to correlate with the criterion *within* the selected group. A study by Fuller (1964) indicates the shrinkage in correlation when the predictor is used to select students. He administered the GRE and MAT to 78 students entering a new doctoral program, which at that time required only a BA degree for admission. Hence, the range of aptitude scores was quite great; raw scores on MAT ranged from

TABLE 6.10 Correlations for Post-First-Year Doctoral Students With Criterion of Faculty Ratings ($N = 34$)

GRE-Verbal	+.234
GRE-Quantitative	+.182
MAT	+.212
PHN-General Favorability	+.333*
PHN-Trustworthiness	+.372*
PHN-Multiplexity	−.119

Note: *$p < .05$

24 to 94. The faculty rated the students after two years. Correlations were as follows: with GRE-V, .46; with GRE-Q, .21; with MAT, .50. But it does appear that if we take the preselected group and then ask what does a better job of relating to performance *within* the group, it is the attitude measure.

These findings are consistent with those of Robertson and Hall (n. d.), who related GRE scores to faculty ratings that were done after the student had been in the doctoral program for one year. Subjects were 73 students and 9 faculty members at the University of Florida. The correlations with faculty ratings were: GRE total score, .25 ($p < .05$); GRE-V, .22; GRE-Q, .18. Comprehensive exam scores did not correlate significantly with GRE scores.

The bewildering problem is that of inconsistent direction of the PHN-rating relationship. At the University of Hawaii, it was negative; in two samples at Peabody, it was positive. We have no ready explanation. It may lie in the type of student or in the basis for judging student quality, although these appear to be similar in the two schools. Perhaps the PHN attitudes of *faculty* at Hawaii and Peabody differ. Or it may simply be a change phenomenon. At any rate, further work, using aptitudes *and* attitudes in a multiple-prediction study is worth doing.

Summary

Three factor analyses of heterogeneous test batteries agree that there exists a coherent "attitudes-toward-people" factor. This factor encompasses measures of the following constructs: philosophies of human nature, Machiavellianism, anomie, alienation, faith in people, and suspicion. Separate correlational studies indicate that philosophies of human nature are also related to locus of control, interpersonal trust, attitudes toward desegregation, and interpretations of the motives behind government policies.

The following constructs were found to be unrelated to philosophies of human nature: attitudes toward appropriate feminine roles, authoritarianism, Reich's consciousness-level typology, and religious attitudes.

The PHN was used along with the Graduate Record Examination scores and Miller Analogies Test scores of graduate students in a study of predictors of success in graduate school. Although none of the predictors accounted for much of the variance in criterion scores, the PHN positive-negative was a better predictor than was the GRE or MAS in three different samples.

CHAPTER SEVEN

Relationship of Philosophies of Human Nature to Interpersonal Behavior

Attitudes are alive and well and gainfully employed in the sphere of action.

—HERBERT KELMAN

Philosophies of human nature have been conceptualized throughout this book as social attitudes. The preceding chapters reviewed evidence that differences in philosophies of human nature exist among groups and that meaningful relationships occur between the PHN measures and other attitudinal variables. The internal consistency, stability, and validity of the PHN scale appear to be within the acceptable limits for such paper-and-pencil measures of attitude. So far, so good.

The pragmatist might say that the measurement of attitudes is useless unless it can be shown that attitudes are related to behavior. While this statement seems to me to be too simplistic, ample evidence exists that a person's philosophy of human nature does affect his or her behavior in a number of ways; it may even be related to the likelihood of having a heart attack. The purpose of this chapter is to review relationships of the PHN scale to behavior: first, to coronary heart disease, and second, to a range of interpersonal behaviors.

Hostility and Coronary Heart Disease

As Fischman (1987) reminds us, "millions of Americans have heard of Type A behavior and know that it leads to heart attacks" (p. 42). But Type A persons are described as having a compendium of characteristics: they are competitive, impatient, distrustful, driven, time-oriented, overworked, and hostile. If a relationship exists, what is central to the link between the amorphous "Type A" syndrome and the very observable heart attack?

Over the last 15 years, a growing body of literature has identified hostility as a key "toxic" element in the relationship between Type A behavior and coronary heart disease (Dembroski & Costa, 1987; Rejeski, Leary, & Gainer, 1988). Among the most impressive of the studies on this topic is the program of research by the Duke University Behavioral Medicine Research Center's Redford Williams, John Barefoot, and their colleagues (Barefoot, Dahlstrom, & Williams, 1983; Barefoot et al., 1987; R. B. Williams, Barefoot, & Shekelle, 1985).

These researchers used the Cook-Medley Hostility scale (W. W. Cook & Medley, 1954), based on items from the Minnesota Multiphasic Personality Inventory (MMPI), as their main measure of hostility. Administering this scale to more than 1,500 patients who had atherosclerotic symptoms, the researchers discovered that those who scored high in hostility were 50% more likely to have clogged arteries than those who scored low. Barefoot et al. (1983) followed up 255 medical students who had completed the MMPI 25 years before; those who had high hostility scores as medical students were more likely to experience coronary heart disease later—in fact, five times more likely. Of the 136 medical students with scores below 14, the average score on hostility, 133 were still alive 25 years later; of the 119 at or above 14 on the hostility score, only 103 were alive. (Of the three below average on hostility who had died, the causes of death were an accident for one, cancer for a second, and myocardial infarction for a third; of the 16 deceased who were above average on hostility, 6 of the deaths were attributed to coronary heart disease or other cardiovascular problems.) Thus in a ratio of 3 dead to 16 dead, Williams concluded that highly hostile people were five times more likely to die before the age of 50.

A later study of middle-aged employees of Western Electric Company in Chicago found that high hostility scores predicted heart attacks and deaths from cardiac problems 10 years later (Shekelle, Gale, Ostfeld, & Paul, 1983), as did another study of attorneys (Blakeslee, 1989).

Just what kind of "hostility" seems to be the mediating factor in the above relationship? Mistrust and cynicism seem central. Scale items such as "Most people lie to get ahead" and "It is safer to trust nobody" distinguished between the two groups. One of the researchers even stated, "People who score high are not angry; they are just cynical" (quoted by Carey & Bruno, 1984). In his most recent book, *The Trusting Heart* (1989), R. B. Williams writes: "Cynicism is a belief system you have about people, and beliefs determine the emotions you experience."

The Philosophies of Human Nature Scale is a strong measure of this cynical hostility; R. B. Williams et al. (1985) define the latter as an attitude that stems from an absence of trust in the basic goodness of others. John Barefoot (personal communication, November 3, 1984) found correlates of -.51 and -.52 between the PHN Trustworthiness scale and the Hostility scale used in the Duke research. Correlations with PHN-Altruism were -.41 and -.43 for undergraduate males and females.

Is there a physiological explanation for the relationship between responses to a paper-and-pencil test and the development of coronary disease? The researchers propose that cynical people produce more "defense reaction" or "fight-or-flight" hormones in a greater range of situations than do the less hostile. These hormones increase the buildup of plaque on the walls of arteries, or "hardening" of the arteries, by depressing levels of HDL, the "good" cholesterol.

Thus R. B. Williams concludes that, *in general,* Type A behavior is not detrimental to one's heart—it is only the cynical component that is. What can be done about this? Can counseling be of assistance? Williams claims that "the benefits of having a "trusting heart," supported by the most modern research, have been understood and counseled by the core teachings of the world's greatest religions for over two millennia" (quoted by Poppy, 1989, p. 103). He considers the Golden Rule to be the best guide.

In *The Trusting Heart,* R. B. Williams (1989) details a 12-step behavior modification program that includes keeping a little notebook, a kind of "hostility log," in which the person records every hostile thought and deed. Eventually, says Williams, recording these events will help you stop such thoughts before they start. Others include:

1. Confessing your problem of too much hostility to others.
2. Putting yourself in others' shoes; try to understand others' "irritating" behavior from their viewpoint.
3. Meditating, or developing the "relaxation response."
4. Substituting assertiveness for aggression (i.e., concentrating on your own needs rather than focusing on the behavior of others).
5. Practicing forgiveness.
6. Learning to laugh at yourself.

PHN and Interpersonal Behavior

It has been claimed that throughout human history the methods we have used to deal with people have been the inevitable outgrowth of our beliefs about the nature of human beings (Combs, Avila, & Purkey, 1971, p. 18). But do PHN attitudes show any relationship to interpersonal behavior? Does a person who expresses a high degree of trust in his or her attitudes about people in general behave in trusting ways when placed in an ambiguous relationship with another person? Does a person who expresses more equivocal beliefs about people seek out more information about another individual before making an important decision to rely upon that person? This chapter describes tests of the relationship of PHN attitudes to interpersonal behavior. First, several diverse demonstrations of such a relationship will be reported. Then, a program of studies on the effects of trusting attitudes upon cooperative behavior in a mixed-motive situation will be reviewed. Finally, a resolution will be sought for the sometimes surprising and usually complex findings.

Student Reactions to a Specific Instructor

One of the ways in which a philosophy of human nature may be used is in making evaluations of a specific person. For example, there are often vast differences in the ways in which students in the same class evaluate a particular instructor, and these differences occur despite the fact that every member of the class may have spent the same amount of time with the instructor. We all can think of reasons for these individual differences in evaluation—for example, the student's performance in the class, the grades he or she has received, and his or her interest in continuing the course (Elliott, 1949; McKeachie & Solomon, 1958). Other less classroom-related factors may also be sources of the variable ratings given to an instructor. A student's philosophy of human nature may color his or her perception of a particular instructor; it may also affect the degree to which the student differentiates the evaluations he or she makes of two different instructors.

To determine if students' substantive beliefs on the PHN scale were related to their evaluations of a particular instructor, Wrightsman (1964a) asked two classes at Peabody College (Ns of 33 and 58) to complete anonymously a teacher-evaluation form and a short form of the PHN scale. In each class, students were divided into positive, neutral, and negative thirds on the basis of the sum of their scores on the substantive dimensions of the PHN scale. The favorableness of the evaluations given the instructor was measured by summing each student's ratings on three questions dealing with the instructor's overall teaching ability, the clarity of class-

TABLE 7.1 Views of Human Nature and Mean Evaluations of the Instructor

| View of Human Nature | | Mean Scores on Teacher-Evaluation Form | | |
(PHN Scale, Short Form)	N	Class 1	N	Class 2
Positive	11	10.7	20	10.2
Neutral	11	9.6	18	9.6
Negative	11	9.7	20	9.4

Source: Adapted from Wrightsman, 1964a, Table 4, p. 749.
Note: In Class 1, the positive group significantly differed from both the neutral and negative groups at the .05 level. In Class 2, the positive group significantly differed from the negative group at the .05 level but did not significantly differ from the neutral group.

room presentation, and the feeling between the teacher and the students. Table 7.1 indicates that in both classes the positive and negative groups on the PHN scale differed significantly in their evaluations of the instructor. That is, those who held positive views of human nature gave favorable evaluations, whereas those who held negative views of human nature gave less favorable or unfavorable evaluations.

In a second study, Wrightsman (1964c) sought to replicate this finding and to determine the influence of multiplex beliefs on teacher evaluations. During the spring quarter of 1963, 97 undergraduate education majors at George Peabody College took two psychology courses concurrently. The courses were Guidance and Adjustment, taught by Mr. X, and Measurement and Evaluation, taught by Mr. Y. The basic differences in the content of the courses are implied by their titles. Guidance and Adjustment was concerned with promoting mental health among schoolchildren; consideration was also given to the philosophy and methods of guidance in schools. Measurement and Evaluation was more concerned with the acquisition of technical and statistical skills, and its content by its very nature was more quantitative and less ambiguous.

At the end of the quarter, after each student had been exposed to each of the instructors for about 22 hours, the student anonymously completed the 84-item PHN scale and a teacher-evaluation form covering each instructor. The teacher-evaluation form consisted of 13 questions covering such matters as the instructor's competence, his breadth of knowledge, his relationships with the students, and his overall teaching ability. Students were classified into three groups for the purposes of analysis. Group I included 42 female secondary education majors; Group II, 33 female elementary education majors, and Group III, 22 men, all but two of whom were secondary education majors. Expected gender differences and group

TABLE 7.2 Correlations Between Multiplex Views of Human Nature and Extent of Differentiation Between Instructors

Group	Multiplexity Subscales Complexity	Variability
I (N = 42)	.36**	.12
II (N = 33)	.35*	.20
III (N = 22)	-.08	.39*

Source: Adapted from Wrightsman, 1964b, Table 4, p. 490.
Note: *Significantly different from zero at .05 level.
**Significantly different from zero at .01 level.

differences occurred on the PHN. For example, mean Trustworthiness scores were: Group I, 6.02; Group II, 11.57; and Group III, 0.27 (differences significant at .01 level). Students who majored in elementary education saw people as very trustworthy and altruistic.

Wrightsman expected that, as in the previous study, the students' PHN-Trustworthiness scores would be related to how favorably they rated their instructors. But this was not true for Instructor X; in his case, the correlations between Trustworthiness scores and favorable ratings were: Group I, -.02; Group II, -.14; and Group III, .09. In contrast, for Instructor Y the results for each group reflected a positive relationship between students' Trustworthiness scores and the favorability of their teacher evaluations. Yet the correlations were not high—Group I, .30; Group II, .19; Group III, .22—and only the correlation for Group I was significantly different from zero. Thus the attempt to replicate the earlier finding was only partially successful.

In the second study, it was also predicted that the evaluations by students with more multiplex views of human nature would differentiate more between Instructors X and Y than would those of students with more simplified views of human nature. Table 7.2 presents the relevant correlations. In both female groups, students who saw human nature as complex differentiated between instructors to a significantly greater degree than did students who saw human nature as relatively simple. This was not true for the men, but the male group did show significant differences on the other multiplexity subscale, Variability. Male students who saw individuals as dissimilar made distinctions between instructors to a significantly greater degree than did men who saw human nature as less variable. This was also true to a minimal extent for the women. But we must conclude that there was only slight confirmation for the expectation that general

beliefs about individual differences are related to degree of differentiation
made between specific persons.

Teacher's Attitudes and Classroom Behaviors

Do teachers reflect their philosophies of human nature by the ways in
which they behave in the classroom? A different sort of teacher-student
interaction was studied by Hopkins (1973), who set forth to determine the
relationship of teachers' philosophies of human nature to the nonverbal-
communication patterns of students and teachers. Hopkins administered
the PHN scale to 99 elementary school teachers and then selected those
with the most extreme positive-negative scores or the most extreme scores
on individual substantive subscales. Hopkins observed nonverbal classroom communication between these teachers and their students three
times, using Galloway's Analysis of Nonverbal Communication (Galloway, 1962, 1966, 1970). (Hopkins did not indicate the length of the observation periods.) Galloway's observation schedule is primarily concerned
with nonverbal acts (gestures, postures, facial expressions, tone or quality
of voice, and physical contact) that maximize or minimize the child's freedom to respond.

Hopkins hypothesized that the nonverbal communications of teachers
with favorable beliefs about human nature would more often be of the
indirect type—that is, they would maximize students' opportunities for
free interaction. For each measure, his hypothesis was confirmed. For example, 7 of the 10 teachers with the highest positive-negative scores
showed indirect nonverbal-communication patterns, while only 1 of the
10 teachers most negative in PHN score showed this indirect type of nonverbal communication (the $\chi^2 = 7.66, p < .05$). If teachers are divided into
groups on the basis of each of the substantive PHN subscales, similar differences occur. For example, 9 of the 10 highest on the Trustworthiness
score used indirect communication, while only 1 of the 10 with the lowest
scores on the Trustworthiness scale use indirect procedures ($\chi^2 = 13.00$,
$p < .05$).

Hopkins also related teachers' PHN scores to the nonverbal-communication patterns of their pupils. Teachers' PHN scores were ranked from
highest to lowest and were correlated (using Spearman's rho) with the
receptivity or inattention of students, as classified by observing students'
eye contact, facial involvement, and attitudes of listening and interest. Of
the 79 teachers tested, only the 10 who scored highest and the 10 who

scored lowest on the PHN scales were used for these analyses. Correlations with pupils' nonverbal-communication patterns were extremely high, which is very unusual for the relationship of one person's attitude to other people's behaviors. The rhos were as follows: positive-negative summated score, .80; Trustworthiness, .76; Altruism, .79; Strength of Will and Rationality, .74; and Independence, .74. How much the use of the extreme 25% of the sample inflates these correlations is unknown and indeterminate; raw data are reported only for the extreme groups and not for the remaining 59 subjects.

As it stands, Hopkins' (1973) study indicates that teachers with favorable beliefs about human nature show nonverbal communication patterns that reflect a desire to permit the open expression of ideas in the classroom, whereas teachers with negative beliefs are more directive and restrictive in their nonverbal communications. Beyond this, the responses of children are highly related to their teacher's attitudes. All of this confirms the speculations of educational philosophers who have told us that a teacher's goals, actions, and judgments are determined by his or her beliefs about human nature. Likewise, proponents of the importance of nonverbal communication, such as Mehrabian (1967), conclude that our real attitudes are often communicated nonverbally, and if the nonverbal message contradicts the verbal one, others tend to believe the nonverbal message. Yet there are some serious weaknesses in Hopkins' study. The use of only the teachers with extreme attitudes limits the generalizability of results and may inflate the relationships. The procedures used in Galloway's Analysis of Nonverbal Communication are not detailed and cannot be followed simply by reading Hopkins' descriptions. Interobserver reliabilities for Hopkins' observations are weak, ranging from .43 to .55. Although the findings are extremely encouraging, more research is necessary before we can accept the general conclusion that a teacher's nonverbal communication is related to his or her philosophy of human nature.

Other Judgments About Specific Persons

Other explorations of the effect of general PHN attitudes upon evaluations of specific individuals were done by Ashcraft (1963) and Nottingham (1969). Ashcraft concentrated her study on the two multiplexity subscales of the PHN. She predicted that (1) individuals whose attitudes indicated a belief in the variability of human nature would reveal greater diversity in their ratings of specific people, and (2) people whose attitudes reflected a belief in the complexity of human nature would demonstrate their beliefs in the ways in which they rated specific people in actual situations. To look at the relationships between behavior and PHN-Variability, she used two procedures focusing on ratings of specific people. First, subjects watched a 12-minute film and then rated the persons in the film on a 9-trait bipolar-rating scale drawn from the factors on the Guilford-Zimmerman Temperament Survey (Guilford & Zimmerman, 1955). (The film presented five people in a family-conflict situation, each reflecting a different temperament. Subjects rated each individual, and the total variance of scores over the five stimulus persons was considered the interindividual-variability-rating score.)

Then, the subjects completed a group form of George Kelly's Role Construct Repertory Test (RCRT) (Kelly, 1955; see also Bieri, 1955). In this test, the respondent lists 12 people in his or her social environment who fit role titles such as "a friend who is popular with others," "your husband or wife or your closest friend of the opposite sex," and "an acquaintance you find hard to understand." In succession, the subject considers different sets of three of these people and, for each set, decides upon a way that two of the individuals are alike and different from the third. For each triad, a construct is thus created. Then, the subject is instructed to place check marks in a grid under the names of those persons who he or she sees as possessing each construct. This procedure yields a matrix of check patterns that represents how the subject perceives and differentiates a group of persons holding different roles. From this procedure a score can be derived that reflects the degree to which the subject has differentiated among people.

Both of Ashcraft's (1963) procedures appear to be reasonable measures of the extent of differentiation that people make in their judgments of specific individuals. Yet their relationships with the PHN-Variability subscale scores were of zero order (.04 for the rating of film characters and .09 for the RCRT score). In further analyses, subjects were divided into three groups on the bases of PHN-Variability scores, and their mean scores on the measures of judgments of specific persons were compared. No significant differences emerged. The correlation between the two specific persons measures was only .07. (These results were based on responses of 100 women who completed the PHN during freshman orientation and the other instruments four months later.)

Ashcraft also sought measures that would reflect the subjects' reactions to the possible complexity of specific individuals and chose two of these measures for comparisons with subjects' responses to the

PHN-Complexity subscale. The first measure was a "Test for Advising Others." In this test, the respondent was given small amounts of information about four hypothetical persons and was asked to list each piece of additional information that would be needed before advising each person in a particular situation. The total number of pieces of information solicited by the subject was considered the score on this measure of "specific complexity."

The second measure was an adaptation of the Role Construct Repertory Test devised by Mayo (1959). Here, as on the Bieri (1955) variation of the RCRT, the subject uses role titles suggested by the experimenter and is asked to compare and contrast people in his or her own environments on constructs of his or her own choosing. The subject reports ways in which Persons #1 and #2 think, feel, or act alike and differently from Person #3. Each of the three-person triads is compared, and the total score is the number of constructs used by the subject to describe the individuals. This test had a time limit of 2½ minutes for each comparison. Mayo reports that the test's results are not related to verbal fluency and that the interjudge reliability of its scoring is .94.

Again, these two procedures would seem to be measuring subjects' orientations regarding the amount of complexity present in specific individuals. Yet the correlations of these measures with PHN-Complexity subscale scores were .08 for the Test of Advising Others and .24 for the Mayo measure of role constructs. Although the latter correlation is significantly different from zero at the .05 level, the PHN-Complexity score accounts for no sizable variance in either specific-persons measure.

The Mayo measure correlated only .38 with the Test of Advising Others, indicating little agreement between the two measures of perceptions of degree of complexity in specific others. However, the significant relationship between the number of constructs employed in answering the Mayo RCRT and the responses to the PHN-Complexity subscale indicates that subjects who regard people in general as complex and difficult to understand will also use a more flexible or varied construct system in judging people whom they know well. That is, friends or relatives cannot be described in one or two all-encompassing terms; rather, they may fit into a variety of descriptions, some conflicting. At the other end of the continuum are the respondents who believe that most people can be forced into particular descriptive slots and can be categorized as "good" or "bad," "friendly" or "unfriendly," and so forth. In this respect, then, Ashcraft's (1963) prediction is supported in that we can assess attitudes in the abstract and then apply these attitudes to predict how subjects will react when asked to rate particular individuals. But the relationship is very weak.

In another study, Nottingham (1969, 1970) also sought indications that people's general philosophies of human nature would influence their information-seeking behavior. But he did not view the attitude as a continuum with linearly operating influences; rather, he proposed that persons with extreme assumptions about human nature (regardless of whether they were positive or negative) would operate differently from those with moderate or neutral attitudes. As Nottingham (1970) states, "It would seem that individuals with moderate attitudes have a less firmly established, a more ambivalent, construct system (i.e., implicit theory of people) for dealing with the world, whereas individuals at the two extremes have already decided what most people are like even before dealing with them" (p. 409). For example, if asked to make a decision about another person, persons with moderate attitudes might seek additional data before making a judgment, whereas those with extreme attitudes would make use of their prevailing attitudinal system—that is, they would seek less additional information.

Hence, Nottingham related PHN attitudes (along with other measures) to information-seeking behavior, with the expectation that those persons with moderate attitudes would be the ones to seek more information before making a decision. The measure of information seeking used was an adaptation of a procedure initiated by Nidorf and Crockett (1964) in their study of impression information. The subjects were provided with three booklets, each of which was titled with a feminine first name and contained 46 pieces of information presented in a first-person format. Each piece of information was on a separate page. Subjects were interviewed individually and were asked to decide how trustworthy each stimulus person was by using information from the booklet. (The specific task for the subject was to decide whether the stimulus person was trustworthy enough to babysit his or her child for a weekend.) Subjects were instructed to tear off each sheet, one at a time, and read it—up to the point at which they had decided that they had enough information to make a decision.

The three booklets differed in regard to the trustworthiness of the stimulus person described. One booklet contained only negative self-descriptive statements, indicating an untrustworthy individual, whereas a second booklet contained only positive statements, implying that the stimulus person was a trustworthy person. The third booklet contained a mixture of positive and negative self-descriptive statements, presenting an ambiguous picture of the stimulus person's trustworthiness.

Subjects were 54 undergraduate women at Peabody College. They were divided into positive-extreme, negative-extreme, or moderate (that is, neutral) groups on the basis of their own PHN-Trustworthiness scores. Contrary to Nottingham's (1970) expectations, subjects with moderate attitudes on the PHN scale did not seek out more information than did subjects with extreme attitudes; there were no significant differences among the three groups. Subjects did, however, seek more information about the stimulus person described by a mixture of positive and negative statements than they did about the stimulus persons described by uniformly positive or uniformly negative statements, and this difference was statistically significant ($F = 5.41$, $df = 2/108$, $p < .01$). In addition, there was a tendency for subjects to seek less information before making negative evaluations of others than they did before making positive judgments. Nottingham (1970) concludes that this finding is to be expected if one considers folk psychology; he states, "Casual observation will document that, in their dealings with others, many individuals tend to place unequal valence on negative information when evaluating people" (p. 410). In seeking interpretations of such findings, Crowdus (1969) concluded (1) that, since good characteristics and behaviors are usually expected, negative decisions are more likely to be noted, and (2) that the costs to the individual for being wrong when he or she makes a negative evaluation are less than those for expecting positive behavior when, in fact, the behavior is negative.

The most substantial finding of Nottingham's (1970) study was a serendipitous one. When Nottingham drew potential subjects with positive, neutral, and negative Trustworthiness scores, his intention was to obtain 18 subjects from each group for his study. Potential subjects were telephoned and asked to participate in a "study of college student attitudes." Only four potential subjects refused to participate, and all had negative PHN-Trustworthiness scores. On the basis of this unexpected turn of events, Nottingham decided to mail questionnaires to all the actual subjects after they had participated in the experiment. The questionnaire asked for information about reasons for participation in the study. Nottingham then tabulated the percentage of subjects in each group who returned this postexperimental questionnaire through the campus mail. Of 18 subjects in each group, only 4 (or 22%) failed to return the questionnaire in both the positive and neutral groups, in contrast to 12 (or 67%) in the negative-trustworthiness group. When analyzed by a chi-square test, the results produced a statistically significant value ($\chi^2 = 8.88$, $df = 2$, $p < .05$). People who believe that others are dishonest, untrustworthy, and irresponsible are more likely to refuse requests for information about their research participation, indicating that our conclusions drawn from studies using volunteer samples may be overly weighted in the direction of people with favorable beliefs about human nature. This variable may be added to Rosenthal and Rosnow's (1969) lists of characteristics that differentiate between volunteer subjects and those who have an opportunity to volunteer and choose not to do so. According to this list, volunteers seem to have higher educational level, superior occupational status, more need for approval, greater intelligence, and less authoritarian tendencies.

Peer Ratings and Philosophies of Human Nature

Do people like you any more if your philosophy of human nature is quite positive? Wrightsman, Richard, and Noble (1966) studied the sociometric choices of 25 guidance counselors who completed a 7-week institute. On their first day they completed a variety of scales, including the PHN scale. At the end of their institute they ranked the other counselors on a series of sociometric questions, such as "Who would you prefer as your own counselor?" "Who is technically most proficient?" "The most intelligent?" "The best liked?" Enrollees who believed that people in general possess strength of will and rationality were preferred as counselors $(r = .60)$, were best liked $(r = .44)$, were considered the best counselors with regard to technical skills $(r = .35)$, and were thought to have the most personal warmth $(r = .34)$. Counselors who believed that people are capable of self-understanding and self-improvement were seen by their peers as more effective in interpersonal relationships, including counseling.

Additional evidence that the effectiveness of counselors is related to their assumptions about human nature comes from a dissertation project by Ligon (1970), who used tape recordings of counseling sessions as the raw material for judging the skills of counselors in training. The degree of facilitative behavior exhibited by the counselor was rated according to the Carkuff-Truax scales for measuring empathy, positive regard, genuineness, and depth of the client's self-exploration. There were modest correlations between counselors' PHN scores and their effectiveness; for example Trustworthiness correlated .33 $(p < .05)$ with positive regard, .22 with empathy, and .18 with genuineness. Yet there was no relationship between degree of counselor's trust and the client's self-exploration. Strength of Will and Rationality scores correlated from .26 to .32 with each of the counselor-effectiveness scores. In contrast, some tendency emerged for Complexity scores to be negatively related to the effectiveness of the counselors; that is, those with less complex beliefs were rated as more genuine and empathic and developed more self-exploration in their clients.

Effects of Experimenters' Philosophies of Human Nature Upon Experimental Outcomes

The most demonstrable effect of a person's philosophy of human nature upon his or her behavior may be an interactive one; Kennedy, Cook, and Brewer (1969) tested this suggestion by studying the role of the experimenter's gender, his or her philosophy of human nature, and his or her expectations about the outcome of an experiment in determining the actual experimental outcome. Four men and 4 women were selected from among 75 graduate students to serve as experimenters in a verbal-conditioning experiment. Two of the men and 2 of the women had extremely positive PHN scores, whereas the other 4 students had extremely negative scores.

Each experimenter was given an expectation for the outcome of the project. Before starting, each was told by the principal investigator that a similar verbal-conditioning experiment conducted the quarter before had led to extremely variable rates of conditioning. But the researchers now could explain the causes; the key factor was the subjects' attitudes. Subjects who were "deterministically oriented" and thus skeptical, would typically not be conditionable while humanistically oriented subjects would be. The student-experimenters were told that the attitudes of their subjects were known and that each experimenter-pair would be assigned five "conditioners" and five "nonconditioners." (Neither the attitudes nor the "conditionability" of the subjects had actually been determined.) Experimenters then led subjects through a standard Tajfel-type conditioning task.

Results indicated that, for seven of the eight experimenters, subjects who were expected to condition had higher mean performance rates than did those not expected to condition. (This difference was significant at the .05 level.) The experimenter's philosophy of human nature did not directly affect subjects' conditioning rates; that is, when a three-way analysis of variance was done on subjects' conditioning performances, there was no significant main effect for PHN scores. But there was a significant interaction between PHN and gender (F = 9.10, df = 1, p < .05). Less conditioning occurred in subjects who had negative-PHN male experimenters than in subjects with positive-PHN male experimenters or negative-PHN female experimenters.

Philosophies of Human Nature and Attitude Change

Chapter 6 described the analysis of a heterogeneous test battery of aptitude, attitude, and personality measures used by Stuart W. Cook (1964) in order to identify potential subjects for an attitude-change project. S. W. Cook's goal was to identify white women with extreme antiblack attitudes. From June 1961 through August 1964, 23 subjects participated, for one month each, in Cook's attitude-change project. They qualified for participation by giving responses that were one or more standard deviations more negative than the mean on several racial-attitude measures. During the month's part-time job, they worked with another white woman and an African-American woman on a group-management task on which the three individuals had to cooperate and interact closely. The prejudiced subjects were not aware that the true purpose of this project was to try to change their racial attitudes; neither did they know that the other two participants were actually confederates of the experimenter. (For further details of the procedures, see S. W. Cook, 1964, 1970, 1971, or Wrightsman, 1972, Chapter 11).

Somewhere between one and nine months after completing the part-time job, each prejudiced subject retook the test battery. Ten of the 23 subjects changed their responses on the various prejudice measures to significantly less negative or more positive attitudes toward African-Americans. The other 13 participants in the attitude-change project showed either essentially the same attitudes as before or even more extreme antiblack attitudes.

What distinguishes between these two classes of subjects? Both were exposed to the same type of interaction; within the limits available, both were subjected to the same conversations, the same group activities, and the same rewards for participation. To find explanations, S. W. Cook and Wrightsman (1967) sought intrapersonal differences between the 10 "changers" and the 13 "nonchangers"—that is, intrapersonal characteristics that would make a prejudiced white person more susceptible to change under the cross-section of Cook's group project. Two constructs were offered as explanations: "self-concept" and "assumptions about people in general." For example, a participant who was dissatisfied with her

TABLE 7.3 A Comparison of Factor Scores of Subjects Whose Attitudes Changed Favorably Versus Subjects Whose Attitudes Did Not Change Favorably

| | | Mean Factor Scores | | |
| | | *Positive Changers* *(N = 10)* | *Non- Changers* *(N = 13)* | *p-Value of Difference Between Means* |
Factor No.	*Factor Title*			
1	Rigidity	+3.23	+3.72	NS
2	Hostility and Anxiety	+1.13	+2.26	NS
3	Antiblack Attitudes	+7.75	+7.27	NS
4	Aptitudes	-1.26	-2.82	NS
5	Positive Attitudes Toward People	+3.68	-4.46	.01
6	Sociability	-0.58	+0.06	NS
7	Tolerance for Unpleasantness	-0.54	+0.95	.025
8	Negativism About Self	+0.46	-1.17	.025
9	Attitudes Toward Teaching	+0.95	+0.08	NS
10	Positive Response Set	+1.52	+0.94	NS
11	Residual	+0.72	+1.27	NS

Source: Adapted from Wrightsman & Cook, 1965, Table 3, p. 10.
Note: NS = Nonsignificant difference

self-concept would be more responsive to such an intervention than would someone who was happy or complacent about her present state of being. Thus a negative self-concept may facilitate or instigate change. But if change is to take place, the prejudiced white person must also be willing to listen to and trust other people, who serve as the vehicles for transmitting change in this project. That is, if a prejudiced young woman holds favorable assumptions about other people, she will accept what others say or do as genuine, correct, and well advised. But if she has unfavorable assumptions about people in general—if she disparages or distrusts what others say and do—she is not likely to be influenced by communications aimed at her. Even a very negative self-concept will not generate attitude change if the recipient distrusts those who attempt to change deeply held attitudes.

To test these speculations, the 10 subjects who became more favorable in their racial attitudes were compared with the 13 subjects who did not. Responses to the initial 12-hour battery of tests were used to compare these two groups (S. W. Cook & Wrightsman, 1967; Wrightsman & Cook, 1965). From this battery, 78 different measures were factor analyzed to determine which measures clustered together or were measuring the same general constructs. Eleven factors emerged from this procedure; they are listed in Table 7.3.

The factors together cover a wide range of intrapersonal characteristics; there are personality traits (Factors 1, 2, 6, 7, and 8), racial attitudes (Factor 3), and other attitudes (Factors 5 and 9). There is also a factor (Factor 4) representing the aptitude and ability measures used in the battery.

By converting raw scores to standard scores and multiplying these by the factor loadings for the test, we can determine composite scores for each of the 11 factors, and the two groups can be compared on each factor (see Table 7.3). Do positive changers, as a group, differ significantly from nonchangers in average score on any of the factors? First of all, let us note some of the factors on which there is no difference in initial score between the positive changers and the nonchangers. For example, those prejudiced whites whose attitudes changed after the group project were no more (or no less) rigid than were the prejudiced participants whose attitudes did not change (Factor 1). They were no more or no less hostile or anxious than were the nonchangers (Factor 2). Surprisingly, their initial antiblack attitudes were no less intense or extreme than those of the nonchangers. Other factors on which the positive changers and nonchangers did not differ in average score are indicated by the "NS" (nonsignificant) in Table 7.3.

Note in Table 7.3 that for each of three factors (Factors 5, 7, and 8) there is a significant p-value indicated. For example, for Factor 5, Positive Attitudes Toward People, the average scores for the two groups were significantly different at the .01 level. The significance level for the other two (Factors 7 and 8) is not as large, but in each case the level of significance is great enough to permit a conclusion that the two groups are truly different in average score. Let us consider each of these factors in turn.

FACTOR 5. POSITIVE ATTITUDES TOWARD PEOPLE

This factor includes high loadings from the following measures: Philosophies of Human Nature Scale, Machiavellianism Scale (negative loading), Anomie Scale (negative loading), Faith-in-People Scale, and Edwards' Social Desirability Scale. Thus Factor 5 definitely represents an accumulation of variables that measure attitudes toward people in general. One aspect of *anomie,* for example, is a belief that other people are uninterested and unsympathetic; the Machiavellianism Scale communicates a cynical belief about others. Note that in Table 7.3 the mean of the positive changers was 3.68, or a positive value, whereas the mean of the nonchangers was -4.46, indicating that as a group the nonchangers did *not* see human nature as good, trustworthy, and so forth. In fact, 11 of the 13 non-changers were below the neutral point on this factor, while only 2 of the positive changers were below neutral (and then only barely). These findings give strong confirmation for one part of our speculations—that is, that subjects who enter an interracial contact experience with cynical, distrusting attitudes toward human nature are *unlikely to come out of it with any more favorable interracial attitudes.*

A replication of this analysis was carried out by Betty Penn (personal communication, July 1, 1971), by analyzing 19 subjects who participated in the Cook attitude-change project after the above analysis was done. Nine of these subjects had significantly less prejudiced attitudes after participation in the interracial project, while the other 10 did not. When Penn compared the initial attitudes of these two groups, she found that the mean PHN-positive-negative score for the changers was 18.44, while the mean score for the nonchangers was 10.60, a difference consistent with the earlier findings but not statistically significant.

FACTOR 7. TOLERANCE FOR UNPLEASANTNESS

This factor is not a clear one because the measures contributing to it do not seem to be conceptually similar. A positive score on this factor appears to mean that its possessor has little need for social approval and is rather escapist in his or her thought patterns. Table 7.3 points out that this description fits the nonchangers more than it does the positive changers. This result is in line with our expectations, but stronger confirmation comes from Factor 8.

FACTOR 8. NEGATIVISM ABOUT SELF

A subject with a score above the mean on Factor 8 is dissatisfied with her self-concept. (The measures of this factor are listed in Table 6.1.) There is a relatively large discrepancy between the way she is and the way she would like to be. Additionally, tests loading on Factor 8 indicate that a subject scoring above the mean on this factor is pessimistic about her personal future and is dependent upon others. It seems appropriate to call this factor Negativism About Self. Consideration of Table 7.3 reflects that the positive changers are, as a group, above the mean on this factor, while the nonchangers lack this negativism toward themselves. Thus the second aspect of the speculation about intrapersonal differences is confirmed. Rokeach and Cochrane's (1972) efforts to induce self-dissatisfaction over conflicts in one's value-attitude system are consistent with these findings, as Rokeach finds that such dissatisfaction mediates changes in attitudes and behavior.

At this point, then, we have evidence that a situation that is carefully designed to bring about a reduction in the amount of prejudice will succeed only in some cases. Two determinants of the likelihood of success reside within the participants themselves—their self-evaluation and their expectations about other people. Positive assumptions about human nature alone, however, are not sufficient to bring about behavior change.

Attitudes and Behavior in a Mixed-Motive Game

Our most extended search for relationships between PHN attitudes and behavior involved cooperative and trusting behaviors in a mixed-motive game situation. Our initial thought was that a subject's beliefs about human nature should be closely related to his or her decision to trust or distrust the other participant in a Prisoner's Dilemma Game or in another mixed-motive situation. After conducting seven studies, considering the nature of the situational factors, and reading Christie and Geis's (1970) analysis, we are much less sure.

The Prisoner's Dilemma Game (PD), the most frequently studied mixed-motive game, requires that each of two participants independently choose between two payoffs. The actual payoff that each participant receives is determined by the choices of both. Usually one choice (called the "competitive choice") enables the subject to maximize personal gain, but if the other subject also chooses to maximize his or her *own* gain, both subjects lose. By making the other choice (called the "cooperative choice") the subject can gain a moderate amount—*if* the other participant also chooses to cooperate. But if the first person chooses to cooperate while the second participant chooses to compete, the competer wins a great deal and the cooperator loses. (Review of research on mixed-motive games may be found in Gallo & McClintock [1965], Rapoport & Chammah [1965], Swingle [1970], and Wrightsman, O'Connor, & Baker [1972].)

In a series of seven studies, PHN attitudes were related to behavior in mixed-motive games. Since these studies have been brought together elsewhere (by Wrightsman, O'Connor, & Baker, 1972) and since their results soon assume a monotonous regularity, they will only be summarized here.

1. Wrightsman (1966) had participants play a two-trial quasi-Prisoner's Dilemma Game, in which the possible payoffs on each trial ranged from zero to six dollars. Each subject chose first on the first trial, after being told that the other participant would be informed of her choice before having to choose. On the basis of her first choice *and* the reasons that she gave for it, each subject was classified as trusting ($N = 27$), distrusting ($N = 19$), or neither ($N = 37$). In Experiment 1, trusting subjects had significantly higher scores on PHN Trustworthiness ($p < .05$), Altruism ($p < 0.5$), and Independence subscales ($p < 0.5$) than did the other two groups. The distrusting group had the most negative PHN scores. In Experiment 2, in which a somewhat different procedure was used, attitude-behavior relationships were replicated but to a less significant degree. Second-trial behavior was also compared to PHN scores. If, on the second trial, the subject found that the other participant had chosen blue (the cooperative response), she was forced to choose between acting in a trustworthy way (by also choosing blue and splitting six dollars between them) and acting in an untrustworthy way (by choosing red and taking the six dollars herself). The subject's PHN attitudes had no significant influence on her choice to act in a trustworthy or untrustworthy way on this second trial.

2. Uejio and Wrightsman (1967) paid 80 undergraduate women at the University of Hawaii to participate in a 50-trial Prisoner's Dilemma Game. Half of the subjects were Caucasians; the others were Japanese-Americans. As in the previous study, the subjects did not see the other participant, but half were told that the other was Japanese-American and half were told that she was Caucasian. The choices of the other player were programmed by the experimenter so that, regardless of what each subject did, the other player chose cooperatively on three-fourths of the trials. The number of cooperative choices that the subject made was compared with her previously obtained scores on a variety of attitude measures, including the PHN subscales. Table 7.4 presents these correlations.

Column 1 of Table 7.4 indicates that when Caucasians played against other Caucasians there were significant relationships between their PHN scores and their degree of cooperation. Similarly, when Japanese-Americans played against Caucasians the expected relationship emerged. But when Caucasians played against Japanese-Americans, there was no relationship between the attitudes and their degree of cooperation. Even more disturbing is the finding that when Japanese-Americans played against other Japanese-Americans there were *negative* relationships between

TABLE 7.4 Product-Moment Correlations Between Attitudes and Extent of Cooperation in the Game by Caucasian (C) and Japanese (J) Players

Attitude Measure	C Versus C	C Versus J	J Versus C	J Versus J	All C	All J	All Versus Same Group	All Versus Diff. Group	All Ss
PHN-Positive-Negative Summation	.46*	-.10	.44*	-.30	.23	.03	.13	.15	.13
PHN-Trustworthiness	.35	-.01	.45*	-.32	.21	.04	.08	.19	.13
PHN-Strength of Will and Rationality	.42*	-.01	.16	-.04	.29*	.02	.25	.07	.16
PHN-Altruism	.56**	.05	.47*	-.22	.23*	.09	.20	.11	.19*
PHN-Independence	.21	-.25	.34	-.38*	.01	-.07	-.09	.01	-.05
PHN-Variability	-.14	.38*	-.34	.09	.09	-.12	-.04	.12	-.03
Political Cynicism	-.37	.01	-.09	.55**	-.18	.23	.02	-.06	-.01
Faith in Human Nature	.19	-.20	.46*	-.15	.06	.12	.10	.10	.08
Machiavellianism	-.53**	.29	-.13	.09	-.18	.03	-.25	.10	-.10

Source: Adapted from Uejio & Wrightsman, 1967, Table 2, p. 569.
Note: *p = .05; **p = .01.

trusting attitudes and cooperative behaviors. The expected relationships did not generalize cross-culturally.

3. Ward (1968) noted that, conceptually, PHN attitudes should be more highly related to the subject's *expectations* about the choices of the other player than to her own choices. An attitude construct that should better predict the subject's own choices would be indexed by her *own* self-reported trustworthiness, altruism, and so forth. Ward constructed a measure of this self-attitude, called the "self-PHN," by changing the stems of PHN items from "most people" or "the average person" to "I."

Not surprisingly, respondents' self-PHN scores were much more favorable than were their PHN scores. For 89 subjects tested on the self-PHN, means, with *SD*s in parentheses, were: Trustworthiness, 23.30 (13.40); Strength of Will and Rationality, 17.90 (10.16); Altruism, 21.25 (11.55); Independence, 16.51 (11.25); Complexity, 3.68 (13.32); Variability, 9.22 (11.66). Interestingly, subjects rated themselves highest in trustworthiness. In contrast to their beliefs about other people, their views of their own degrees of strength of will and rationality are not so favorable as are their views on trustworthiness and altruism.

Ward administered both forms of the PHN scale to 36 male subjects who later played a 30-trial PD game. Table 7.5 shows the correlations between self-PHN and PHN scores. On each trial, subjects recorded on a tally sheet what they planned to choose and what they expected the other player to choose. Four correlations were obtained to determine if Ward's conceptualization had led to higher correlations than those that had been previously found. As Ward predicted, the correlation between the self-PHN and the number of cooperative choices made by the subject (.17) was higher than that between the self-PHN and the number of cooperative choices that subject expected the other player to make (−.08). The difference was not significant, however, and each correlation produced a disappointingly low relationship between attitude and behavior. Contrary to expectation, the correlation between PHN and the number of cooperative choices expected of the other player (−.06) was not significantly greater than the correlation between self-PHN and the number of cooperative choices by the subject (−.23). Both were negative in direction, and neither was significantly different from zero. Even though Ward found a slight degree of confirmation for her expectations, her findings did not show a solid relationship between any paper-and-pencil measure and any game-related behavior. The two paper-and-pencil measures correlated .37 with each other ($p < .05$), and the number of cooperative choices

TABLE 7.5 Correlations Between PHN and Self-PHN Subscales

		Self-PHN Subscales				
Regular PHN Subscales	*Trust-worthy*	*Strength of Will & Rationality*	*Altruism*	*Indepen-dence*	*Complexity*	*Variability*
Trustworthiness	.471	.250	.328	.137	−.021	−.131
Strength of Will and Rationality		.490	.146	.053	−.163	−.087
Altruism			.150	.032	−.013	−.071
Independence				.016	−.025	−.220
Complexity					.335	.173
Variability						.443

Note: N = 87 undergraduates at Peabody College

expected from the other player correlated .35 ($p < .05$) with the subject's cooperativeness.

4. Wrightsman et al. (1967) used 80 female undergraduates in a 30-trial PD game in which two characteristics of the other player—race and strategy of choice—were varied. Each subject thought she was playing against either a black woman or a white woman. Depending upon her experimental condition, she soon found that the other player's choices were cooperative on 90% of the trials, were competitive on 90% of the trials, or matched her choice on every trial. (In a fourth condition, subjects played all 30 trials without any feedback about the other person's choices.) The

TABLE 7.6 Correlates of Extent of Cooperation with Attitudes and with Ratings Given the Other Player

	Experimental Condition				All Subjects Combined
Attitude Measure	*90% Coop.*	*90% Comp.*	*Matching*	*No Info.*	
Trustworthiness of Human Nature (PHN Scale)	.151	.298	−.090	−.111	.003
Altruism of Human Nature (PHN Scale)	.254	.409*	.015	−.028	.093
Attitude Toward School Segregation (Komorita)	.278	.251	−.466	.541*	.125

Source: Adapted from Wrightsman, Davis, Lucker, et al., 1967.
Notes: N per condition = 20 and combined N = 80 for Rows 1 and 2; for Row 3, only the Ss with black partners were used, N per condition = 10 and combined N = 40.
*Significantly different from .00 at .05 level.

TABLE 7.7 Correlations Between PHN Subscale Scores and Extent of Cooperation

	Strategy Condition		
PHN Subscale	*90% Coop.*	*90% Comp.*	*Matching*
Trustworthiness	-.06	.19	.28
Strength of Will and Rationality	-.12	.33	.23
Altruism	.09	.07	.35*
Independence	-.05	-.03	.02
Positive-Negative Score (sum of above four subscales)	.01	.16	.31

Source: Adapted from Wrightsman, Bruininks, Lucker, & Anderson, 1972.
Note: All subjects completed the PHN scale: of the 48 in each strategy condition PHN-scale scores were available for 32 in the 90%-cooperative condition, 30 in the 90%-competitive condition, and 33 in the matching condition
*Significantly different from zero at .05 level.

number of cooperative choices made by each subject was compared to her PHN score. Table 7.6 indicates that relationships between attitudes and degree of cooperation are limited. Of eight PHN-cooperation correlations, only one is significantly different from zero.

5. A similar study (Wrightsman, Bruininks, Lucker, & Anderson, 1972) used 72 freshmen and 72 seniors, all women, in a 30-trial game employing one of three strategy-of-other conditions (90% cooperative, 90% competitive, or matching). Correlations of degree of cooperation with PHN attitudes are generally of zero order, as Table 7.7 indicates. Only one of the 12 subscale correlations was statistically significant.

6. Another 30-trial game in the same series (Wrightsman, Baxter, Nelson, & Bilsky, 1969) varied the other player's strategy and information given to the subject about the other player's personality. Strategy conditions were the same as in the two previous studies. Additionally, each subject was led to believe that the personality of the other participant (another woman) was either very cooperative or very competitive. All conditions were collapsed together, however, when correlations with paper-and-pencil measures were determined. Table 7.8 presents these, including other measures of Attitudes Toward People besides the PHN. The relationships are overwhelmingly nonexistent.

7. Baxter's (1973b) study looked at the effect of the other person's race and personality upon cooperation in a 30-trial game. All 90 subjects found that the other participant chose cooperatively on 90% of the trials. As Table 7.9 shows, manifestations of any significant relationship between PHN scores and various indications of cooperation were scarce. In addi-

TABLE 7.8 Correlations Between Attitude and Personality Measures and Number of Cooperative Responses

| Measure | Correlation with Extent of Cooperation | | | |
	Total Trials	On First 10 Trials	On Second 10 Trials	On Third 10 Trials
California F Scale	-.092	-.176	-.054	-.054
Machiavellianism	-.028	.010	-.038	-.037
Risk Avoidance	.118	.037	.092	.165
Social Desirability				
(Marlowe-Crowne)	-.255*	-.205	-.261*	-.227*
PHN:				
Trustworthiness	-.095	-.159	-.057	-.069
Strength of Will				
and Rationality	-.079	-.065	-.074	-.075
Altruism	.034	-.070	.067	.062
Independence	-.072	-.093	-.051	-.062
Complexity	-.026	.069	-.048	-.060
Variability	-.043	-.086	-.002	-.041
Self PHN:				
Trustworthiness	-.172	-.185	-.141	-.155
Strength of Will				
and Rationality	-.090	-.074	-.064	-.102
Altruism	-.176	-.105	-.204	-.158
Independence	.028	.033	.041	.007
Complexity	.035	-.006	.081	.014
Variability	.094	-.032	.095	.152
Personal Orientation Inventory:				
Nature of Man	-.166	-.078	-.159	-.191
Synergy	-.149	-.110	-.195	-.104
Acceptance of Aggression	.036	.005	.058	.029

Source: Adapted from Wrightsman, Baxter, Nelson, & Bilsky, 1969.
Notes: $N = 89$
*$p < .05$.

tion to the number of cooperative choices on total trials, such indications as cooperation on the first trial, on the first 2 trials, and on the first 10 trials, as well as Rapoport's (1966) stochastic variables (measures of cooperation), were also used, but no relationship emerged.

A related study is Richman's (1971), in which 194 male and 204 female subjects participated in three situations that required the making of cooperative or competitive choices. These included a two-trial variation of the PD game similar to the one in Wrightsman's (1966) study, a PD game designed to maximize cooperative play, and a PD game designed to min-

TABLE 7.9 Correlations Between PHN Subscale Score and Various Measures of Cooperation

PHN Subscale	Total No. Choices	Coop. on Trial 1	Coop. on Trials 1-2	Coop. on Trials 1-10	Stochastic Variables			
					Trust-worthiness	Forgiveness	Repentance	Trust
Trustworthiness	.02	-.08	-.14	.13	.07	.06	-.05	-.12
Strength of Will and Rationality	-.09	-.01	-.14	-.18	-.03	-.09	-.13	-.03
Altruism	-.16	.03	-.25*	-.24	-.12	.01	-.15	.05
Independence	-.06	.09	-.09	-.16	.00	-.03	-.06	-.21*

Note: *Significantly different from zero at .05 level.
Stochastic variables from Rapoport (1964, 1966), defined as below.

Trial X		Trial Y	
Player chooses	Exper. programs	Player chooses	Disposition
Cooperation	Cooperation	Cooperation	Trustworthiness
Competition	Cooperation	Cooperation	Repentance
Cooperation	Competition	Cooperation	Forgiveness
Competition	Competition	Cooperation	Trust

Source: Adapted from Baxter, 1969, Table 11, pp. 69-70.

imize cooperative play. In addition, the following paper-and-pencil measures were given: three subscales from the PHN, Sawyer's Altruism Scale (1966), and Richman's Malevolence-Benevolence Scale (Richman, 1970). These eight measures were factor analyzed. The four questionnaire measures of beliefs about human nature (Trustworthiness, Altruism, Independence, and Malevolence-Benevolence) defined the first factor for each gender. The second factor reflected the two traditional PD-game procedures. Both the modified PD game and the Altruism subscale were independent of the first two factors and of each other.

Thus results of the follow-up studies scrub any conclusion of a general relationship between philosophies of human nature and PD-game cooperative behavior, regardless of experimental conditions. (In contrast, a study by Schlenker, Helm, & Tedeschi [1973] reported modest correlations between Rotter's Interpersonal Trust scores and cooperation in a modified Prisoner's Dilemma Game.)

Given the pattern of results, the next step in a research analysis might be the identification of situational characteristics that delimit the influence of philosophies of human nature. For example, one replicated conclusion is that the subject's attitude plays a greater role in a one-trial game than in a multitrial game (Terhune, 1968; Wrightsman, 1966). In a multitrial game, the subject continually receives inputs about the other's choice that may override his or her basic trust or distrust, even though the subject may have relied upon his or her attitude on the first trial. (In actuality, in a multitrial game even the subject's choices on the first trial do not seem to be based upon beliefs about human nature, as studies by Baxter [1969] and Terhune [1968] have shown.)

Situational factors that influence the relationship between attitudes toward people and behavior have already been specified for Machiavellian attitudes (Christie & Geis, 1970). In some ways, Machiavellianism can be considered the opposite of a favorable philosophy of human nature, although Machiavellianism also includes a motivational component that the PHN concept lacks. Highly Machiavellian persons need to manipulate people; they also believe that flattery, threat, and deceit are the most successful ways of getting people to conform to their thinking (Christie & Geis, 1968).

Geis and Christie (1970) reviewed 38 studies that related Machiavellianism to interpersonal behavior in experimental situations. (Not all of these were PD games, but a number of them put two or more motives in conflict within each subject.) After a careful consideration of cases in which Machiavellianism did and did not make a difference, Geis and

Christie concluded that the following three factors contribute to the emergence of a significant relationship: (1) face-to-face interaction, (2) the degree of latitude for improvisation (that is, the opportunity to exaggerate, amplify, or innovate responses), and (3) the degree of irrelevant affect that can be manifested. In cases in which these three conditions prevail, highly Machiavellian subjects were more successful in achieving their goals on an interpersonal task than were less Machiavellian subjects. In general, Geis and Christie (1970) concluded that "high Machs" were most successful when given the opportunity to improvise in a face-to-face situation, whereas in the same situation, "low Machs" were distracted by feelings that are responses to essentially irrelevant details. In such cases, high Machs "manipulate more, win more, are persuaded less, persuade others more, and otherwise differ significantly from Low Machs" (Geis & Christie, 1970, p. 312).

We note that none of these three conditions appears to be manifested in a typical Prisoner's Dilemma Game situation. Typically, the two subjects are not face to face; in fact, no direct communication is permitted between them. Second, the usual game permits no latitude for improvisation on a particular trial, for the response repertory is limited to two alternatives. The presence of distracting irrelevant affect in PD games is harder to assess. Geis and Christie classify some PD games as possessing irrelevant affect and some as lacking such affect; others they leave unclassified.

Despite the ambiguity with regard to irrelevant affect, the conclusion remains that PD games as a group lack the qualities that facilitate success by highly Machiavellian subjects. Thus it is to be expected that Machiavellian attitudes will not usually be related to cooperativeness on the standard PD game. Geis and Christie find, for example, that in 13 of the 14 situations that possessed all three qualities—face-to-face contact, latitude for improvisation, and irrelevant affect—high-Mach subjects were more "successful." Yet in each of the 11 studies in which none of these conditions were present—including some PD studies—highly Machiavellian subjects were not significantly more successful than less Machiavellian subjects.

The thorough analysis made by Geis and Christie facilitates the understanding of the role of philosophies of human nature in determining interpersonal behavior, and it is highly likely that the general conclusion they derive for the Machiavellianism Scale applies to the PHN scale and other measures of attitudes toward people as well.

Geis and Christie's approach points out that situational characteristics can severely delimit or even eliminate the effect of attitudes upon behavior.

Wicker (1971) took a somewhat different approach in his studies of the attitude-behavior relationship. He noted that many defenders of the role of attitudes claim that if other variables were taken into account better predictions about behavior could be made from knowledge of attitudes (Weissberg, 1965). Wicker (1971) labeled one of these additional variables "perceived consequences of behavior"—that is, "what a person believed would follow from his engaging in a given action" (1971, p. 19). A second variable is the person's evaluation of different behaviors, and a third covers the subject's perception of the relative influence of unplanned, extraneous events upon his or her behavior. Wicker studied the effects of these variables, along with religious attitudes, upon religious behavior (such as attendance at Sunday worship service, contributions to the church, and participation in church activities). Prediction of behavior improved significantly when these three indicators were used in addition to attitude measures. The best single predictor of behavior was the subject's perceived influence of extraneous events (mean $r = .36$), followed by his or her evaluation of related behaviors (mean $r = .26$) and by his or her scores on the religious attitude measures ($r = .15$). Even when all of these predictors were employed, however, Wicker was still unable to account for about 75% of the variance in behavior.

Nevertheless, the application of these concepts to the study of trusting behavior might be fruitful. For example, with regard to cooperative behavior in a PD game, Ajzen and Fishbein (1970, 1980) proposed and demonstrated that there is a close relationship between behavioral intentions to perform a certain act (that is, to cooperate on a certain trial) and the actual performance of the act. Some would prefer that the concept of "attitude" be narrowed to express a person's disposition to act in a specific event as indicated by a verbal report prior to action—for example, "my attitude toward choosing blue or red on a particular trial"—and, through such a revision, it can be shown that attitudes relate to behavior more impressively. But such a revision throws out the assumptions of breadth and consistency—assumptions that have been central in making the concept of attitude the "building block in the edifice of social psychology" (Allport, 1935). "Well," say some, "that's the way the edifice crumbles." Instead, we believe that there remains a place in the determination of behavior for attitudes as traditionally conceived. The major difficulties have been the assumption that this construct is the *sole* determinant of behavior, and the overreliance upon paper-and-pencil measures of these attitudes.

In pursuing the elusive relationship between attitudes and behavior, Ajzen and Fishbein (1980) have developed what has been called a theory of "reasoned action." The term *reasoned action* implies that most behaviors are carried out for a purpose—that people think about the consequences of their actions and make deliberate decisions to achieve some outcomes and avoid others. More recent research, for example Fazio (1986), has emphasized whether an attitude is accessible to working memory. This conclusion causes us to ask, once more, how salient beliefs about human nature are to varying individuals who must choose to act in trusting or suspicious ways.

Summary

Persons with high levels of hostility and cynicism were found to be at greater risk of a heart attack. The PHN scale seems to tap into this ideology, as it correlates with the Ho scale.

Several types of approaches were used to determine the relationship of philosophies of human nature to interpersonal behavior.

Students' evaluations of a particular instructor were found to be related to the students' general beliefs about human nature, indicating that these beliefs serve as initial orientations in determining reactions to specific people. Similarly, those students who believed that human nature is complex and variable made greater distinctions in their evaluations of two different instructors.

Teachers who differ in philosophies of human nature also differ in the type of nonverbal communication that they display in the classroom. These attitude differences also influence the behavior of their students.

If highly antiblack college students are placed in a month-long job working with a black, only some of the prejudiced participants develop less prejudiced attitudes. Those who do change in this direction may be distinguished from the others on the basis of two characteristics; they possess significantly more favorable beliefs about human nature, and they possess significantly more negative self-concepts. In other words, they are dissatisfied with themselves and they trust others as influence agents.

Behavior in a mixed-motive game would appear to be determined by philosophies of human nature, as this choice situation requires the trial. In one-trial tasks, persons with favorable philosophies of human nature were more likely to trust the other player to share with them. On multitrial games, however, the number of cooperative responses made by a subject is usually unrelated to the subject's expressed attitudes about human nature; situational determinants overcome attitudinal ones as influences upon interpersonal behavior. Post-hoc analysis indicates that behavior in the mixed-motive game situation, as it is usually employed, may not be related to attitudes because of built-in constraints in the procedure, including the absence of face-to-face communication, the limited number of possible responses, and the lack of an opportunity to capitalize on irrelevant affect.

CHAPTER EIGHT

Determinants of Philosophies of Human Nature

LOIS STACK
CARL E. YOUNG
LAWRENCE S. WRIGHTSMAN

No beliefs will be more important to education than those we hold about the nature of man and the limits of his potentials.

—YEARBOOK COMMITTEE,
Association for Supervision and
Curriculum Development

Why does one person trust other people while his or her neighbor does not? Antecedent experiences and training, of course, are the general causes, but this chapter presents data on a more specific determinant—"parental training during childhood." We propose that specific actions of the parents, particularly those of the mother, instill in the young child a positive, negative, or neutral orientation toward people in general. To support this hypothesis we will describe a study that relates maternal behaviors to the degree of trust and positive attitudes toward people held by 3-year-old children. Further evidence regarding relationships between the attitudes of children and those of their parents will also be reported.

We will then consider other questions related to the development of philosophies of human nature in children. Do the common experiences of childhood in our culture affect children's attitudes? Are these attitudes less positive in older children than in younger ones? Finally, we will report on the construction, administration, and interpretation of a scale to measure children's attitudes.

The Development of Trust

Erik Erikson's psychosocial theory (1963; see also Evans, 1967) postulates that as people develop their own identity and integrate their own life cycles with those of others, they must pass through several stages or crises. The first of these stages Erikson has termed "basic trust versus basic mistrust." Erikson defines *basic trust* as a general sense of the correspondence between one's needs and one's world, whereas *basic mistrust* is a readiness for danger or an anticipation of discomfort. The most decisive period for the development of trust is believed to be the first year of life, when the infant has his or her initial interpersonal interactions with those nearby. To develop a favorable balance of basic trust over basic mistrust, the child needs to develop a reliance upon the sameness and continuity of the behavior of his or her immediate providers—the parents. Trust depends upon caretakers who respond to the infant's physical and emotional needs in expectable ways.

In successfully resolving this first crisis of life, the infant will have developed a favorable ratio of basic trust over basic mistrust. This ratio will persist to some extent throughout the person's life, claims Erikson, although it will be subject to constant modification as situations, persons, and events add new data to feelings about people and the world in general.

According to Erikson, trust is a basic human attitude that includes a deep faith in the self, in other persons, and in culture and society. Persons who possess such a faith will be able to view themselves and their life spans in a time perspective that includes hope for the future. "Trust," in Erikson's sense, goes beyond a trust of specific other persons and encompasses a trust of life itself that "forms the basis in the child for a sense of identity which will later combine a sense of being 'all right,' of being oneself, and of becoming what other people trust one will become" (Erikson, 1963, p. 249). This distinction between trust of specific other persons and trust in life itself seems to correspond to two environmental characteristics that Erikson proposes as important for the development of trust. These characteristics are a trustworthy maternal environment, in which the child develops a sense of mutuality or "friendly otherness," and a trustworthy social environment, which helps the child develop a sense of the meaning of life.

Since Erikson theorizes that interpersonal interactions during infancy are of major importance in the development of basic trust, we will review three aspects of caretaker behaviors that may influence the character of these early interpersonal interactions. These aspects of the "trustworthy maternal environment" are social reciprocity, variety of stimulation, and consistency.

SOCIAL RECIPROCITY

The first aspect of caretaker behavior refers to the establishment of mutual regulation between the mother and child and involves the adaptation of each participant to the responses of the other. This mutual adaptation may occur during such routine infant-care procedures as feeding, bathing, and dressing, but it is not necessarily an outgrowth of these procedures. For instance, while a mother feeds her infant her attention might be on a book, the television screen, or the mechanical action of the milk flowing from the bottle. Mutual adaptation of responses between the pair, however, could occur only if her attention were on the infant itself and if the infant's attention were on the mother. Mutual attention and interacting responses lead to the establishment of social reciprocity—a kind of mutually regulated pattern of social interaction.

In a review of social development in infancy, Ferguson (1971) discussed the importance of such reciprocal responses as the basis for all human interaction:

> From its earliest beginnings in infancy, social interaction consists of closely reciprocal, often mutually very similar sets of responses. Thus, a given response (vocalizing, watching, smiling) from one participant serves as the eliciting stimulus for a similar or corresponding response in the other participant, and, in this way, self-sustaining sequences or chains of responses are set up. Imitation is only one special and rather obvious class of such mutual or reciprocally matching responses. I would suggest that these responses form the supporting structure for almost all human interactions, beginning with those of the first months of extra-uterine life. (p. 127)

Assessing the infant's level of arousal within the interaction itself, as well as previous to it, is an important aspect of the maternal adaptation involved in social reciprocity. The intensity of the mother's stimulation should facilitate an optimal state of animation in the infant—neither so exciting that the child loses behavioral control nor so low-keyed that the stimulation fails to gain the infant's attention. If the mother adapts herself to the infant so that these states of optimal animation occur during direct encounters with her (rather than while the infant is alone), reciprocity and more complex behavior integrations seem to be facilitated.

In a study of mothers and infants, Escalona (1968) noted that the development of social reciprocity seemed to depend on both occasional high peaks of excitation and subtle, sustained interactions with the mother. These subtle interactions often included mutual gazing, imitation of vocal patterns, reciprocal changes in facial expression, and use of small gestures and inflections. The particular responses observed in any given pair often seemed to depend on the characteristic mode of response displayed by the infant—another example of reciprocal adaptation on the mother's part.

The 32 mothers studied by Escalona differed in the extent to which they converted routine infant-care procedures into occasions for social interaction. While some mothers considered feeding, bathing, and dressing their babies prescribed duties to be dispatched, others took advantage of such opportunities to interact socially with their infants, only incidentally accomplishing the routine physical tasks. Although most mothers did provide their infants with adequate pleasure, comfort, and stimulation, there were real differences in the social character of these interactions. For example, some mothers seemed to invite reciprocity by imitating the infant's vocalizations, by holding a spoon close to the infant's mouth and waiting for him or her to seize it, or by extending a toy to the child rather than placing it in the child's hand. Such actions probably focus the infant's attention on the mutuality of the situation—on the partner's response as well as his or her own response—and thus foster both the sense of "friendly otherness" that Erikson (1963) sees as an integral part of the development of trust and the sense of self for which basic trust forms the foundation.

It has been demonstrated in other contexts that one's expectations about another person's responses can influence the actual responses of that person. For example, expectations of experimenters and data collectors can affect the responses that they obtained from subjects (Rosenthal, 1964, 1966), and the expectations of teachers concerning a child's potential for accelerated intellectual progress have been related to subsequent measures of intelligence (Rosenthal & Jacobson, 1968). Although these conclusions have not been accepted uniformly (see critical reactions by Barber & Silver [1968] and by Snow [1969]), even some of the critics admit that the hypothesized effects have been demonstrated in some of the studies. It is not too difficult to extend the conclusion to one that deals with the effect of the expectations of mothers upon the behavior of their children.

In Stack's (1972a) study, to be described in this chapter, the subjects were 3-year-olds rather than infants. Although we have been discussing social reciprocity as applied to mother-infant pairs, it was assumed that such relationship would also be applicable to mother-child pairs at the 3-year-old level and that differences in reciprocity observed would be even greater due to the increased duration of the relationship.

VARIETY OF STIMULATION

Reciprocity is not the only feature of a trustworthy maternal environment. A second aspect noted by Erikson is the importance of presenting a variety of stimuli to the developing child. Because infants explore with their visual, tactile, and auditory senses, "we must see to it that we deliver to their senses stimuli as well as food in the proper intensity and at the right time; otherwise, their willingness to accept may change abruptly into diffuse defense—or into lethargy" (Erikson, 1959, p. 57).

Early studies of institutionalized infants (Casler, 1961; Dennis & Najarian, 1957; Spitz, 1945) showed that physical care alone was not enough for infants to develop normally. In later studies of similar populations, the amount and kind of perceptual stimulation provided for infants seemed to emerge as independent and important aspects of early experience (Sayegh & Dennis, 1965; H. R. Schaffer, 1965). Whether it is the perceptual stimulation itself or the affective bond that is built up in the stimulation process that facilitates development is difficult to determine, since most institutions that provide rich and appropriate stimulation are also institutions that provide individualized care by a relatively small number of adults with whom the children do in fact develop intense personal relationships (Escalona, 1968, p. 13).

Evidence that reciprocating mothers provide a greater variation of stimuli for their infants than do nonreciprocating mothers is offered by Rubenstein (1967). The attentive behaviors of 44 mothers toward their 6-month-old infants were time-sampled in their homes. Observers counted the number of times a mother looked at, touched, held, or talked to her baby during three of the child's waking hours. (This measure was a rough approximation of reciprocity, since it considered only maternal behaviors.) During a later observation of each infant, a count of the number of toys within the child's reach revealed that highly attentive mothers offered a significantly greater variety of toys than did less attentive mothers. The total number of toys did not differ, however. In addition, attentive mothers offered significantly more social-play opportunities, and such social play is in itself a rich source of varied stimulation. To the extent that the attentiveness observed by Rubenstein (1967) included the mutuality of response necessary for social reciprocity, reciprocity and varied stimulation seem to be related aspects of good caretaking. When the infants were tested one month later, the infants with more attentive mothers showed significantly more exploratory behavior than did those whose mothers showed only average or limited degrees of attentiveness. Maternal reciprocity and varied stimulation thus resulted in more advanced infant development. Would they also result in a more trusting infant? Erikson's theory implies that they would.

CONSISTENCY

The third dimension of a trustworthy maternal environment deals with the predictability of the mother's actions toward the child. In discussing the means by which trust is strengthened in a child, Allport (1961, p. 102) has noted that consistency in handling the child seems to help the child predict the actions of others and thus seems to elevate his or her sense of trust in people. If parents consistently respond to the infant's cry of hunger or discomfort, he or she will develop an expectancy of consistent reinforcement, and if the child's interactions with people are consistently reinforced, we would expect the child to have a favorable, or trusting, attitude that presumably generalizes to other people with whom he or she comes in contact. Gradually the child establishes what Rotter (1954) considered a generalized expectancy about other people and their reinforcement value. This generalized expectancy is forged out of all the child's past experiences with people.

It should be noted that consistency is quite compatible with varied stimuli. It is possible for a mother to provide a variety of stimuli at the same time that her behavior toward the child is basically consistent and predictable. Consistency is the main theme in the mother-child relationship; the variation of stimuli that the mother provides around this theme helps the child to differentiate and generalize aspects of his or her world and thus to expand his or her powers of prediction to a wider range of objects and persons.

A trustworthy maternal environment, as described by Erikson, is of prime importance in helping the child experience a sense of relaxed mutuality or "friendly otherness." Such a trustworthy environment provides the child with social reciprocity, a variety of stimuli, and consistent, predictable behaviors from people close by.

ENVIRONMENTAL SOCIAL STRUCTURE

According to Erikson, the development of a favorable ratio of basic trust over basic mistrust depends on the infant's reliance on the sameness and continuity of his or her providers—not only of the immediate caretakers but also of the entire environmental social structure, which provides an outer wholeness of life. The infant is a social being born into a social world. He or she needs the unifying continuity of a trustworthy mother, a family to protect the mother, society to support the structure of the family, and the traditions that give cultural continuity to systems of tending and training. Thus the caretakers themselves need to experience a trustworthy environment if they are to be able to provide such an environment for their child. Support for this hypothesis is offered by evidence that people from lower socioeconomic groups tend to score lower than people from middle-income groups on adult and elementary school measures of trust (Phypers, 1967; Rotter, 1967; Wrightsman & Satterfield, 1967) and by the frequent characterization of urban ghetto dwellers as extremely distrustful (Hess, 1969; Pavenstadt, 1965). But would such socioeconomic differences in trust appear as early as 3 years of age?

Empirical Tests of Trust in Young Children

Stack (1972a) set forth to look at the role of caretaker behaviors and of the environmental social structure in determining the degree of trusting behavior manifested by young children. Because she considered measuring trust in infants too difficult, Stack chose 3-year-old children as the focus of her study. She developed, as a measure of the child's trust, a behavior rating scale composed of 10 behaviors.

Each child was rated first by an observer and then by the director of the research section of the Demonstration and Research Center for Early Education at Peabody College. These ratings were based on observation of each child in his or her own home. The rho values between the ratings of the original observers and the ratings of the research-section director were .80, .80, and .44 for the three original observers (see Appendix F for a copy of the instrument).

The 24 subjects were drawn from three groups—8 each from urban lower-class, urban middle-class, and rural middle-class families. All lower-class families had Hollingshead ratings (measures of social class) of 6 or 7, and in most both parents had failed to complete high school.

Income level for the lower-class families fell below that recommended by the U.S. Office of Economic Opportunity as a maximum income for families receiving Head Start services. In the middle-class families (Hollingshead rating of 1 or 3), all fathers had completed college and most had graduate training; all mothers had some college experience, and most had a degree. Income level in most of these families was well above the national average.

Groups were equally divided with regard to sex and ethnic background. No black subjects were included in the rural sample, however, since the population area from which this group was drawn contained no black families. As far as possible, children were matched across groups for family size and position of the child within the family. All participating families lived in middle Tennessee.

To derive measurements of caretakers' behaviors, Stack relied on coded specimen records (Barker & Wright, 1951; H. F. Wright, 1967) of the subjects' home-life experiences drawn from observations of social interaction in the home. At least eight observations, ranging in length from 10 to 47 minutes, were obtained for each child. In total, 198 specimen records (5,477 minutes of observation) were developed to final form and utilized. The behavior in each behavior setting was then coded according to 26 descriptive variables, and all data were computerized. (For further information about the group of specimen records gathered in this project, see Schoggen & Schoggen, 1971.)

For the study on trust, computerized data were retrieved for all mother-child interactions. Ten variables were selected to represent the three dimensions drawn from Erikson's theory (social reciprocity, variety of stimulation, and consistency). To study the degree of social reciprocity in each mother-child pair, Stack used four variables: information exchange, success, goal congruence, and interpersonal score. Information exchange was the proportion of maternal activities devoted to understanding the child's position and to helping the child understand his or her own position. Included were instances in which the mother requested that the child tell or repeat something, informed the child of others' feelings, or offered other information to the child. Success was simply the percentage of interactions in which the mother's goal for the child was achieved. (Highly reciprocal mothers were expected to be more successful.) The maternal goal for each interactive activity was rated for the degree to which it was congruent with the child's own goal; goal congruence was the percentage of activities that were rated as fully harmonious with the child's own wishes. This was the only variable that took into account simultaneously behavior of both mother and child; this focus on mutual interaction makes goal congruence perhaps the clearest indicator of social reciprocity. The fourth variable, interpersonal score, was derived by rating maternal affect and investment (from 1 point for anger to 6 points for a warmly enthusiastic interaction) and summing these scores over all interactions. High scores thus represented a high frequency of positive social interaction.

Variety of stimulation, the second Erikson dimension, not only entered into the interpersonal score by virtue of the fact that frequent social interchange is a means of providing variety, but it was also represented specifically by three additional variables: positive activities, isolated structure, and simple signs and contact. The first variable examined the content of activities provided by the mother; the percentage of activities concerned with giving affection, help, objects, or fun became the score for positive activities. The structure of mother-child interactions was also diagrammed and classified. Some goal activities occurred singly, while others overlapped, enclosed, or were enclosed by adjacent activities. Since isolated interactions were considered to provide less variety than did other types, a high percentage of isolated activities was judged indicative of a lack of maternal provision for variety. Another indication was the mother's reliance on simple gestures, body contact, or murmurs, as opposed to verbal communication which has more possibilities for variety.

Maternal directions to the child were classified into several types, two of which—specific directions and negative directions—seemed to be of interest in studying maternal consistency. Consistent mothers were expected to use a high proportion of very specific directions and a low proportion of negative directions (such as "stop that!"). The final variable—ignore—examined maternal consistency in responding to the child when he or she tried to interact. In retrospect, Stack concluded that the directions variables were not adequate indicators of consistency across time, although the ignore variable was adequate.

Stack found that the more trusting children—as identified by the rating scale—displayed more pleasure in interpersonal relations and a more advanced level of language development than did the other children. Contrary to expectations, they did not exhibit more mature feelings of personal control; neither did they initiate more interactions with others. Once interactions had been initiated, however, the more trusting children were more consistently rewarding to their play partners and displayed a higher rate of interaction with all partners (both adults and children).

The caretaker behaviors that were significant predictors of children's trust were (1) the frequency of maternal interaction and its emotional

TABLE 8.1 Correlations Showing Related Aspects of Maternal Functioning and Children's Trust in Stack's Study

	Maternal Interpersonal	Maternal Goal Congruence	Children's Trust Ratings
Information Exchange	.65***	.77***	.52**
Success	.39	.68***	.45*
Goal Congruence	.66***	—	.58**
Interpersonal	—	.66***	.48*
Positive Activities	.46*	.44*	-.02
Isolated Structure	-.68***	-.66***	-.54**
Simple Signs	-.55**	-.63**	-.43*
Specific Directions	.43*	.50*	.34
Negative Directions	-.81***	-.83***	-.43*
Ignore	-.60**	-.67***	-.39

Note: *$p < .05$; **$p < .01$; ***$p < .001$

investment ($F = 5.00$; df 1, 16; $p < .05$) and (2) the rated harmony between the mother's and child's goals in each observed interaction ($F = 4.09$; df 1, 16; $p < .05$). Harmony of goals was used as an indicator of social reciprocity, whereas the interpersonal score reflected both the reciprocity and variety of stimulation. Support was thus offered for the importance of these two aspects of caretaker behavior. The dimensions, however, cannot be completely separate, as is indicated by the fact that most of the other maternal variables studied were significantly related to these two predictor variables as well as to children's trust (see Table 8.1). Children who were rated as trusting had mothers who encouraged communication, especially verbal communication; who were generally successful in their attempts to direct the child; who acted reciprocally in their choice of activities for the child; who interacted frequently and warmly; who often had several mother-child activities going at the same time; and who did not generally direct the child in a negative manner. One surprising finding was the lack of relationship between children's trust and such maternal activities as gently teasing, offering affection or permission, joining the child's activities, or helping the child. Mothers of trusters engaged in these activities as often as did mothers of mistrusters.

Erikson's theory predicts that socioeconomic group membership affects the development of trust. This prediction was confirmed in Stack's (1972a) sample of 3-year-olds, as it had been in other age groups; children from low-income families had significantly lower trust ratings than did children from middle-income families (F = 6.65, df 1, 13, p < .05), and mothers in the low-income group treated their 3-year-olds differently than did middleincome mothers. No gender or race differences occurred in Stack's sample.

Relationship of Parents' and Children's Belief About Human Nature

Another way to approach the role of parental influence is to relate parental attitudes about human nature to those of their children. There is a body of research literature (for example, E. Q. Campbell, 1958; Newcomb & Svelha, 1937; Wrightsman, 1964b) indicating that positive relationships exist between parents' attitudes and their children's attitudes on such diverse topics as religion, politics, and the likelihood of a nuclear war. More specifically, it has been often demonstrated that attitudes of racial prejudice are transmitted from parents to children (Bird, Monachesi, & Burdick, 1952; Quinn, 1954; R. C. Schaffer & Schaffer, 1958; R. M. Williams, 1964).

In a relevant research project, Baxter (1973a) studied the PHN scores of families who attended churches in Bristol, TN. He tested 548 persons attending Baptist, Methodist, Presbyterian, Episcopal, and Disciple of Christ churches. Out of that total, there were 88 family groups. (A family group was defined as at least one parent plus at least one child of junior or senior high school level.) Out of the 88 family groups, there were 71 mothers, 54 fathers, 37 senior high school sons, 20 junior high school sons, 43 senior high school daughters, and 29 junior high school daughters. Thus there were eight possible types of relationships available for correlational analysis. The resulting correlations are presented in Table 8.2. There is certainly little to indicate strong parent-child relationships in Table 8.2. Only 5 of 64 correlations are beyond the .05 level of significance (we would expect at least 3 by chance alone), and the significant correlations are neither internally consistent in direction nor localized in one subscale or one type of family relationship. For example, there is a significant positive relationship between the degrees of multiplexity seen in human nature by fathers and their senior high school daughters (r = .56), but the correlation between fathers and their junior high sons on this measure is negative (-.59). Although it is tempting to interpret specific correlations in a post-hoc manner, it is unwise and unjustified to do so.

TABLE 8.2 Correlations Between PHN Scores of Parents and Children

Type of Relationship	Number of Pairs	Trust-worthiness	Strength of Will & Rationality	PHN Scale: Altruism	Indepen-dence	Complexity	Vari-ability	Positive-Negative	Multi-pexity
Mother and senior high school daughter	31	-.134	-.190	.085	-.173	.035	.210	-.052	.260
Mother and junior high school daughter	20	.208	.116	.459*	-.403	.279	.153	.229	.218
Mother and senior high school son	16	.325	-.177	-.093	.040	.250	.374	-.061	.408
Mother and junior high school son	16	.241	-.142	.329	-.429	.165	-.234	-.066	-.079
Father and senior high school daughter	18	.325	-.245	.054	-.022	.418	.517*	.016	.557**
Father and junior high school daughter	19	-.037	-.041	.123	-.392	.194	-.016	-.144	.135
Father and senior high school son	16	-.268	-.048	-.108	.028	.560*	.001	-.209	.420
Father and junior high school son	12	.518	-.100	-.167	.115	-.175	-.326	.165	-.589

Source: Adapted from Baxter, 1973a.
Note: $*p < .05$; $**p < .02$

Further research is necessary to determine whether relationships are present between parents' philosophies and those of their younger children.

The Development of Philosophies of Human Nature in Children

The inappropriateness of the PHN scale as a measuring instrument for school-age children may partially account for the lack of relationship between parents' and children's attitudes found by Baxter (1973a). An informal study done in a private school that attracts academically talented students found that junior high students had difficulties with both the complexity and vocabulary of PHN items. For this reason, and in order to determine developmental trends in philosophies of human nature, a children's form was constructed.

More specifically, the Children's Philosophies of Human Nature Scale (or C-PHN) was developed by C. E. Young and Wrightsman (1968) to overcome the three limitations of the use of the PHN with junior high school students: (1) item complexity, (2) advanced vocabulary, and (3) excessive length of test. The vocabulary problem was ameliorated by using only words from the basic fourth-grade vocabulary list published by Dale and Eicholz (1960). The issue of item complexity, although related to vocabulary, presented other problems. Junior high students have difficulty with such PHN items as "Most people will change the opinion they express as a result of an onslaught of criticism, even though they really don't change the way they feel." The ideal item seemed to be one that consisted of a simple declarative sentence pertinent to the children's immediate environment—for example, "Most students do not cheat when taking an exam." An adequate length for the new scale posed a third problem. Since decreasing the number of items in each of the six PHN subscales would threaten the scale's validity, Young and Wrightsman chose instead to decrease the number of subscales.

Trustworthiness, Strength of Will and Rationality, and Complexity were retained. Trustworthiness seemed to be a particularly important attitude to measure. It has been a theme of this book that this construct underlies much of our interpersonal behavior; specifically here, it was seen as related to such salient attitudes in children as their school morale. Also, a number of studies have been concerned with various aspects of children's honesty, a factor directly related to trustworthiness (Kohlberg, 1963). Altruism was not included, since it is highly correlated with Trustworthiness on the adult PHN scale. Strength of Will and Rationality was chosen because of its motivational and self-concept implications and because of its potential relationships with attitudes toward poverty and racial groups. Complexity was chosen because it might have the clearest developmental trends—that is, education and chronological age should bring increased awareness of the complexity of human behavior.

CONSTRUCTION OF ITEMS FOR C-PHN SUBSCALES

For each of the three C-PHN subscales, statements with which the student could agree or disagree were composed. Statements from the adult PHN scale were paraphrased in the hope of making the C-PHN a downward chronological-age extension of the PHN. The initial product contained 12 items in each of the three subscales: Trustworthiness, Strength of Will and Rationality, and Complexity. The six Likert-type response categories used in the PHN are also used in the C-PHN: -3 = strongly disagree, -2 = disagree somewhat, -1 = slightly disagree, $+1$ = slightly agree, $+2$ = agree somewhat, and $+3$ = strongly agree. To minimize possible response bias, the 12 items in each subscale include 6 favorable statements and 6 unfavorable statements. A copy of this scale with subscales and directions marked is included in Appendix G.

EVIDENCE OF VALIDITY

The C-PHN was administered to more than 3,700 students from grades 4 through 12 and to 630 college freshmen at a private university, through the efforts of Christina Satterfield and Dale Irwin, who collected most of these data.

Three evidences of validity will be discussed—school differences, gender differences, and correlations with the adult PHN. Three schools, New Providence Junior High School in Clarksville, TN, and East Side Junior High School and Hardy Junior High School, both in Chattanooga, TN, were chosen for the original validation study. New Providence, which drew students from middle-class backgrounds, had an air-conditioned, innovative building, a team-teaching program, and an enthusiastic faculty. About 60% of the New Providence students were children of military personnel stationed at Fort Campbell, but these military families usually lived off the base in private housing. About 10% of the New Providence students were black. East Side Junior High drew its students from lower-middle-class backgrounds (about 20% were black). Hardy Junior High

TABLE 8.3 C-PHN Subscale Means from Three Junior High School Student Bodies

School	Grade	Sex	N	Trustworthiness		Strength of Will & Rationality		Complexity	
				Mean	SD	Mean	SD	Mean	SD
New Providence	7	F	162	5.59	10.71	6.60	7.75	11.00	9.91
	7	M	173	1.55	10.61	7.12	7.50	8.32	7.85
	8	F	162	3.97	11.58	8.44	11.72	14.25	13.96
	8	M	153	2.71	11.24	8.12	7.51	11.05	15.50
	9	F	106	7.42	15.22	8.26	6.95	17.75	9.63
	9	M	100	2.11	11.73	7.36	7.36	14.43	9.37
East Side	7	F	49	.96	9.13	6.60	5.70	9.28	7.97
	7	M	54	-.09	11.03	4.73	6.98	9.51	8.80
	8	F	63	2.06	11.25	6.73	7.25	15.47	10.31
	8	M	83	-.98	9.82	5.36	7.01	10.60	8.43
	9	F	86	.40	11.79	8.10	6.43	15.87	9.66
	9	M	62	.24	9.45	5.41	7.09	11.46	8.87
Hardy	7	F	66	-3.30	9.35	4.57	6.46	10.16	8.12
	7	M	58	-3.78	8.18	4.22	6.45	10.44	9.44
	8	F	57	-2.69	8.37	4.67	6.37	11.03	8.51
	8	M	51	-3.90	6.81	6.44	6.65	10.15	8.21

School, which was located adjacent to a low-income housing project, also had an old traditional school building and was about 30% to 40% black. Approximately 30% of Hardy students came from one-parent families, whereas less than 10% of New Providence students were in this category.

These schools were appropriate for an initial validation study because of their distinct differences. It was hypothesized that New Providence students would have higher Trustworthiness and Strength of Will and Rationality scores than would East Side students and that East Side students would have higher scores on these two scale than would students at Hardy. Furthermore, it was expected that girls would have more positive scores than boys and that there would be an increase in Complexity scores with advance in grade.

C-PHN data on these three junior high student bodies are presented in Table 8.3, which reveals consistent gender and school differences. Girls had significantly higher ($p < .01$) Trustworthiness and Complexity scores at both New Providence and East Side than did boys. The gender difference on Strength of Will and Rationality at East Side ($p < .01$) was also significant. These gender differences were in keeping with the school-morale differences reported by Wrightsman, Nelson, and Taranto (1968) and with the usual findings regarding gender differences in social attitudes.

In each of the three schools, seventh-graders had lower Complexity scores than did eighth-graders. Eighth-graders saw human nature as less complex than did the ninth-graders in the two schools in which there was a ninth grade. Grade differences on the other two subscales were less clear-cut; in fact, grade differences on Trustworthiness were inconsistent from school to school. There was a slight tendency for beliefs about Strength of Will and Rationality to heighten with increased age.

New Providence students had significantly higher Trustworthiness and Complexity scores than did East Side students ($p < .01$), and East Side students had significantly higher scores on these two subscales than did the students at Hardy ($p < .01$). We believe that these differences are most parsimoniously accounted for by the differing environmental social structures of the children at the three schools. Lower-class children have lower ability levels and less success in school than middle-class children do, and they may have goals different from those of middle-class children. The environment of a housing project creates different attitudinal expectations toward the behavior of others than does a community of single-family houses.

The findings in Table 8.4 reaffirm such a socioeconomic explanation of differences on the C-PHN. These data are drawn from fourth- and fifth-graders in four Tullahoma, TN, elementary schools. South Jackson ranked lowest in socioeconomic standing and East Lincoln was next lowest, while Bel Aire and Robert E. Lee were upper-middle-class schools.

The data in Table 8.4 indicate that the Trustworthiness-subscale rankings corresponded with the school's socioeconomic ranking. Robert E. Lee and Bel Aire were significantly higher than South Jackson and East Lincoln on Trustworthiness, Robert E. Lee at the .01 level and Bel Aire at the .05 level. The fifth-graders were higher than the fourth-graders in all four schools on Trustworthiness, and this difference was significant at South Jackson and East Lincoln ($p < .05$). Girls had higher Trustworthiness scores than did boys at East Lincoln and Robert E. Lee ($p < .05$); however, boys had higher scores than did girls at Bel Aire.

Complexity scores were higher for fifth-graders than for fourth-graders in three of the four schools. There was little grade-level difference in mean Strength of Will and Rationality at any school.

The data presented in Tables 8.5 and 8.6 indicate that neither social desirability nor ability level is significantly correlated with the C-PHN successes. The F scale used was the Children's Authoritarianism Scale, a

TABLE 8.4 C-PHN Data from Four Elementary Schools

School	Grade	Sex	N	Trustworthy Mean	Strength of Will Mean	Complexity Mean
South Jackson	4	F & M	101	-.56	6.85	14.21
	5	F & M	110	1.70	6.08	14.38
	4 & 5	F & M	211	.62	6.45	14.30
East Lincoln	4	F	33	1.36	6.21	12.12
	4	M	45	-3.33	4.91	10.49
	4	F & M	78	-1.35	5.46	11.18
	5	F	38	2.81	6.87	14.57
	5	M	36	2.39	5.30	17.00
	5	F & M	74	2.61	6.11	15.70
	4 & 5	F & M	152	.58	5.78	13.41
Bel Aire	4	F	59	1.81	6.34	21.29
	4	M	52	3.32	8.30	16.46
	4	F & M	111	2.52	7.26	19.03
	5	F	59	1.42	6.30	19.86
	5	M	39	6.15	8.82	15.25
	5	F & M	98	3.30	7.30	18.03
	4 & 5	F & M	209	2.88	7.28	18.55
Robert E. Lee	4	F & M	63	3.41	5.46	12.81
	5	F & M	62	4.90	6.77	15.18
	4 & 5	F & M	125	4.15	6.11	13.98
	4 & 5	F	57	6.56	6.46	16.35
	4 & 5	M	68	2.13	5.82	12.00

set of 16 Likert-type items that are mostly a revised, simplified version of the items from the California F Scale of Authoritarianism (Adorno, Frenkel-Brunswik, Levinson, & Sanford, 1950). The Social Desirability Scale (CSD) was developed by V. C. Crandall, Crandall, and Katkovsky (1965). The School Morale Scale was developed by Wrightsman, Nelson, and Taranto (1968).

RELATIONSHIP OF C-PHN TO ADULT PHN

The C-PHN and the PHN were administered to 400 freshman men at Vanderbilt University during freshman testing in 1967 to determine the relationship between the two scales. Administration of the two scales was counterbalanced to minimize order effects. The correlations are presented

TABLE 8.5 Correlations Among C-PHN Subscales and Related Variables

Item	School Morale Total	Trustworthiness	Strength of Will & Rationality	Complexity	Children's F Scale
		School A; Total Jr. High; N = 992			
Trustworthiness	.24				
Strength of Will and Rationality	.21	.28			
Complexity	.07	.00	.04		
Children's F Scale	-.23	-.42	-.18	-.14	
Social Desirability	.24	.09	.11	-.13	.05
		School B; Grade 5; N = 94			
Trustworthiness	.19				
Strength of Will and Rationality	.13	.21			
Complexity	.06	.18	.05		
Children's F Scale	-.30	-.48	.01	-.34	
Social Desirability	.20	.07	-.09	-.38	.15
		School B; Grade 4; N = 79			
Trustworthiness	.22				
Strength of Will and Rationality	-.02	.07			
Complexity	.15	.18	-.16		
Children's F Scale	-.27	-.40	.11	-.34	
Social Desirability	.07	-.08	.04	-.00	.11

in Table 8.7. The heterogeneous-method, homogeneous-attitude correlations of .508, .734, .570 are not so high as might be expected; however, a comparison of factor analyses between the PHN and the C-PHN helps account for the outcome. The items on the C-PHN-Trustworthiness subscale load on three factors, only two of which are interpretable and shared by the PHN. The other two C-PHN subscales load on five factors each, only two of which seem to be definitely interpretable and shared by the PHN. It is reasonable to assume that correlations of subscale items that are common to shared, interpretable factors on the PHN and the C-PHN account for the size of the correlations; thus if more Trustworthiness items, for example, loaded on factors common to the two scale formats, the correlations would be higher.

An additional factor analysis of the C-PHN using another population did not differ significantly from the first factor analysis. In both factor analyses, the first factor represents a negative attitude toward other people and contains six negatively scored Trustworthiness items and one Strength of Will and Rationality item. The second factor represents a positive

TABLE 8.6 Correlations Among C-PHN Subscales and Related Variables at School D

Item	IQ	School Morale Total	Grade-Point Average	Trustworthiness	Strength of Will & Rationality
		9th-Grade Males; N = 100			
School Morale Total	.17				
Grade-Point Average	.42	.22			
Trustworthiness	.21	.48	.18		
Strength of Will and Rationality	.07	.31	-.09	.39	
Complexity	.29	.29	.28	.03	-.06
		9th-Grade Females; N = 106			
School Morale Total	.20				
Grade-Point Average	.53	.25			
Trustworthiness	.15	.30	.09		
Strength of Will and Rationality	.15	.33	.18	.04	
Complexity	.21	.16	.06	.04	.07
		7th-Grade Females; N = 162			
School Morale Total	.27				
Grade-Point Average	.71	.45			
Trustworthiness	.35	.36	.22		
Strength of Will and Rationality	.28	.24	.22	.17	
Complexity	.43	.06	.34	.14	.15

attitude toward others and contains four positively scored Trustworthiness items. The third factor represents a Complexity dimension and contains two negatively scored and three positively scored Complexity items. The other five factors do not seem to fit any general descriptive title.

A third factor analysis of the Children's Philosophies of Human Nature Scale (C-PHN) (not described in detail here) found similar factor matrices. The subjects in these three analyses were (1) males only, (2) females only, and (3) males and females combined. In each of these analyses, the first three factors are interpretable, but the other factors are not interpretable. (The 36 items are arranged by factors in Appendix G, in the table entitled "Factor Scales on C-PHN.") The first factor is composed of six negative Trustworthiness items and one negative Strength of Will and Rationality item and represents a general attitude of "pessimism." The second factor is composed of four positive Trustworthiness items and represents a general attitude of altruism. Like the factor analyses of the

TABLE 8.7 PHN and C-PHN Subscale Correlations for University Males, $N = 400$

	Strength of Will & Rationality	Trust-worthiness	Indepen-dence	Altruism	Vari-ability	Com-plexity	Positive-Negative	Multiplexity	C-PHN Trust-worthiness	C-PHN Strength of Will
Adult PHN:										
Trust.	.39									
Indep.	.37	.57								
Alt.	.30	.66	.59							
Var.	-.02	.04	.01	-.08						
Comp.	-.13	.08	-.04	-.04	.38					
Pos.-Neg.	.64	.84	.81	.83	-.01	-.04				
Multi.	-.10	.08	-.02	-.07	.80	.86	-.03			
C-PHN:										
Trust.	.41	.73	.52	.60	.01	.05	.72	.04		
St. W. & R.	.51	.28	.28	.21	-.02	-.10	.40	-.08	.35	
Comp.	.04	.05	-.05	-.10	.51	.57	-.02	.65	.03	.08

adult form described in Chapter 4, the positively scored and negatively scored Trustworthiness items split into separate factors. The third factor is composed of five Complexity items and represents a general attitude of complexity.

In the original validation study (C. E. Young & Wrightsman, 1968), the Trustworthiness subscale consistently produced statistically significant differences, with girls having higher scores than boys and with students in middle-class schools having higher scores than students in lower-class schools. Since the first two interpretable factors in the factor analyses were predominantly composed of Trustworthiness items and since the Trustworthiness scale was the best-discriminating scale in the original validation study, it was decided to retain those items in the first two factors and to create additional items that might load on these same two initial factors. The purpose here was to add items that would increase the reliability and the validity of the two new empirical scales called Pessimism and Altruism.

The resulting set contained 13 items from the original scale and 29 new items. These items are included in Appendix G, under the title "Revised Item Pool for C-PHN." This new scale was then administered to a new junior high school sample (N = 503), and the new data were then factor analyzed.

Two definite factors again emerged. The first factor is composed of positively scored items that represent pessimism, and the second factor is composed of positive items that represent altruism. There are 12 items in the first factor and 10 in the second with loadings of .30 or higher.

Two of the items that had loadings less than -.30 on the second factor were rewritten as positive items to balance the two scales. This final scale of 24 items is given in Table 8.8.

This new scale, the Revised C-PHN, yields two subscale scores and an overall positive-negative score (P-N). The two subscales are called Pessimism and Altruism. These scales are not mutually exclusive. Thus the negative of one does not affirm the other; neither does the affirmation of one negate the other. Nevertheless, their sum (P-N) represents a potentially important attitudinal construct in the study of children. At this time, the C-PHN (rev.) has not been administered to new criterion groups. Since there are no normative data available on this new scale, the Trustworthiness subscale on the C-PHN is still the most valuable measure of children's positive-negative philosophies of human nature.

Research using the C-PHN (rev.) should make it possible, however, to determine the extent to which various environmental phenomena are

TABLE 8.8 Revised C-PHN Scale

Pessimism Items
1. You cannot trust politicians.
2. Most businessmen are not "fair and square" anymore.
3. In a game, most people will cheat to win.
4. No one really cares about me and my problems.
5. If most people found a wallet, they would keep the money in it.
6. More people hate than love these days.
7. You must have luck to succeed in life.
8. A person should never trust anybody but himself.
9. Most people do not tell the truth anymore.
10. Other kids don't care what I'm worried about.
11. Most adults don't care about what happens to kids.
12. Everything in this world is getting worse.

Altruism Items
1. A person should try to like everybody.
2. A person should never hurt other people to make money.
3. Most people will not cheat to win in a game.
4. Helping people makes one feel good.
5. Selfishness is wrong.
6. It is important to listen when someone is talking about his problems.
7. Most neighbors will help each other out.
8. It is a good idea to always share with others.
9. A person should always trust others.
10. A person should always be willing to help others.
11. Everyone should fight poverty.
12. A person should be kind to everyone.

---

related to the development of children's positive-negative attitudes toward life in general. This might be done by administering both the C-PHN (rev.) and the Science Research Associates' Junior Inventory to the same sample of students. Since the latter test measures attitudes toward school, home, self, people, and health, correlations between the Revised C-PHN and scores on each of five parts' scores of the Junior Inventory would give estimates of the relationship of these five areas to positive-negative assumptions. It should also be interesting to study the relationship between the PHN and aggression, social behavior, school-dropout rate, and other such areas.

Summary

Erik Erikson's (1963) theory of the emergence of trust versus mistrust as an initial conflict during infancy generated hypotheses that mothers' caretaker behaviors and the environmental social structure would be related to the presence of trust in 3-year-olds. Stack (1972a) developed a rating scale of the trusting behavior of 3-year-olds and found that the ratings given children were related to the behavior of their mothers toward them. Additionally, there were social-class differences in the degree of trusting behavior shown by these children as well as social-class differences in the mothers' behaviors.

The other major concern of this chapter was the development of assumptions about human nature beyond the basic trust of early childhood. Baxter's (1973a) findings of no relationship between PHN attitudes of adolescents and those expressed by their parents suggested that the adult form of the PHN may be inappropriate for use with children. A downward extension of the scale, called the Children's Philosophies of Human Nature Scale, or C-PHN, was constructed to assess the attitudes of elementary school children. Only three of the original subscales were relied upon—Trustworthiness, Strength of Will and Rationality, and Complexity.

CHAPTER NINE

The Zeitgeist and Philosophies of Human Nature, or, Where Did All the Idealistic, Imperturbable Freshmen Go?

NORMA J. BAKER

LAWRENCE S. WRIGHTSMAN

> Today's youth have no heroes.
>
> —Headline in a Sunday-
> supplement magazine article

The "Zeitgeist," or "spirit of the times," is many faceted and always changing. Take the United States in the early 1960s as an example. A feeling of optimism surged through the country. A new administration had taken over the government, and it had generated a contagious vibrant style. Even if its substance was yet to be demonstrated, the new administration conveyed an excitement and zest to many Americans, especially young people. The Zeitgeist was to change, however. By the end of the 1960s, the spirit was diametrically different; in fact, the United States was a rather dispirited nation. By then, both contemporary professional journals and popular magazines were generously sprinkled with references to the disillusionment and discontent of many Americans, particularly young people. For example, in an article in *Parade* magazine (Oct. 29, 1967), Lloyd Shearer (1967) reported a survey that had asked 2,100 American young people, ages 16-23, "Is there any living American or foreign public figure whom you admire and respect or with whom you identify?" More than half, 53.1%, could give no answer.

If, as D. L. Kanter and Mirvis (1989) claim, "the cynical American" has become the prototype, we can look to events in the 1960s as sources for the current cluster of prevailing attitudes. Thirty years later, the 1960s remain the decade of most profound change in this century.

This chapter asks if changes in the spirit of the times are reflected in changes in young people's philosophies of human nature. A longitudinal study that tested the same people in 1961 and again in 1969 would not have given a clear answer to this question, because changes in these individuals over such a long time interval would also be influenced by their own unique personal experiences. A cross-sectional study that tested different groups of young people all at the same stage in life but at different points in time would better permit a clear-cut answer to the question.

But where do we obtain samples with similar backgrounds who are at the same stage in life but who arrived at that stage at different points in time? Our solution was to test successive freshman classes at the same college. We will evaluate the adequacy of the assumptions behind this decision later in this chapter.

Our basic procedure was to administer the Philosophies of Human Nature Scale and the Taylor Manifest Anxiety Scale to entering freshman classes at George Peabody College from 1959 through 1971. But before reporting the findings, we will examine the professional literature to see if social scientists had anticipated changes in student responses that reflected the Zeitgeist.

American college students and other young people have traditionally carried forward the traits of optimism, idealism, and faith in a future full of opportunity. Nevitt Sanford (1962a), in describing the developmental status of the freshmen entering Vassar College in the early 1960s, said: "the typical entering freshman is idealistic, sociable, well-organized, and well-behaved" (p. 253).

Most descriptions of college students in the 1950s referred to them—as the students of the 1980s would later be characterized—as docile and serious about their own work but apathetic about larger social concerns. The most widely cited one, Jacob's (1957) description of college students as "gloriously contented" in 1957, was far removed from the image of the American undergraduate prevalent a short decade later. Jacob's comprehensive survey of studies dealing with student values included the following conclusions:

> The traditional moral virtues are valued by almost all students. . . . American students are . . . dutifully responsive toward government. . . . International problems are the least of the concerns to which they expect to give much personal attention during their immediate future. . . . Students by and large set great stock by college in general and their own college in particular. (Jacob, 1957, pp. 2-3)

Thus went the early 1950s. The label "privatism" was used by Jacob to describe this value pattern that included a pronounced absence of concern for social problems and the wider world, along with a feeling of estrangement and distance from what older generations represented. From his survey of college students' values, Jacob estimated that, at that time, 75% or 80% of the college population had a privatistic value system.

Other surveys in the 1950s concurred with the evaluation of college students as apathetic and politically uninterested, reflecting the Zeitgeist of the somnolent Eisenhower era. Goldsen, Rosenberg, Williams, and Suchman (1960) saw students' apathy as a withdrawal from the increasing complexities of their generation.

Discussing social change and American youth, Keniston (1962) stressed the decline in political involvement among college youth as a corollary of their emphasis on the private and the present. Underlying their preference for an aesthetic rather than a political commitment was a feeling of public powerlessness. Keniston used the term *alienated* to describe students whose feelings of powerlessness extended beyond matters of political and social interest. Alienation included the feeling that their influence could not be felt in any area beyond their own personal spheres.

In what appeared to be an attempt to see beyond students' withdrawal or feelings of alienation, Mogar (1964) reported results that contradicted Jacob's earlier conclusion that students were "gloriously contented" with regard to their outlook for the future. In the early 1960s, Mogar found that a significant minority of students were struggling with their current "valuelessness." He suggested that their withdrawal could be interpreted as a rebellion against convention and popular values.

Indeed, rebellion came to the campus in the school year of 1964-1965. That was not a year for swallowing goldfish, staging panty raids, or stacking students in telephone booths. Instead, the Free Speech Movement at Berkeley, student demonstrations, and teach-ins made it appear that American students had taken a fresh look at the world and that they did not like what they saw.

From about 1965, the university has become a major vehicle of dissent. Protest (Cowan, 1966), ferment (Mallery, 1966), anomie (Goodman, 1966), unrest (Crane, 1967), stress (D. R. Brown, 1967), radicalism (Flacks, 1967), and cynicism (Greeley, 1968) were offered as terms to describe American college students in the 1960s.

Everyone seems to have concluded that the 1960s were years of rapid social change, accompanied by crucial changes in the behavior of college students. But even though much has been written about student unrest, there have been relatively few empirical studies of underlying personalities and attitudes that might have generated the behavior of dissent and protest.

In one attempt to find personality correlates of moral reasoning and political-social behavior, Haan, Smith, and Block (1968) studied Free Speech Movement arrestees, activists, "nonstudents," Peace Corps volunteers, and randomly selected students from the University of California at Berkeley and San Francisco State University. Using Kohlberg's (1963) system for measuring moral judgment, they analyzed differences among five moral types with respect to family-social backgrounds and self-descriptions. In general, Haan et al. found that students who reflected principled moral reasoning (Kohlberg Stages 5 and 6), as contrasted with those who were conventionally moral, were more active in political-social matters, particularly in protest. The self- and ideal descriptions of the principled moralists emphasized interpersonal reactivity and obligation, self-expressiveness, and a willingness to live in opposition to immoral values.

Drawing implications from Durkheim's concept of anomie, Goodman (1966) saw some positive aspects in student behavior of the late 1960s. She suggested that some college students were moving from limitless self-indulgence to remarkably Spartan and unqualified commitment. It was perhaps a move away from inertia, through hedonism, toward social activity.

Activists have directed attention to the campus; yet the results of several studies have led to the conclusion that, prior to May 1971, most instances of student activism involved only a minority of students in a few selected colleges and universities. Peterson (1967) found that only about 9% of any student body was reported as involved in protest movements up to that time and that protest occurred disproportionately often at select institutions of high quality. Keniston (1967) made a distinction between the activists and the alienated and said that dissent was by no means the dominant mood of American college students. Summarizing a number of surveys, he concluded that apathy and privatism were still far more dominant than was dissent. Although extreme acts such as the invasion of Cambodia or the Kent State student killings could trigger massive protest, such occurrences were and are rare.

Feuer (1969) reviewed the American student movement, as symbolized by the Berkeley uprising, and concluded that activism was peripheral to the philosophies and lives of the vast majority of American students. But although it may be true that most students are not activists, they might still have reflected what Feuer calls "the secondary consequences of student activism, which brought dangers to the United States" (Feuer, 1969, p. 88). Among those dangers he listed the activists' example of violence and of contempt for democratic procedure and their intimidation of the majority.

With this in mind, we hypothesized that if the questionnaire responses of freshman classes from 1959 through 1968 were analyzed, they would show a progressive increase in disillusionment and a "creeping pessimism" about society. We expected the trend to begin to stabilize with the 1969 freshmen.

To look at changes, we administered questionnaires to 2,568 freshmen at Peabody College in 10 entering classes from 1959 through 1971. (The classes of 1961, 1963, and 1964 were not tested.) The testing battery did not always contain the same tests, but two scales were administered enough years to permit a look at cross-decade trends. The Taylor Manifest Anxiety Scales (Taylor, 1953) was administered to entering freshmen in 1959, 1960, 1965, 1966, 1967, 1968, 1969, 1970, and 1971. The PHN scale was administered to freshmen in 1962 and each year from 1965 through 1971. Each freshman class was tested at the completion of freshman-orientation week, with the same instructions, in the same room, and by the same examiner (who was not able to keep constant his physical appearance from 1959 through 1971). Explanations of the purpose of the testing were the same for each class.

Since previous research has indicated gender differences on most PHN subscales, data were analyzed separately for men and women. The mean scores for each freshman class are presented in Table 9.1, with the women's averages on the left and the men's averages on the right. If you read down the columns for each of the PHN substantive subscales, you will note a unidirectional trend toward a more negative view of human nature from 1962 through 1968. This is the case for both men and women.

The 1962 freshmen of both genders had the most favorable beliefs about human nature on each of the four substantive dimensions. The mean score for women on the Trustworthiness subscale dropped from 9.80 in 1962 to 0.41 in 1968; from 1968 through 1971, it remained rather stable. An even greater decline on the Trustworthiness subscale was found for the men; their mean went from 8.38 in 1962 to -5.38 in 1968 and then regressed slightly in 1969, 1970, and 1971. The women's mean score on Altruism dropped from 5.10 in 1962 to -3.91 in 1968. In 1971, the mean was about the same, -3.19. For men, the Altruism mean was 1.54 for the 1962 freshmen but was -11.58 for the 1968 freshmen. These are declines of one standard deviation or more. From 1965 through 1968, each class was less

TABLE 9.1 Mean PHN and Taylor MAS Scores for Peabody Freshman Classes, 1959-1971

	Women								Men							
Year	N	PHN Trust.	PHN St. W. & R.	PHN Alt.	PHN Indep.	PHN Comp.	PHN Var.	MAS	N	PHN Trust.	PHN St. W. & R.	PHN Alt.	PHN Indep.	PHN Comp.	PHN Var.	MAS
1959	176	)	Not given					14.20	58	)	Not given					14.22
1960	175	)						14.33	60	)						13.88
1961		)						N.G.		)						N.G.
1962	250	+9.80	+15.30	+5.10	+4.30	+8.80	+16.20	N.G.	63	+8.38	+13.21	+1.54	+2.95	+7.06	+15.87	N.G.
1963		N.G.	N.G.	N.G.	N.G.	N.G.	N.G.	N.G.		N.G.	N.G.	N.G.	N.G.	N.G.	N.G.	N.G.
1964		N.G.	N.G.	N.G.	N.G.	N.G.	N.G.	N.G.		N.G.	N.G.	N.G.	N.G.	N.G.	N.G.	N.G.
1965	261	+6.93	+12.52	-0.46	+2.36	+6.88	+17.47	17.01	84	+3.98	+9.86	-4.80	+0.17	+4.90	+14.36	16.68
1966	189	+3.57	+12.27	-3.16	-0.26	+6.48	+16.46	18.76	56	-0.43	+8.55	-7.95	-2.05	+5.59	+15.41	19.07
1967	170	+4.38	+10.11	-1.54	-0.11	+8.81	+17.88	19.80	54	+0.50	+9.22	-3.37	-2.00	+6.39	+16.31	19.04
1968	165	+0.41	+9.08	-3.91	-1.17	+9.17	+16.99	21.50	50	-5.38	+8.30	-11.58	-4.66	+5.48	+16.02	19.24
1969	175	+1.86	+9.33	-1.46	-0.11	+7.90	+18.23	22.11	70	-4.80	+4.46	-11.17	-5.37	+6.13	+15.27	19.38
1970	231	+2.00	+9.22	-1.72	+0.18	+7.87	+17.14	20.06	50	-4.10	+6.76	-8.30	-5.06	+8.84	+15.70	17.80
1971	202	+0.50	+9.09	-3.19	-2.13	+9.24	+18.39	20.41	47	-3.34	+8.93	-10.08	-4.36	+9.21	+14.47	19.68

Note: N.G. = not given

TABLE 9.2 F Values for Mean Differences in PHN Scores and MAS Scores of Peabody Freshmen, 1959-1968

Measure	Women's F Value	p	Men's F Value	p
Trustworthiness	29.83	.01	9.40	.01
Strength of Will				
and Rationality	54.45	.01	2.37	.05
Altruism	15.93	.01	8.63	.01
Independence	8.11	.01	3.39	.01
Complexity	2.43	.05	0.37	NS
Variability	2.95	.05	0.45	NS
Taylor MAS	38.67	.01	9.42	.01

Note: The PHN was administered to five classes (1962, 1965, 1966, 1967, 1968), and the MAS was administered to six classes (1959, 1960, 1965, 1966, 1967, 1968).

positive or more negative than the previous class on these substantive dimensions, with the exception of a slight regression in the 1967 freshman class. Analyses of variance indicated that both the male and female groups from 1962 through 1968 differed significantly on each of the four PHN substantive dimensions. F values of $p < .01$ were obtained for female groups on all four positive-negative subscales. F values of $p < .01$ were obtained for men on the Trustworthiness, Altruism, and Independence subscales, F values of $p < .05$ were obtained on the Strength of Will and Rationality subscale. The means and F values for both men and women are shown in Table 9.2.

F values of $p < .05$ were obtained for women on the two individual-differences dimensions of the PHN, but those scores did not follow the linear pattern of the substantive subscales. For men, differences among classes on these two individual-differences dimensions were not significant. These dimensions, Complexity and Variability, deal with beliefs about the differences in human nature and may not be conceptualized on an evaluative dimension. They were not expected to show consistent changes over time and, in fact, did not.

Mean scores on the Taylor Manifest Anxiety Scale also showed significant differences among the classes from 1959 through 1968; the trend was toward increasingly greater expressions of anxiety in the later classes. MAS scores can range from 0 to 50. The mean score for women in 1959 was 14.20, rising to 21.50 in 1968 and 22.11 in 1969 before regressing slightly in 1970 and 1971. For men, the mean score went from 14.22 in 1959 to 19.24 in 1968, 19.38 in 1971. The F values are shown in Table 9.2.

TABLE 9.3 Test for Trend by Orthogonal Polynomials Linear-Trend Analysis, Using 1959-1968 Freshman Classes

Scale	Women		Men	
	F Linear	*p*	*F Linear*	*p*
PHN-Trustworthiness	66.862	0.0001	34.099	0.0001
PHN-Strength of Will and Rationality	54.425	0.0001	6.227	0.0126
PHN-Altruism	40.474	0.0001	21.919	0.0001
PHN-Independence	25.696	0.0001	12.394	0.0008
PHN-Complexity[a]	1.065	0.3026	—	—
PHN-Variability[a]	0.349	0.5617	—	—
Manifest Anxiety Scale	139.096	0.0001	21.550	0.0001

Note: a. For males, PHN Complexity and PHN Variability were not included in the trend analysis because the analysis-of-variance *F* values were not significant.

From 1959 to 1968, each female sample's mean was higher than that of the previous class; this was also true of men, except for the 1960 freshmen. High scores on the MAS indicate overt admissions of anxiety. Thus each year through 1968, freshmen expressed more anxiety symptoms than did members of the previous class. (The MAS had slight negative correlations with PHN substantive subscales [*r*s of -.05 to -.18].)

Do these changes reflect a consistent trend from the early 1960s through 1968? On the MAS and on each of the PHN subscales that showed a significant *F* ratio, a post hoc test for trend by orthogonal polynomials was made (Winer, 1962). A significant linear component emerged for both male and female groups on the PHN substantive subscales—that is, the mean scores could be plotted along a straight line. The MAS scores for male and female groups also showed a significant linear trend. For example, the linear *F* for women on the Trustworthiness subscale was 66.86, which is significant beyond the .0001 level. The trend analysis for female groups showed linear *F* values for all four PHN substantive subscales and for the MAS that were significant beyond .0001. The linear *F* values for men were significant beyond .0001 on the Trustworthiness, Altruism, and Independence subscales, and on the MAS; and the linear *F* on the Strength of Will and Rationality subscale showed *p* < .01. Table 9.3 indicates the values obtained in the trend analysis.

An analysis of the standard deviations for each class on these measures indicated that there was no tendency for the scores to become either more widespread or less widespread in the later classes. Standard deviations remained from 9 to 12 points on the PHN subscales and between 7.9 and 9.4 on the MAS.

From 1968 through the rest of the testing period, the pattern of PHN scores and anxiety scores remained relatively stable. The changes from the 1968 freshmen through their 1971 counterparts showed neither a linear trend nor a consistent direction. We may conclude that the functional ending of the change was in 1968. How may we account for this apparent increase in cynicism and anxiety? Were there differences in the composition of the classes that were the cause?

To see if there were ability differences or demographic differences among classes that would explain the increasing cynicism and anxiety, we made several further analyses. Ability scores on the American College Test (ACT) (American College Testing Program, 1965) were available for the freshman classes of 1963 and of 1965 through 1968.

One-way analyses of variance were made of these classes' ACT percentile scores. The ACT composite scores did not show a significant difference for women. For men, the F value for mean differences in ACT composite scores was 24.64, with $p < .01$. The highest mean score on ACT composite for men was in 1966, however, and there was no consistent increase from year to year. ACT scores were not available for the years prior to 1963. Table 9.4 indicates the mean ACT percentile scores and F values for English, mathematics, social science, natural science, and an ACT composite score. As Table 9.4 shows, the changes in ACT mean percentiles do not follow the linear trend of the PHN and MAS scores. Thus we may rule out ability differences as an explanation of the apparent increases in cynicism and anxiety.

But perhaps *other* variables would differentiate between the classes— variables that would change in line with the changes produced by the PHN and the MAS. We sought background information about the members of different classes and selected for analysis 10 items from the College Student Questionnaire, Part I (Educational Testing Service, 1965). The College Student Questionnaire (CSQ) elicits background information (size of home town, parents' education, religion, respondent's reasons for attending college, and so on) and was completed by members of the freshman classes of 1966, 1967, and 1968. (CSQ data were not available for all the classes included in the previous comparisons.) Chi-square tests were made separately for men and women. The following types of information were compared for the three classes: age at time of testing, philosophy of higher education (that is, vocational orientation, academic orientation, collegiate orientation, and nonconformist orientation), parents' marital

TABLE 9.4 Mean ACT Percentile Scores for Peabody Freshman Classes of 1963 and 1965-1968

		Women							Men			
Year	N	Eng.	Math.	Soc. Sci.	Nat. Sci.	Comp.	N	Eng.	Math.	Soc. Sci.	Nat. Sci.	Comp.
1963	201	61.05	45.83	54.27	46.58	51.37	58	46.40	45.83	54.91	54.55	52.28
1965	311	60.68	48.13	60.74	51.06	55.59	110	49.55	57.78	59.27	59.46	58.15
1966	180	66.68	50.76	61.37	53.96	58.92	49	53.04	55.84	66.41	65.23	60.96
1967	128	66.14	51.22	54.73	52.83	56.65	54	50.53	49.74	56.53	57.12	54.16
1968	113	65.27	77.31	55.23	51.14	57.36	30	60.67	52.87	59.10	61.30	59.30
F		2.72*	3.82**	3.42**	2.09	2.25		3.51**	4.47**	7.33**	3.20*	24.64**

Note: $*F$ ($p < .05 = 2.37$)
$**F$ ($p < .01 = 3.32$)

233

status, birth order, parents' child-rearing policy, reaction to cheating, and feelings about competing. Of all these, only one—the comparison of ages of the male groups—yielded a chi-square value that was significant ($p < .05$). (Frequency distributions for these chi-square comparisons are included in Appendix H at the end of this book.) It appears that there were no demographic or background characteristics that would explain the changes in PHN and MAS scores. Adding strength to this conclusion is an analysis by Nottingham (1968) that correlated information on the CSQ with PHN scores within the 1967 freshman class and found that freshmen's substantive-subscale scores were unrelated to their CSQ responses.

If we then rule out the possibility that the samples are from different populations, two other possible explanations occur: (1) the change reflects an increasing willingness to admit negative things about oneself and others, and (2) loss of trust and increases in anxiety reflect changes in the Zeitgeist during the 1960s.

The first of these explanations is plausible. Certainly the post-World War II years have seen an increase in the value placed on honesty, openness, and authenticity by American youth. Similarly, a person is less stigmatized now than several decades ago if he or she admits to having an emotional difficulty. So it may be that the changes from 1962 through 1968 reflected not increased cynicism and anxiety but rather a willingness to bring out into the open some beliefs and personal feelings that have always been present. We have no way of testing this alternative explanation.

We prefer the second explanation, of course. That is, the 1960s saw a progressive disillusionment with the capacity of our country to solve its problems of poverty, racism, and war. The summer of 1968 must have been the low point. Two major figures much revered by American youth were assassinated in the spring and summer of 1968. Riots occurred in many major cities. It became increasingly clear that the war in Vietnam was not to be solved easily. The outcome of the demonstration at the 1968 Democratic Party convention in Chicago occurred three weeks before members of the 1968 freshman class took pencils in hand to indicate their attitudes.

It would appear that from 1968 to 1971 things did not greatly improve, but they did not become perceptibly worse. We expected the 1969 freshmen to show less cynicism and less anxiety than their 1968 counterparts, because there was a brief flush of optimism around the edges of the Zeitgeist in early 1969—a new administration, a period in which everyone was encouraged to "cool it," and a wait-and-see attitude. But the 1969 freshmen did not appreciably differ from the 1968 freshmen. Neither did the 1970 or 1971 freshmen differ very much.

We recognize that we are drawing large implications from findings generated on only one campus. Is there any evidence for the same trend on other campuses? Yes, although the same instruments were not used. Hochreich and Rotter (1970) administered Rotter's Interpersonal Trust Scale to elementary psychology classes at the University of Connecticut, starting in the fall of 1964 and continuing through September 1969. In total, 4,605 students were tested under comparable testing conditions. Hochreich and Rotter report a significant drop in interpersonal trust means each year. In September 1964, the mean score was 72.4; in 1969, it was 66.6. Standard deviations ranged from 8.31 to 11.20. This means that a 1969 student who was in the middle of the distribution would have been in the most distrusting one third of the 1964 group.

Hochreich and Rotter found no difference in their groups with regard to class rank, college entrance examination scores, or ethnic-group composition. Likewise, they reject an explanation that the change in mean scores occurred because it is now less socially desirable to express trust, and they support their conclusion by reporting that the size of correlations between interpersonal trust and the Marlowe-Crowne (M-C) (Crowne & Marlowe, 1960) measure of social desirability does not differ significantly over the period studied. Hochreich and Rotter (1970) do not report the magnitudes of these correlations, but elsewhere they report that previous studies (Hochreich, 1968; Mulry, 1966; Rotter, 1967) found correlations of .21 to .27 between the Marlowe-Crowne Social Desirability Scale and Rotter's Interpersonal Trust Scale. In four samples, the correlations between M-C social desirability and positive-negative score on the PHN were .235, .308, .320, and .302.

As much as we would like to concur, we fail to see how this rules out changes in social desirability as an explanation. Is there no drop in the mean social-desirability scores for 1964-1969? That would be stronger evidence.

In addition, the Detroit Area Study, directed by Otis Dudley Duncan (see Lear, 1972), included cross-sectional surveys of the attitudes of adults living in Detroit and produced results that reflect changes in the beliefs of Detroiters about their fellow human beings. For example, in 1956, 33% of Detroit adults agreed with the statement, "Most people don't care about the next fellow." In 1971, 50% agreed (Lear, 1972). Two statements reflecting feelings of anomie, with which only 13% and 26% of the 1956 respondents agreed, were agreed with by 35% and 39% of the 1971 sample. Do such changes simply mean that different types of people lived in Detroit in 1956 and in 1971? Or are the changes more pervasive?

Numerous explanations have been offered for the changes in trust and anxiety found among young people. One way to bring some organization to these explanations is to categorize such as sympathetic, critical, or neutral regarding the students (Halleck, 1968).

Explanations sympathetic to the student, view the student as the victim of human-made circumstances and see student unrest as a legitimate and rational effort to change these circumstances. The more obvious social conditions seen as causing this unrest were the Vietnam War, the pressures on the student to compete, the anonymity associated with technology and bigness, and the identification of the student with the racial minorities and the poor.

If students are asked the reasons for the changes, a theme of being a pawn of others or a victim of circumstances emerges. In an attempt to solicit explanations from college students themselves, we met with some Peabody College students who were among those in the classes analyzed in this study. These students were members of an educational-psychology class section selected for participation in a tutoring project with Head Start children. We presented a brief report of the findings of our analysis of freshman classes and asked the students to react. Their responses were tape-recorded. No one in the group expressed surprise at the direction of the findings. When asked why college freshmen would have reported less positive views of human nature and would have shown increases in anxiety, the students' most frequent answers were: Vietnam, pressures to make high grades to get into college, racial rioting, and assassinations of public figures. The following comments were typical:

> Oh, I think it's Vietnam. The guys feel pressure to make the grades so they won't be drafted. The girls feel anxious about Vietnam, because there goes the husband pool.

> When you see riots in the streets on your TV every day, why wouldn't you be anxious?

> About those independent scores . . . a person feels very little control over his environment . . . it all ties into the war.

> Young people don't trust the government. There's been a tendency for young people not to feel involved in government, but that's changing now. The little

man can't be heard in government, and young people are identifying with these "out" groups.

Every year it gets harder to get into college. The competition gets worse.

When we were in junior high, they started this big thing on critical thinking. We were taught to question everything. Before, we thought everything was OK. Then, when we learned to question, we became more distressed.

Being in this section of educational psychology makes me anxious! Tutoring those kids and seeing how bad things really are makes me depressed.

The last quotation suggests that greater exposure to the effects of impoverished environments may contribute to anxiety and loss of trust in the basic goodness of human nature. With the emphasis on the Peace Corps, VISTA, and community involvement, the students in the 1960s developed a more realistic view of the effects of poverty and of inequalities of opportunity.

The feeling that increasing competition for college admission is an obstacle to youthful idealism has been articulated by Greeley (1968). The psychosocial moratorium of late adolescence is cut short for most young Americans because, if they are to succeed, they must choose that right college, take the right courses, and pass the right exams. This kind of pressure does not allow time for the process of identity formation.

Flacks (1967) referred to the high degrees of impersonality and competitiveness in high schools and universities. He hypothesized that student unrest grew out of the incompatibility between an emerging pattern of familial relations and institutional expectations. In many upper-middle-class, professional homes there has been an emphasis on democratic, egalitarian relations and a high degree of permissiveness stressing values other than achievement. Young people reared in this kind of family setting find it difficult to submit to adult authority and to a high degree of competition. They are intolerant of the hypocrisy of adults who express values different from those indicated by their life-styles.

One student's explanation regarding the emphasis on critical thinking suggests the hypothesis that, each year, students are simply more accustomed to looking for faults in others. It is possible that responding negatively to items such as those of the PHN has acquired social-desirability value. Edwards (1957) has shown that subjects generally attribute desirable characteristics to themselves. But what is "desirable"? Perhaps it is now fashionable to pontificate cynically about one's fellows. If the schools have emphasized the need for critical thinking, a negative stance may have come to be viewed as socially desirable. It would be interesting to repeat Edwards's social-desirability research to see if, in the interval, there have been changes in the average desirability values given to statements.

Some hypothesized explanations of student discontent are not so sympathetic to the students. The affluence hypothesis says that the child reared in an affluent society does not learn to use work as a means of mastering some aspect of the world and is thus trapped in a never-ending search for new diversions and new freedoms (Halleck, 1968). Protest and cynicism are simply the diversions of the day.

The permissiveness hypothesis lays blame upon parents who have abdicated their responsibility to discipline their children, thus rearing a generation of spoiled, greedy youth. Even rational forms of discipline, such as being required to master basic concepts before moving on to more abstract ideas, bother them (Halleck, 1968).

In addition to explanations sympathetic to or critical of students, there are further hypotheses that may be seen as neutral in that they refer to more subtle societal changes that affect the values of youth. As an example, Keniston (1967, 1968a, 1968b) has suggested that, with the accelerating rate of innovation, the wisdom and skills of parents can no longer be transmitted to children with any assurance that they will be appropriate for them. This means that truth must just as often be created by children as learned from parents.

Another social force to be considered is the pervasive influence of television viewing. Although the psychological impact of television has not been completed determined, there is reason to believe that contemporary youth have been exposed to negative information about human behavior more rapidly and at an earlier age than ever before. The effect of this premature emergence of "both sides" of human nature may have helped create a deep skepticism as to the validity of authority (Halleck, 1968). The pervasiveness of the media prevents any easy inference that the sole cause for increasing cynicism is a deterioration in the quality of life in the society. It may not be so much that life is getting worse as that we are constantly exposed, through television and other media, to human behavior that is less than trustworthy and altruistic. We are thinking here not only of violent dramatic programs but also of scenes of murder, war, riots, and other hostile acts on news programs. As Otto (1969) has written:

The consistent emphasis in the news on criminal violence, burglarizing, and assault makes slow but pervasive inroads into our reservoir of trust. As we hear and read much about the acts of violence and injury men perpetrate upon one another, year after year . . . we begin to trust our fellow man less, and we thereby diminish ourselves. It is my conclusion the media's excessive emphasis on violence, like the drop of water on the stone, erodes and wears away the trust factor in man. (p. 16)

Thus this onslaught of images may subtly affect our basic philosophy of human nature. Television has also made possible an instant awareness of the gaps between the ideals professed by American society and the practices that contradict that preference.

Summary

Changes in philosophies of human nature may be influenced by the Zeitgeist, or the spirit of the times. During the decade of the 1960s the idealism reflected in such projects as the Peace Corps and Head Start changed into a pessimism and distrust that reflected the effects of ghetto riots, assassinations, and police brutality. Such changes were manifested in differences in PHN scores of freshmen entering Peabody College from 1962 through 1968; more recent classes consistently saw human nature as more untrustworthy, more irrational, more selfish, and more conforming. Increases in anxiety scores also occurred in the more recent classes. Alternative explanations based on different populations as sources of different freshman classes were rejected.

CHAPTER TEN

Philosophies of Human Nature: How Much Change Is Possible?

GEORGE W. BAXTER, Jr.
ROBERT N. CLAXTON
LAWRENCE S. WRIGHTSMAN

> The man who never alters his opinion is like standing water, and breeds reptiles of the mind.
>
> —WILLIAM BLAKE,
> *The Marriage of Heaven and Hell*

After reviewing the voluminous evidence on the consistency of personality, Walter Mischel (1969) concluded that our assumptions about people are formed early in life and that our later experiences are construed so as to conform to these assumptions. He wrote: "There is a great deal of evidence that our cognitive constructions about ourselves and the world—our personal theories about ourselves and those around us . . . often are extremely stable and highly resistant to change" (p. 1012).

But does this apply to attitudes? How much do a person's attitudes change between two attitude ratings? Does a fundamental change in a person's environment cause this person to develop a different set of attitudes? Do deliberate attempts to change philosophies of human nature have any effect? This chapter explores these and related questions.

All studies reported in this chapter are longitudinal ones that involve the retesting of the same subjects. From study to study, however, the time interval between test and retest is quite different, as is the nature of the intervening experience. The studies deal with four types of possible change in philosophies of human nature: (1) change resulting from the passage of time and its associated uncontrolled experiences, (2) change resulting from some dramatic happening in one's world, (3) change resulting from experience on a job, and (4) change resulting from direct attempts to alter one's attitudes. We will consider each of these in turn.

Changes Over Time

Studies in which the same subjects are tested and then retested on the same instrument after an interval of many years are hard to come by; researchers devoted to doing such studies may perish before they can publish. We must be content with something less. In fact, we have found only two studies in which several months passed before PHN attitudes of heterogeneous groups were retested. They are Baxter's (1968) project, which reassessed the attitudes of students near the end of their first or second year of college, and Bayless's (1971) study, which retested freshmen after their first semester of college. In both studies, students had been tested at the beginning of their freshman year.

If we were to ask how much change occurs in a person's philosophy of human nature in a *representative* four to eight months of his or her life, the four to eight months immediately after college entrance would certainly not be the ideal ones to consider. For most college freshmen, those months mark their first extended period away from home, as well as the beginning of a new stage in life, with new friends, new activities, and new insights about themselves and the world. However, if any period in a person's life past adolescence should cause a change in his or her philosophy of human nature, it should be the freshman year in college. Consider the environmental changes for a young woman from rural upstate New York who matriculates at Columbia University, in the midst of the Harlem ghetto—or for an only child who has always enjoyed the quietude of a room of his own and who now must share space with a garrulous roommate.

Yet not all observers would agree that the college experience makes any real difference. Jacob (1957), in his pessimistic review of the literature on changing values in college, concluded: "The changes which have been observed . . . are mainly changes on the surface of personality. They do not really involve the fundamental values which shape a student's life pattern" (p. 53). But rebuttals (Barton, 1959; Riesman, 1958) pointed out that many of the studies that Jacob reviewed used inadequate methodologies and that Jacob failed to evaluate the quality of these studies. In fact critics claimed Jacob had not even attempted to adequately define and measure values.

Jacob's bombshell of a book also generated more well-designed studies of value change in college, but such studies generally avoided concern with students' assumptions about human nature. Although the Cornell Values Study (Goldsen, Rosenberg, Williams, & Suchman, 1960) found that many attitudes toward religious, political, and social issues could be explained by assumptions about human nature, it used these assumptions only as constants and never as variables that might change in their own right. Nevertheless, many studies of change in student values may cast some light on expectations about changes in philosophies of human nature.

The most relevant findings have involved concepts of tolerance, dogmatism, rigidity, authoritarianism, and prejudice. Compared with freshmen, seniors were found to be more tolerant toward people (Jacob, 1957; Lehmann & Dressel, 1962; N. Sanford, 1962b); toward individual differences (Freedman, 1961); toward diversity of opinion, radical ideas, and unconventional people (Jacob, 1957; Lehmann & Dressel, 1962; Lehmann, Sinha, & Harnett, 1966); toward ambiguity (D. R. Brown, 1967); and toward other religions (Lehmann & Dressel, 1962). At the same time, seniors were less dogmatic and authoritarian (Beach, 1967; D. R. Brown, 1967; Foster, 1961; Plant, 1962), less inflexible regarding human nature (Jacob, 1957), less rigid and conventional (K. P. Cross, 1968), and less stereotypic in thinking and beliefs (D. R. Brown, 1967; Jacob, 1957; Lehmann & Dressel, 1962; Lehmann et al., 1966). And clearly, college seniors had become less ethnocentric (Beach, 1967; D. R. Brown, 1967; K. P. Cross, 1968; Foster, 1961; Jacob, 1957; Plant, 1958, 1962; Plant & Telford, 1966; Webster, 1958).

In citing these, we must always be aware that contradictory interpretations can result from the same data. Feldman (1972) shows how data are often interpreted to fit the investigator's theory that the college experience is a maturing one. For example, Heath (1968) found that, after seven months of college, freshmen were less "autonomous" and emotionally self-sufficient than they were when they entered. But he concluded that the apparent regression was necessary for the students to become even more autonomous later!

Although most of the above conclusions were based on questions concerning selected political, societal, and religious situations (Smith, 1958), they still seem related to the Complexity and Variability dimension of philosophies of human nature. Increased openness, sophistication, flexibility, and awareness and acceptance of individual differences suggest that seniors should score higher than freshmen do on these PHN subscales. Evidence of increased acceptance of other people might also suggest that, over time, college students should show a more positive attitude toward human nature as measured by PHN substantive subscales. Related literature, however, should also be considered. For example, some indirect indications of changes in the trustworthiness dimension are available. McConnell (1962), in a cross-sectional study, reported increased permissiveness by seniors in answers to questions on such topics as censorship of books and the employment of former Communists. Using similar questions, the Cornell Values Study (Goldsen et al., 1960; Suchman, 1958) found that those students—of any class—with more faith or trust in people were more permissive. Since trust and trustworthiness go together, such replies by seniors suggest that they see other people as more trustworthy than freshmen do. Beyond this, other studies have found seniors freer of stereotypic images of good and bad (D. R. Brown, 1967), less fearful that evil forces were in the world (Jacob, 1957), and less cynical about people (Freedman, 1967).

These findings have compared seniors with freshmen. In contrast, Baxter's (1968) study using the PHN compared the scores of end-of-year freshmen and end-of-year sophomores with their own scores as entering freshmen. Was Baxter's time interval adequate to show change? Evidence from the literature says that it was. Several researchers (Foster, 1961; Freedman, 1961, 1967; Lehmann, 1965; Lehmann & Dressel, 1962; Plant, 1962) reported that the major change occurred during the first two years of college, and some (Freedman, 1967; Lehmann, 1965; Lehmann & Dressel, 1962) concluded that more change occurred during the first year than during the second year.

The subjects for Baxter's (1968) study were male and female freshmen who entered George Peabody College for Teachers in September 1965 or in September 1966. Freshmen who enrolled without prior college experience, who took the orientation-week battery of tests, and who had been full-time students during the interim were contacted for retesting in late April and early May 1967. After eliminating students who did not meet those conditions, Baxter had 112 women and 31 men as potential subjects from the 1965 freshman class and 152 women and 39 men from the 1966 freshman class. Of 215 freshman from 1966, 191 were actually included as subjects (the other 24 did not appear for retesting), and this number was considered to be an adequate representation of the entire group. However, of the 213 eligible freshmen from 1965 (sophomores at the time of retesting), only 143 were retested. Therefore, the original PHN scores of retested subjects were compared with those of unretested subjects to determine if the retested subjects represented some self-selection on the PHN scale. Men (Ns of 31 retested and 21 not retested) were compared separately from women (Ns of 112 and 49). Of the 12 t tests (6 subscales for 2 genders), only the comparison of Complexity scores for women was statistically significant at the .05 level. It was concluded that the retested and unretested sophomores were sufficiently similar to assume that the 143 retested subjects were an adequate representation of the eligible group.

Table 10.1 reports the changes in mean PHN scores for women who were retested at the end of their freshman year. Of the six subscales, only Complexity manifested a significant shift in either direction. That is, eight months later, freshman women believed human nature to be more complex than they had when they enrolled in college. Although the women tended to see people as more trustworthy, more independent, and less selfish than they had previously, these changes were not statistically significant. Table 10.1 also indicates that, for every measure, the spread of scores on retest was somewhat greater than it was on first testing. For two subscales— Trustworthiness and Strength of Will and Rationality—the difference in variance was significant, as it was for multiplexity and positive-negative scores.

The pattern for men retested after eight months was not consistent with that for the women (see Table 10.2). In fact, things were topsy-turvy. For the men, attitudes toward the substantive qualities of human nature became more favorable; the shift is statistically significant on the Trustworthiness, Strength of Will and Rationality, and Altruism subscales and is in the same direction for Independence. None of these changed in the female sample. Changes in Complexity scores, which were significant for the women, were not so for the men, although the shift was in the same direction. And although the spread of women's scores on all measures had become greater, the spread for the men's scores decreased on seven of the eight measures. (In no case was the decrease statistically significant, though.)

With this degree of confusion apparent for the 8-month retest results, what emerges in the 20-month retest? Table 10.3 shows the means for the 112 women retested after 20 months is remarkably similar to that for the different set of women who were retested after 8 months. These women also saw human nature as significantly more complex than they had previously, but no other subscale showed any significant change. Over the

TABLE 10.1 Mean PHN Subscale Scores for Freshman Women Retested After Eight Months ($N = 152$)

PHN Scale	Mean on 1st Test	Mean on 2nd Test	t for Difference	SD on 1st Test	SD on 2nd Test	t for Difference	r for Two Testings
Trustworthiness	3.74	5.11	1.54	12.13	13.85	2.14*	.65*
Strength of Will and Rationality	12.61	11.16	-1.53	9.33	11.48	2.75*	.38*
Altruism	-2.82	-2.06	0.71	13.06	14.54	1.57	.55*
Independence	-0.22	1.28	1.56	12.35	13.80	1.70	.60*
Complexity	6.15	9.11	3.26*	10.74	12.10	1.72	.53*
Variability	16.30	16.78	0.80	10.36	10.81	0.61	.51*
Positive-Negative	13.32	15.49	0.77	38.09	45.55	2.98*	.67*
Multiplexity	22.45	25.89	2.66*	16.33	18.38	3.04*	.58*

Note: *Significant at .05 level.

245

TABLE 10.2 Mean PHN Subscale Scores for Freshman Men Retested After Eight Months ($N = 39$)

PHN Scale	Mean on 1st Test	Mean on 2nd Test	t for Difference	SD on 1st Test	SD on 2nd Test	t for Difference	r for Two Testings
Trustworthiness	-1.92	3.44	3.49*	11.88	10.99	-0.65	.65*
Strength of Will and Rationality	6.10	10.28	2.09*	9.45	0.26	-0.12	.10
Altruism	-9.41	-4.00	3.19*	12.50	10.22	-1.52	.58*
Independence	-1.87	-0.10	1.41	10.53	8.71	-1.59	.68*
Complexity	7.36	9.26	0.98	10.78	11.49	0.43	.42*
Variability	15.56	13.38	-1.64	10.34	9.53	-0.68	.65*
Positive-Negative	-7.10	9.62	3.91*	34.93	31.36	-0.90	.68*
Multiplexity	22.92	22.64	-0.07	18.21	16.75	-0.63	.58*

Note: *Significant at .05 level.

20 months, the scores on Trustworthiness and Altruism increased slightly, as they did in the 8-month retest.

Did men in the 20-month retest show patterns consistent with those of men in the 8-month retest? Table 10.4 presents their mean scores. Each male sample showed, to a nonsignificant degree, the increased beliefs in complexity present in the female samples. But in the most important ways, the 20-month retest for men reversed the findings of the 8-month retest. After the 20-month interval, men had significantly *more negative* beliefs about trustworthiness and altruism. Views about independence were also more negative, but the differences were not statistically significant.

Thus freshman women retested after 8 months or 20 months had higher Complexity scores, suggesting that they had become more mature and sophisticated about human behavior. The sheer amount of change over 20 months was only slightly greater than the change over 8 months. Female freshmen showed no consistent tendency to believe that human nature was any more or less favorable upon retest than they did originally. On the other hand, although men also saw human nature as more complex, their differences were not significant. After 8 months of college, men described people as more trustworthy and altruistic and as possessing more strength of will. But after 20 months of college, the second group of men saw people as less trustworthy and altruistic. The means provide an explanation for the apparent contradiction between the two male groups. A very marked phenomenon of regression toward the mean seems to be at work within each male sample. The trend lines cross on all dimensions except Variability and the related multiplexity dimension, and convergence is seen on these two. In all cases except Independence, the difference between the two groups had become less by spring of 1967. (Admittedly, we do not know how the 1965 male freshmen (20-months subjects) would have scored at the end of one year.) The number of men in both samples was also relatively small. However, an explanation for the marked regressions may be that men constitute only one-fourth of the freshman class and may have associated more closely and known one another better than they would have under other conditions. That likelihood seems great, since all resident males lived in the same dormitory.

In general, slightly more change in PHN scores occurred after 20 months than after 8, but clearly the greatest change came during the first year. In studies using other instruments, Lehmann (1965) and Freedman (1967) also found that changes in attitudes occurred mostly during the first year of college.

TABLE 10.3 Mean PHN Subscale Scores for Freshman Women Retested After 20 Months ($N = 112$)

PHN Scale	Mean on 1st Test	Mean on 2nd Test	t for Difference	SD on 1st Test	SD on 2nd Test	t for Difference	r for Two Testings
Trustworthiness	6.53	7.05	0.42	12.24	11.93	-0.29	.38*
Strength of Will and Rationality	12.73	11.30	-1.38	9.49	11.21	1.97	.45*
Altruism	-0.36	0.30	0.49	12.03	13.61	1.40	.38*
Independence	3.71	2.61	-0.89	11.20	11.24	0.04	.31*
Complexity	6.42	9.04	2.55*	11.19	12.06	0.96	.57*
Variability	16.81	16.69	-0.11	9.79	11.32	1.61	.32*
Positive-Negative	22.62	21.27	-0.35	35.53	38.04	0.77	.38*
Multiplexity	23.23	25.72	1.46	17.57	19.03	0.99	.52*

Note: *Significant at .05 level.

TABLE 10.4 Mean PHN Subscale Scores for Freshman Men Retested After 20 Months ($N = 31$)

PHN Scale	Mean on 1st Test	Mean on 2nd Test	t for Difference	SD on 1st Test	SD on 2nd Test	t for Difference	r for Two Testings
Trustworthiness	5.52	-0.48	-3.38*	9.65	11.76	1.32	.59*
Strength of Will and Rationality	7.94	10.06	1.09	8.85	10.93	1.26	.41*
Altruism	-0.94	-5.38	-2.11*	11.18	14.36	1.70	.60*
Independence	-0.10	-1.87	-0.93	9.90	9.67	-0.14	.41*
Complexity	5.81	9.84	1.76	10.38	10.54	0.14	.26
Variability	13.61	11.68	-0.98	9.92	12.37	1.41	.53*
Positive-Negative	12.42	2.32	-2.17*	29.18	35.71	1.54	.70*
Multiplexity	19.42	21.52	0.75	17.76	18.40	0.21	.42*

Note: *Significant at .05 level.

In conflict with each other are the reports on whether students become more homogeneous in attitude as a result of sharing the same campus environment. Jacob (1957) interpreted the literature as showing more homogeneity and consistency of values. But Newcomb (1943) found that Bennington seniors were "scarcely at all more homogeneous in attitude than freshmen" (p. 147) and showed "little or no increase in homogeneity until the senior year" (p. 206). Lehmann and Dressel (1962) and Webster (1958) found less homogeneity among seniors than among freshmen; only on measures of authoritarianism and tolerance were seniors more homogeneous. Senior men were also more homogeneous on a dogmatism measure. In both of these studies, the standard deviations varied greatly, rising and falling throughout the four years. In Baxter's PHN study, the women retested after 20 months showed an increase in variance on five of the six subscales, although no increase was significant. The women retested after 8 months showed increased variance on all subscales, and two (Trustworthiness and Strength of Will and Rationality) were significantly larger on retest. Clearly, greater heterogeneity of attitudes has occurred among the retested women. The variances for the men retested after 20 months were larger on five of six subscales, and the decrease on the sixth scale was negligible. None of the changes was statistically significant. But, for the 8-month retest, five subscales showed a variance decrease—again none being significant. The seemingly contradictory pattern presented by the two male groups could be a part of their regression toward a common mean.

Certainly pressures toward homogeneity of attitude will be stronger in some colleges than in others. Greater heterogeneity could imply that the school does not present a clear image to which the student could conform. It could also suggest a weak peer influence. At Peabody College at the time of testing 45% of the students were commuters and another 10% came from nearby parts of the state and often spent weekends at home. There was a feeling of "live and let live" on campus, with different segments of the student body free to "do their own thing." These factors could account for the increase in heterogeneity in three of the four retested groups.

In another study of changes during the first year of college, Bayless (1971) retested the entire 1969 freshman class ($N = 927$) in the Arts and Sciences College of Oklahoma State University at the end of the first semester. Table 10.5 indicates that the changes in mean PHN-subscale scores were minor; none was statistically significant. As in most of

TABLE 10.5 Mean PHN Subscale Scores for Oklahoma State University Freshmen Retested at End of First Semester (N = 927)

PHN Subscale	Mean on 1st Test	Mean on 2nd Test	SD on 1st Test	SD on 2nd Test
Trustworthiness	1.89	1.81	11.51	11.94
Strength of Will and Rationality	12.72	10.83	9.88	10.13
Altruism	-2.52	-1.93	12.21	13.28
Independence	0.37	0.15	10.76	11.57
Complexity	9.14	10.50	11.36	11.58
Variability	10.37	10.29	9.14	9.99

Source: Adapted from Bayless, 1971, Table XV, p. 70.

Baxter's samples, the tendency for the spread of scores was to increase upon retest.

Changes Resulting from a Dramatic Event

The previous evidence indicates that by the time a person reaches college his or her attitudes toward human nature have become relatively stable. However, a dramatic event—if it contains implications regarding human nature—may lead to changes in long-held beliefs. One such event was the assassination of President John F. Kennedy on November 22, 1963. In discussing immediate reactions to the events of that weekend, we noticed that the response of several people was a general disillusionment with human nature.

Wrightsman and Noble (1965) attempted to find out if this disillusionment was a standard reaction among those most upset by the assassination. A total of 30 college students of both genders (but predominantly female), who had originally taken the PHN scales as freshmen 14 months earlier, were readministered the PHN scale and then were given a questionnaire dealing with their reactions to Kennedy's death. The questionnaire was designed to assess the degree of the respondent's agreement with the President's policies and the tone of his or her reaction to the assassination. The first question presented four issues (civil rights, the tax cut, the nuclear-test ban, and foreign policies) and asked the respondent to indicate whether he or she agreed, disagreed, or had no opinion about the President's stand. The second question dealt with reactions to the preassassination publicity about the Kennedy family, but since 25 of the 30 subjects checked the same response ("I was interested in reading articles and watching TV programs about the Kennedy family"), this question was not used in the analysis. The final question asked which of five statements came closest to the respondent's own reaction to the President's death; the statements ranged from "I felt as if a member of my family or close personal friend had died" to "I felt that a national figure whom I did not admire had died."

Each person answered the PHN scale without being told the purpose of the retesting and before seeing the questionnaire on reactions to the President's death. Nineteen of the subjects completed these tests one day after the funeral (November 26); the other 11 completed them on Thursday, December 5. Since chi-square analysis of responses to each question indicated that there were no differences in the questionnaire responses as a function of day on which they were completed, the two groups were pooled for analysis.

Wrightsman and Noble (1965) hypothesized that those subjects who most agreed with the President's policies and who were most upset by his death would change in the direction of less favorable views of human nature. It was found that of the 15 subjects who agreed with Kennedy's stand on each of the four issues, 4 changed to more favorable views of human nature while 11 changed to less favorable views. Of the 15 people who disagreed with Kennedy's stand on one or more of the issues, 10 changed to more favorable views of human nature while 5 changed to less favorable views. A chi-square test of the 2 × 2 table was significant at the .05 level (chi square = 4.82).

It appears that the majority of the people sympathetic with Kennedy's views developed a less favorable view of human nature, whereas most of those not in sympathy with his views did not. The different direction of changes between groups cannot be explained on the basis of regression toward the mean, for there was no significant difference in means between groups on the original PHN positive-negative summed scores. The original means were +39.11 (for subjects agreeing with JFK's stands) and +25.40 (for subjects disagreeing with his stands); the t value for the difference was only 1.28.

Similar trends were found when the 30 subjects were divided on the basis of their reactions to questions about the President's death. Persons who chose the most extreme response ("I felt as if a member of my family or a close personal friend had died") were compared with those who chose other responses. Most of the others chose "I felt that a national figure whom I respected had died, but I felt no personal loss." Analysis indicates that 12 of the 18 "extreme reactors" changed in the direction of less favorable views of human nature, whereas only 3 of the 12 "less-severe reactors" changed in an unfavorable direction. As before, the chi square for the 2 × 2 table was significant at the .05 level (chi square = 5.00).

Thus it appears that those subjects most disturbed by Kennedy's death generally reflected their feelings with a devaluation of human nature. Again, the different direction of changes between the "severe-reaction" and "less-severe-reaction" groups cannot be explained on the basis of regression toward the mean, for there was no significant mean difference between groups on the original PHN measure.

These findings lead to several questions. First, why did the majority of those who disagreed with Kennedy and who were less affected by his death develop more favorable views of human nature? Data from a test-retest reliability study with the PHN scale (40 Ss, three-month interval) indicate no systematic tendency for repeated scores to be more or less favorable than the original scores. Perhaps those not personally affected reacted more immediately to the worldwide sympathetic response to the President's death and to the ability of government leaders to make an orderly transition.

The second question deals with the permanency of the disillusionment on the part of the pro-Kennedy subjects. If their changes were caused by the President's murder, was this just a temporary phenomenon or a more lasting one? To gain some information about this, in the latter part of March 1964—four months after the assassination—the researchers again asked the 30 subjects to complete the PHN scale. Twenty-eight of the 30 subjects complied with this request; the other 2 subjects were no longer enrolled and did not respond to two requests sent to their permanent addresses.

Mean positive-negative summated scores for those who agreed with the President's policies changed from +33.35 (November) to +46.28 (March); thus four months after the President's death those 14 subjects who had agreed with his policies now possessed more positive PHN scores than they had before. On the other hand, the 14 who disagreed changed negligibly from their November 1963 mean (from +34.40 to +34.35). An analysis of variance for repeated measurements on two independent groups (Edwards, 1950, pp. 288-296) revealed that neither the changes nor the interaction was significant.

Similarly, those who had felt a great personal loss developed more favorable views of human nature between November and March, while those who had felt no personal loss did not. (Approximately two thirds of those who agreed with Kennedy's policies felt a "great personal loss.")

The lack of statistical significance makes any conclusions difficult. But it appears that whatever reactions were felt by the pro-Kennedy subjects were temporary. Their attitudes toward human nature were more favorable in March than they had been in either previous test.

Interpreted most generously, this study demonstrates the sensitivity of the PHN scale to the changes in attitudes toward human nature resulting from exposure to overwhelming new information. The differential patterns of shift in attitude reflect this to a statistically significant degree, but the analysis of mean differences does not. All of the mean differences are in the predicted direction, however, and the conclusion of this study—advanced with caution—is that the effect of that November weekend in Dallas did strongly, if temporarily, alter some persons' general attitudes toward human nature.

Changes Resulting from Job Experience

All of us probably began our first job with certain expectations about the nature of the job, the qualities of our fellow employees, and the adequacy of our own skills. These expectations may have been altered after several months on the job. Does working in a "hard, cruel world" also influence one's philosophy of human nature? Several studies deal with this question.

Novice teachers and education majors doing their practice teaching doubtless have teaching strategies that they have derived from their beliefs about the nature of the learner and the learning process. Are such beliefs maintained in the face of a group of schoolchildren who don't learn or won't learn as the teaching strategies said they would?

Two studies provide consistent answers. In the first, Altman and Castek (1971) measured the effects of a semester of practice teaching on philosophies of human nature. Their subjects were 121 of the 122 practice teachers in elementary education at Wisconsin State University-La Crosse during the fall and spring semesters of the 1970-1971 school year. The experimental design was a rather unusual one, however, in which no specific practice teacher was retested. Instead, practice teachers participated in one of three formats—the usual student-teaching situation, an internship program, or a microteam program. All of the analyses by Altman and

TABLE 10.6 Preteaching and Postteaching Mean PHN Scores

PHN Scale	Semester	Student Teachers		Microteams		Interns	
		Controls	Experimentals	Controls	Experimentals	Controls	Experimentals
Trustworthiness	Fall	8.21	11.91	12.36	4.33	11.00	9.20
	Spring	7.31	9.76	11.26	0.66	8.00	5.25
Strength of Will	Fall	7.00	15.33	13.18	9.75	9.33	13.80
and Rationality	Spring	13.75	12.82	15.60	2.00	3.66	5.50
Altruism	Fall	1.42	9.91	2.63	2.91	3.33	1.60
	Spring	4.37	2.35	5.93	-2.55	2.66	2.25
Independence	Fall	-2.50	9.91	2.45	-0.92	-3.00	3.20
	Spring	2.81	2.00	2.93	-2.22	-2.66	-4.75
Complexity	Fall	8.35	10.50	12.00	15.83	23.33	14.60
	Spring	13.18	11.23	4.53	13.88	19.33	13.50
Variability	Fall	15.00	16.16	15.90	16.91	19.66	17.00
	Spring	20.06	16.35	13.20	18.11	15.33	13.00
Positive-Negative	Fall	14.14	47.08	30.63	16.08	10.66	27.80
	Spring	28.25	26.94	35.73	-2.11	11.66	8.25
Multiplexity	Fall	23.35	26.66	27.90	32.75	43.00	31.60
	Spring	33.25	27.58	17.73	32.00	34.66	26.50

Note: Ns were as follows: Control group, fall semester, 14 student teachers, 11 microteam members, 3 interns; spring semester, 16 student teachers, 15 microteam members, 3 interns; experimental group, fall semester, 12 student teachers, 12 microteam members, 5 interns; spring semester, 17 student teachers, 9 microteam members, 4 interns.

Castek (1971) are broken down by formats, and no overall averages are reported.

It is unfortunate that the researchers decided that it would not be possible to retest the same practice teachers; yet, even with the limitations of their design, some potentially useful findings emerge. Table 10.6 presents the mean PHN scores for experimentals and controls for each semester.

The results in Table 10.6 are not consistent from one semester's group to the next. The only significant differences occurred for the spring-semester groups, in which there was a significant decrement ($p < .05$) in positive-negative summed scores for the experimentals, as compared with the controls. That is, those who took the PHN at the end of the semester had more negative scores than did those who took it at the beginning. On Strength of Will and Rationality, there were significant differences between experimentals and controls in all three formats as well as a significant interaction (all ps at .05 level). Table 10.6 shows that, for the spring semester, there was a slight decrease in PHN positive-negative score for the student-teacher group, a decrease of more than a standard deviation for the microteam group, and a slight increase for the interns. It is not surprising that only significant differences occurred in the spring group, since, in the fall, pretesting was not completed until the practice teachers had been in the field for three weeks.

After the fact, we would expect that Strength of Will and Rationality is the subscale most subject to negative change during practice-teaching. First, it is a dimension on which the average student teacher's score is quite favorable—hence, there is room for deterioration. Second, the practice teacher's score reflects a projection of self-concept and adherence to middle-class American beliefs about the successful outcomes of hard work. When a teacher is placed in a classroom of heterogeneous children, the realization that not all of the children share the teacher's beliefs about the benefits of disciplined willpower may be sudden and dramatic. This realization should be reflected in changes in the Strength of Will and Rationality score.

A better designed study by Yeargan (1973) confirms this expectation. Yeargan administered the PHN to a self-selected group of practice teachers on three occasions: at the beginning of their student-teaching semester, at the end, and four weeks after the end. (However, only 14 of the original 39 subjects completed the third testing.) The subjects, education majors (27 in secondary education, 12 in elementary education) from three colleges, had volunteered to participate in an innovative inner-city teacher-training project. The practice teaching was done in inner-city schools.

When the scores obtained for the 39 student teachers before and after their student-teaching experience were compared, the only substantive subscale to show a statistically significant change was Strength of Will and Rationality. The mean preexperience score was +13.79, whereas the mean postscore was +8.38. The difference had a t value of 3.76, significant at the .001 level, using a two-tailed test. Mean changes on the other substantive subscales were quite small, but the change in overall positive-negative score approached statistical significance ($p < .07$, two-tailed test).

Further analysis by Yeargan (1973) indicated that the greatest change on the Strength of Will and Rationality scale occurred for the elementary education majors (mean 1 = +15.25; mean 2 = +4.25; $t = 4.32, p < .001$). The decrease for secondary education majors was less extreme (from 13.14 to 10.22, $t = 1.90, p < .07$).

To one who would expect that experience has a beneficial effect upon attitudes, such results can only be considered quite disturbing. Yet they certainly are confirmed by other studies that have dealt with the effects of student teaching upon attitudes. Minnesota Teacher Attitude Inventory scores have become more negative after student teaching (Weinstock & Peccolo, 1970). Student teachers' educational philosophies have also become less consistent (Newsome, Gentry, & Stephens, 1965). And attitudes and behavior have become more rigid, more controlling, and more authoritarian (Hoy, 1967; Jacobs, 1968). A next research step should be to interview student teachers and observe their behavior, in order to gain insights into specific determinants of their disillusionment.

For neophyte social workers, the equivalent of practice teaching may be participation in a summer-long manpower-retraining program in which they are exposed to people in extreme states of poverty. Dretz and Dretz (1969) measured changes in PHN scores of 52 social work students participating in such programs.

The participants were social work students who had completed one year of graduate work toward their Master of Social Work degrees. Each was administered the PHN scale during orientation and planning sessions in Washington, D.C., in mid-June 1968. Retests were completed in early August 1968, when the participants reassembled in Kansas City after eight weeks of work with the poor. Of 54 participants, 52 completed both pre- and posttests.

The participant sample was composed of 21 men and 31 women, ranging in age from 20 to 42 years (mean = 26.9). Thirty were single, 21 married, and 1 divorced. There were 37 whites, 12 African-Americans, and 3

TABLE 10.7 Preinternship and Postinternship Mean PHN Scores for 52 Social-Work
Students

PHN Scale	Initial Test Mean	Retest Mean	Difference in Means	t of Mean Difference
Trustworthiness	8.76	8.53	0.23	0.14
Strength of Will				
and Rationality	7.01	6.32	-0.69	0.54
Altruism	3.21	2.75	-0.46	0.37
Independence	0.19	0.63	0.44	0.29
Complexity	8.65	8.11	-0.54	0.47
Variability	11.25	10.26	-0.99	0.76
Positive-Negative	19.19	17.75	-1.46	0.35
Multiplexity	19.92	18.38	-1.51	0.82

Source: Adapted from Dretz & Dretz, 1969, p. 52.

Orientals. These social workers were divided into seven teams and sent to
seven different states, where they spent the majority of the summer retraining the extreme poor for new occupations.

Table 10.7 presents the two sets of mean scores for this group. Changes
are very slight. Although we are given the satisfaction that the scales are
measuring something consistently, we have no indication that eight weeks
of working with the poor influenced the social workers' attitudes in one
direction or the other. To see if there were changes in subgroups that were
not present for the entire group, Dretz and Dretz divided the group on the
basis of age, gender, race, marital status, past experience in social work,
and the state in which the summer work was done. The outcome of these
subanalyses may be summarized as follows:

1. *Age.* When the group was dichotomized into younger—that is, under
26—and older members, the older members scored lower on the retest
than they had initially for all scales except Altruism, whereas the younger
group scored higher for all scales except Altruism and Variability. But no
change was statistically significant.

2. *Gender.* On retest, women's scores decreased for Trustworthiness,
Strength of Will and Rationality, Altruism, Variability, and positive-negative
score, and increased for Independence, Complexity, and multiplexity.
When retested, men scored higher on Trustworthiness, Altruism, Independence, and positive-negative score, and lower on Strength of Will and Rationality, Variability, multiplexity, and Complexity. On complexity, the
change was statistically significant ($t = 2.44$, $df = 20$, $p < .05$); at the end

of the summer, men viewed people as less complex and less hard to understand than they had at the beginning of the summer.

3. *Race.* Participants were dichotomized as white or nonwhite. On retest, members of the nonwhite group scored higher than they did initially on all dimensions except Strength of Will and Rationality; the white subsample scored lower on all dimensions on retest. No differences were statistically significant.

4. *Marital status.* No subgroup changes were statistically significant, and little difference in trends occurred as a result of subgrouping by marital status.

5. *Previous work experience in social work.* Sixteen of the 52 participants had more than one year's previous employment in social work. In this group, retest scores were significantly lower on Complexity ($t = 2.49$, $df = 15$, $p < .05$) and multiplexity ($t = 2.58$, $df = 15$, $p < .05$). No changes in the less-experienced group were significant.

6. *Regional team.* Each participant was assigned to one of seven teams that operated in different states. Since the number of participants per team was so small (6 to 8), results have little meaning. It is interesting, however, that changes were inconsistent from team to team. They are summarized as follows:

a. Arizona ($N = 8$): on retest, lower on all variables.

b. Colorado ($N = 8$): on retest, lower on all variables except Trustworthiness, Independence, and positive-negative score.

c. Maine ($N = 6$): increases on all variables except Altruism and Variability, on which there was a slight decrease.

d. Maryland ($N = 8$): higher on all PHN variables except Trustworthiness, on which there was a very slight change in the negative direction. Differences in Variability and multiplexity were statistically significant (ts of 3.33 and 3.24, $df = 7$, $p < .05$).

e. Mississippi ($N = 6$): decrease on all dimensions except Variability, which showed a slight increase.

f. Texas ($N = 8$): decrease on all dimensions except Trustworthiness, which showed a slight increase.

g. Wisconsin ($N = 8$): higher on retest on the substantive dimensions and lower on the individual-differences measures.

Thus specific groups produce different outcomes, implying that particular experiences may be influential—if anything is—in changing the beliefs of adults.

Induced Changes: Attempts to Change Beliefs

The last type of change to be reviewed is change resulting from deliberate attempts to alter philosophies of human nature. We will present two examples of such attempts. One is the encounter group, which has among its many aims the development of greater trust in others. The other is a study by Claxton (1971) that had as its goal a change in the attitudes of unskilled adults undergoing manpower retraining. Let us consider Claxton's study first.

CHANGING ATTITUDES OF UNSKILLED WORKERS

Claxton's subjects were participants in a Manpower Development and Training (MDT) program, administered by the Department of Labor and the Department of Health, Education, and Welfare. The program provided occupational training or retraining in a classroom setting for unemployed or underemployed persons 16 years of age and older. Training usually consisted of six hours per day of occupational training, two hours of remedial basic education, and some individual and group counseling. Courses varied in length from 20 to 52 weeks.

Claxton's subjects were 273 trainees in 16 Manpower Development and Training classes. The occupations for which different groups were being trained included stenographer, cook, welder, auto mechanic, and general office clerk. The classes, locations, and group classifications used by Claxton are listed in Table 10.8. All subjects were of low socioeconomic status; 66% were male and 65% were black. The age range was from 17 to 72, with a mean age of 24.5 years.

The incorporation of an attitude-change intervention was quite consistent with the philosophy of the program. The Department of Labor has stressed the need to modify attitudes, aspirations, achievement motivation, self-images, and other factors that might be social psychological barriers to employment (Doeringer, 1969). The 1968 Manpower Report (cited by Etzioni, 1972) supports "the necessity of direct efforts to modify the attitudes of the disadvantaged before introducing them to job situations."

At the end of the first week of orientation to the occupational training programs, the PHN Scale was administered to participants in all groups except Groups K and P. The instructions were carefully read aloud to ensure that all subjects understood the method of rating the statements on the scale. Care was taken to emphasize that the statements should apply

TABLE 10.8 Occupational Area and Location of Groups in Claxton's Study

Class	Occupational Area	Location
A	Stenographer	Nashville
B	Cook I	Nashville
C	Electrical Appliance Repair I (E.A.R.)	Nashville
D	Welder I	Nashville
E	Auto Body Repair I	Nashville
F	Auto Mechanic I	Nashville
G	Woodworking	Cleveland, TN
H	General Office Clerk	Cookeville, TN
I	Auto Mechanic II	Nashville
J	Welder II	Nashville
K	Clerk-Typist, Keypunch I	Nashville
L	Cook II	Nashville
M	E. A. R. II	Nashville
N	Auto-Body II	Nashville
O	Clerk-Typist, Keypunch II	Nashville
P	Clerk-Typist, Keypunch III	Nashville

to "most people," male and female, black and white. The attitude statements were then read aloud slowly and reread when required. The PHN scale was given to all groups in the same manner. Group A and Groups I through N were also given the Personal Efficacy Scale (P. Gurin, Gurin, Lao, & Beattie, 1969) during the first week of training.

The occupational-training groups (Groups G and H) received six months of routine training under provisions of the MDT Act. Counseling activities for these groups consisted of two hours per week of program orientation, presentation of materials related to getting a job (interview techniques, dress, and personal grooming), field trips to local businesses, and guest speakers from various private and governmental agencies. There was no specific attempt to alter PHN-related attitudes in Groups G and H.

The training and counseling groups (A through F plus K) received occupational training, basic education, and approximately two hours of group counseling per week for six months. In addition, individual vocational and problem-centered guidance service was available to the trainees. Group counseling consisted of activities similar to those for Groups G and H but, in addition, included activities related to interpersonal attitudes. Topics for discussion included trust in other people, unselfishness, and differences among individuals. The concepts of strength of

TABLE 10.9 Training Period, Class, Group, and Counselor for PHN Training

| Training Period | Subject Class | Counselors | | |
		Multiplexity Group	Trust Group	Passive Group
I	A,K	C	A	B
II	O	A	B	C
III	B,C,D,E	B	C	A

Source: Adapted from Claxton, 1971.

will, independence, and locus of control were not introduced or discussed with the staff or trainees. All topics were related to employment and adjustment to job requirements. Techniques included use of audiovisual materials, group discussions guided by a program counselor, and role-playing exercises. The PHN was readministered to Groups A through H and K after approximately six months of training but prior to specific-goal-oriented counseling sessions.

These goal-oriented counseling sessions involved subjects from Groups A through E plus Groups K and O. Subjects were randomly assigned to one of three treatment conditions: (1) multiplexity (active participation), (2) trust-altruism (active participation), and (3) a passive control condition. Subjects participated in only one of the three 90-minute training sessions. Counselors were rotated through each training condition (multiplexity, trust-altruism, and passive) to control for counselor effects. Thus each subject experienced one of the three conditions, and each counselor conducted all three conditions (see Table 10.9).

Training sessions were aimed at developing favorable attitudes on a specific PHN dimension—that is, on multiplexity for Group I, on Trustworthiness and Altruism for Group II, and on multiplexity, Trustworthiness, and Altruism for Group III. Groups I and II required active involvement and improvisation from the subjects. Group III used the same discussion outlines and had the same time limits as Group I and Group II but activity was limited to lecture, passive exposure to persuasive communication, and discussion with no additional group participation. (Specific procedures for each training group are described in detail in Claxton [1971].) All groups were posttested on the PHN on the same day with no opportunity for subjects from different groups to discuss activities with others.

TABLE 10.10 PHN Differences as a Result of Six Months of Occupational Training and "Routine MDT Counseling" (Groups G and H of Claxton's Study)

PHN Subscale	PHN at Program Entry (N = 27)		PHN After Six Months of Training		t Value for Mean Differences	p Value (One-Tailed)
	Mean	SD	Mean	SD		
Trustworthiness	2.38	12.81	-1.52	12.36	.33	NS
Strength of Will and Rationality	12.51	9.22	9.07	10.06	1.75	< .05
Altruism	.66	18.74	-3.63	14.23	1.40	NS
Independence	4.55	11.66	3.03	9.28	.83	NS
Complexity	3.85	8.08	1.92	9.98	1.01	NS
Variability	11.96	13.22	8.74	14.20	1.23	NS

At the same time, each group was asked to fill out a staff-rating form and an exercise-satisfaction item. The staff-rating sheet concerned the trainees' view of the sincerity and altruistic motives of the program staff.

After the subjects completed approximately six weeks of training, instructors were asked to rate trainees according to instructions given them on a rating sheet. Descriptions of trustworthiness, altruism, complexity, and variability were provided as aids in rating trainees.

Information on tardiness, absenteeism, and demographic data was obtained from program records. Ninety days after trainees had completed training and became employed, a follow-up inquiry with trainees and employers provided data on employment status and earning of trainees. Inquiries included mail, telephone, and personal contact. No staff member or trainee had any knowledge of the PHN or personal-efficacy scores prior to ratings, evaluations, training sessions, and follow-up inquiries.

What was the effect of these interventions? Apparently, the occupational training and routine MDT counseling did not have any major effects. Table 10.10 reports the mean scores for Claxton's Groups G and H. On only one subscale was there a notable change; on Strength of Will and Rationality, the mean dropped from +12.51 to +9.07, a difference that is statistically significant only if a one-tailed test is used ($t = 1.75$, $df = 26$, $p < .05$ one-tailed).

Groups participating in a program of occupational training plus a counseling program designed to change PHN attitudes, however, did show the expected changes. Within these experimental groups, there were gains in scores on Trustworthiness ($p < .05$) (see Table 10.11). An analysis of variance was used to determine if PHN gains were significantly greater for the experimental groups than for the control groups; those for Altruism ($p < .02$) and Complexity ($p < .05$) were greater.

Claxton (1971) hence found support for his hypothesis that an increase in mean scores would result from the use of specific techniques to affect PHN dimension. Support also existed for his prediction that active participation and improvisation would be more effective than passive exposure to persuasive communication and discussion. There was a substantial increase in Altruism scores for the active trust-altruism group and only a very slight increase for the passive group ($F = 4.98$, $p < .009$) (see Table 10.12). There was no increase in Altruism scores for the active multiplexity group. Although the same pattern appeared in the Trustworthiness scores (that is, the greatest increase for the active trust-altruism group, slight gains for the discussion group, and no increase in the active

TABLE 10.11 PHN Differences as a Result of Six Months of Training at the Nashville Occupational Training Program (N.O.T.P.)

PHN Subscale	PHN at Program Entry (N = 67)		PHN After Six Months of Training		t Value for Mean Differences	p Value (One-Tailed)
	Mean	SD	Mean	SD		
Trustworthiness	-8.32	11.43	-5.30	10.04	2.20	<.02
Strength of Will and Rationality	14.00	9.61	8.68	8.16	4.66	<.0001
Altruism	-5.47	13.97	-2.75	10.80	1.85	<.05
Independence	3.85	11.05	3.02	9.81	.65	NS
Complexity	5.31	10.68	7.31	10.45	1.90	<.05
Variability	11.62	12.04	12.13	11.52	.39	NS

TABLE 10.12 Mean PHN Altruism Score Change by Group

Group	Pretest	Posttest
Active Multiplexity	-2.23	-4.74
Active Trust-Altruism	-3.23	1.07
Passive Multiplexity and Trust-Altruism	-2.00	-1.81
	Mean PHN Trust Score Change by Group	
Group	Pretest	Posttest
Active Multiplexity	-5.78	-7.19
Active Trust-Altruism	-5.70	-1.85
Passive Multiplexity and Trust-Altruism	-6.22	-5.70

multiplexity group), the differences did not reach statistical significance (see Table 10.12).

There were significant interaction effects between counselor and technique, however, with regard to the amount of change in Trustworthiness scores ($F = 3.67$, $p < .009$). Apparently Counselor C was the most effective counselor when a discussion format was used, while Counselor B was the most effective counselor for active participation. Counselor B actually caused a substantial decrease in Trustworthiness scores when using the discussion technique.

A substantial increase in Complexity scores occurred in the active multiplexity group, lesser gains in the passive discussion group, and virtually no change in Complexity scores for the group actively trained in trust-altruism ($F = 9.47$, $p < .0004$). See Table 10.13 for mean changes.

TABLE 10.13 Mean PHN Complexity Score Change by Group

Group	Pretest	Posttest
Active Multiplexity	3.56	15.67
Active Trust-Altruism	8.22	8.70
Passive Multiplexity and Trust-Altruism	6.44	13.67
	Mean PHN Variability Score Change by Group	
Group	Pretest	Posttest
Active Multiplexity	6.44	16.37
Active Trust-Altruism	13.96	12.96
Passive Multiplexity and Trust-Altruism	12.11	15.04

A significant gain also occurred in mean Variability scores for those actively trained in multiplexity, lesser gains for the passive discussion group, and no increase in Variability scores for the group actively trained in trust-altruism ($F = 3.06$, $p < .02$). Counselor A appeared to be the most effective of the counselors in using the discussion technique and also the most effective in the active-participation technique. Counselor B again apparently caused a slight decline in Variability scores by using the discussion technique.

There were no significant differences in the means for the Strength of Will and Rationality and Independence subscales as a result of the training in trust-altruism and multiplexity; neither were any changes expected, as training and subject matter did not include these concepts.

An analysis of variance was performed to determine if there were differences among groups with regard to degree of satisfaction after training sessions, and significant differences emerged ($F = 9.008$, $p < .0005$). Active participation in the multiplexity session was most enjoyed (mean = 4.26), with active participation in trust-altruism sessions next in degree of satisfaction (mean = 3.33). The discussion sessions were least enjoyed (mean = 3.07).

In summary, it appears that if significant changes in attitude are to occur as a result of Manpower Development Training programs, explicit programs must be used to change them. Changes occurred only in those groups in which the beliefs were a part of the subject matter of counseling and group activities. But do such interventions influence the behavior of the trainees? Claxton (1971) related the trainees' PHN scores to several types of variables: tardiness and absenteeism during training, program drop out, ratings from instructors, and employment status 90 days after placement on a job; in all, there were 21 different performance variables. Significant correlations were found in about 25% of the relationships between initial PHN scores and these variables.

Tardiness rate during the training period correlated .228 ($p < .05$) with Altruism scores, indicating a slight tendency for participants with more altruistic beliefs to be tardy more often. But contrary to these, absenteeism correlated -.232 ($p < .05$) with Altruism. Program dropout during training correlated negatively ($r = -.225$, $p < .05$) with Variability. Since these correlations are so low and since significant negative ones are infrequent, we may conclude that PHN scores did not predict behavior during training.

Some instructor ratings of participants on trust-altruism were not related to the participants' actual PHN scores on Trustworthiness or Altruism. The instructors, however, tended to agree with one another about which trainees had the most favorable attitudes; the instructors also tended to see the same trainees as possessing favorable and multiplex attitudes. The correlations were from .51 ($p < .01$) to .77 ($p < .01$).

Turning to behavioral measures, Claxton found that PHN measures were not correlated with whether or not trainees were employed three months after placement. There was, however, a correlation ($r = .423, p < .05$) between trainees' earnings after three months of employment and their Variability scores.

A t test for independent means was computed to check for possible PHN differences between those who were employed three months after placement and those who were not. No significant differences were found for any PHN dimension. In essence, Claxton's study demonstrates that a specific training program can change expressed attitudes toward human nature. There is, however, no evidence from this study that initial or changed attitudes have any relationship to behavior.

SENSITIVITY-TRAINING GROUPS

One of the goals of sensitivity training is the development of greater trust in others. A less articulated but equally relevant goal is the realization of the differences between people in their perceptions of the same actions and events. Therefore, changes on both major aspects of the PHN scale may be expected as the result of participation in sensitivity-training or human-growth courses. Two studies, by J. R. Young (1970) and by Kleeman (1972), deal with the effects of such programs on beliefs about the nature of human beings.

Young studied the changes in PHN scores of 38 undergraduates who participated in a weekend T-group lab. They were all majors in an innovative program called Human Behavior and were acquainted with one another. The first session of the lab was on a Friday evening and lasted four hours. During this session, the participants were assigned to four training groups, each with eight or nine female members, one male member, and two male trainers.

On Saturday and Sunday the participants attended the training groups all day (10 hours per day). Meals were served in the laboratory setting, and subjects returned to their homes or dormitory rooms each night.

The goals of this particular training-group exercise were "(a) an increase in self-insight and self-awareness, (b) an increased sensitivity to the behavior of others, and (c) increased awareness and understanding of

TABLE 10.14 Mean Scores for *T*-Group Participants and Controls in Young's Study

PHN Scale	Experimentals			Controls		
	Pretest	*Immediate Posttest*	*Delayed Postest*	*Pretest*	*Immediate Posttest*	*Delayed Posttest*
Trustworthiness	3.13*	9.15*	8.00	4.21	4.36	6.17
Strength of Will and Rationality	10.88	12.30	12.49	10.73	11.19	12.55
Altruism	-3.82	4.95	1.15	2.13	1.56	0.44
Independence	-1.11	0.82	0.90	-1.47	0.49	2.49
Complexity	14.47	14.77	15.41	10.63	13.22	15.08
Variability	18.10	18.92	16.09	18.31	18.57	16.88
Positive-Negative	13.39	26.68	22.60	16.68	17.23	23.73
Multiplexity	31.86	33.73	31.23	29.15	31.73	32.08

Source: Adapted from J. R. Young, Table 2, p. 20.
Note: *N* = 38 each for experimentals and controls. Pretest occurred four days before the weekend *T* group, immediate posttest four days afterward, and delayed posttest two months afterward.
*Means significantly different at .01 level.

269

the types of processes that facilitate or inhibit group functioning and the interactions between group members" (J. R. Young, 1970, pp. 7-8). Group activities included micro-lab and nonverbal exercises, small T grouping, community exercises, group-on-group interactions and assessment, and a final community assessment.

All subjects took the PHN scales three times: four days before the training lab, four days after the lab, and two months after the lab. The subjects were drawn randomly from a pool of 76 possible participants. The remaining 38 students, who did not participate in the weekend lab, were tested at the same time as the subjects and hence served as controls.

Mean scores at the three testings are included in Table 10.14. None of the changes in the control group were significant. But in the case of sensitivity-training participants, the mean Trustworthiness score increased from 3.13 to 9.15 upon first retest, a change that was significant at the .01 level (F = 6.72), using an analysis of covariance. At the time of the delayed retesting, the mean Trustworthiness score had regressed slightly, to 8.00—still about one-half standard deviation above the pretest mean. The Altruism mean had a tendency to increase (pretest = 3.82; initial posttest = 4.95), but the F-value of 2.47 fell short of significance. Neither of the individual-differences subscales showed a significant change.

J. R. Young divided his subjects into three groups on the basis of their initial positive-negative summated scores and looked at the changes in each group. Initially high scores in the experimental group became even higher on the first posttest (means of 17.92 and 24.51, F of 6.19, p < .01). This group also had increased multiplexity views upon retest (means of 48.84 and 53.33, F of 14.43, p < .001). The T-group experience also affected the most negative group, bringing about changes of a standard deviation or more on Trustworthiness and Altruism scores. The group with moderate PHN scores was not influenced by the T-group experience.

The intervention used by Kleeman (1972) differed in length and content from the one used by J. R. Young. At eight colleges in different parts of the country, students took a one-semester human development course designed to reflect the goals and activities of Kendall College Human Potential Seminar. Six of the colleges were two-year, public community junior colleges, one was a private, liberal arts junior college, and the remaining one was a four-year state college. Students enrolled for the human potential seminar (HPS) as a regular course, attended it twice a week, and completed the PHN scale before and immediately after completing the course. The number of students participating in the human-potential seminar ranged from 13 at one college to 98 at another. A total of 188 students completed both pretests and posttests. Classes in psychology, literature, biology, history, and other subjects were used as control groups. These 140 control subjects also completed the PHN at the beginning and the end of the semester.

The Kendall College Human Potential Seminar is a group project built around a series of specific activities and exercises that are designed to develop more positive self-concepts in its participants. The leader of the seminar is usually a counselor; an HPS leader's manual is available. The seven major phases of the seminar, as described by McHolland (1971), are the following:

1. The "in-depth unfoldment experience," developed by Herbert Otto (1966) is used in the first phase. Participants recount significant life experiences as well as their happiest moments. The goal of this exercise is the development of empathy among the group members.

2. An "acknowledgment-of-successes" phase follows, in which the participants' successful experiences are studied by the group in order to remove factors that prevent the realization of the person's full potential. A goal here is an understanding of one's own motivations.

3. In the "value-clarification" phase, participants share their answers to questionnaire items. This phase is "designed to provide a basis for self-determination" (Kleeman, 1972, p. 15).

4. In the "strength-acknowledgment" phase, group members identify strengths of each individual participant and give attention to whatever hindrances prevent his or her development. A group fantasy is constructed by sharing participants' projections of what one participant "might be doing successfully in five years" (Kleeman, 1972, p. 15).

5. In the next phase, participants are invited to reflect upon and share areas of latent potential, thus helping each to rediscover his or her abilities and to focus on self-determination. Alternate or additional exercises during this phase are the recalling and sharing of peak experiences and formative experiences.

6. A method of conflict resolution that relies upon goal setting and value choices is used in the next phase. Each participant is encouraged to identify his or her conflicts in values and to state whether they are primarily interpersonal, intrapersonal, or institutional in nature. The group aids each individual in planning a course of action consonant with his or her value system and motivational pattern.

7. The final phase is oriented toward long-range goal setting. Implications of the entire HPS process are also discussed. Participants are encouraged to keep in touch with the others in order to communicate how well

they have actualized their potentials. The basic goal of the HPS emphasized at this point "is to encourage each participant to transfer what he has learned in the group to a style of life outside the group" (Kleeman, 1972, p. 16).

Table 10.15 presents the mean scores on the PHN substantive subscales for experimental and control subjects at the beginning of the semester and at the end. The preexperience means for the two groups were quite similar; in no case was the difference between them more than 1.15 points. Upon retest, the controls changed significantly on only one subscale; their attitudes on Altruism became slightly more favorable (from -1.17 to 0.40). In contrast, the students who participated in the human-potential seminar developed significantly more favorable attitudes on each dimension. The average changes were 3.42 points on Trustworthiness, 2.62 points on Strength of Will and Rationality, 4.22 points on Altruism, and 3.76 points on Independence. These differences are not large, but they are consistent. Although the experimental subjects had less favorable beliefs than did the controls on the pretest, on the posttest the experimentals were more favorable than were their counterparts on all subscales.

Kleeman's (1972) study indicates that, after voluntarily participating in a course directed at self-growth, students changed their beliefs about human nature. Whether the activities of the class were themselves the causes of the changes, we cannot say. It may be that participants expected that their attitudes would be changed by such an experience; hence, they responded so as to show changes. (In other words, they reflected a philosophy of human nature that emphasizes an assumption of change.)

Implications for the Real World

As Etzioni (1972) points out, attempts to treat social problems in the United States have reflected two quite different sets of assumptions about people: (1) that people are quite pliable—that if persuaded, explained to, or propagandized, they will change—and (2) that people will not change; the environment must be changed if social problems are to be ameliorated. Etzioni is pessimistic about the validity of the first assumption. He states that "social scientists like myself have begun to re-examine our core assumption that man can be taught almost anything and quite readily" (1972, p. 45). The research reported in this chapter may be interpreted as offering some support to Etzioni's conclusion. Although direct attempts to intervene have some effects, they are limited and transitory.

TABLE 10.15 PHN Pre- and Posttest Means for Experimental and Control Subjects in Kleeman's Study of the Human Potential Seminar

| | Pretests | | | | | Posttests | | | | |
| PHN Subscale | Experimentals | | Controls | | Pretest Mean Difference | Experimentals | | Controls | | Posttest Mean Difference |
	Means	SD	Means	SD		Means	SD	Means	SD	
Trustworthiness	0.88	11.16	0.96	11.27	-0.12	4.30*	12.54	1.20	12.29	3.10
Strength of Will and Rationality	8.07	10.44	8.58	10.66	-0.51	10.69*	11.91	8.99	12.26	1.70
Altruism	-2.32	11.63	-1.17	12.23	-1.15	1.90*	13.28	0.40*	12.69	1.50
Independence	-1.00	11.23	0.09	10.44	-0.91	2.76*	12.10	0.05	10.79	2.71

Source: Adapted from Kleeman, 1972, Table 2, p. 65.
Note: Ns = Experimental, 188; control, 140.
*Pre- versus posttest difference between means significant at .05 level.

Work experiences, such as teaching in a ghetto school, may change attitudes, but not in a direction favored by social change agents. Manpower development programs that seek to develop new attitudes in soon-to-be-employed workers may change their attitudes, but there is no indication that the change brings about any change in behavior. New approaches to our social problems need to alter the circumstances surrounding the problem as well as the attitudes of participants.

Summary

The title of this chapter posed the question of how much change in philosophies of human nature is possible. Now we can give some tentative answers.

First of all, the continuity of philosophies of human nature is much more impressive than the changes. It seems likely that philosophies of human nature do not change much after a person reaches adolescence. Even the potential upheaval of the first year of college, with its new environment, new freedoms, and new peers, has no demonstrated effect upon *substantive* beliefs about human nature. The first year of college does have an effect upon beliefs in individual differences; the change is in the direction of beliefs that people are complex and different from one another.

If it is true that everyday experiences have little influence once attitudes have been established, what of dramatic events? The little evidence available is that such events change substantive beliefs, but only for a temporary period.

Likewise, specific activities developed for the purpose of changing philosophies of human nature have been shown to produce their intended effects. When actively involving the participants, training programs for unskilled workers have brought about greater beliefs in the trustworthiness, altruism, and complexity of people. Participation in sensitivity groups or semester-long courses oriented toward developing human potential has changed attitudes, while the attitudes of subjects in control groups have remained the same. The long-term effects of such interventions appear to be less strong, however; three months later there is regression toward the original attitudes.

CHAPTER ELEVEN

A Time for Taking Stock

JONATHA ATYAS
LAWRENCE S. WRIGHTSMAN

There is no general mythology today, nor can there ever be again. Our lives
are too greatly various in their backgrounds, aims, and possibilities for any
single order of symbols to work effectively on us all.

—JOSEPH CAMPBELL

Within the span of a few months, American readers saw the publication of
two important books that reflected views of human nature that were totally at odds with each other.

In *Chance and Necessity*, Jacques Monod (1972), a Nobel Prize-winning French biochemist, proposed that

life arose on earth by chance, that man is alone in a dead universe, and that
there is no rational foundation for any belief that man's existence serves a
purpose, is part of Somebody's plan, is progressing toward a "higher" end, or,
indeed has any discernible goal save the biological goals common to living
organisms. (Bliven, 1972, p. 75)

For Monod, evolution is an incorrect conception if it assumes continuous
improvement of biological organisms. To the degree that biological life is
said to have a preference, that preference is not to evolve into something
higher but instead to remain the same.

In contrast, Arthur Koestler (1972), in *The Roots of Coincidence*,
claimed that "all things, living and nonliving, are interconnected—a one,
a Unity, to which we all belong" (Bliven, 1972, p. 76). He reviewed with
favor the evidence from scientific investigations of ESP and parapsychol-
ogy and discussed some other challenges to the basic laws of physics—in
particular, the immaterial forces and messages that he claims most of us

275

Box 11.1
A Need for Myths

Joseph Campbell, (1972) the author of a four-volume study of world mythologies, has proposed that myths are "public dreams"—that is, that they tell
us a great deal about our deepest fears, sorrows, joys, and hopes. To Campbell, a myth is a dreamlike "symbol that evokes and directs psychological
energy." Mythology's most important function is to guide the individual,
stage by stage, through the inevitable psychological crises of life. However,
old myths are no longer working for us. We must, he claims in his *Myths to
Live By* (1972), have life-sustaining illusions, and we are now at the stage of
discovering new mythologies for ourselves.

---

have tuned out of our receptor systems. According to Koestler, we have
potentialities for growth and development that we hardly realize.

So we see that no moratorium exists on pronouncements about the nature and abilities of humankind. Because of a continuing need to understand human nature, speculation and oratory persist, although little
enlightenment occurs. In fact, in this age of uncertainty, there may be a
need for new myths about the human condition (see Box 11.1). We may
also need to look at assumptions about human nature in fresh ways, in
ways that use different types of empirically oriented methodology.

Where Do We Stand Now?

Let us stop to consider the empirical data that we possess about the
philosophies of human nature of people in general. Although areas of
doubt and confusion remain, some conclusions can be stated with confidence. Employing the PHN-scale score as an indication of a person's philosophy of human nature, we find that different respondents possess
widely ranging beliefs. Clear-cut distinctions exist between the responses
of different racial, religious, and occupational groups and of the two genders. These differences have persisted over the 25 years of research with
the scale. The general results are in keeping with predictions based on
other group characteristics or on our past experiences. Yet great diversity
in philosophies may exist between two members of any one of these

groups. The PHN scale cannot be used as a screening device to select persons for admission to an occupation; simply not enough within-group homogeneity in attitudes is present.

We are also confident that direct interventions to change philosophies of human nature can be successful. That is, personal development courses, encounter groups, and job retraining programs with an attitude-based curriculum can shift participants' philosophies of human nature in the desired directions. But so far, we have little evidence that such programs have long-term effects; we need investigations to determine if respondents retain the more positive conceptions of human nature that they express immediately after participation in such programs. We also need to determine if their heightened trust in others is reflected in changes in their interpersonal behavior.

When we study the determinants of interpersonal behavior, we discover that the attitudes of the individuals involved may sometimes be quite salient, but at other times philosophies of human nature have limited influence. If situational factors are of a certain type, attitudes do make a difference. For example, a person's philosophy of human nature is more related to behavior when (1) he or she has no information about or contact with the other person with whom the first person is interacting and (2) he or she is given no instructions or orientation regarding the framework from which to respond. But once we can see and can talk to the individuals with whom we are interacting, we can alter our behavior on the basis of their reactions. In such cases and in cases in which we have definite goals, our beliefs about human nature have lessened influence. For example, some car buyers may believe that certain used car dealers are out to cheat them blind. Other buyers may be more likely to take the salesperson at his or her word. But in this kind of interaction, the price of the car takes on such importance that individual differences in car buyers' philosophies of human nature probably have little influence.

Here we are seeking some qualification of a point made by Christie and Geis, which we reviewed in Chapter 7. In the case of Machiavellian attitudes, Christie and Geis (1970) found that the more similar an interpersonal experimental task is to tasks in the nonlaboratory world, the more likely it is that the highly Machiavellian person will be successful at it. They conclude this because many of their laboratory tasks permitted no real communication between subjects or restricted interpersonal responses to "right" and "left" or "yes" and "no." In such restricted encounters, the respondent often has little more to go on than his or her assumptions about the nature of the other respondent. Once he or she sees how the other person is responding, however, this new information over-balances or counteracts beliefs about human nature. Thus attitudes may or may not make a difference in a laboratory task, and Christie and Geis's analysis of the qualities of a situation offers an excellent beginning for a greater understanding of the role of attitudes in determining behavior. We need further research to determine how attitudes and environmental factors interact to determine specific behaviors. As noted in Chapter 7, in the last few years a renewed interest in conceptualizing the structure of attitudes has emerged (see Pratkanis, Breckler, & Greenwald, 1989, for examples).

Where Do We Go from Here?

Perhaps at this point we should consider innovative ways of studying assumptions about human nature. Past approaches have produced encouraging findings but, still, new paradigms are needed for the study of social behavior and attitudes.

As used in Kuhn's (1962) influential book, *The Structure of Scientific Revolutions,* a *paradigm* is a pattern or model that sets the rules for the game of science. The paradigm determines the legitimate objects and methods of study as well as the significant modes of conceptualization. For example, in the 18th century, the field of physical optics operated within a paradigm that conceptualized light as composed of material particles, and the topics and methods of study followed this particular conceptualization. But such a paradigm did not generate satisfactory explanations of its phenomena; in the 19th century a new paradigm developed that conceived of light as transverse wave motion. It was followed by a 20th-century synthesis (that light is represented by photons, which have some wavelike properties and some particlelike properties).

According to Kuhn, scientific revolutions occur when existing paradigms cease to function adequately. Although Kuhn's analysis was directed mainly at the physical sciences, it may be useful for social psychology today. Clearly there has been a crisis over methodology and findings, and consideration of new approaches may be fruitful.

Two different ways of studying assumptions about people are proposed here: the first, an analysis of the assumptions of one individual based on his or her literary writings, and the second, a study of the relationship of the assumptions about human nature to the communal movement. They are not entirely new ways, but they are fresh in their avoidance of laboratory manipulation and paper-and-pencil methods of attitude assessment—the methodologies now under the most criticism. They also propose new units of analysis.

The Analysis of the Written Work of One Individual

One approach is to identify the consistent ways in which people describe and classify specific individuals whom they know well. From this analysis, we may gain insight into their conceptions of human nature. For example, Rosenberg and Jones (1972) have applied content analysis and factor analysis to determine the assumptions about human nature and the implicit personality theory of one person. They chose as their object of study Theodore Dreiser, author of *Sister Carrie,* (1971) and *An American Tragedy* (1978).

Dreiser was chosen because of his book *A Gallery of Women,* published in 1929, which contained detailed character descriptions. Called "underestimated" by a recent critic (Aaron, 1990), *A Gallery of Women* consists of 15 different stories, each a portrayal of a different woman known or encountered by Dreiser. Thus each person is described in 20 to 50 contiguous pages, and a variety of people are so described. Most of the subjects were, in Aaron's terms, "frustrated, ambitious women in search of intellectual, artistic, and sexual fulfillment" (Aaron, 1990, p. 36). By listing each character mentioned in any of these stories and each trait ascribed to him or her, Rosenberg and Jones identified 241 characters and 6,761 descriptive units from the book. Box 11.2 gives an example.

The basic task of analysis was to determine what traits clustered together. An involved statistical analysis revealed that, in Dreiser's writings, traits associated with men were quite different from those associated with women. Men were seen by Dreiser as "poetic," and "sincere" and as "geniuses." Terms used to describe women included "defiant," "intelligent," "cold," "clever," "reads much," "attractive," "graceful," and "sensual." The dimensions of conformity versus nonconformity also emerged as an important construct in Dreiser's descriptions of people. Conformity was not associated only with the female gender, as the usual stereotype would predict; to Dreiser, women could be as nonconforming as men. Additionally, he associated nonconforming behavior with the following personality descriptions: "sad," "suffering," "lonely," and "troubled."

Do the descriptions of human characteristics revealed in Dreiser's writings have any relationship to his real-life behavior? Apparently so. Dreiser

Box 11.2
An Example of Rosenberg and Jones's Analysis

One of the minor characters in *A Gallery of Women* is Olive Brand's father. Below are the units extracted from the book that describe him:

Source of the Description	Descriptive Unit
Dreiser	mathematics, occupied the chair of
Dreiser	Professor
Dreiser	banker
Dreiser	elder in a church
Dreiser	vestryman in a church
Dreiser	baptist
Dreiser	quiet, his home was in a — street
Dreiser	solemn, his home was very
Dreiser	middle-western, his home was very
Dreiser	long face
Dreiser	grave face
Dreiser	bearded
Olive Brand	solemn
Olive Brand	profound
Olive Brand	conspicuous ornament of his church
Olive Brand	ornament, conspicuous — of his church
Dreiser	*bearded*
Dreiser	whiskers
Dreiser	commonplace, represented all the — s
Dreiser	solemn, represented all the —ities
Olive Brand	commonplace

(Adapted from Rosenberg & Jones, 1972, p. 374.)

liked unconventional women with style and boldness, especially if they possessed intelligence and business acumen (Lingeman, 1990). He was sexually promiscuous and even carried on affairs with several women at the same time; he was fired from one job because of his open affair with a 17-year-old girl. Swanberg's (1965) biography of Dreiser proposes "Dreiser's Law," which has two assumptions: (1) beliefs held by the multitude, the bourgeois, and their leaders are likely to be wrong per se, and (2) unconventionalists' beliefs, which fly in the face of orthodoxy, are in all probability correct.

In a somewhat different approach, Swede and Tetlock (1986) used the writings of Henry Kissinger to form conclusions about his implicit theory of personality, that is, which human characteristics he saw as going together.

An analysis of written work is a refreshing approach, not only because it relies on people to generate their own individualized constructs but also because its extensive materials are produced far away from the usual test-taking situation. We may all agree that there is much of Dreiser in his description of others. But where do we find such extensive and deeply expressed materials for other people? Could the letters of recommendation we write ad infinitum be used? Perhaps even the works of other novelists would not produce enough for a reliable analysis. We might test the possibility of using the works of John P. Marquand, who wrote five or six major novels that deal with the New England upper-middle-class families he knew from personal experiences. Many of the salient traits of his characters reflect aspects of Marquand's own personality and experiences (Birmingham, 1972). A feasibility study is necessary to determine if an analysis like the one by Rosenberg and Jones (1972) could produce enough raw data from other respondents to generate reliable descriptive clusters.

It is certainly true that most of us do not write novels annually; neither do we frequently produce other detailed documents that reflect our views of specific others. But we all possess—in the back of our heads—detailed descriptions of each of our relatives, friends, and business or school associates. Probing interviews can generate descriptions of specific individuals that can be analyzed as Rosenberg and Jones did Dreiser's writings.

Assumptions About Human Nature in the Communal Movement

A second approach capitalizes on the communal movement that had its renascence in the United States 20 years ago. Some challenging possibilities for research emerge when we look at communes from two theoretical perspectives: (1) the interaction of assumptions about human nature and the design of social structures, and (2) the relationships of ideology, utopian thought, and social reality suggested by people like Karl Mannheim. Before we can grasp the significance of the recent communal movement, we must have clearly in mind the nature and implications of these two theoretical perspectives.

As we noted in Chapter 2, it seems safe to assert that our view of human nature is an important determinant of the type of social structure that we deem desirable for group living, whether we are considering a family, communal group, or society at large. Our design for a society must be congruent with what we see as the possibilities and limitations of human nature. On the one hand, the structures adopted must satisfy each individual's needs and allow the expression of his or her capabilities; on the other hand, these social structures must provide the kind of social order required to compensate for each person's limitations.

But the relationship between assumptions about human nature and social structures is far more complex than one of simple linear causality. Although the structures adopted by a group are influenced by prevailing views of human nature, the reverse is also true: the prevailing views of human nature may be determined in part by the existing social structures. Whatever the truth regarding human nature, the appearance of social reality lends credence to a particular belief (P. Berger & Luckmann, 1967). Argyris (1957) has noted this process in industry: specialization has the effect of requiring and hence rewarding immature behavior. The top-to-bottom chain of command develops a dependent posture in the low-level employee who must act in accord with the "word from the top." In addition, since specialization taps only small portions of every employee's reservoirs of talent, interests, and aspirations, all employees must compress themselves into very narrowly defined units at work and seek satisfaction for the neglected portions of their beings in the time left over. In other words, employees are paid to be dissatisfied much of the time and, further, to do nothing about their dissatisfactions. The effects of this condition are dependence, passivity, impotence, and even avoidance of work (Argyris, 1957; Hess, 1970). It is a small step for a plant manager or an office worker to move from the observation of these behaviors to the development of a set of assumptions about people that reflects what McGregor (1960) called "Theory X"—a theory that states that the average worker is "by nature indolent," unambitious, desirous of being led, avoidant of responsibility, self-centered, indifferent to the needs of the organization, change-resistant, credulous, and "not very bright" (p. 6). On the basis of such a view, certain organizational procedures are employed to direct, motivate, and control people. Recent developments in industry, such as the General Motors plant in Spring Hill, TN, designed to build Saturn automobiles, attempt to deflect this specialization by using work teams who share decisions and emphasize a collaborative effort focused on the assembly of a complete product (Gwynne, 1990). It will be interesting to evaluate the effects of the working arrangements on beliefs about human nature.

One deleterious consequence of a fragmented bureaucratic structure is that, as the organization expands, its members come to see themselves as powerless to affect the system. Yet—by virtue of their anonymity among great numbers—they also see themselves as relatively safe from retribution and hence not responsible for their individual acts of petty thievery or neglect of public property (Coleman, 1970). Such acts as taking light bulbs from the office stockroom for use at home or leaving tools or equipment in dirty disarray at the end of the workday corroborate a view of humanity as irresponsible and uncommitted. Thus social structure created to control abuses by the powerful few have altered the conceptions of people held by many.

By promoting certain kinds of human behavior, the social structure gives a kind of validity to particular perceptions of human nature (see Box 1.6 for an example), Philip Slater (as quoted in Melville, 1972) summarized some of the dominant features of Western society that may be considered to have evolved from such interactions. According to Slater, property rights are valued over personal rights, "technological requirements over human needs, competition over cooperation, violence over sexuality, concentration over distribution, producer over consumer, means over ends, secrecy over openness, social forms over personal expression, striving over gratification, and Oedipal love over communal love" (Melville, 1972, p. 19). It seems clear that survival in such a system is dependent upon acting out of self-interest, and, hence, a coping behavior may come to be seen as a characteristic of human nature. That is, humankind is not altruistic: People must be dealt with in terms of their basic selfishness.

The persistence of outmoded beliefs about social reality also contributes to the relationship between social structure and assumptions about human nature. For example, the economic condition of scarcity led our society to conclude that hoarding and selfishness were acceptable human characteristics—although not, of course, with this nomenclature. One could act competitively—indeed, such behavior was necessary for survival—and the resources that one accumulated (stocks and bonds, real estate, inflated bank accounts, and other material nonessentials) were testimony to one's personal success. As communards and recent critics of society remind us, this amassing of capital makes less sense in a state of economic and material abundance than in a state of scarcity; sharing rather than hoarding should be the sign of the successful human being, and status should be determined less by what one has than by what one is. But in actuality, people—and the social system—continue to operate on the assumption of scarcity, delaying gratification and assuming the necessity of competitive behavior. "Greed" even became a key motive in the 1980s. In fact, the assumption is commonly made that the appetite for material goods is infinite and that consumption may even pass the point of satiety (Melville, 1972).

On the individual level, as well as on the social-systems level, the persistent manifestation in the culture of assumptions made obsolete by new economic realities can lead to an erroneous conclusion that certain behaviors, necessary under the old conditions, spring from an unalterable human nature. Individuals may then govern their own behavior in ways seen as consistent with that view of human nature—for example, they may deal with competition with increased competitiveness. If perceptions of "innate" competitiveness do elicit a competitive response, how can such an established cyclic relationship be broken? We may, of course, attempt to alter the particular social structures themselves, but historically this has proved to be a circular task. For example, even violent revolutions tend to perpetuate, under new labels, much of the structure and behavior they ostensibly sought to change. Perhaps an attack can be more successful if we challenge erroneous perceptions of social reality instead of social structures and, by this means, attack the resultant assumptions about human nature. The phenomenon of the communal movement during the 1970s constituted just such a challenge.

In seeking to understand the challenge to assumptions about human nature that is inherent in the relationship among attitudes, behavior, and social structure of a communal group, we return to the proposition that a person's philosophy of human nature is intertwined with his or her societal experience (P. Berger & Luckmann, 1967; Mannheim, 1936)—and herein lies an important consideration for social-psychological research. As Roberts (1971) notes, "trust, openness, and love are not reinforced in the business world" (p. 104). As a matter of fact, research on large organizations reported by Argyris (1969) has produced evidence that norms in most task groups discouraged risk taking, openness, and trust among participants (Pattern A groups) and, moreover, that the group members were blind to this condition, even in the face of feedback from the researchers. Argyris concludes that, if one does not study groups in which norms permit expressing feelings, taking risks, and helping others (Pattern B groups), one runs the risk of developing a conception of man in which the "natural" behavior is hiding feelings, not taking risks, showing little concern, individuality, and trust. This will tend to occur naturally because individuals will turn to descriptive research to develop their views of man. What *is* becomes what *ought to be*. Existing theory is used to explain aggressive behavior. Thus, black militants have defended their aggressive behavior by citing psychological research that "proves" aggression is an expected response to frustration. The covert and silent analyzing of other people and unilaterally attributing motives to them can be shown to follow from present conceptions of attribution theory. (Argyris, 1969, p. 101).

It seems, then, that studying groups that are functioning in a limited way may be inadequate for finding the means of fostering healthy group behavior, just as concentrating solely on pathology at the individual level is inadequate for understanding the healthy person. But it is doubly unfortunate that naturally occurring Pattern B groups are rare; in fact, they are often thought of as "deviant" from prevailing social norms! Yet, if opportunities and means to study such groups are not soon found, our knowledge and theories about the development of high interpersonal competence and satisfying group life will be severely limited (Argyris, 1969). The experiments in communal living, most of which attempt to develop Pattern B norms, may be the answer to this dilemma.

STUDYING THE ASSUMPTIONS
ABOUT HUMAN NATURE HELD BY COMMUNES

Although the late 1960s and the 1970s are recalled as the peak period for communes, an estimated 3,000 still exist across the United States (Larrabee, 1990). Among them are The Farm, a commune of 300 members founded in 1971 and located in a rural area near Summertown, TN; Twin Oaks, a commune in Virginia established in 1967 and based on principles espoused by B. F. Skinner in his novel *Walden Two* (1948), and Communidad los Horcones, another Skinner-based commune located at an isolated ranch in Northern Mexico (Rohter, 1989). Tremendous variety exists with respect to their size, location, and source of income.

Although our goal is to study beliefs of contemporary communards, we recognize that the problems in doing research on communes are manifold. Even though many communes have considered educating the public an important mission, the time and energy consumed by visitors, as well as the deleterious effect of the constant presence of unassimilated persons in the group, have often caused strict limitations on when, how, and even *if* visiting would be allowed, particularly in the better-known communes. Further, living as a visitor with a group even for extended periods of time can offer only partial insights into the communal way of life. A transient's personal experience hardly approximates that of someone whose immediate and future survival may depend on the effective functioning of the group as a whole and on the quality of his or her relationship with other group members. In addition, communards' comments to an investigator regarding their motives for joining and their communal experience may be colored by group loyalty, internal-dissonance reduction, or insufficient awareness of their own dynamics and those of the group. Similarly, the extensive variety of recent communes makes generalizations from experience with a few somewhat dubious, and the sporadic development of the communal movement precludes reliable data at this time.

Furthermore, several factors act against an investigator's focusing on individuals rather than on social structures or groups: (1) the relative anonymity of communards, resulting partly from the prevailing ethic in many communes that a person must be accepted for what he or she now is (which negatively sanctions questions about one's past) and partly from the legal jeopardy or harassment that may be incurred if individuals are too clearly identified (see Roberts, 1971); (2) the high turnover rates and great mobility among communal members; (3) the questionable validity of ex post facto attempts to understand the motivation or personality dynamics that preceded an individual's involvement in the communal movement; and (4) even the sensitive reluctance of the investigator to invade the privacy of the individual. Finally, there is the rejection by the counterculture of the scientific method in general, and particularly of the instruments of behavioral scientists as a means of knowing (Roszak, 1969). As Melville (1972) has pointed out, descriptive surveys and sociological questions may fail to reveal what communal life "feels like." He also quotes the caution offered by a member of an Oregon commune:

> Any family, any commune, is like a Rorschach test. What you see when you come here says more about who you are than what it is. Visitors come expecting to see free love, naked bodies, scruffy, idle, nonproductive hippies. And what they observe is some people embracing others, a few people walking around naked, and a lot of us just sitting around. But they completely miss what's really going on, because they don't see what these things mean to us. (Melville, 1972, p. 138)

THE COMMUNE'S CONTRIBUTION TO
NEW WAYS OF THINKING ABOUT HUMAN NATURE

Most communal groups, even those in the city, act on assumptions that appear to challenge "social reality," while other groups accept urban life on its own terms. In understanding this distinction we bring in the work of Mannheim (1936), who made a distinction between two modes of thought, both of which transcend social reality. One of these is ideology, which functions to legitimize the existent social reality. In effect, an ideology maintains that social reality conforms to the ideal—in this case, what *is* is what *ought to be*. Although the term *ideology* has broader reference in general usage, we will use it only in Mannheim's sense. The other transcendent mode is utopian thought, which challenges the theoretical framework (ideology) of social reality and is aimed at changing it.

Both ideology and utopian thought are complexes of ideas that constitute particular perspectives on social reality and thus focus attention on certain elements of it. They are not representations of truth; rather, they may involve considerable distortion or selective attention to some aspects of reality at the expense of others. Both ideology and utopian thought, however, provide an alternative to a mode of thought that accepts existent social reality as a matter of fact, not as a matter subject to human manipulations. Insofar as ideology is usually resorted to as a means of justifying the status quo, it is only utopian thinking that allows us to perceive discrepancies between our social constructions and transcendent ideals, thereby enabling us to retain mastery of our existence. Without the perception of such discrepancies, we would lose our "will to shape history, and therewith [our] ability to understand it" (Mannheim, 1936, p. 236).

Until the simple disaffection of the beatniks and hippies was transformed into the positive living designs of the communal movement in the late 1960s and the 1970s, social observers had begun to deplore the absence of utopian thought. In his preface to the 1936 translation of Mannheim's *Ideology and Utopia*, Louis Wirth described our Western society as having lost the sense of a common reality and with it the ability to express and communicate our experiences. Not only was individual experience fragmented, but so was any previous cultural and group solidarity, and, as a result, a condition of anomie prevailed. Such a condition inevitably gives rise to increased rates of crime, neuroticism, alcoholism, drug addiction, and suicide, and to a sense of meaninglessness in the individual (Etzioni, 1970; Mannheim, 1936).

These conditions are not, of course, unique to recent times. The same processes and conditions were deplored by such thinkers of the 19th and early 20th centuries as Nietzsche and Kierkegaard, who warned of the consequences of the object-subject split and the repression of human drives.

Statements like these have been expressed by Keniston (1965), Reich (1970), Roszak (1969), Slater (1970), and Toffler (1970). It seems that the emergence of anomie is a reflection of the breakdown or absence of both ideology and utopian thought. Keniston (1968b), in his exploration of the antecedents of the alienation afflicting youth, stated that our society systematically undermines idealism and utopian spirit; Keniston applauded the communal movement for providing a utopian inspiration that sensitizes us to our common plight.

Utopian thought, which is fundamental to a positive development of society, can operate to sharpen one's awareness of the complex of ideas supporting the prevailing social order (the ideology) as well as to make clear the shortcomings, fallacies, and incongruities inherent in that social order. The first of these effects may account for the dominant culture's tolerance for the counterculture in general and for the communal movement in particular, both of which are perceived as deviant from the cultural mainstream. That is, deviance may serve a positive function for the dominant group (T. M. Mills, 1967). By making clear what should not be done, deviant behavior helps clarify what ought to be done, thereby making more explicit the group's norms. The aversive consequences resulting from deviant behavior can also help group members see the virtue of regulating their own behavior in accord with conventional norms. Still further, deviance can increase the group's awareness of its own identity:

> Comparisons which deviance makes possible help establish the range in which the group operates, the extent of its jurisdiction over behavior, the variety of styles it contains . . . [which] are among the essential dimensions which give a group identity and distinctiveness. . . . A group is distinguished in part by the norms it creates for handling deviance and by the forms of deviance it is able to absorb and contain. (Dentler & Erikson, quoted in T. M. Mills, 1967, p. 78)

The second effect of utopian thought—exposing the negative aspects of the prevailing social order—suggests that deviant behavior may sometimes be healthy behavior, a rebellion against environmental conditions that can be dehumanizing and destructive (Argyris, 1969; Rhodes, 1972). Cross-cultural comparative studies indicate that some social norms are abrasive and frustrating in any culture, leading one to conclude that some types of norms are more suited than others to fulfilling human needs. This observation alters the way we look at deviance. Is the person deviant for not conforming, or is society deviant for departing from the "natural"— that is, for not being congruent with human needs (Etzioni, 1970)?

Not only does utopian thought comment upon and clarify the existing social reality, but it also often suggests viable alternatives to the prevailing social structures—alternatives that can perfect the nature of humankind. Paul Goodman has stated that "the great task of anthropology is to ascertain what of human nature has been lost and to find the means of its recovery" (Melville, 1972, p. 28). Communes and intentional communities have often been experiments toward achievement of this goal (R. M. Kanter, 1972; Roberts, 1971). But perhaps, as we have already suggested, the task is neither to mount a frontal attack on existing social structures nor to establish alternative scripts that will change human nature, thereby leading them to adopt structures that allow for the emergence of positive aspects of human nature.

One impact of the hippie movement first and of the burgeoning of communes that came later was to demonstrate that prevailing conceptions of human nature, closely bound as they are to a specific set of social circumstances, are insufficient, if not inaccurate. For example, Argyris (1969) proposed that our understanding of social behavior derives from the study of situations in which conforming behavior and conflict reduction are both required and rewarded. But in many communes, as well as T groups, conflict and toleration of differences are prized as difficult but highly productive means of increasing self-awareness and interpersonal competence.

The development of the communal movement also sharply defined the discrepancy between, on the one hand, a philosophy of human nature asserting that we can be free and can influence our environment, and, on the other, a perception of social reality that says we cannot change society and are powerless to affect our life in all except the most personal spheres of activity—and with limited power even in these areas (Melville, 1972). As long as they remain within the dominant culture, individuals may perceive their locus of control to be largely external. Once they reject the dominant culture and move to establish their own social forms, they demonstrate two things: (1) that the apparent powerlessness of the individual in the dominant social structure is not a matter of fact but a construction of human origin, and (2) that a person is able to create structures congruent with a differing view of human nature.

The acceptance by an individual of an ideology without his or her being able to participate in society according to that ideology brings its own peculiar horrors—as, for example, when the Protestant work ethic assigns dignity and worth to a person on the basis of productivity, but that person is unable to find a job (Westhues, 1972b). The consequences of such an orientation have been explored both in fact, as in research on low-income and minority groups, and in fiction, one example being Malamud's (1982) *The Fixer.*

But what happens when an ideology is brought into question and the social reality is no longer seen as satisfying human needs? Or when culturally entrenched philosophies of human nature are exposed as inadequate or erroneous? In such cases, such persons may engage in revolutionary activity, or they may withdraw from the prevailing social system and establish their own alternative. In life, we recognize that these two alternatives do not seem mutually exclusive and that there exist many possibilities that combine radical activity with communal living. We believe, however, that a dominant purpose or orientation can be identified even for those groups that seem to integrate both alternatives.

As Westhues (1972a) has pointed out, theories of the origins of revolution and of counterculture phenomena both point to the same factors: dissatisfaction with contemporary life, deprivation, stress, dislocation, and alienation. But there is little to suggest why an individual chooses one course over the other. Stark (cited in Westhues, 1972a) has hypothesized that sectarian movements are more likely to arise in "cesaro-papist societies" in which there is a national religion. But an alternative hypothesis might be offered. A particular philosophy of human nature in which humankind is seen as perfectible would tend to lead the alienated individual toward efforts to establish an intentional community that aims to change society by changing human nature (Bettelheim, 1969; Westhues, 1972a). In contrast, a view of human nature as imperfect and fixed, thereby requiring the regulation of an appropriate social order, might tend to lead the individual toward revolutionary activity with society as the target for change. Melville (1972) observed that belief in the perfectibility of human nature is central for communards, whereas political activists believe that "changing heads" is not enough.

But a third alternative may exist as well. H. J. Cross and Pruyn (1972) stated that, for some people, there may be enough social space within the dominant society for those who reject its values to live in accordance with their own—even without their colleagues' awareness of their divergence. Coleman (1970) developed a related but somewhat different view in depicting possible social inventions that must arise to meet the weakening of existing systems like the nation. He envisioned the availability to individuals of two simultaneously existing options. Society might come to consist of a matrix of communes in which matters such as marriage norms, use of drugs, and other policies would be determined by the commune rather than by a larger political entity like the state. Those persons who dislike the character of communal living might elect to live in the interstices between communes, so to speak, as autonomous individuals relatively unaffected by the kinds of pressures that develop in highly cohesive group life. Building a society with these alternatives could come about only as a result of a belief in both the complexity and variability of human nature. This appears to be one aftermath of the communal movement of two decades ago.

One may speculate further on the implications of a successful challenge to generally accepted philosophies of human nature. According to the model of social change proposed by D. C. Klein (1968), the "innovation curve" begins with a try-out by atypical figures. That may be what we have witnessed in the communal movement. If society does evolve in the direction of living groups larger than the nuclear family, we may need to develop a new kind of expertise, one that can deal with the problems inherent in macrosystems. Both D. C. Klein (1968) and Bennis (1970) view microsystems as involving interfaces among groups, in which theory applicable to macrosystems may not suffice for understanding. Bennis (1970) sees the need for developing "interstitial" people who will link and facilitate interorganizational transactions. It may be important to study assumptions about the nature of groups as well as assumptions about the nature of humankind.

Further, whether one chooses revolution or escape to the communes as a means of reacting against an unacceptable perception of social reality, one must still face the essential questions of how to relate with one's colleagues (Roberts, 1971). Communards have shown a laudable concern for congruence between the means used and the ends served (Melville, 1972). Unhappily, the confusion between methods of social organization and the ends or ideologies these methods perpetuate may lead designers of communes to reject organization blindly and thus preordain failure of the group. For example, it is not the existence of rules per se that makes established society so intolerable; rather, it is the inflexibility, the imperviousness to individual influence, and the degree of inclusiveness of those rules, as well as the manner of their enforcement.

The main question in setting up a communal endeavor is not whether to have an organizational structure at all, but rather what organizing principle to follow. The anarchist's assumption is that self-regulation is best, whereas the liberal assumption is that institutions must be created to safeguard personal liberty. Clearly divergent philosophies of human nature are reflected in these views. As Carr indicates, although anarchy is valuable as a critique of society, it is less useful as a social program (Melville, 1972). No matter what the source or focus of interest, observers seeking to identify variables that contribute to the success of groups emphasize the necessity of social structures in order to implement essential processes. Moreover, the processes seen as the most important are always the same no matter who is the observer (Griebe, 1972; R. M. Kanter, 1972; D. C. Klein, 1968; Melville, 1972; T. M. Mills, 1967; Moffatt, 1972; Roberts, 1971). Invariably they boil down to issues of integration patterns (including communication), conflict management, decision making and leadership, boundary maintenance, and attitudes toward (and strategies for) change (D. C. Klein, 1968).

Thus a future direction for the study of assumptions about human nature is an observation-interview study of the planning and operation of a variety of living arrangements. What assumptions about humans and society are verbalized by persons who found or join communal-living groups? How do they see these assumptions implemented by the organizational structure of the group and its regulatory procedures? Do assumptions about human nature change as a result of living in a commune for an extended period of time? Has, as this chapter implies, a change occurred in the perceptions of internalized locus of control in their own lives? We must await future research for empirical answers to these questions.

Summary

This chapter has a broad and somewhat detached view of the place of assumptions about human nature in contemporary society. As assumptions, philosophies of human nature have been shown to be meaningful devices that people use to organize their beliefs about others. The stability of philosophies of human nature, as well as the varying philosophies held by different races, occupations, and sexes, indicates a useful construct for further social-psychological study.

There is much still to be learned, however. Further research needs to be done to answer the following questions:

1. Although we know that interventions and specialized training can change negative philosophies of human nature into more positive ones, are such changes in attitude transmitted into different behaviors? If not, why not?

2. Although it has been shown that trust in 3-year-old children is related to certain behaviors by their mothers, what happens to these trusting attitudes as the child grows older? Are these "initial" states of trust predictive of future states, as Erikson claims?

3. Are there certain patterns or profiles of philosophies of human nature characteristic of certain stages in life or of certain socioeconomic groups? Although we know that differences exist between occupations on specific scales, a profile analysis might give greater understanding of the underlying dimensions.

Beyond such research questions, this chapter advocates new methodologies and sources for a continued inquiry into assumptions about people. One such approach is a detailed exploration of the assumptions held by a specific individual. This may be achieved by an analysis of written work—novels, diaries, or letters of recommendation—if such are available. The work by Rosenberg and Jones (1972), using the literary efforts of Theodore Dreiser, is a model.

A second new approach capitalizes on the recent communal movement in order to determine the relationship of assumptions about human nature to conceptions of society. We are living in a time when the conventional wisdom about human nature and the nature of society is under attack. Technology has run amok; many now question our ability to bring technology under manageable control. Bureaucracy—a social structure originally established to provide for personal growth—now stifles human development and generates a philosophy that human nature is lazy, irresponsible, and extrinsically motivated. The communal movement has challenged a pessimistic drift in our society. Through study of the movement's assumptions, aims, procedures, and outcomes, we may gain an understanding of the future of philosophies of human nature.

APPENDIX A

PHN Scale, in Its Usual Format

This questionnaire is a series of attitude statements. Each represents a commonly held opinion, and there are no right or wrong answers. You will probably disagree with some items and agree with others. We are interested in the extent to which you agree or disagree with matters of opinion.

Read each statement carefully. Then, on the separate answer sheet, indicate the extent to which you agree or disagree by circling a number for each statement. The numbers and their meanings are as follows:

If you agree strongly, circle +3.
If you agree somewhat, circle +2.
If you agree slightly, circle +1.
If you disagree slightly, circle -1.
If you disagree somewhat, circle -2.
If you disagree strongly, circle -3.

First impressions are usually best in such matters. Read each statement, decide if you agree or disagree and determine the strength of your opinion, and then circle the appropriate number on the answer sheet. *Be sure to answer every statement.*

If you find that the numbers to be used in answering do not adequately indicate your own opinion, use the one that is *closest* to the way you feel.

PHN Scale

1. Great successes in life, such as great artists and inventors, are usually motivated by forces of which they are unaware.
2. Most students will tell the instructor when he has made a mistake in adding up their scores, even if he has given them *more* points than they deserved.
3. Most people will change the opinion they express as a result of an onslaught of criticism, even though they really don't change the way they feel.
4. Most people try to apply the Golden Rule, even in today's complex society.
5. A person's reaction to things differs from one situation to another.
6. I find that my first impression of a person is usually correct.

7. Our success in life is pretty much determined by forces outside our own control.

8. If you give the average person a job to do and leave him to do it, he will finish it successfully.

9. Nowadays many people won't make a move until they find out what other people think.

10. Most people do not hesitate to go out of their way to help someone in trouble.

11. Different people react to the same situation in different ways.

12. People can be described accurately by one term, such as "introverted" or "moral" or "sociable."

13. Attempts to understand ourselves are usually futile.

14. People usually tell the truth, even when they know they would be better off by lying.

15. The important thing in being successful nowadays is not how hard you work but how well you fit in with the crowd.

16. Most people will act as "Good Samaritans" if given the opportunity.

17. Each person's personality is different from the personality of every other person.

18. It's not hard to understand what really is important to a person.

19. There's little one can do to alter his fate in life.

20. Most students do not cheat when taking an exam.

21. The typical student will cheat on a test when everybody else does, even though he has a set of ethical standards.

22. "Do unto others as you would have them do unto you" is a motto that most people follow.

23. People are quite different in their basic interests.

24. I think I get a good idea of a person's basic nature after a brief conversation with him.

25. Most people have little influence over the things that happen to them.

26. Most people are basically honest.

27. It's a rare person who will go against the crowd.

28. The typical person is sincerely concerned about the problems of others.

29. People are pretty different from one another in what "makes them tick."

30. If I could ask a person three questions about himself (assuming that he would answer them honestly), I would know a great deal about him.

31. Most people have an unrealistically favorable view of their own capabilities.

32. If you act in good faith with people, almost all of them will reciprocate with fairness toward you.
33. Most people have to rely on someone else to make their important decisions for them.
34. Most people with fallout shelters would let their neighbors stay in them during a nuclear attack.
35. Often a person's basic personality is altered by such things as a religious conversion, psychotherapy, or a charm course.
36. When I meet a person, I look for one basic characteristic through which I try to understand him.
37. Most people vote for a political candidate on the basis of unimportant characteristics, such as his appearance or name, rather than on the basis of his stand on the issues.
38. Most people lead clean, decent lives.
39. The average person will rarely express his opinion in a group when he sees that the others disagree with him.
40. Most people would stop and help a person whose car was disabled.
41. People are unpredictable in how they'll act from one situation to another.
42. Give me a few facts about a person, and I'll have a good idea of whether I'll like him or not.
43. If a person tries hard enough, he will usually reach his goals in life.
44. People claim that they have ethical standards regarding honesty and morality, but few people stick to them when the chips are down.
45. Most people have the courage of their convictions.
46. The average person is conceited.
47. People are pretty much alike in their basic interests.
48. I find that my first impressions of people are frequently wrong.
49. The average person has an accurate understanding of the reasons for his behavior.
50. If you want people to do a job right, you should explain things to them in great detail and supervise them closely.
51. Most people can make their own decisions, uninfluenced by public opinion.
52. It's only a rare person who would risk his own life and limb to help someone else.
53. People are basically similar in their personalities.
54. Some people are too complicated for me to figure out.
55. If people try hard enough, wars can be prevented in the future.
56. If most people could get into a movie without paying and be sure that they were not seen, they would do it.

57. It is achievement, rather than popularity with others, that gets you ahead nowadays.
58. It's pathetic to see an unselfish person in today's world, because so many people take advantage of him.
59. If you have a good idea about how several people will react to a certain situation, you can expect most people to react the same way.
60. I think you can never really understand the feelings of other people.
61. The average person is largely the master of his own fate.
62. Most people are not really honest for a desirable reason; they're afraid of getting caught.
63. The average person will stick to his opinion if he thinks he's right, even if others disagree.
64. People pretend to care more about one another than they really do.
65. Most people are consistent from situation to situation in the way they react to things.
66. You can't accurately describe a person in just a few words.
67. In a local or national election, most people select a candidate rationally and logically.
68. Most people would tell a lie if they could gain by it.
69. If a student does not believe in cheating, he will avoid it even if he sees many others doing it.
70. Most people inwardly dislike putting themselves out to help other people.
71. A child who is popular will be popular as an adult, too.
72. You can't classify everyone as good or bad.
73. Most persons have a lot of control over what happens to them in life.
74. Most people would cheat on their income tax if they had a chance.
75. The person with novel ideas is respected in our society.
76. Most people exaggerate their troubles in order to get sympathy.
77. If I can see how a person reacts to one situation, I have a good idea of how he will react to other situations.
78. People are too complex to ever be understood fully.
79. Most people have a good idea of what their strengths and weaknesses are.
80. Nowadays people commit a lot of crimes and sins that no one else ever hears about.
81. Most people will speak out for what they believe in.

82. People are usually out for their own good.

83. When you get right down to it, people are quite alike in their emotional makeup.

84. People are so complex that it is hard to know what "makes them tick."

PHN Subscale Items, Grouped by Subscale

Trustworthiness	Correlation of Item with Subscale	Mean Response 400 Women	Mean Response 307 Men
Positively Scored Items			
2. Most students will tell the instructor when he has made a mistake in adding up their scores, even if he has given them *more* points than they deserved.	.407	-0.067	-0.495
8. If you give the average person a job to do and leave him to do it, he will finish it successfully.	.438	0.912	0.632
14. People usually tell the truth, even when they know they would be better off by lying.	.505	-0.535	-0.609
20. Most students do not cheat when taking an exam.	.489	0.885	1.127
26. Most people are basically honest.	.435	1.090	1.009
32. If you act in good faith with people, almost all of them will reciprocate with fairness toward you.	.435	1.317	1.127
38. Most people lead clean, decent lives.	.522	0.987	0.638
Negatively Scored Items			
44. People claim that they have ethical standards regarding honesty and morality, but few people stick to them when the chips are down.	-.603	0.095	0.400
50. If you want people to do a job right, you should explain things to them in great detail and supervise them closely.	-.430	-0.620	-0.156
56. If most people could get into a movie without paying and be sure that they were not seen, they would do it.	-.589	0.120	0.576
62. Most people are not really honest for a desirable reason; they're afraid of getting caught.	-.558	-0.122	0.172
68. Most people would tell a lie if they could gain by it.	-.657	-0.067	0.228
74. Most people would cheat on their income tax if they had a chance.	-.597	-0.192	0.394
80. Nowadays people commit a lot of crimes and sins that no one else ever hears about.	-.408	1.057	1.371

Strength of Will and Rationality	Correlation of Item with Subscale	Mean Response 400 Women	307 Men
Positively Scored Items			
43. If a person tries hard enough, he will usually reach his goals in life.	.326	1.687	1.508
49. The average person has an accurate understanding of the reasons for his behavior.	.263	-0.852	-0.791
55. If people try hard enough, wars can be prevented in the future.	.321	0.397	0.462
61. The average person is largely the master of his own fate.	.535	0.940	1.029
67. In a local or national election, most people select a candidate rationally and logically.	.459	-0.862	-0.814
73. Most people have a lot of control over what happens to them in life.	.538	0.927	1.237
79. Most people have a good idea of what their strengths and weaknesses are.	.415	1.135	0.938
Negatively Scored Items			
1. Great successes in life, such as great artists and inventors, are usually motivated by forces of which they are unaware.	-.402	0.310	-0.026
7. Our success in life is pretty much determined by forces outside our own control.	-.475	-1.200	-1.137
13. Attempts to understand ourselves are usually futile.	-.402	-0.932	-0.723
19. There's little one can do to alter his fate in life.	-.440	-1.955	-2.146
25. Most people have little influence over the things that happen to them.	-.490	-1.457	-1.394
31. Most people have an unrealistically favorable view of their own capabilities.	-.282	-0.270	0.648
37. Most people vote for a political candidate on the basis of unimportant characteristics, such as his appearance or name, rather than on the basis of his stand on the issues.	-.426	0.407	0.427

Altruism

	Correlation of Item with Subscale	Mean Response 400 Women	307 Men
Positively Scored Items			
4. Most people try to apply the Golden Rule, even in today's complex society.	.544	-0.232	-0.745
10. Most people do not hesitate to go out of their way to help someone in trouble.	.632	0.362	-0.084
16. Most people will act as "Good Samaritans" if given the opportunity.	.631	0.510	0.348
22. "Do unto others as you would have them do unto you" is a motto that most people follow.	.599	-0.345	-0.964

28. The typical person is sincerely concerned about the problems of others.	.613	0.015	-0.394
34. Most people with fallout shelters would let their neighbors stay in them during a nuclear attack.	.425	0.425	0.140
40. Most people would stop and help a person whose car was disabled.	.533	0.415	-0.332
Negatively Scored Items			
46. The average person is conceited.	.459	-0.022	0.218
52. It's only a rare person who would risk his own life and limb to help someone else.	.595	0.050	0.296
58. It's pathetic to see an unselfish person in today's world, because so many people take advantage of him.	.546	-0.452	0.182
64. People pretend to care more about one another than they really do.	.589	0.522	0.742
70. Most people inwardly dislike putting themselves out to help other people.	.539	-0.872	-0.283
76. Most people exaggerate their troubles in order to get sympathy.	.370	1.030	1.228
82. People are usually out for their own good.	.546	1.052	1.260

Independence

Positively Scored Items			
45. Most people have the courage of their convictions.	.551	0.335	0.120
51. Most people can make their own decisions, uninfluenced by public opinion.	.548	-0.940	-0.934
57. It is achievement, rather than popularity with others, that gets you ahead nowadays.	.537	-0.120	0.075
63. The average person will stick to his opinion if he thinks he's right, even if others disagree.	.675	0.367	0.055
69. If a student does not believe in cheating, he will avoid it even if he sees many others doing it.	.468	1.777	1.348
75. The person with novel ideas is respected in our society.	.413	0.572	0.452
81. Most people will speak out for what they believe in.	.616	0.537	0.280
Negatively Scored Items			
3. Most people will change the opinion they express as a result of an onslaught of criticism, even though they really don't change the way they feel.	-.499	0.777	0.771
9. Nowadays many people won't make a move until they find out what other people think.	-.531	1.392	1.384
15. The important thing in being successful nowadays is not how hard you work but how well you fit in with the crowd.	-.400	-0.285	-0.319
21. The typical student will cheat on a test when everybody else does, even though he has a set of ethical standards.	-.531	-0.485	-0.143
27. It's a rare person who will go against the crowd.	-.464	1.105	1.465

	Correlation of Item with Subscale	Mean Response 400 Women	307 Men
Independence (contd)			
33. Most people have to rely upon someone else to make their important decisions for them.	-.518	-0.645	-0.296
39. The average person will rarely express his opinion in a group when he sees that the others disagree with him.	-.474	0.750	0.853
Complexity			
Positively Scored Items			
48. I find that my first impressions of people are frequently wrong.	.520	0.682	0.452
54. Some people are too complicated for me to figure out.	.368	1.227	1.270
60. I think you can never really understand the feelings of other people.	.395	-0.175	-0.068
66. You can't accurately describe a person in just a few words.	.435	2.280	1.843
72. You can't classify everyone as good or bad.	.487	2.465	1.892
78. Most people are too complex to ever be understood fully.	.537	1.265	1.328
84. People are so complex that it is hard to know what makes them tick.	.561	1.287	1.205
Negatively Scored Items			
6. I find that my first impression of a person is usually correct.	-.435	-0.375	-0.482
12. People can be described accurately by one term, such as "introverted" or "moral" or "sociable."	-.446	-2.127	-1.941
18. It's not hard to understand what really is important to a person.	-.438	-0.707	-0.504
24. I think I get a good idea of a person's basic nature after a brief conversation with him.	-.522	-0.130	0.400
30. If I could ask a person three questions about himself (assuming that he would answer them honestly), I would know a great deal about him.	-.483	-0.082	-0.104
36. When I meet a person, I look for one basic characteristic through which I try to understand him.	-.407	-0.485	-0.521
42. Give me a few facts about a person, and I'll have a good idea of whether I'll like him or not.	-.433	-1.007	-0.619

Variability

Positively Scored Items

5. A person's reaction to things differs from one situation to another.	.327	2.245	2.133
11. Different people react to the same situation in different ways.	.323	2.820	2.567
17. Each person's personality is different from the personality of every other person.	.363	2.752	2.368
23. People are quite different in their basic interests.	.488	1.502	1.586
29. People are pretty different from one another in what "makes them tick."	.508	1.610	1.407
35. Often a person's basic personality is altered by such things as a religious conversion, psycho-therapy, or a charm course.	.314	0.527	0.596
41. People are unpredictable in how they'll act from one situation to another.	.447	1.140	1.149

Negatively Scored Items

47. People are pretty much alike in their basic interests.	-.559	-0.597	-0.778
53. People are basically similar in their personalities.	-.607	-1.645	-1.671
59. If you have a good idea about how several people will react to a certain situation, you can expect most people to react the same way.	-.433	-0.382	-0.234
65. Most people are consistent from situation to situation in the way that they react to things.	-.462	-0.582	-0.312
71. A child who is popular will be popular as an adult, too.	-.396	-0.430	-0.384
77. If I can see how a person reacts to one situation, I have a good idea of how he will react to other situations.	-.589	-0.557	-0.416
83. When you get right down to it, people are quite alike in their emotional makeup.	-.458	-0.905	-0.889

Note: Item-subscale correlations adapted from O'Connor, 1971, Tables 1C-6C, pp. 57-62.

APPENDIX C

Revised Subscales for PHN Scale

Subscale A: Cynicism (10 items, all scored in a positive direction; high score indicates cynicism.)

Item No.	Statement	Original Scale
56.	If most people could get into a movie without paying and be sure that they would not be seen, they would do it.	T
62.	Most people are not really honest for a desirable reason; they're afraid of getting caught.	T
46.	The average person is conceited.	A
74.	Most people would cheat on their income tax if they had a chance.	T
68.	Most people would tell a lie if they could gain by it.	T
44.	People claim that they have ethical standards regarding honesty and morality, but few people stick to them when the chips are down.	T
70.	Most people inwardly dislike putting themselves out to help other people.	A
64.	People pretend to care more about one another than they really do.	A
58.	It's pathetic to see an unselfish person in today's world, because so many people take advantage of him.	A
21.	The typical student will cheat on a test when everybody else does, even though he has a set of ethical standards.	I

Subscale B: Internal Locus of Control (5 items, 3 scored in reversed direction; high score indicates a belief in internal locus of control.)

Item No.	Statement	Original Scale
61.	The average person is largely the master of his own fate.	SWR
73.	Most persons have a lot of control over what happens to them in life.	SWR
7.	Our success in life is pretty much determined by forces outside our control. (Reversed item.)	SWR
19.	There's little one can do to alter his fate in life. (Reversed item.)	SWR
25.	Most people have little influence over the things that happen to them. (Reversed item.)	SWR

Subscale C: Beliefs That People Are Conventionally Good (12 items; high score indicates a belief in conventional goodness.)

Item No.	Statement	Original Scale
4.	Most people try to apply the Golden Rule, even in today's complex society.	A
10.	Most people do not hesitate to go out of their way to help someone in trouble.	A
16.	Most people will act as "Good Samaritans" if given the opportunity.	A
22.	"Do unto others as you would have them do unto you" is a motto that most people follow.	A
40.	Most people would stop and help a person whose car was disabled.	A
67.	In a local or national election, most people select a candidate rationally and logically.	SWR
14.	People usually tell the truth, even when they know they would be better off by lying.	T
63.	The average person will stick to his opinion if he thinks he's right, even if others disagree.	I
57.	It is achievement, rather than popularity with others, that gets you ahead nowadays.	A
28.	The typical person is sincerely concerned about the problems of others.	A
81.	Most people will speak out for what they believe in.	I
45.	Most people have the courage of their convictions.	I

Subscale D: Complexity (6 items, all positively scored; high score indicates a belief in complexity.)

Item No.	Statement	Original Scale
54.	Some people are too complicated for me to figure out.	C
60.	I think you can never really understand the feelings of other people.	C
66.	You can't accurately describe a person in a few words.	C
78.	People are too complex to ever be understood fully.	C
84.	People are so complex that it is hard to know what "makes them tick."	C
41.	People are unpredictable in how they'll act from one situation to another.	V

Subscale E: Variability (7 items, 2 reversed; high score indicates a belief in variability.)

Item No.	Statement	Original Scale
5.	A person's reaction to things differs from one situation to another.	V
11.	Different people react to the same situation in different ways.	V
17.	Each person's personality is different from the personality of every other person.	V
23.	People are quite different in their basic interests.	V
29.	People are pretty different from one another in what "makes them tick."	V
47.	People are pretty much alike in their basic interests. (Reversed item.)	V
53.	People are basically similar in their personalities. (Reversed item.)	V

Subscale F: First Impressions (5 items, 1 reversed; high score indicates a belief in the accuracy of first impressions.)

Item No.	Statement	Original Scale
48.	I find that my first impressions of people are frequently wrong. (Reversed item.)	C
24.	I think I get a good idea of a person's basic nature after a brief conversation with him.	C
18.	It's not hard to understand what is really important to a person.	C
6.	I find that my first impression of people is usually correct.	C
30.	If I could ask a person three questions about himself (assuming that he would answer them honestly), I would know a great deal about him.	C

Behavior Insight Test

Directions: The following are descriptions of situations that might occur every day. Your task is to write your response to the questions asked after the situation is described. Sometimes you may feel as if you want more information before answering, but your task is to answer as best you can *with the information given,* even if your answer is only a "best guess."

Be sure to answer each question after each situation. There is no time limit on this test.

1. The scene is a cashier's stand at a cafeteria. The customer hands the cashier a $5 bill to pay for his meal. The cashier mistakes it for a $10 bill and gives him change for $10 instead of for $5. The customer is immediately aware of the mistake.

What should the customer do?
What does the customer do?
What would you do if you were the customer?

2. Bob is a teenager who has just completed high school. He is trying to decide whether to go to college. He greatly desires a college education but has always made very poor grades in school even though he tried hard. His high school counselor has told Bob that he has very little chance of succeeding in college. Bob has been offered a position in a sales-trainee program if he will join right away. If he joins, he must make a commitment to stay in the program for two years and in sales work for two more years. Job prospects would then be good, but Bob still prefers to go to college.

What should Bob do?
What will Bob probably do?
What would you do in Bob's position?

3. John, a college student living in the dormitory, plans to spend the evening studying for the weekly quiz scheduled the next morning in his 8:00 a.m. class. The rest of the gang are going across town to see a movie that John would like to see. This is the last night in town for this movie. All of the gang come into John's room and try to talk him into going to the movie with them.

What should John do?
What does John do?
What would you do if you were John?

4. In addition to his regular full-time job, for which income tax is deducted from his paycheck, Art occasionally acts as a tutor for college students. The students pay him cash by the hour, and Art makes about $300 a year this way. Art is now filling out his income-tax return and has to decide whether to put down this extra income. If he does, it will cost him about $60 extra in income tax. If he does not, he will save the $60 with very little risk of being caught.

What should Art do?
What does Art do?
What would you do in Art's position?

5. Frank and his date and three other couples are at an amusement park. Everybody else wants to ride the roller coaster, but Frank is convinced it is dangerous. Frank's date asks him to go with them and says he's "chicken" if he doesn't.

What does Frank do?
What should Frank do?
What would you do if you were Frank and felt the way he did?

6. Scene: a college library. A student leaves the stacks with a library book in hand. Instead of stopping at the checkout desk, he walks past it and out the front door. (There are many people crowded around the checkout desk, and no one notices him.)

Why do you think he failed to have the book checked out?
Would most people agree with you as to the reason for the student's behavior?

7. A tenth-grade class is taking a final exam in algebra. The instructor tells the students that they are on their honor not to cheat during the test. He leaves the room. Sue has had a great deal of difficulty in the course—in fact, she has been told by the instructor that she will fail the course if she does not pass the final. Sue sees that it is easy for her to look at the work being done by one of the best students in the class. There is little chance that she will be detected copying, even by the other students. There is no honor system in the school.

Should Sue copy or not?
Does she copy?
What would you do in this situation (assuming that you, too, were on the brink of failing)?

8. A convicted thief, who is 35 years of age and has served five terms in prison for burglary or theft, states that he has been converted by the chaplain at the penitentiary and that he is going to "go straight" when he is released next week.

Do you think he really intends to "go straight"?
Will he avoid a life of crime in the next five years?

9. Tom, who is sitting in his room in the dormitory, gets up and walks down to Sam's room. He knocks on the door, gets no answer, turns the knob, finds it unlocked, and enters. He picks up three dollar bills lying on the dresser and walks out.

Why do you think Tom took the money?
What reason would most people give for Tom's behavior?

10. Jane is overweight. Her family doctor has told her that the cause of her weight problem is purely psychological. She realizes that the stresses of life cause her to eat much more than she needs to. Many of her friends have told her that if she tries hard enough she will be able to cut down on her diet. Although the stresses upon her are as great as ever, Jane decides to switch to a rigid diet in order to lose weight.

Should she diet?
How well is she able to keep on the diet?
How well would you be able to?

11. Ed and Emily have been married 12 years and have quarreled constantly. Three years ago, they separated. Two months ago, their son had a serious operation, and, for the first time in several years, Ed and Emily have had a reason to be together. They decided to give their marriage another try. Their son is now well.

Do you think the marriage will work?
How do you think most people would feel about the future success of the marriage?

12. Mrs. Smith and Mrs. Jones are both third-grade teachers in the same school. The students in one class are quite similar to those in the other. Mrs. Smith believes that the best way to ensure learning is to make children fear the consequences of misbehaving. She believes in punishment for errors. Mrs. Jones believes that the best way to ensure learning is to encourage a feeling of self-confidence in the student. She believes in giving rewards for right answers.

Which is the more successful teacher?
Which class learns better?
Would your answers be different if it was a 12th-grade class?

13. Mr. Browne is the director of a group of 12 Sea Scouts. He has had some difficulty lately in getting them to maintain order at their meetings. What is the best way for him to get them to behave—to threaten them, to reason with them, to punish them when they misbehave, to ignore them, or what?

What does Mr. Browne do?
What would you do if you were Mr. Browne?

14. Walter Burns is 21 years of age. He is graduating from college and must decide which of two job offers to accept. One (Job A) involves the kind of work he really wants to do but would pay only a bare "living wage." The other (Job B) is not stimulating to him, but the pay is much better—high enough so that he could have a life free of desperate financial pressures. In other respects, the jobs are equivalent.

Which job should he choose?
Which job does he choose?
Which would you choose in his position?

15. Mr. and Mrs. Stewart have a 17-year-old daughter, Sally, who has stayed out on dates beyond her curfew time on several nights lately. They have said nothing to her about it yet but have been discussing how they might get Sally in on time.

What procedures do you think Mr. and Mrs. Stewart should use to get Sally in on time?
Which do they use?
What would you do if you were one of Sally's parents?

Interpretations of Government Policy Scale

Directions: Why do our government and its leaders act in the ways they do? The following set of statements attempts to assess your opinion of why our government has adopted certain policies. Notice that, for each statement, there are two possible reasons for the government policy, marked "A" and "B." You are to decide which reason *you think* is nearer the *real reason* for the government's policy. Place the letter (A or B) of your choice in the blank by the statement. Since these are opinions, there is no right or wrong answer. If you have any questions, ask the test administrator.

_____ 1. The main reason why our government helps the underdeveloped countries of Africa is that:

      A. it is our responsibility as a Christian nation to try to improve the standard of living of less fortunate countries.

      B. if we don't help these countries, the Communists will take them over and they will end up in an enemy camp.

_____ 2. Much of our policy toward Russia is based on:

      A. the belief of our leaders that Russia wants to attack us as soon as the time is ripe.

      B. the belief of our leaders that Russia does not want wars any more than we do.

_____ 3. Our leaders are confident about our eventual triumph over Russia because:

      A. they know that Communism is evil and that it will not succeed.

      B. they know that we have an advantage in goods, manpower, and know-how.

_____ 4. If our leaders knew for sure that they could attack Russia and Red China and destroy them without loss of American life or destruction of American property:

      A. they would attack.

      B. they would not attack.

_____ 5. The purpose of American missile bases in countries surrounding Russia (such as Turkey, Greece, and Iran) is:

A. to protect the peoples of these countries from attack by Russia.

B. to aid us in a quick retaliation if Russia attacks us and to serve as offensive weapons if we decide to attack Russia first.

_____ 6. The reason why we keep American troops within the city of West Berlin is that:

A. if we didn't, the million citizens of West Berlin would fall under Communist domination.

B. it is embarrassing to the Russians and strategically important for us to have a base far within the territory of a Russian satellite country.

_____ 7. Some prominent Americans advocate our invading Cuba. Their reason for this is:

A. Cuba is developing into an embarrassment to America's prestige in the Western hemisphere.

B. the people of Cuba are oppressed and should be freed from the Castro dictatorship.

_____ 8. If America were to stop testing atom bombs and destroy its supply:

A. Russia would develop its stockpile to a sufficient size and then attack us.

B. Russia would stop testing its atom bombs, too.

_____ 9. The government's main reason for pressuring for the integration of schools is that:

A. black children have a right to the same opportunities that white children have.

B. the votes of blacks in the North are very crucial in deciding many elections.

_____10. Several years ago, Francis Gary Powers was shot down while flying an American U-2 plane. America had U-2 planes flying over Russia:

A. primarily for defensive reasons—to guard us against a surprise attack by the Russians.

B. primarily because America, like every other major power nowadays, must spy on other countries.

_____11. The basic reason why our government sends wheat to India is that:

A. getting rid of our surpluses saves the government money in storage costs and keeps the wheat farmers happy because it increases the cost of wheat.

B. feeding the hungry people of the world is our duty and responsibility as a prosperous nation.

_____12. The reason why the American government wants members of the American Communist Party to register is that:

A. the American Communist Party is directly controlled by Moscow, and its members seek the overthrow of our government.

B. most members of the American Communist Party, while not revolutionaries, are misguided idealists who may be led astray by revolutionaries.

_____13. The reason why our government might share its atom secrets with its allies is that:

A. this will further discourage the Russians from attacking us.

B. it is our duty to treat our allies as we would like them to treat us—to share our benefits with them.

_____14. The reason why we no longer send U-2 planes over Russia is that:

A. it is immoral to spy, even in today's international affairs.

B. we are afraid of getting caught and precipitating another crisis.

_____15. The U.S. government's aid in the development and rearming of West Germany:

A. is motivated by our national spirit of forgiveness and our willingness to give a former enemy a chance to get back on its feet.

B. is basically done to protect ourselves—to give us an extra buffer state between us and the Russians.

_____16. When asked why Russia has refrained from greater military aggression, our leaders would reply that:

A. Russia is afraid of our superior military strength.

B. Russia really does not want to go to war any more than we do.

Item Analysis and Scoring Procedures for Interpretations of Government Policy Scale

For the purpose of item analysis, the IGP scale was administered to 101 male and 92 female college students at three colleges in the South and Midwest.[1] Since summated scores on the 16 items indicated a sex difference, a separate item analysis was done for each sex. The men were divided into high (N = 24), medium (N = 52), and low (N = 25) groups on the basis of the summated scores on the 16 items. Responses to each item were tabulated for the members of each group, and a 2 × 3 chi-square test of independence was performed for each item (H. M. Walker & Lev, 1953, p. 95). On four of the items (Items 4, 8, 9, and 14), the three groups did not

TABLE E-1 Scoring Key and Percentage Responses for Each Item

Item No.	Content	"Soft-Headed" Choice	Percentage of of Men Making "Soft-Headed Choice"	Percentage of Women Making "Soft-Headed "Choice
1ª	Help underdeveloped nations	A	17	25
2ª	Russia to attack?	B	52	60
3ª	Why our triumph?	A	35	47
4	Attack if safe?	B	71	71
5	Missiles near USSR	A	27	11
6ª	Troops in W. Berlin	A	71	76
7ª	Invade Cuba	B	42	31
8	If we stop testing	B	6	5
9	Push for integration	A	75	80
10ª	Why U-2s?	A	32	24
11ª	Why wheat to India?	B	58	61
12ª	Register communists	B	39	54
13ª	Share atom secrets	B	32	53
14	No more U-2s	A	6	4
15ª	Rearm W. Germany	A	20	21
16	USSR refrained	B	66	77
	Average percentage for all 16 items		40.6	43.7
	Average percentage for 10 items on the scale		39.8	45.2

Note: a. Only these items survived the item analysis and will be scored in future uses of the scale.

differ significantly at the .05 level of significance or better. The same analysis was repeated for the 92 female subjects. They were also divided into high (N = 26), medium (N = 38), and low (N = 28) groups. For the women, responses to the same four items did not significantly differentiate the three groups. Items 5 and 16 also did not survive the item analysis.

Thus, for each sex, Items 1, 2, 3, 6, 7, 10, 11, 12, 13, and 15 were each validated by the method of summated ratings. These 10 items constitute the original Interpretations of Government Policy Scale. It is recommended that the 16-item format be used, however, as this is the format that was used when the scale was validated.

Each time the "soft-headed reason" is chosen, one point is scored. No points are scored for a choice of the "hard-headed" response or for an omission. Table E-1 gives the "soft-headed choice" for each item (including those items that did not survive the item analysis), as well as the percentage of men and women who chose this alternative.

Reliability. The split-half reliability of the 10-item scale was determined by dividing the scale into halves, computing subjects' scores for each half, correlating the scores, and applying the Spearman-Brown Prophecy Formula. The reliability coefficient for the total group was +.60 (for the men, +.55; for the women, +.63). These reliabilities, while not high, are acceptable for group comparisons. Their lowness is perhaps the price one pays for a short scale in a rather unclear conceptual area.

Note

1. The author wishes to express his thanks to Walter Collins of George Peabody College, Jack Kennedy of Belmont College, and Onas Scandrette of Wheaton (IL) College for their assistance in administering the scale.

APPENDIX F

Stack's Trust Rating Scale

For each item, check the box that best applies to this child.

Subject No. _____

	Very much like child all the time	Somewhat like child most of the time	Neutral; sometimes yes, sometimes no	Usually not like that	Definitely not like that
A peaceful and untroubled person					
Incapable of absorbing frustration; everything seems to frustrate child					
Accessible to new ideas					
Can't share things with anybody					
Imperturbable optimist					
Never gets what he really wants					
Pessimistic, little hope					
Able to take things as they come					
Basic mistrust of other people					
Deep, unshakable faith in self					

How well do you remember this child?

Not well at all   Reasonably well   Extremely well

How confident do you feel in your judgment of this child?

0%   50%   100%

APPENDIX G

Children's PHN Scale

Each of the following statements represents something with which some people agree and some disagree. There are no right or wrong answers. You will probably disagree with some statements and agree with others. We are interested in how much you agree or disagree with them.

Read each statement carefully. Then, by the side of each statement, show how much you agree or disagree. Do this by drawing a circle around one of the numbers. The numbers and their meanings are as follows:

If you agree strongly, mark +3.
If you agree somewhat, mark +2.
If you agree slightly, mark +1.
If you disagree slightly, mark –1.
If you disagree somewhat, mark –2.
If you disagree strongly, mark –3.

The first answer you think about is usually the best one to mark. Remember to read each statement, decide if you agree or disagree and how much so, and then carefully mark your answer. Make *only one* mark for each statement. Always use the answer that *is closest* to the way you feel.

Here are some examples:

	Strongly disagree	Disagree somewhat	Slightly disagree	Slightly agree	Agree somewhat	Strongly agree
1. Vanilla is the best flavor of ice cream.	–3	–2	–1	+1	+2	(+3)
(Notice that the person has circled +3. That means he strongly agrees with the statement. He does believe vanilla is the best flavor.)						
2. A Ford is my favorite kind of car.	–3	(–2)	–1	+1	+2	+3
(Notice that the person has circled –2. He disagrees somewhat with the statement. Some other kind of car is his favorite.)						

Read each statement and decide whether you agree or disagree. Then decide how much you agree or disagree, and circle the number.

Part I
C-PHN Scale

Scale and Direction		Strongly disagree	Disagree somewhat	Slightly disagree	Slightly agree	Agree somewhat	Strongly agree
T+	1. Most people tell the truth.	-3	-2	-1	+1	+2	+3
SWR+	2. Most people understand why they do things.	-3	-2	-1	+1	+2	+3
C-	3. Most people are really alike.	-3	-2	-1	+1	+2	+3
SWR+	4. Most people who try hard do well in life.	-3	-2	-1	+1	+2	+3
T-	5. Most people cheat when taking a test.	-3	-2	-1	+1	+2	+3
C+	6. It is hard to understand people.	-3	-2	-1	+1	+2	+3
C+	7. You can't describe everyone as good or bad.	-3	-2	-1	+1	+2	+3
SWR-	8. In life, luck is more important than ability.	-3	-2	-1	+1	+2	+3
T+	9. Most people obey laws.	-3	-2	-1	+1	+2	+3
SWR-	10. Most people don't know their good points and bad points.	-3	-2	-1	+1	+2	+3
C-	11. Everyone is much the same as everyone else.	-3	-2	-1	+1	+2	+3
SWR-	12. Most people can't do anything to change what happens to them.	-3	-2	-1	+1	+2	+3
T-	13. Most people will not keep a promise.	-3	-2	-1	+1	+2	+3
C-	14. I can tell what a person is like by looking at him.	-3	-2	-1	+1	+2	+3
C+	15. It is hard to know the reasons why people do things.	-3	-2	-1	+1	+2	+3
SWR+	16. Anybody can make a lot of money if he tries hard enough.	-3	-2	-1	+1	+2	+3
T-	17. Most people would steal something if they knew they wouldn't get caught.	-3	-2	-1	+1	+2	+3
SWR+	18. When people do things wrong, it is usually their own fault.	-3	-2	-1	+1	+2	+3
T+	19. If you help someone else out, he will help you out.	-3	-2	-1	+1	+2	+3
C-	20. It only takes a few minutes to get to know somebody.	-3	-2	-1	+1	+2	+3
T-	21. In a game, most people will cheat to win.	-3	-2	-1	+1	+2	+3
SWR-	22. Most people think that they can do more things than they can actually do.	-3	-2	-1	+1	+2	+3
C-	23. You can understand a person by looking at the clothes he wears.	-3	-2	-1	+1	+2	+3
SWR+	24. In a game, the best person always wins.	-3	-2	-1	+1	+2	+3
T+	25. Most people will do the right thing even if no one is watching them.	-3	-2	-1	+1	+2	+3
C+	26. Many people do the same thing for different reasons.	-3	-2	-1	+1	+2	+3
T+	27. If they could, most people would help a stranger who was in trouble.	-3	-2	-1	+1	+2	+3

C−	28. Most people are easy to understand.	−3	−2	−1	+1	+2	+3
T−	29. If most people found a wallet, they would keep the money in it.	−3	−2	−1	+1	+2	+3
SWR−	30. Good people are luckier than bad people.	−3	−2	−1	+1	+2	+3
C+	31. It takes a long time to really understand people.	−3	−2	−1	+1	+2	+3
SWR+	32. If people try hard enough, there will be no more wars.	−3	−2	−1	+1	+2	+3
T−	33. Most people will tell a lie to keep from getting into trouble.	−3	−2	−1	+1	+2	+3
C+	34. You can't tell what a person is like by looking at him.	−3	−2	−1	+1	+2	+3
T+	35. Most people will report a crime when they see it.	−3	−2	−1	+1	+2	+3
SWR−	36. If a person is born poor, he will always stay poor.	−3	−2	−1	+1	+2	+3

Part II

Children's Authoritarianism Scale

Directions: Read each statement below and decide whether you agree or disagree with it. Then circle either "I agree" or "I disagree" by the side of the statement.

1. The best rule is to play fair with your own gang and let the other children look out for themselves. I agree I disagree
2. There are only two kinds of people: the weak and the strong. I agree I disagree
3. Teachers should not tell the children what to do and should not worry about what the children want. I agree I disagree
4. I have often been punished unfairly. I agree I disagree
5. If a person doesn't like the way our country does things, he should just keep his mouth shut. I agree I disagree
6. I refuse to play some games because I am not good at them. I agree I disagree
7. I often feel as if I had done something wrong or bad. I agree I disagree
8. Most people will cheat if they can gain something from it. I agree I disagree
9. Most people are honest only because they are afraid of being caught. I agree I disagree
10. Most of the other countries of the world are really against us but are just afraid to show it. I agree I disagree
11. Most people hate it when they have to help someone else. I agree I disagree
12. It is really true that you will have bad luck if a black cat crosses your path. I agree I disagree
13. I have more than my share of things to worry about. I agree I disagree

Part II (contd)

14. It is all right to get around the law if you don't actually break it.	I agree	I disagree
15. If a person is not happy, it is just his own fault.	I agree	I disagree
16. I think most people would tell a lie to get ahead.	I agree	I disagree

PHN Score Sheet (C-Form)
PHN Scales

Trustworthiness		Strength of Will and Rationality		Multiplexity	
+	-	+	-	+	-
1. ___	5. ___	2. ___	8. ___	6. ___	3. ___
9. ___	13. ___	4. ___	10. ___	7. ___	11. ___
19. ___	17. ___	16. ___	12. ___	15. ___	14. ___
25. ___	21. ___	18. ___	22. ___	26. ___	20. ___
27. ___	29. ___	24. ___	30. ___	31. ___	23. ___
35. ___	33. ___	32. ___	36. ___	34. ___	28. ___
Sum =	Sum =	Sum =	Sum =	Sum =	Sum =
	Reverse sign		Reverse sign		Reverse sign
Grand Sum =		Grand Sum =		Grand Sum =	

Children's Authoritarianism
(Part II)

1. A D
2. A D
3. A D
4. A D
5. A D
6. A D
7. A D
8. A D
9. A D
10. A D
11. A D
12. A D
13. A D
14. A D
15. A D
16. A D

Factor Scales on C-PHN

Factor 1—Labeled "Pessimism"

T-	Most people cheat when taking a test.
T-	Most people will not keep a promise.
T-	Most people would steal something if they knew they wouldn't get caught.
T-	In a game, most people will cheat to win.
SWR-	Most people think that they can do more things than they can actually do.
T-	If most people found a wallet, they would keep the money in it.
T-	Most people will tell a lie to keep from getting into trouble.

Factor 2—Labeled "Altruism"

T+	If you help someone else out, he will help you out.
T+	Most people will do the right thing even if no one is watching them.
T+	If they could, most people would help a stranger who was in trouble.
T+	Most people will report a crime when they see it.

Factor 3—Labeled "Complexity"

C-	It only takes a few minutes to get to know somebody.
C+	Many people do the same thing for different reasons.
C-	Most people are easy to understand.
C+	It takes a long time to really understand people.
C+	You can't tell what a person is like by looking at him.

Factor 4—Not Labeled

C-	Most people are really alike.
SWR-	In life, luck is more important than ability.
C-	Everyone is much the same as everyone else.
SWR-	Most people can't do anything to change what happens to them.
C-	I can tell what a person is like by looking at him.
C-	You can understand a person by looking at the clothes he wears.
SWR-	If a person is born poor, he will always stay poor.

Factor 5—Not Labeled

T+	Most people tell the truth.
SWR+	Most people understand why they do things.
T+	Most people obey laws.

Factor 6—Not Labeled

SWR+	When people do things wrong, it is usually their own fault.
C+	It is hard to know the reasons why people do things.
C+	You can't describe everyone as good or bad.
SWR-	Most people don't know their good points and bad points.

Factor 7—Not Labeled

SWR+	Most people who try hard do well in life.
SWR+	Anybody can make a lot of money if he tries hard enough.
SWR+	In a game, the best person always wins.
SWR-	Good people are luckier than bad people.
SWR+	If people try hard enough, there will be no more wars.

Factor 8—Not Labeled

C+	It is hard to understand people.

Revised Item Pool for C-PHN

1. Most people cheat when taking a test.
2. If you help someone else out, he will help you out.
3. Most people will not keep a promise.
4. Most people will do the right thing even if no one is watching them.
5. Most people would steal something if they knew they wouldn't get caught.
6. If they could, most people would help a stranger who was in trouble.
7. In a game, most people will cheat to win.
8. Most people will report a crime when they see it.
9. If most people found a wallet, they would keep the money in it.
10. Most neighbors will help each other out.
11. Most people will tell a lie to keep from getting into trouble.
12. You can always trust people who go to church.
13. A person should never trust anybody but himself.
14. There is more good than bad in people.
15. Most people do not tell the truth anymore.
16. A person should always be willing to help others.
17. Most adults don't care about what happens to kids.
18. A person should be kind to everyone.
19. Everything in this world is getting worse.
20. More people in the world are learning to like each other.
21. There are going to be more wars in the future.
22. A person should try to like everybody.
23. You cannot trust politicians.
24. A person should never hurt other people to make money.
25. Most businessmen are not "fair and square" anymore.
26. Most people will stop to help someone who is having car trouble.
27. It is hard to find a good deal when buying most things.
28. Helping people makes one feel good.
29. No one really cares about me and my problems.
30. It is important to listen when someone is talking about his problems.
31. More people hate than love in these days.
32. It is a good idea to always share with others.
33. You must have luck to succeed in life.
34. Most people will try to feed someone who is hungry.
35. Even your best friend will tell your secrets if he gets a chance.

36. Most people are courteous to everyone they meet.
37. Other kids don't care what I'm worried about.
38. Everyone should fight poverty.
39. No one likes to be friends with kids who are "different."
40. Selfishness is wrong.
41. Everyone breaks some laws on purpose.
42. Most people will help those who live in slum areas.

APPENDIX H

Chi-Square Comparisons of CSQ Data

CSQ Item 2
Age

Age	Females 1966	1967	1968	Males 1966	1967	1968
16	2	2	1	1	0	0
17	46	49	30	8	11	11
18	128	116	116	32	32	23
19	8	4	12	6	3	7
20	3	2	3	0	0	3
21	0	0	1	4	0	0
22	1	0	0	2	0	0
23	1	1	1	0	1	0
24+	2	4	7	4	1	1
	N = 191	178	171	N = 57	48	45
		chi square = 16.54			chi square = 27.21	

Table value of chi square with 16 df = 26.30, p < .05
Adapted from Educational Testing Service, 1965.

CSQ Item 49
Educational Philosophy A
(Vocational Orientation)

Choice	Females 1966	1967	1968	Males 1966	1967	1968
1. most accurate	47	38	34	21	15	12
2. 2nd most accurate	81	69	76	19	18	16
3. 3rd most accurate	55	60	42	14	11	15
4. least accurate	12	10	19	3	4	2
	N = 191	178	171	N = 47	48	45
		chi square = 8.28			chi square = 2.72	

Table value of chi square with 6 df = 12.59, p < .05

CSQ Item 50
Educational Philosophy B
(Academic Orientation)

Choice	Females			Males		
	1966	*1967*	*1968*	*1966*	*1967*	*1968*
1. most accurate	45	29	25	9	7	9
2. 2nd most accurate	68	62	56	23	22	14
3. 3rd most accurate	71	71	77	22	14	16
4. least accurate	10	16	12	5	5	6
	N = 194	178	170	*N* = 59	48	45
		chi square = 7.94			chi square = 2.91	

Table value of chi square with 6 *df* = 12.59, *p* < .05

CSQ Item 51
Educational Philosophy C
(Collegiate Orientation)

Choice	Females			Males		
	1966	*1967*	*1968*	*1966*	*1967*	*1968*
1. most accurate	95	100	104	18	16	19
2. 2nd most accurate	31	33	23	10	7	13
3. 3rd most accurate	47	28	32	14	20	8
4. least accurate	21	15	10	10	5	6
	N = 194	176	169	*N* = 52	48	46
		chi square = 9.94			chi square = 9.02	

Table value of chi square with 6 *df* = 12.59, *p* < .05

CSQ Item 52
Educational Philosophy D
(Nonconformist Orientation)

Choice	Females			Males		
	1966	*1967*	*1968*	*1966*	*1967*	*1968*
1. most accurate	9	7	5	8	8	5
2. 2nd most accurate	11	15	18	7	4	4
3. 3rd most accurate	21	17	18	7	3	5
4. least accurate	152	140	129	38	33	31
	N = 193	179	170	*N* = 60	48	45
		chi square = 3.67			chi square = 1.96	

Table value of chi square with 6 *df* = 12.59, *p* < .05

CSQ Item 103
Parents' Marital Status

Choice	Females 1966	Females 1967	Females 1968	Males 1966	Males 1967	Males 1968
1. living together	160	153	140	42	39	33
2. divorced, separated	10	0	15	5	3	7
3. father deceased	17	8	13	9	5	3
4. mother deceased	0	3	2	1	0	0
5. both parents deceased	0	1	2	1	1	1
N = 187		171	172	N = 58	48	44
		chi square = 12.43			chi square = 5.95	

Table value of chi square with 8 df = 15.51, $p < .05$

CSQ Item 106
Birth Order

Choice	Females 1966	Females 1967	Females 1968	Males 1966	Males 1967	Males 1968
1. only child	16	22	16	6	6	4
2. oldest child	80	63	64	20	23	16
3. youngest child	42	40	40	14	11	8
4. in-between child	47	41	49	17	7	15
N = 185		166	169	N = 57	47	43
		chi square = 3.60			chi square = 5.80	

Table value of chi square with 6 df = 12.59, $p < .05$

CSQ Item 128
Parents' Child-Rearing Policy

Choice	Females 1966	Females 1967	Females 1968	Males 1966	Males 1967	Males 1968
1. authoritarian	28	29	28	13	13	10
2. permissive	11	6	6	6	7	2
3. mutuality	148	139	133	43	27	31
N = 187		174	167	N = 62	47	43
		chi square = 1.79			chi square = 3.75	

Table value of chi square with 4 df = 9.49, $p < .05$

CSQ Item 139
Reaction to Cheating

Choice	Females			Males		
	1966	*1967*	*1968*	*1966*	*1967*	*1968*
1. not disturbed	10	18	16	7	7	6
2. disturbed	88	73	86	18	19	16
3. action depends ...	20	21	21	5	6	7
4. talk to cheater	45	40	30	21	11	13
5. report without naming	22	17	11	4	3	1
6. report student	4	5	6	2	2	0
	N = 189	174	170	*N* = 57	48	43
		chi square = 9.92			chi square = 6.19	

Table value of chi square with 10 *df* = 18.3, *p* < .05

CSQ Item 145
Feelings About Competing

Choice	Females			Males		
	1966	*1967*	*1968*	*1966*	*1967*	*1968*
1. dislike	50	47	67	12	10	11
2. neutral	72	71	54	22	18	14
3. enjoy	62	57	54	23	21	20
	N = 184	175	175	*N* = 57	49	45
		chi square = 7.71			chi square = 4.25	

Table value of chi square with 4 *df* = 9.5, *p* < .05

References

Aaron, D. (1990, November 12). Brother Theodore. *New Republic,* pp. 34-37.

Adorno, T. W., Frenkel-Brunswik, E., Levinson, D. J., & Sanford, R. N. (1950). *The author-itarian personality.* New York: Harper & Row.

Abramowitz, S. I. (1973). Internal-external control and social-political activism: A test of the dimensionality of Rotter's internal-external scale. *Journal of Consulting and Clinical Psychology, 40,* 196-201.

Ajzen, I., & Fishbein, M. (1970). The prediction of behavior from attitudinal and normative variables. *Journal of Experimental Social Psychology, 6,* 466-487.

Ajzen, I., & Fishbein, M. (1980). *Understanding attitudes and predicting social behavior.* Englewood Cliffs, NJ: Prentice-Hall.

Allan, M., Hunter, D., & Lum, K. (1971). *Male juvenile delinquents and their philosophies of human nature.* Unpublished manuscript, University of British Columbia.

Allport, G. W. (1935). Attitudes. In C. Murchison (Ed.), *Handbook of social psychology* (pp. 789-844). Worcester, MA: Clark University Press.

Allport, G. W. (1958). What units shall we employ? In G. Lindzey (Eds.), *Assessment of human motives* (pp. 239-260). New York: Holt, Rinehart & Winston.

Allport, G. W. (1961). *Pattern and growth in personality.* New York: Holt, Rinehart & Winston.

Allport, G. W. (1962). The general and unique in psychological science. *Journal of Personality, 30,* 405-422.

Allport, G. W. (1966). Traits revisited. *American Psychologist, 21,* 1-10.

Allport, G. W. (1968). The historical background of modern social psychology. In G. Lindzey & E. Aronson (Eds.), *Handbook of social psychology* (2nd ed.) (Vol. 1, pp. 1-80). Reading, MA: Addison-Wesley.

Allport, G. W., Vernon, P. E., & Lindzey, G. (1960). *Manual: A study of values* (rev. ed.). Boston: Houghton-Mifflin.

Alter, J. (1990, October 15). Real life with Garry Trudeau. *Newsweek,* pp. 60-66.

Altman, B. E., & Castek, J. E. (1971, September). *A comparative evaluation of the effectiveness of student teaching, interning, and micro-team teaching in undergraduate teacher training* (Final report, Project No. 0-E155). Washington, DC: U.S. Department of Health, Education, and Welfare, Office of Education, Bureau of Research.

328

American College Testing Program. (1965). *Technical report.* Iowa City: ACT, Research and Development Division.

Anderson, J. P. (1940). *The relationships between certain aspects of parental behavior and attitudes of junior high pupils.* New York: Teachers College, Columbia University.

Anderson, R. L. (1969). *Philosophy of human nature as a function of political preference, political involvement, and age.* Unpublished master's thesis, Central Washington State College.

Argyris, C. (1957). *Personality and organization.* New York: Harper & Row.

Argyris, C. (1969). The incompleteness of social-psychological theory: Examples from small group, cognitive consistency, and attribution research. *American Psychologist, 24,* 893-908.

ASCD Yearbook Committee (A. W. Combs, Chairman). (1962). *Perceiving, behaving, becoming.* Washington, DC: Association for Supervision and Curriculum Development.

Ashcraft, C. W. (1963). *The relationship between conceptions of human nature and judgments of specific persons.* Unpublished doctoral dissertation, George Peabody College for Teachers.

Ashcraft, C. W. (1964, April). *Relationship between religious attitudes and the perception of others in varied environmental settings.* Paper presented at the meetings of the Southeastern Psychological Association, Gatlinburg, TN.

Ashcraft, C. W. (1967, April). *Relationship of philosophies of human nature to self disclosure.* Paper presented at the meetings of the Southeastern Psychological Association, Atlanta.

Bach, R. (1970). *Jonathan Livingston Seagull.* New York: Macmillan.

Baker, J. R. (1983). Introduction. In J. R. Baker & A. P. Ziegler, Jr. (Eds.), *William Golding's "Lord of the flies"* (pp. xiii-xxiv). New York: Perigee.

Baker, N. (1972). *The typology in* The greening of America: *Its relation to philosophies of human nature and acceptance of change.* Unpublished doctoral dissertation, George Peabody College for Teachers.

Baldwin, A. L. (1955). *Behavior and development in childhood.* New York: Dryden.

Baldwin, J. (1963). *The fire next time.* New York: Dial.

Ballantyne, R. M. (1927). *The Coral Island, a tale of the Pacific Ocean.* New York: Nelson.

Bannister, D. (Ed.). (1970). *Perspectives in personal construct theory.* New York: Academic Press.

Bar-Tal, D., & Greenberg, M. S. (1973, May). *Stability attributions of 115 adjectives commonly used to describe persons.* Paper presented at the meetings of the Midwestern Psychological Association, Chicago.

Barber, T. X., & Silver, M. J. (1968). Pitfalls in data analysis and interpretation: A reply to Rosenthal. *Psychological Bulletin, 70*(6, Pt. 2), 48-62.

Barefoot, J. C., Dahlstrom, W. G., & Williams, R. B., Jr. (1983). Hostility, CHD incidence, and total mortality: A 25-year follow-up study of 255 physicians. *Psychosomatic Medicine, 45*(1), 59-63.

Barefoot, J. C., Siegler, I. C., Nowlin, J. B., Peterson, B. L., Haney, T. L., & Williams, R. B. (1987). Suspiciousness, health, and mortality: A followup study of 500 older adults. *Psychosomatic Medicine, 45,* 59-63.

Barker, R. G., & Wright, H. F. (1951). *One boy's day.* New York: Harper & Row.

Barton, A. H. (1959). *Studying the effects of college education.* New Haven, CT: Hazen Foundation.

Batson, C. D. (1990). How social an animal? The human capacity for caring. *American Psychologist, 45,* 336-346.

Baumhart, R. C. (1961). How ethical are businessmen? *Harvard Business Review, 39,* 6-19.

Baxter, G. W., Jr. (1968). *Changes in PHN after one year and two years in college.* Unpublished master's thesis, George Peabody College for Teachers.

Baxter, G. W., Jr. (1969). *The effects of information about other player and race of other players upon cooperation in a two-person game.* Unpublished doctoral dissertation, George Peabody College for Teachers.

Baxter, G. W., Jr. (1973a, April). *Perception of the human nature in the generalized other across two and one-fourth generations.* Paper presented at the meetings of the Southeastern Psychological Association, New Orleans.

Baxter, G. W., Jr. (1973b). Race of the other player, information about other player, and cooperation in a two-person game. *Journal of Conflict Resolution, 17,* 131-161.

Bayless, J. A. (1971). *A comparative study of freshman arts-and-sciences majors as to their perceptions of human nature and tendencies toward dogmatism.* Unpublished doctoral dissertation, Oklahoma State University, College of Education.

Beach, L. R. (1967). Study of personality in the church-related liberal-arts college. *Journal of College Student Personnel, 8,* 105-108.

Bell, P. A., & Byrne, D. (1978). Repression-sensitization. In H. London & J. E. Exner, Jr. (Eds.), *Dimensions of personality* (pp. 449-485). New York: John Wiley.

Bennis, W. G. (1970). *Organization development: Its nature, origins, and prospects.* Reading, MA: Addison-Wesley.

Berendt, J. (1990, July). Reading us like a book. *Esquire,* p. 30.

Berger, E. M. (1951). The relation between expressed acceptance of self and expressed acceptance of others. *Journal of Abnormal and Social Psychology, 47,* 778-782.

Berger, P., & Luckmann, T. (1967). *The social construction of reality: A treatise in the sociology of knowledge.* New York: Anchor Press.

Bettelheim, B. (1943). Individual and mass behavior in extreme situations. *Journal of Abnormal and Social Psychology, 38,* 417-452.

Bettelheim, B. (1969). *The children of the dream: Communal child rearing and American education.* New York: Avon.

Bieri, J. (1955). Cognitive complexity-simplicity and predictive behavior. *Journal of Abnormal and Social Psychology, 21,* 263-269.

Bird, C., Monachesi, E., & Burdick, H. (1952). Studies of group tensions: III. The effect of parental discouragement of play activities upon the attitudes of white children toward Negroes. *Child Development, 23,* 295-306.

Birmingham, S. (1972). *The late John P. Marquand.* Philadelphia: J. B. Lippincott.

Blake, R., & Dennis, W. (1943). The development of stereotypes concerning the Negro. *Journal of Abnormal and Social Psychology, 38,* 525-531.

Blakeslee, S. (1989, January 17). Cynicism and mistrust linked to early death. *The New York Times,* p. 21.

Bliven, N. (1972). Head to head. *New Yorker, 48*(25), 75-77.

Bossom, J., & Maslow, A. H. (1957). Security of judges as a factor in impressions of warmth in others. *Journal of Abnormal and Social Psychology, 55,* 147-148.

Bracher, F. (1959). *The novels of James Gould Cozzens.* New York: Harcourt Brace & World.

Brown, D. R. (1967). Student stress and the institutional environment. *Journal of Social Issues, 23,* 92-107.

Brown, L. F. (1967, January). [Book review of *Thomas Woodrow Wilson*]. *Book of the Month Club News,* p. 8.

Bruner, J. S., & Tagiuri, R. (1954). The perception of people. In G. Lindzey (Ed.), *Handbook of social psychology* (Vol. 2, pp. 634-654). Cambridge, MA: Addison-Wesley.

Bryan, J. H. (1970). Children's reactions to helpers: Their money isn't where their mouths are. In J. Macaulay & L. Berkowitz (Eds.), *Altruism and helping behavior* (pp. 61-76). San Diego: Academic Press.

Bryan, J. H., & Test, M. (1967). Models and helping: Naturalistic studies in aiding behavior. *Journal of Personality and Social Psychology, 6,* 400-407.

Burgess, A. (1963). *A clockwork orange.* New York: Norton.

Butler, J. M., & Haigh, G. V. (1954). Changes in the relation between self-concepts and ideal concepts consequent upon client-centered counseling. In C. R. Rogers & R. F. Dymond (Eds.), *Psychotherapy and personality change* (pp. 55-57). Chicago: University of Chicago Press.

Byrne, D. (1961). The repression-sensitization scale: Rationale, reliability, and validity. *Journal of Personality, 29,* 334-349.

Byrne, D., Barry, J., & Nelson, D. (1963). Relation of the revised repression-sensitization scale to measures of self-description. *Psychological Reports, 13,* 323-334.

Byrne, D. & Sheffield, J. (1965). Response to sexually arousing stimuli as a function of repressing and sensitizing defenses. *Journal of Abnormal Psychology, 70,* 114-118.

Campbell, D. T., & Fiske, D. W. (1959). Convergent and discriminant validation by the multitrait-multimethod matrix. *Psychological Bulletin, 56,* 81-105.

Campbell, E. Q. (1958). Some psychological correlates of character in attitude change. *Social Forces, 36,* 335-340.

Campbell, J. (1972). *Myths to live by.* New York: Viking.

Camus, A. (1969). *The rebel* (A. Bower, Trans.). New York: Knopf.

Capek, K. (1923). *R. U. R.* Garden City, NY: Doubleday.

Carey, J., & Bruno, M. (1984, September 10). Why cynicism can be fatal. *Newsweek,* p. 68.

Carlson, E. R. (1966, April). *Concepts of man and attitudes on social issues.* Paper presented at the meetings of the Western Psychological Association, Long Beach, CA.

Casler, L. (1961). Maternal deprivation: A critical review of the literature. *Monographs of the Society for Research in Child Development, 26* (Serial No. 80).

Cattell, R. B. (1966). The scree test of the number of significant factors. *Multivariate Behavioral Research, 1,* 245-276.

Christie, R. (1970). Relationships between Machiavellianism and measures of ability, opinion, and personality. In R. Christie & F. L. Geis (Eds.), *Studies in Machiavellianism* (pp. 35-52). New York: Academic Press.

Christie, R., & Geis, F. (1968). Some consequences of taking Machiavelli seriously. In E. F. Borgatta & W. W. Lambert (Eds.), *Handbook of personality theory and research* (pp. 959-973). Chicago: Rand McNally.

Christie, R., & Geis, F. (Eds.). (1970). *Studies in Machiavellianism.* San Diego: Academic Press.

Clark, R. D., III, & Word, L. E. (1971, April). *A case where the bystander did help.* Paper presented at the meetings of the Eastern Psychological Association, New York City.

Claxton, R. N. (1971). *Changes in the philosophies of human nature of a disadvantaged group as a function of occupational and attitudinal training.* Unpublished master's thesis, George Peabody College for Teachers.

Coleman, J. (1970). Social inventions. *Social Forces, 49,* 163-173.

Coleman, J., Campbell, E., Hobson, C., McPartland, J., Mood, A., Weinfield, F., & York, R. (1966). *Equality of educational opportunity.* Washington, DC: Government Printing Office.

Collins, B. E. (1974). Four separate components of the Rotter I-E Scale: Belief in a difficult world, a just world, a predictable world, and a politically responsive world. *Journal of Personality and Social Psychology, 29,* 381-391.

332   ASSUMPTIONS ABOUT HUMAN NATURE

Collins, W. E., & Wrightsman, L. S. (1966). *Philosophies of human nature held by Marine Corps recruits*. Unpublished manuscript, George Peabody College for Teachers.
Combs, A. W., Avila, D. C., & Purkey, W. W. (1971). *Helping relationships: Basic concepts for the helping professions*. Boston: Allyn & Bacon.
Conger, J. J., & Miller, W. C. (1966). *Personality, social class, and delinquency*. New York: John Wiley.
Converse, P. E. (1964). The nature of belief systems in mass publics. In D. Apter (Ed.), *Ideology and discontent*. New York: Free Press.
Cook, S. W. (1964, July). *An experimental analysis of attitude change in a natural social setting*. [Small contract proposal submitted to the U.S. Commissioner of Education.]
Cook, S. W. (1970). Motives in a conceptual analysis of attitude-related behavior. In W. J. Arnold & D. Levine (Eds.), *Nebraska Symposium on motivation, 1969* (pp. 179-231). Lincoln: University of Nebraska Press.
Cook, S. W. (1971, August). *The effect of unintended racial contact upon racial interaction and attitude change* (Final report, Project No. S-1320, Contract No. OEC-4-7-051320-0273). Washington, DC: U.S. Office of Education.
Cook, S. W., & Wrightsman, L. S. (1967, April). *The factorial structure of "positive attitudes toward people."* Symposium paper presented at the meetings of the Southeastern Psychological Association, Atlanta.
Cook, W. W., & Medley, D. M. (1954). Proposed hostility and pharisaic-virtue scales for the MMPI. *Journal of Applied Psychology, 38,* 414-418.
Cowan, J. L. (1966). *Freedom, protest, and university environment*. Paper presented at the meeting of the American Psychological Association, New York City.
Cox, D. W. (1972). *A comparative study of philosophies of human nature of students, faculty, counselors, and administrators in a community college*. Unpublished doctoral dissertation, University of Illinois, School of Education.
Crandall, V. J., & Bellugi, U. (1954). Some relationships of interpersonal and intrapersonal conceptualizations to personal-social adjustment. *Journal of Personality, 23,* 224-232.
Crandall, V. C., Crandall, V. J., & Katkovsky, W. (1965). A children's social desirability questionnaire. *Journal of Consulting Psychology, 29,* 27-36.
Crandall, V. C., Katkovsky, W., & Crandall, V. J. (1965). Children's beliefs in their own control of reinforcements in intellectual-achievement situations. *Child Development, 36,* 91-109.
Crane, R. M. (1967). Unrest on campus—Revolution or evolution? *College and University, 42,* 209-217.
Crockett, W. H. (1965). Cognitive complexity and impression formation. In B. A. Maher (Ed.), *Progress in experimental personality research* (Vol. 2, pp. 47-90). Orlando, FL: Academic Press.
Cronbach, L. J. (1955). Processes affecting scores on "understanding of others" and "assumed similarity." *Psychological Bulletin, 52,* 177-193.
Crowne, D. P., & Marlowe, D. (1960). A new scale of social desirability independent of psychopathology. *Journal of Consulting Psychology, 24,* 349-354.
Cross, H. J., & Pruyn, E. L. (1972). Adjustment and the counter culture. In J. F. Adams (Ed.), *Psychology of adjustment*. New York: Holbrook Press.
Cross, K. P. (1968). Student values revisited. *Research Reporter, Center for Research and Development in Higher Education* (University of California, Berkeley), *3*(1), 2-5.
Crowdus, S. (1969). *The effects of positive and negative information on person perception*. Unpublished manuscript, Vanderbilt University.
Dale, E., & Eicholz, G. (1960). *Children's knowledge of words: An interim report*. Unpublished manuscript, Ohio State University.

Darley, J. M., & Latané, B. (1968a). Bystander intervention in emergencies: Diffusion of responsibility. *Journal of Personality and Social Psychology, 8,* 377-383.

Darley, J. M., & Latané, B. (1968b). When will people help in a crisis? *Psychology Today,* 2(7), 54-57; 70-71.

Davids, A., & Silverman, M. (1960). A psychological case study of death during pregnancy. *Journal of Abnormal and Social Psychology, 61,* 287-291.

Davis, O. C. (1971). *The relationships between the perceptions of the organizational climate of a school and the philosophies of human nature of members of the staff.* Unpublished doctoral dissertation, George Peabody College for Teachers, Department of Education.

Dawes, R. M. (1988). *Rational choice in an uncertain world.* San Diego: Harcourt Brace Jovanovich.

Dembroski, T. M., & Costa, P. T. (1987). Coronary-prone behavior: Components of the Type A pattern and hostility. *Journal of Personality, 55,* 211-235.

Dennis, W., & Najarian, P. (1957). Infant development under environmental handicap. *Psychological Monographs, 71*(No. 436).

Dixon, W. J. (Ed.). (1965). *BMD: Biomedical computer programs.* Los Angeles: University of California at Los Angeles, Health Sciences Computing Facility, School of Medicine.

Doeringer, P. B. (Ed.) (1969). *Programs to employ the disadvantaged.* Englewood Cliffs, NJ: Prentice-Hall.

Dole, A. A., Nottingham, J. A., & Wrightsman, L. S. (1969). Beliefs about human nature held by clinical, counseling, and rehabilitation students. *Journal of Counseling Psychology, 16,* 197-202.

Doyle, C. (1965). *Psychology, science, and the Western democratic tradition.* Unpublished doctoral dissertation, University of Michigan.

Doyle, C. (1966, September). *An empirical study of the attitudes of psychologists and other scientists and humanists toward science, freedom, and related issues.* Paper presented at the meetings of the American Psychological Association, New York City.

Dreiser, T. (1978). *An American tragedy.* Cambridge, MA: Bentley. (Reprint of 1948 ed.)

Dreiser, T. (1929). *A gallery of women.* New York: Liveright.

Dreiser, T. (1971). *Sister Carrie.* Cambridge, MA: Bentley.

Dretz, C. J., & Dretz, J. P. (1969). *Attitudes and attitude changes among social work student participants in Manpower for Social Services Head Start Program in 1968.* Unpublished master's thesis, University of Tennessee, School of Social Work.

Duke, R. B., & Wrightsman, L. S. (1968). Relation of repression-sensitization to philosophies of human nature. *Psychological Reports, 22,* 235-238.

Educational Testing Service. (1965). *Supervisor's manual for the college student questionnaire.* Princeton, NJ: Educational Testing Service.

Edwards, A. L. (1950). *Experimental design in psychological research.* New York: Holt.

Edwards, A. L. (1957). *The social desirability variables in personality assessment research.* New York: Dryden.

Elliott, D. N. (1949). *Characteristics and relationships of various criteria of teaching.* Unpublished doctoral dissertation, Purdue University.

Eriksen, C. (1951). Some implications for TAT interpretation arising from need and perception experiments. *Journal of Personality, 19,* 282-288.

Eriksen, C. (1952). Individual differences in defensive forgetting. *Journal of Experimental Psychology, 44,* 442-446.

Eriksen, C., & Lazarus, R. (1952). Perceptual defense and projective tests. *Journal of Abnormal and Social Psychology, 47,* 302-308.

Erikson, E. H. (1950). *Childhood and society.* New York: Norton.

Erikson, E. H. (1959). Identity and the life cycle. *Psychological Issues, 1,* 18-164.

Erikson, E. H. (1963). *Childhood and society* (2nd ed.). New York: Norton,
Erikson, E. H. (1964). *Insight and responsibility.* New York: Norton.
Escalona, S. K. (1968). *The roots of individuality: Normal patterns of development in infancy.* Chicago: Aldine.
Etzioni, A. (1970). Man and society: The inauthentic condition. In F. F. Korten, S. W. Cook, & J. I. Lacey (Eds.), *Psychology and the problems of society* (pp. 451-459). Washington, DC: American Psychological Association.
Etzioni, A. (1972). Human beings are not very easy to change after all. *Saturday Review, 55*(23), 45-47.
Evans, R. I. (1967). *Dialogue with Erik Erikson.* New York: Harper & Row.
Eysenck, H. (1960). The place of theory in psychology. In H. Eysenck (Ed.), *Experiments in personality.* London: Routledge & Kegan Paul.
Fales, E. D., Jr., & Seder, P. (1973, May 13). Whom can you trust? *Parade,* p. 11.
Fazio, R. H. (1986). How do attitudes guide behavior? In R. M. Sorrentino & E. T. Higgins (Eds.), *Handbook of motivation and cognition.* New York: Guilford.
Feldman, K. A. (1972). Some theoretical approaches to the study of change and stability in college students. *Review of Educational Research, 42,* 1-26.
Ferguson, L. R. (1971). Social development in infancy. *Merrill-Palmer Quarterly, 17,* 119-138.
Feuer, L. S. (1969). *The conflict of generations: The character and significance of student movements.* New York: Basic Books.
Fey, W. F. (1955). Acceptance by others and its relation to acceptance of self and others: A revaluation. *Journal of Abnormal and Social Psychology, 50,* 274-276.
Fischman, J. (1987, February). Type A on trial. *Psychology Today,* pp. 42-50.
Fischman, J. (1987, December). Getting tough. *Psychology Today,* pp. 26-28.
Flacks, R. (1967). The liberated generation: An explanation of the roots of student protest. *Journal of Social Issues, 23,* 52-75.
Fletcher, G.J.O. (1983). The analysis of verbal explanations for marital separation: Implications for attribution theory. *Journal of Applied Social Psychology, 13,* 245-258.
Fletcher, G.J.O., Danilovics, P., Fernandez, G., Peterson, D., & Reeder, G. D. (1986). Attributional complexity: An individual differences measure. *Journal of Personality and Social Psychology, 51,* 875-884.
Foster, J.F.S. (1961). *The impact of a value-oriented university* (Project No. 729, Cooperative Research Program). Washington, DC: U.S. Department of Health, Education, and Welfare, Office of Education.
Freedman, M. B. (1961). *Measurement and evaluation of change in college women.* Poughkeepsie, NY: Mellon Foundation, Vassar College.
Freedman, M. B. (1967). *The college experience.* San Francisco: Jossey-Bass.
Freud, E. L. (Ed.). (1960). *Letters of Sigmund Freud.* New York: Basic Books.
Freud, S. (1949). *The future of an illusion.* London: Hogarth Press.
Freud, S., & Bullitt, W. C. (1967). *Thomas Woodrow Wilson.* Boston: Houghton-Mifflin.
Freyd, M. (1923). Measurement in vocational selection: An outline of research procedure. *Journal of Personnel Research, 2,* 215-249.
Friedrich, O. (1987, March 16). Upside down and vice versa. *Time,* pp. 79-80.
Fromm, E. (1959). *Sigmund Freud's mission.* New York: Harper & Row.
Fulghum, R. (1988). *All I really need to know I learned in kindergarten.* New York: Random House.
Fuller, P. R. (1964, May). *The relationship of the Miller Analogies Test to faculty ratings and to professional position ten years subsequent to testing in an unusually heterogeneous*

group of psychology graduate students. Paper presented at the meetings of the Rocky Mountain Psychological Association, Salt Lake City.

Furnham, A. (1988). *Lay theories: Everyday understanding of problems in the social sciences.* Oxford: Pergamon.

Furnham, A., Johnson, C., & Rawles, R. (1985). The determinants of beliefs in human nature. *Personality and Individual Differences, 6,* 675-684.

Gallo, P., & McClintock, C. G. (1965). Cooperative and competitive behavior in mixed-motive games. *Journal of Conflict Resolution, 9,* 68-78.

Galloway, C. M. (1962). *An exploratory study of observational procedures for determining teacher nonverbal communication.* Unpublished doctoral dissertation, University of Florida.

Galloway, C. M. (1966). Teacher nonverbal communication. *Educational Leadership, 24,* 55-63.

Galloway, C. M. (1970). *Teaching is communicating: Nonverbal language in the classroom* (NEA Bulletin No. 29). Washington, DC: Association for Student Teaching.

Gamson, W. A., & Modigliani, A. (1966). Knowledge and foreign policy opinions: Some models for consideration. *Public Opinion Quarterly, 30,* 187-199.

Gardiner, H. W. (1972). Philosophies of human nature among Roman Catholic sisters. *Psychological Reports, 30,* 369-370.

Geis, F. L. (1978). Machiavellianism. In H. London & J. Exner (Eds.), *Dimensions of personality* (pp. 305-363). New York: John Wiley.

Geis, F. L., & Christie, R. (1970). Overview of experimental research. In R. Christie & F. L. Geis, *Studies in Machiavellianism* (pp. 285-313). San Diego: Academic Press.

Gibbs, N. R. (1988, September 5). Begging: To give or not to give. *Time,* pp. 68-70.

Gibran, K. (1923). *The prophet.* New York: Knopf.

Goldberg, L. R. (1972). Parameters of personality construction and utilization: A comparison of prediction strategies and tactics. *Multivariate Behavioral Research Monographs, 7,* No. 2.

Golding, W. (1954). *Lord of the flies.* New York: Putnam.

Golding, W. (1967). *The hot gates and other occasional pieces.* New York: Pocket Books.

Goldsen, R., Rosenberg, M., Williams, R., & Suchman, E. (1960). *What college students think.* Princeton, NJ: Van Nostrand.

Goodman, M. (1966). Campus youth in an age of anomie. *National Association of Women Deans and Counselors Journal, 29,* 188-193.

Gouldner, A. W. (1970). *The coming crisis in Western sociology.* New York: Basic Books.

Greeley, A. (1968). The college blight on idealism. *Educational Record, 49,* 429-434.

Griebe, K. (1972). Selecting members for your commune. *Communities,* No. 1, 12-15.

Guilford, J. P., & Zimmerman, W. S. (1955). *Manual: Guilford-Zimmerman Temperament Survey.* Beverly Hills, CA: Sheridan Supply Company.

Guion, R. M. (1970, September). *Some orthodoxies in personnel testing.* Paper presented at the meetings of the American Psychological Association, Miami Beach.

Gurin, G. (1968). *Inner-city Negro youth in a job-training project* (Final report, Contract No. 82-21-14). Washington, DC: U.S. Department of Labor.

Gurin, P., Gurin, G., Lao, R., & Beattie, M. (1969). Internal-external control of the motivational dynamics of Negro youth. *Journal of Social Issues, 25*(3), 29-54.

Gwynne, S. C. (1990, October 29). The right stuff. *Time,* pp. 74-84.

Haan, N., Smith, M. B., & Block, J. (1968). Moral reasoning of young adults: Political-social behavior, family background, and personality correlates. *Journal of Personality and Social Psychology, 10,* 183-201.

Halleck, S. L. (1968, November). Hypotheses of student unrest. *Education Digest,* pp. 13-17.

Hamrick, M. R. (1970, May). *A comparative study of the philosophies of human nature of university trustees, administrators, faculty, and students.* Unpublished master's thesis, Wake Forest University, Department of Education.

Hamsher, J. H., Geller, J. D., & Rotter, J. B. (1968). Interpersonal trust, internal-external control, and the Warren Commission Report. *Journal of Personality and Social Psychology, 9,* 210-215.

Harris, C. W. (Ed.). (1963). *Problems in measuring change.* Madison: University of Wisconsin Press.

Harvey, O. J., Hunt, D. E., & Schroder, H. M. (1961). *Conceptual systems and personality organization.* New York: John Wiley.

Hase, H. D., & Goldberg, L. R. (1967). The comparative validity of different strategies of deriving personality inventory scales. *Psychological Bulletin, 67,* 231-248.

Havighurst, R. J., & Taba, H. (1949). *Adolescent character and personality.* New York: John Wiley.

Hearn, B. (1972). *Analysis of college student attitudes regarding women's roles.* Unpublished master's thesis, George Peabody College for Teachers.

Heath, D. H. (1968). *Growing up in college.* San Francisco: Jossey-Bass.

Heider, F. (1958). *The psychology of interpersonal relations.* New York: John Wiley.

Heilbroner, R. L. (Ed.). (1972). *In the name of profit.* Garden City, NY: Doubleday.

Heinlein, R. (1961). *Stranger in a strange land.* New York: Putnam.

Heller, J. (1961). *Catch-22.* New York: Simon & Schuster.

Hendrickson, A. E., & White, P. O. (1964). Promax: A quick method for rotation to oblique structure. *British Journal of Statistical Psychology, 17,* 65-70.

Hersch, P. D., & Scheibe, K. E. (1967). Reliability and validity of internal-external control as a personality dimension. *Journal of Consulting Psychology, 31,* 609-613.

Hess, R. D. (1969, January). *Parental behavior and children's school achievement: Implications for Head Start.* Paper presented at Head Start Research Seminar #5, Washington, DC.

Hess, R. D. (1970). Social class and ethnic influences on socialization. In P. H. Mussen (Ed.), *Carmichael's manual of child psychology* (3rd ed.) (Vol. 2, pp. 457-557). New York: John Wiley.

Hillegas, M. R. (1967). *The future as nightmare: H. G. Wells and the anti-Utopians.* New York: Oxford University Press.

Hiltner, S. (1962). The dialogue on man's nature. In S. Doniger (Ed.), *The nature of man* (pp. 237-261). New York: Harper & Row.

Hinkle, D. N. (1970). The game of personal constructs. In D. Bannister (Ed.), *Perspectives in personal construct theory* (pp. 91-110). San Diego: Academic Press.

Hoagland, E. (1969). The problem of the Golden Rule. *Commentary, 48*(2), 38-42.

Hochreich, D. J. (1968). *Refined analysis of internal-external control and behavior in a laboratory situation.* Unpublished doctoral dissertation, University of Connecticut.

Hochreich, D. J., & Rotter, J. B. (1970). Have college students become less trusting? *Journal of Personality and Social Psychology, 15,* 211-214.

Holland, R. (1970). George Kelly: Constructive innocent and reluctant idealist. In D. Bannister (Ed.), *Perspectives in personal construct theory* (pp. 111-132). San Diego: Academic Press.

Hopkins, W. S. (1973). *Philosophies of human nature and nonverbal communication patterns.* Unpublished doctoral dissertation, Oklahoma State University, Department of Elementary Education.

Houriet, R. (1971). *Getting back together.* New York: Coward, McCann & Geoghegan.

Hoy, W. K. (1967). Organizational socialization: The student teacher and pupil control ideology. *Journal of Educational Research, 61,* 153-155.

Humphreys, L. G. (1956). The normal curve and the attenuation paradox in test theory. *Psychological Bulletin, 53,* 472-476.

Hunt, R. A. (1963). *An exploratory study of some relationships between personality variables and achievement in seminary.* Unpublished manuscript, Texas Christian University.

Hunter, J. E., Gerbing, D. W., & Boster, F. J. (1982). Machiavellian beliefs and personality: Construct invalidity of the Machiavellianism dimension. *Journal of Personality and Social Psychology, 43,* 1293-1305.

Huxley, A. (1932). *Brave new world.* New York: Harper & Row.

Jacob, P. (1957). *Changing values in college.* New York: Harper & Row.

Jacobs, E. B. (1968). Attitude change in teacher education: An inquiry into the role of attitudes in changing teacher behavior. *Journal of Teacher Education, 19,* 410-415.

Jankowicz, A. D. (1987). Whatever became of George Kelly? Applications and implications. *American Psychologist, 42,* 481-487.

John, K. E. (1988, March 7-13). In media we trust-less. *Washington Post National Weekly Edition,* p. 37.

John, O. P. (1990). The "big five" factor taxonomy: Dimensions of personality in the natural language and in questionnaires. In L. A. Pervin (Ed.), *Handbook of personality: Theory and research* (pp. 67-100). New York: Guilford.

Johnson, W. A. (1969). *A comparison of the philosophies of human nature of Negro and white high school seniors.* Unpublished master's thesis, George Peabody College for Teachers.

Johnson-George, C., & Swap, W. C. (1982). Measurement of specific interpersonal trust: Construction and validation of a scale to assess trust in a specific other. *Journal of Personality and Social Psychology, 43,* 1306-1317.

Jonas, G. (1972). Onward and upward with the arts: S. F. *New Yorker, 48*(23), 33-52.

Jourard, S. (1964). *The transparent self.* Princeton, NJ: Van Nostrand.

Kaiser, H. F. (1960). The application of electronic computers to factor analysis. *Educational and Psychological Measurement, 20,* 141-151.

Kanfer, S. (1972, February 7). Holden today: Still in the rye. *Time,* pp. 50-51.

Kanfer, S. (1990, July 2). Sermons from Rev. Feelgood. *Time,* pp. 58-60.

Kanter, D. L., & Mirvis, P. H. (1989). *The cynical Americans: Living and working in an age of discontent and disillusion.* San Francisco: Jossey-Bass.

Kanter, R. M. (1972). *Commitment and community: Communes and utopias in sociological perspective.* Cambridge, MA: Harvard University Press.

Kawamura, W. I., & Wrightsman, L. S. (1969, January). *A factorial study with 18 measures of religiosity and 29 measures of personality.* Paper presented at the meetings of the Society for the Scientific Study of Religion, Atlanta.

Kayloe, J. C. (1976). *Personality variances on scales of Machiavellianism, philosophies of human nature, and values among students in different fields of specialization.* Unpublished master's thesis, University of Dayton.

Kelley, H. H. (1972). *Causal schemata and the attribution process.* Morristown, NJ: General Learning Press.

Kelley, H. H. (1973). The processes of causal attribution. *American Psychologist, 28,* 107-128.

Kelly, G. A. (1955). *The psychology of personal constructs.* New York: Norton.

Kelly, G. A. (1963). *A theory of personality: The psychology of personal constructs.* New York: Norton.

338   ASSUMPTIONS ABOUT HUMAN NATURE

Kelly, G. A. (1970). A brief introduction to personal construct theory. In D. Bannister (Ed.), *Perspectives on personal construct theory* (pp. 1-30). San Diego: Academic Press.

Kennedy, J. J., Cook, P. A., & Brewer, R. R. (1969, March). *An examination of the effects of three selected experimenter variables in verbal conditioning research.* Paper presented at the meetings of the Southeastern Psychological Association, New Orleans.

Keniston, K. (1962). Social change and youth in America. *Daedalus, 91,* 145-171.

Keniston, K. (1965). *The uncommitted: Alienated youth in American society.* New York: Harcourt Brace Jovanovich.

Keniston, K. (1967). The source of student dissent. *Journal of Social Issues, 23,* 108-137.

Keniston, K. (1968a). Heads and seekers. *American Scholar, 38,* 97-112.

Keniston, K. (1968b). *Young radicals: Notes on committed youth.* Orlando, FL: Harcourt Brace Jovanovich.

Kerlinger, F. N. (1958). Progressivism and traditionalism: Basic factors of educational attitudes. *Journal of Social Psychology, 48,* 111-135.

Kerlinger, F. N. (1961). Factor invariance in the measurement of attitudes toward education. *Educational and Psychological Measurement, 21,* 273-285.

Kerlinger, F. N. (1967a). The first- and second-order factor structures of attitudes toward education. *American Educational Research Journal, 4,* 191-205.

Kerlinger, F. N. (1967b). Social attitudes and their criterial referents: A structural theory. *Psychological Review, 74,* 110-122.

Kimber, J.A.M. (1947). The insight of college students into the items of a personality test. *Educational and Psychological Measurement, 7,* 411-420.

Kinder, D. (1986). Presidential character revisited. In R. Lau & D. O. Sears (Eds.), *Political cognition* (pp. 233-256). Hillsdale, NJ: Lawrence Erlbaum.

King, M. (1971). *Correlation of PHN scores with scores on a semantic-differential form of the scale.* Unpublished manuscript, George Peabody College for Teachers.

Kirkpatrick, C. (1936). The construction of a belief-pattern scale for measuring attitudes toward feminism. *Journal of Social Psychology, 7,* 421-437.

Kleeman, J. L. (1972). *The Kendall College human potential seminar model and philosophies of human nature.* Unpublished doctoral dissertation, University of Illinois, College of Education.

Klein, D. C. (1968). *Community dynamics and mental health.* New York: John Wiley.

Klein, G. S. (1951). The personal world through perception. In R. R. Blake & G. V. Ramsey (Eds.), *Perception: An approach to personality* (pp. 328-359). New York: Ronald Press.

Kluckhohn, F. R. (1953). Dominant and variant value orientations. In C. Kluckhohn, H. A. Murray, & D. M. Schneider (Eds.), *Personality in nature, society, and culture* (2nd ed.) (pp. 342-357). New York: Knopf.

Kobasa, S. C. (1979). Stressful life events, personality, and health: An inquiry into hardiness. *Journal of Personality and Social Psychology, 37,* 1-11.

Koepper, R. C. (1966). *Psychological correlates of teacher attitudes toward school desegregation.* Unpublished doctoral dissertation, George Peabody College for Teachers, School of Education.

Koestler, A. (1972). *The roots of coincidence.* New York: Random House.

Kohlberg, L. (1963). Moral development and identification. In H. W. Stevenson (Eds.), *Child psychology: The sixty-second yearbook of the National Society for the Study of Education, Part I.* Chicago: University of Chicago Press.

Kohn, A. (1987, May). Whatever happened to human potential? *Psychology Today,* pp. 99-100.

Krasner, L. (1965). The behavior scientist and social responsibility: No place to hide. *Journal of Social Issues, 21*(2), 9-30.

Kroeber, A. L. (1955). On human nature. *Southwestern Journal of Anthropology, 11,* 195-204.

Kuhn, T. S. (1962). *The structure of scientific revolutions.* Chicago: University of Chicago Press.

Kushner, H. S. (1981). *When bad things happen to good people.* New York: Schocken.

LaForge, R., & Suczek, R. (1955). The interpersonal dimension of personality: III. An interpersonal checklist. *Journal of Personality, 24,* 94-112.

Lapham, L. (1971). What movies try to sell us. *Harpers, 243*(1458), 106-115.

LaPiere, R. I. (1959). *The Freudian ethic.* New York: Duell, Sloan, & Pearce.

Larrabee, J. (1990, November 23). Age of Aquarius lives. *USA Today,* p. 8A.

Lasater, T. M., & Ramirez, A. (1970, May). *Lack of correlation among several current measures of helplessness: I-E, anomie, and powerlessness.* Paper presented at the meetings of the Rocky Mountain Psychological Association, Salt Lake City.

Latané, B., & Darley, J. (1968). Group inhibition of bystander intervention in emergencies. *Journal of Personality and Social Psychology, 10,* 215-221.

Latané, B., & Darley, J. (1970a). Social determinants of bystander intervention in emergencies. In J. Macaulay & L. Berkowitz (Eds.), *Altruism and helping behavior* (pp. 13-27). San Diego: Academic Press.

Latané, B., & Darley, J. (1970b). *The unresponsive bystander: Why doesn't he help?* New York: Appleton-Century-Crofts.

Latané, B., Nida, S. A., & Wilson, D. W. (1981). The effects of group size on helping behavior. In J. P. Rushton & R. M. Sorrentino (Eds.), *Altruism and helping behavior: Social, personality, and developmental perspectives.* Hillsdale, NJ: Lawrence Erlbaum.

Latané, B., & Rodin, J. (1969). A lady in distress: Inhibiting effects of friends and strangers on bystander intervention. *Journal of Experimental Social Psychology, 5,* 189-202.

Lazarus, R., Eriksen, C., & Fonda, C. (1951). Personality dynamics and auditory-perceptual recognition. *Journal of Personality, 19,* 471-482.

Lazarus, R., & Longo, N. (1953). The consistency of psychological defense against threat. *Journal of Abnormal and Social Psychology, 48,* 495-499.

Lear, J. (1972). Where is society going? The search for landmarks. *Saturday Review, 55*(16), 34-39.

Lefcourt, H. M. (1991). Locus of control. In J. P. Robinson, P. R. Shaver, & L. S. Wrightsman (Eds.), *Measures of personality and social psychological attitudes* (pp. 413-499). San Diego: Academic Press.

Lehmann, I. J. (1965). American college students and the socialization process. In W. B. Brookover, D. Gottlieb, I. J. Lehmann, R. Richards, J. F. Thaden, & A. M. Verner (Eds.), *The college student* (pp. 58-77). New York: Center for Applied Research in Education.

Lehmann, I. J., & Dressel, P. L. (1962). *Critical thinking, attitudes, and values in higher education.* East Lansing: Michigan State University.

Lehmann, I. J., Sinha, B. K., & Harnett, R. T. (1966). Changes in attitudes and values associated with college attendance. *Journal of Educational Psychology, 57*(2), 89-98.

Lerner, M. J. (1966, September). *The unjust consequences of the need to believe in a just world.* Paper presented at the meetings of the American Psychological Association, New York City.

Lerner, M. J. (1970). The desire for justice and reactions to victims. In J. Macaulay & L. Berkowitz (Eds.), *Altruism and helping behavior* (pp. 205-230). San Diego: Academic Press.

Lerner, M. J. (1971). Justice, guilt, and veridical perception. *Journal of Personality and Social Psychology, 20,* 127-135.

Lerner, M. J. (1974). Social psychology of justice and interpersonal attraction. In T. Huston (Ed.), *Perspectives on interpersonal attraction.* San Diego: Academic Press.

Lerner, M. J. (1980). *The belief in a just world: A fundamental delusion.* New York: Plenum.

Lerner, M. J., & Elkinton, L. (1970). *Perception of injustice: An initial look.* Unpublished manuscript, University of Kentucky.

Lerner, M. J., & Miller, D. T. (1978). Just world research and the attribution process: Looking back and ahead. *Psychological Bulletin, 85,* 1030-1051.

Lerner, M. J., & Simmons, C. (1966). Observer's reaction to the "innocent victim": Compassion or rejection? *Journal of Personality and Social Psychology, 4,* 203-210.

Levanway, R. W. (1955). The effect of stress on expressed attitudes toward self and others. *Journal of Abnormal and Social Psychology, 50,* 225-226.

Levinson, D. J., & Huffman, P. E. (1953). Traditional family ideology and its relation to personality. *Journal of Personality, 22,* 101-117.

Ligon, C. L. (1963). *Religious backgrounds and philosophies of human nature.* Unpublished manuscript, George Peabody College for Teachers.

Ligon, C. L. (1970). *The relationship between scores on the Philosophies of Human Nature scale and levels of facilitation among counselors in preparation.* Unpublished doctoral dissertation, Florida State University, College of Education.

Lincoln, H., & Levinger, G. (1972). Observer's evaluations of the victim and the attacker in an aggressive incident. *Journal of Personality and Social Psychology, 22,* 202-210.

Lingeman, R. (1990). *Theodore Dreiser: An American journey, 1908-1945.* New York: Putnam.

Lovejoy, A. D. (1961). *Reflections on human nature.* Baltimore, MD: Johns Hopkins Press.

Lupfer, M., & Wald, K. (1984). *An exploration of adults' religious orientations and their philosophies of human nature.* Unpublished manuscript, Memphis State University.

MacDonald, A. P., Jr. (1971a). *Derogation of a victim: Justice or guilt?* Unpublished manuscript, West Virginia University.

MacDonald, A. P., Jr. (1971b). *Intercorrelations of I-E measures.* Unpublished manuscript, West Virginia University.

Machiavelli, N. (1952). *The prince.* New York: Modern Library.

Maddi, S. R. (1976). *Personality theories: A comparative analysis* (3rd ed.). Homewood, IL: Dorsey.

Maddock, R. C., & Kenny, C. T. (1972). Philosophies of human nature and personal religious orientation. *Journal for the Scientific Study of Religion, 11,* 277-281.

Maher, B. (Ed.). (1969). *Clinical psychology and personality: The selected papers of George Kelly.* New York: John Wiley.

Malamud, B. (1982). *The fixer.* New York: Washington Square Press.

Mallery, D. (1966). *Ferment on the campus: An encounter with the new college generation.* New York: Harper & Row.

Mannheim, K. (1936). *Ideology and Utopia: An introduction to the sociology of knowledge* (L. Wirth, Trans.). New York: Harcourt Brace & World.

Manuel, F. (Ed.). (1966). *Utopias and utopian thought.* Boston: Beacon.

Marcus, G. B. (1986). Stability and change in political attitudes: Observe, recall, and "explain." *Political Behavior, 8,* 21-44.

Martin, J. M., & Fitzpatrick, J. P. (1964). *Delinquent behavior: A redefinition of the problem.* New York: Random House.

Marx, K. (1963). *Karl Marx: Selected writings in sociology and social philosophy* (T. B. Bottomore & M. Rubel, Eds. and Trans.). London: Penguin.

References 341

Maslow, A. H. (1962). *Toward a psychology of being.* Princeton, NJ: Van Nostrand.
Maslow, A. H. (1965). A philosophy of psychology: The need for a mature science of human nature. In F. T. Severin (Ed.), *Humanistic viewpoints in psychology* (pp. 17-33). New York: McGraw-Hill.
Maslow, A. H., & Mittelman, E. (1941). *Principles of abnormal psychology.* New York: Harper & Row.
Maslow, B. G. (Compiler). (1972). *Abraham H. Maslow: A memorial volume.* Pacific Grove, CA: Brooks/Cole.
Mason, R., Jr. (1966). *A comparative study of the relationships between seminary students and counselor trainees in their perceptions of human nature and tendencies toward authoritarianism.* Unpublished doctoral dissertation, University of Georgia.
May, E. P. (1971). *A study of therapists' and homosexuals' philosophies of human nature and attitudes toward deviant behavior.* Unpublished doctoral dissertation, University of Illinois, Department of Educational Psychology.
May, R. (1982). The problem of evil: An open letter to Carl Rogers. *Journal of Humanistic Psychology, 22,* 10-21.
Mayo, C.M.W. (1959). *Cognitive complexity and conflict resolution in impression formation.* Unpublished doctoral dissertation, Clark University.
McCandless, B. R. (1961). *Children and adolescents: Behavior and development.* New York: Holt, Rinehart & Winston.
McClosky, H., Hoffman, P. J., & O'Hara, R. (1960). Issue conflict and consensus among party leaders and followers. *American Political Science Review, 54,* 406-427.
McConnell, T. R. (1962). Differences in student attitudes toward civil liberties. In R. L. Sutherland, W. H. Holtzman, E. A. Koile, & B. K. Smith (Eds.), *Personality factors on the college campus* (pp. 29-42). Austin, TX: Hogg Foundation for Mental Health.
McGregor, D. (1960). *The human side of enterprise.* New York: McGraw-Hill.
McGregor, D. (1966). The human side of enterprise. In W. G. Bennis & E. H. Schein (Eds.), *Leadership and motivation: Essays of Douglas McGregor* (pp. 3-20). Cambridge: MIT Press.
McHolland, J. D. (1971). Human potential seminars. In T. O'Banion (Ed.), *New directions in community college student personnel programs.* Washington, DC: American Personnel and Guidance Association.
McIntyre, C. J. (1952). Acceptance by others and its relation to acceptance of self and others. *Journal of Abnormal and Social Psychology, 47,* 624-625.
McKeachie, W. J., & Solomon, D. (1958). Student ratings of instructors: A validity study. *Journal of Educational Research, 51,* 379-382.
Mehrabian, A. (1967). Orientation behavior and nonverbal communication. *Journal of Communication, 17,* 328-342.
Melville, K. (1972). *Communes in the counter culture: Origins, theories, styles of life.* New York: William Morrow.
Meyerson, E. (1930). *Identity and reality.* New York: Macmillan.
Milgram, S. (1963). Behavioral study of obedience. *Journal of Abnormal and Social Psychology, 67,* 371-378.
Milgram, S. (1965). Some conditions of obedience and disobedience to authority. *Human Relations, 18,* 57-76.
Milgram, S. (1970). The experience of living in cities. *Science, 167,* 1461-1468.
Milgram, S. (1972). Interpreting obedience: Error and evidence. In A. G. Miller (Ed.), *The social psychology of psychological research* (pp. 138-154). New York: Basic Books.
Milgram, S. (1974). *Obedience to authority.* New York: Harper & Row.

Miller, A., Wattenberg, M., & Malanchuk, O. (1986). Schematic assessments of candidates. *American Political Science Review, 80,* 521-540.

Miller, G. A. (1969). On turning psychology over to the unwashed. *Psychology Today, 3*(7), 53-54, 66-71.

Mills, C. W. (1959). *The sociological imagination.* New York: Oxford University Press.

Mills, T. M. (1967). *The sociology of small groups.* Englewood Cliffs, NJ: Prentice-Hall.

Mischel, W. (1968). *Personality and assessment.* New York: John Wiley.

Mischel, W. (1969). Continuity and change in personality. *American Psychologist, 24,* 1012-1018.

Moffatt, G. (1972). Community axioms. *Communities,* No. 1, pp. 6-7.

Mogar, R. (1964). Value orientation of college students: Preliminary data and review of the literature. *Psychological Reports, 5*(Pt. 15).

Monod, J. (1972). *Chance and necessity: An essay on the natural philosophy of modern biology.* New York: Knopf.

Morgenthau, H. J. (1951). *In defense of the national interest.* New York: Knopf.

Morris, C. (1956). *Varieties of human value.* Chicago: University of Chicago Press.

Mulry, R. C. (1966). *Personality and test-taking behavior.* Unpublished doctoral dissertation, University of Connecticut.

Myers, H. J., Borgatta, E. F., & Jones, W. C. (1965). *Girls at vocational high.* New York: Russell Sage Foundation.

Neal, A. G., & Rettig, S. (1967). On the multidimensionality of alienation. *American Sociological Review, 32,* 54-64.

Newcomb, T. M. (1943). *Personality and social change.* New York: Dryden.

Newcomb, T. M., & Svelha, G. (1937). Intrafamily relationships in attitude. *Sociometry, 1,* 180-205.

Newsome, G. L., Gentry, H. L., & Stephens, L. D. (1965). Changes in consistency of educational ideas attributable to student teaching experiences. *Journal of Teacher Education, 16,* 319-323.

Nidorf, L. J., & Crockett, W. H. (1964). Some factors affecting the amount of information sought about others. *Journal of Abnormal and Social Psychology, 69,* 98-101.

Niebuhr, R. (1953). Human nature and social change. *Christian Century, 50,* 360-363.

Nisbett, R. A. (1961). Voting practices vs. democratic theory. *Commentary, 31,* 60-65.

Nisbett, R. A., & Wilson, T. (1977). Telling more than we can know: Verbal reports on mental processes. *Psychological Review, 84,* 231-259.

Noll, V. H. (1951). Simulation by college students of a prescribed pattern on a personality scale. *Educational and Psychological Measurement, 11,* 478-488.

Nottingham, J. A. (1968). *The relationship between philosophies of human nature and liberalism-conservatism.* Unpublished manuscript, George Peabody College for Teachers.

Nottingham, J. A. (1969). *The effect of extremity of attitude on information-seeking behavior.* Unpublished doctoral dissertation, George Peabody College for Teachers.

Nottingham, J. A. (1970). Extremity of attitude and information seeking behavior. *Proceedings, 78th Annual Convention, APA, 5,* 409-410.

Nottingham, J. A., Gorsuch, R., & Wrightsman, L. S. (1970). Factorial replication of the theoretically derived subscales on the Philosophies of Human Nature Scale. *Journal of Social Psychology, 81,* 129-130.

Oakeshott, M. J. (1962). *Rationalism in politics and other essays.* New York: Basic Books.

O'Connor, J. (1971). *Multimethod analysis of the Philosophies of Human Nature Scale.* Unpublished manuscript, George Peabody College for Teachers.

Oldsey, B. S., & Weintraub, S. (1965). *The art of William Golding.* New York: Harcourt Brace & World.

Omwake, K. T. (1954). The relation between acceptance of self and acceptance of others shown by three personality inventories. *Journal of Consulting Psychology, 18,* 443-446.

Orlansky, H. (1949). Infant care and personality. *Psychological Bulletin, 46,* 1-48.

Orne, M. T., & Holland, C. C. (1968). On the ecological validity of laboratory deceptions. *International Journal of Psychiatry, 6*(4), 282-293.

Orwell, G. (1983). *1984.* New York: Harcourt Brace Jovanovich.

Osgood, C. E., Suci, G. J., & Tannenbaum, P. H. (1957). *The measurement of meaning.* Urbana: University of Illinois Press.

Oskamp, S. (1972). Social perception. In L. S. Wrightsman (Ed.), *Social psychology in the seventies* (pp. 430-457). Pacific Grove, CA: Brooks/Cole.

Otto, H. A. (Ed.). (1966). *Explorations in human potentialities.* Springfield, IL: Charles C Thomas.

Otto, H. A. (1969). New light on human potential. *Saturday Review, 52*(51), 14-17.

Painton, P. (1990, April 6). Shrugging off the homeless. *Time,* pp. 14-16.

Paulhus, D. L. (1991). Measurement and control of response bias. In J. P. Robinson, P. R. Shaver, & L. S. Wrightsman (Eds.), *Measures of personality and social psychological attitudes* (pp. 17-59). San Diego: Academic Press.

Pavenstadt, E. (1965). A comparison of the child-rearing environment of upper-lower and very low class families. *American Journal of Orthopsychiatry, 35,* 89-98.

Peck, R. F., & Havighurst, R. J. (1960). *The psychology of character development.* New York: John Wiley.

Perloe, S. (1960). Inhibition as a determinant of perceptual defense. *Perceptual and Motor Skills, 11,* 59-66.

Peter, E., Jr. (1961). There will always be dragons to fight in the public interest. *The Quill, 49,* 7-8ff.

Peterson, R. (1967). Organized student protest in 1964-65. *National Association of Women Deans and Counselors Journal, 30,* 50-56.

Phillips, E. L. (1951). Attitudes toward self and others: A brief questionnaire report. *Journal of Consulting Psychology, 15,* 79-81.

Phypers, J. M. (1967). *Delay of gratification and adjustment in elementary school children.* Unpublished doctoral dissertation, University of Colorado.

Pierce-Jones, J., Reid, J. B., & King, F. J. (1959). Adolescent racial and ethnic group differences in social attitudes and adjustment. *Psychological Reports, 5,* 549-552.

Piliavin, I., Hardyck, J., & Vadum, A. R. (1967, August). *Reactions to a victim in a just or nonjust world.* Paper presented at the meetings of the Society of Experimental Social Psychology, Bethesda, MD.

Plant, W. T. (1958). Changes in ethnocentrism associated with a four-year college education. *Journal of Educational Psychology, 49,* 162-165.

Plant, W. T. (1962). *Personality changes associated with a four-year college education* (Project 348 [SAE 7666]). Washington, DC: U.S. Office of Education, Cooperative Research Branch.

Plant, W. T., & Telford, C. W. (1966). Changes in personality for groups completing different amounts of college over two years. *Genetic Psychology Monographs, 74*(1), 3-36.

Poppy, J. (1989, October). Soothing the savage heart. *Esquire,* pp. 103-104.

Pratkanis, A. R., Breckler, S. J., & Greenwald, A. G. (Eds.). (1989). *Attitude structure and function.* Hillsdale, NJ: Lawrence Erlbaum.

Prytula, R., Champagne, J. J., Grigsby, C. F., & Soltys, A. J., Jr. (1972, December). The personality and characteristics of police officers and their attitudes toward others. *Police Chief,* p. 54.

Quinn, O. (1954). The transmission of racial attitudes toward white Southerners. *Social Forces, 33,* 41-47.

Radke, M. J. (1946). *The relationship of parental authority to children's behavior and attitudes.* Minneapolis: University of Minnesota Press.

Rapoport, A. (1966). *Two person game theory: The essential ideas.* Ann Arbor: University of Michigan Press.

Rapoport, A., & Chammah, A. (1965). *Prisoner's dilemma.* Ann Arbor: University of Michigan Press.

Raspberry, W. (1990, November 5-11). No conspiracy. *Washington Post National Weekly Edition,* p. 28.

Read, S. J. (1983). Once is enough: Causal reasoning from a single instance. *Journal of Personality and Social Psychology, 45,* 323-334.

Reich, C. A. (1970). *The greening of America.* New York: Random House.

Rejeski, W. J., Leary, M. R., & Gainer, L. (1988, August). *Cynical hostility and cardiovascular reactivity.* Paper presented at the meetings of the American Psychological Association, Atlanta.

Rempel, J. K., & Holmes, J. G. (1986, February). How do I trust thee? *Psychology Today,* pp. 28-34.

Rempel, J. K., Holmes, J. G., & Zanna, M. P. (1985). Trust in close relationships. *Journal of Personality and Social Psychology, 49,* 95-112.

Rhodes, W. C. (1972). *Behavioral threat and community response.* New York: Behavioral Publications.

Richard, W. C., Mates, C. B., & Whitten, L. (1967, April). *Personality traits and attitudes of adolescent girls with behavior disorders.* Paper presented at the meetings of the Southeastern Psychological Association, Atlanta.

Richman, J. (1970). *An analysis of the concept of cooperation in the Prisoner's Dilemma game: Some need structure correlates.* Unpublished doctoral dissertation, Syracuse University.

Richman, J. (1971). Concept of cooperation in the Prisoner's Dilemma and other tasks: Some need structure correlates. *Proceedings, 79th Annual Convention, APA, 5,* 227-228.

Riesman, D. (1958). The "Jacob report." *American Sociological Review, 23,* 732-738.

Riesman, D., in association with Glazer, N., & Denny, R. (1955). *The lonely crowd.* Garden City, NY: Doubleday.

Roberts, R. E. (1971). *The new communes: Coming together in America.* Englewood Cliffs, NJ: Prentice-Hall.

Robertson, M., & Hall, E. (no date). *Predicting success in graduate study.* Unpublished manuscript, Western Michigan University.

Rogers, C. R. (1949). A coordinated research in psychotherapy: A non-objective introduction. *Journal of Consulting Psychology, 13,* 169-175.

Rogers, C. R. (1957). A note on "the nature of man." *Journal of Consulting Psychology, 4,* 199-203.

Rogers, C. R. (1982). Reply to Rollo May's letter to Carl Rogers. *Journal of Humanistic Psychology, 22,* 85-89.

Rohter, L. (1989, August 7). A desert group lives by Skinner's precepts. *The New York Times,* pp. 17-18.

Rokeach, M., & Cochrane, R. (1972). Self-confrontation and confrontation with another as determinants of long-term value change. *Journal of Applied Social Psychology, 2,* 283-292.

Rosenberg, S., & Jones, R. A. (1972). A method for investigating a person's implicit theory of personality: Theodore Dreiser's view of people. *Journal of Personality and Social Psychology, 22,* 372-386.

Rosenthal, R. (1964). The effect of the experimenter on the results of psychological research. In B. A. Maher (Ed.), *Progress in experimental personality research* (Vol. I, pp. 79-114). San Diego: Academic Press.

Rosenthal, R. (1966). *Experimenter effects in behavioral research.* New York: Appleton-Century-Crofts.

Rosenthal, R., & Jacobson, L. (1968). *Pygmalion in the classroom: Teacher expectation and pupils' intellectual development.* New York: Holt, Rinehart & Winston.

Rosenthal, R., & Rosnow, R. L. (1969). The volunteer subject. In R. Rosenthal & R. L. Rosnow (Eds.), *Artifact in social research.* San Diego: Academic Press.

Roszak, T. (1969). *The making of a counter culture.* Garden City, NY: Anchor Books.

Rotter, J. B. (1954). *Social learning theory.* Englewood Cliffs, NJ: Prentice-Hall.

Rotter, J. B. (1966). Generalized expectancies for internal vs. external control of reinforcement. *Psychological Monographs, 80,* 1-28.

Rotter, J. B. (1967). A new scale for the measurement of interpersonal trust. *Journal of Personality, 35,* 651-665.

Rotter, J. B. (1971). Generalized expectancies for interpersonal trust. *American Psychologist, 26,* 443-452.

Rousseve, R. J. (1969). "Counselor, know thyself." *Personnel and Guidance Journal, 47,* 628-633.

Rubenstein, J. (1967). Maternal attentiveness and subsequent exploratory behavior in the infant. *Child Development, 38,* 1089-1100.

Rubin, Z., & Peplau, A. (1973). Belief in a just world and reaction to another's lot: A study of participants in the national draft lottery. *Journal of Social Issues, 29,* 73-93.

Rubin, Z., & Peplau, L. A. (1975). Who believes in a just world? *Journal of Social Issues, 31,* 65-90.

Russell, G. (1990). *Hans J. Morgenthau and the ethics of American statecraft.* Baton Rouge: Louisiana State University Press.

Sabine, G. H. (1961). *A history of political theory* (3rd ed.). New York: Holt, Rinehart & Winston.

Salinger, J. D. (1951). *The catcher in the rye.* Boston: Little, Brown.

Sanford, F. H. (1961). *Psychology: The scientific study of man.* Belmont, CA: Wadsworth.

Sanford, N. (1962a). Developmental status of the entering freshmen. In N. Sanford (Ed.), *The American college* (pp. 253-282). New York: John Wiley.

Sanford, N. (1962b). The effects of college education. In N. Sanford (Ed.), *The American college* (pp. 805-810). New York: John Wiley.

Sanford, N. (1965). Will psychologists study human problems? *American Psychologist, 20,* 192-202.

Sanford, N., Adkins, M. M., Miller, R. B., & Cobb, E. A. (1943). Physique, personality, and scholarship. *Monographs of the Society for Research in Child Development, 8*(1).

Sarbin, T., Taft, R., & Bailey, D. (1960). *Clinical inference and cognitive theory.* New York: Holt, Rinehart & Winston.

Sartre, J. P. (1947). *No exit and three other plays.* New York: Knopf.

Sawyer, J. (1966). The altruism scale: A measure of cooperative, individualistic, and competitive interpersonal orientation. *American Journal of Sociology, 71,* 407-416.

Sayegh, J., & Dennis, W. (1965). The effect of supplementary experiences upon the behavioral development of infants in institutions. *Child Development, 36,* 81-90.

Schaffer, H. R. (1965). Changes in developmental quotient under two conditions of maternal separation. *British Journal of Social and Clinical Psychology, 4,* 39-46.

Schaffer, R. C., & Schaffer, A. (1958). Socialization and the development of attitudes toward Negroes in Alabama. *Phylon, 19,* 274-285.

Schlenker, B. R., Helm, B., & Tedeschi, J. T. (1973). The effects of personality and situational variables on behavioral trust. *Journal of Personality and Social Psychology, 25,* 419-427.

Schlesinger, A., Jr. (1971). The necessary amorality of foreign affairs. *Harpers, 243*(1455), 72-77.

Schneider, D. J. (1971, September). *Non-linguist aspects of trait implication.* Symposium paper presented at the meetings of the American Psychological Association, Washington, DC.

Schoggen, M., & Schoggen, P. (1971). Environmental forces in the home lives of three-year-old children in three population subgroups. *DARCEE Papers and Reports,* No. 5, George Peabody College for Teachers.

Schroder, H. M., Driver, M. J., & Streufert, S. (1967). *Human information processing.* New York: Holt, Rinehart & Winston.

Scott, T. (1976). *Lord Chesterfield and his letters to his sons.* Folcroft, PA: Folcroft.

Scott, W. A. (1960). Measures of trait homogeneity. *Educational and Psychological Measurement, 20,* 751-757.

Scott, W. A. (1968). Attitude measurement. In G. Lindzey & E. Aronson (Eds.), *Handbook of social psychology* (2nd ed.) (Vol. 2, pp. 204-273). Reading, MA: Addison-Wesley.

Shayon, R. L. (1967). Which H. G. Wells was right? *Saturday Review, 50*(4), 50.

Shearer, L. (1967, October 29). The plight of American youth: No more heroes. *Parade,* pp. 4-7.

Shekelle, R. B., Gale, M., Ostfeld, A. M., & Paul, O. (1983). Hostility, risk of coronary heart disease, and mortality. *Psychosomatic Medicine, 45,* 109-114.

Shils, E. (1961). The calling of sociology. In T. Parsons, E. A. Shils, K. D. Naegele, & J. R. Pitts (Eds.), *Theories of society* (Vol. 2, pp. 1405-1450). New York: Free Press.

Silva, R. J. (1972). *The relationship between self/ideal-self congruence and philosophy of human nature.* Unpublished manuscript, George Peabody College for Teachers.

Simon, G. C. (1970). *Construction of a univocal measure of positive attitudes toward people and its relation to change in attitude toward amputees.* Unpublished doctoral dissertation, New York University.

Simon, G. C. (1972). The factorial invariance of attitudes toward people (ATP). *Journal of Social Psychology, 86,* 315-316.

Simons, C. W., & Piliavin, J. A. (1972). Effect of deception on reactions to a victim. *Journal of Personality and Social Psychology, 21,* 56-60.

Skinner, B. F. (1938). *The behavior of organisms.* New York: Appleton-Century-Crofts.

Skinner, B. F. (1948). *Walden two.* New York: Macmillan.

Skinner, B. F. (1971). *Beyond freedom and dignity.* New York: Knopf.

Slater, P. E. (1970). *The pursuit of loneliness: American culture at the breaking point.* Boston: Beacon.

Smith, J. E. (1958). *Value convictions and higher education.* New Haven, CT: Hazen Foundation.

Snow, R. E. (1969). Review of Rosenthal and Jacobson's "Pygmalion in the classroom." *Contemporary Psychology, 14,* 197-198.

Sowell, T. (1987). *A conflict of visions: Ideological origins of political struggles.* New York: William Morrow.

Spitz, R. (1945). Hospitalism: An inquiry into the genesis of psychiatric conditions in early childhood. In International Psychoanalytic Association (Ed.), *The psychoanalytic study of the child* (Vol. 1). New York: International Universities Press.

Spranger, E. (P.J.W. Pigors, Trans.). (1928). *Types of men.* Halle, Germany: Niemyer.

Stack, L. C. (1972a). *An empirical investigation of Erik Erikson's theory of the development of basic trust in three-year-old children.* Unpublished doctoral dissertation, George Peabody College for Teachers.

Stack, L. C. (1972b). *The philosophies of human nature of two groups of crisis-call volunteers.* Unpublished manuscript, George Peabody College for Teachers.

Stack, L. C. (1978). Trust. In H. London & J. E. Exner, Jr. (Eds.), *Dimensions of personality* (pp. 561-599). New York: John Wiley.

Stagner, R. (1961). *Psychology of personality* (3rd ed.). New York: McGraw-Hill.

Steinitz, H. (1987). *Fear versus hope: The comparative motivating effects of fear appeals and efficiency enhancement on attitudes and behavior toward nuclear weapons policy.* Unpublished master's thesis, University of Kansas.

Stevenson, L. (1987). *Seven theories of human nature* (2nd ed.). New York: Oxford University Press.

Suchman, E. A. (1958). The values of American college students. In A. E. Traxler (Ed.), *Long-range planning for education.* Washington, DC: American Council on Education.

Sullivan, J. L., Aldrich, J. H., Borgida, E., & Rahn, W. (1990). Candidate appraisal and human nature: Man and superman in the 1984 election. *Political Psychology, 11,* 459-484.

Swanberg, W. A. (1965). *Dreiser.* New York: Scribner.

Swede, S. W., & Tetlock, P. E. (1986). Henry Kissinger's implicit theory of personality: A quantitative case study. *Journal of Personality, 54,* 617-646.

Swingle, P. (Ed.). (1970). *The structure of conflict.* San Diego: Academic Press.

Tauber, P. (1971). *The sunshine soldiers.* New York: Ballantine.

Taylor, J. (1953). A personality scale of manifest anxiety. *Journal of Abnormal and Social Psychology, 48,* 285-290.

Terhune, K. W. (1968). Motives, situation, and interpersonal conflict within the Prisoner's Dilemma. *Journal of Personality and Social Psychology, 8,* 1-24.

Thomas, L. (1990, August 15). Next life, I'll be white. *The New York Times,* p. A15.

Tobias, A. (1989, July 31). I was a teenage Communist. *Time,* p. 39.

Toffler, A. (1970). *Future shock.* New York: Bantam Books.

Tryon, R. C., & Bailey, D. E. (1965, July 31). *User's manual of the BC TRY system of cluster and factor analysis* [Tape version for IBM 709, 7092, 7094 programs]. University of Colorado.

Tryon, R. C., & Bailey, D. E. (1966). The BC TRY computer system of cluster and factor analysis. *Multivariate Behavioral Research, 1,* 34.

Tryon, R. C., & Bailey, D. E. (1970). *Cluster analysis.* New York: McGraw-Hill.

Tuchman, B. W. (1967). The historian's opportunity. *Saturday Review, 50*(8), 27-31ff.

Tversky, A., & Kahneman, D. (1974). Judgment under uncertainty: Heuristics and biases. *Science, 185,* 1124-1131.

Tversky, A., & Kahneman, D. (1983). Extensional versus intuitive reasoning: The conjunction fallacy in probability judgment. *Psychological Bulletin, 90,* 293-315.

Tyler, L. E. (1965). *The psychology of human differences.* New York: Appleton-Century-Crofts.

Uejio, C. K., & Wrightsman, L. S. (1967). Ethnic-group differences in the relationship of trusting attitudes to cooperative behavior. *Psychological Reports, 20,* 563-571.

Underwood, B. J. (1957). *Psychological research.* New York: Appleton-Century-Crofts.

Unger, R. K. (1990, August). *Cross-cultural aspects of the Attitudes Toward Reality Scale.* Paper presented at the meetings of the American Psychological Association, Boston.

Unger, R. K., Draper, R. D., & Pendergrass, M. L. (1986). Personal epistemology and personal experience. *Journal of Social Issues, 42*(2), 67-79.

Valentine, E. (1982). *Conceptual issues in psychology.* London: Allen & Unwin.

Wainwright, L. (1964). The dying girl that no one helped. *Life, 56*(21), 21.

Wakefield, D. (1963). The search for love. In H. A. Grunwald (Ed.), *Salinger: A critical and personal portrait* (pp. 193-210). New York: Pocket Books.

Walker, D. E. (1956). Carl Rogers and the nature of man. *Journal of Counseling Psychology, 3,* 89-92.

Walker, E. L. (1970). *Psychology as a natural and social science.* Pacific Grove, CA: Brooks/Cole.

Walker, H. M., & Lev, J. (1953). *Statistical inference.* New York: Holt.

Wallach, M. A., & Wallach, L. (1983). *Psychology's sanction for selfishness: The error of egoism in theory and therapy.* San Francisco: Freeman.

Ward, L. M. (1968). *Separating the contributions of personality and attitudinal determinants of choice behavior in a two-person game.* Unpublished master's thesis, George Peabody College for Teachers.

Watson, G. (1957). Some personality differences in children related to strict or permissive parental discipline. *Journal of Personality, 44,* 227-249.

Weber, M. (1930). *The Protestant ethic and the spirit of capitalism.* London: Allen & Unwin.

Webster, H. (1958). Changes in attitude during college. *Journal of Educational Psychology, 49,* 109-118.

Wegner, D. M., & Vallacher, R. R. (1977). *Implicit psychology: An introduction to social cognition.* New York: Oxford University Press.

Weigert, E. (1962). The psychoanalytic view of personality. In S. Doniger (Ed.), *The nature of man* (pp. 3-21). New York: Harper & Row.

Weinstock, H. R., & Peccolo, C. M. (1970). Do students' ideas and attitudes survive practice teaching? *Elementary School Journal, 70,* 210-218.

Weir, J. A. (1990). *Judgments about rape victims: Blame, causality, and responsibility.* Unpublished manuscript, University of Kansas, Department of Psychology.

Weissberg, N. C. (1965). On DeFleur and Westie's "Attitude as a scientific concept." *Social Forces, 43,* 422-425.

Wells, H. G. (1971). *The time machine: An invention.* Cambridge, MA: Bentley. (Original work published 1895)

Wells, H. G. (1981). *The island of Dr. Moreau.* Cambridge, MA: Bentley. (Original work published 1896)

Westhues, K. (1972a). Hippiedom 1970: Some tentative hypotheses. *Sociological Quarterly, 13,* 81-89.

Westhues, K. (1972b). *On marginality and its solutions in contemporary society.* A lecture presented at St. Francis Xavier University, Antigonish, Nova Scotia.

Weyant, R. G. (1971, September). *Helvetius and Jefferson: Studies of human nature and government in the eighteenth century.* Paper presented at the meetings of the American Psychological Association, Washington, DC.

Whyte, W. H. (1957). *The organization man.* Garden City, NY: Doubleday.

Wicker, A. W. (1971). An examination of the "other variables" explanation of attitude-behavior inconsistency. *Journal of Personality and Social Psychology, 19,* 18-30.

Wiener, M., Carpenter, B., & Carpenter, J. (1956). Determination of defense mechanisms for conflict areas from verbal material. *Journal of Consulting Psychology, 20,* 215-219.

Wiggins, J. S. (1973). *Personality and prediction: Principles of personality assessment.* Reading, MA: Addison-Wesley.

Wilkinson, L. D., & Hood, W. D. (1973). Student responses to the Philosophies of Human Nature Scale. *Journal of College Student Personnel, 14*(5), 434-437.

Will, G. F. (1989, May 8). In the grip of gambling. *Newsweek,* p. 78.

Williams, R. B. (1989). *The trusting heart: Great news about Type A behavior.* New York: Random House.

Williams, R. B., Barefoot, J. C., & Shekelle, R. B. (1985). The health consequences of hostility. In M. A. Chesney, S. E. Goldston, & R. H. Rosenman (Eds.), *Anger, hostility, and behavioral medicine* (pp. 173-186). New York: Hemisphere.

Williams, R. M., Jr. (1964). *Strangers next door.* Englewood Cliffs, NJ: Prentice-Hall.

Winer, B. J. (1962). *Statistical principles in experimental design.* New York: McGraw-Hill.

Winter, G. (1966). *Elements for a social ethic.* New York: Macmillan.

Winter, M. S. (1969). *Risk taking and philosophical orientation among students in rehabilitation counseling and other selected social service and non-social service graduate programs.* Unpublished doctoral dissertation, University of Pittsburgh.

Wirth, L. (1936). Preface. In K. Mannheim, *Ideology and utopia: An introduction to the sociology of knowledge* (L. Wirth, Trans.). New York: Harcourt Brace Jovanovich.

Witkin, H. A., Lewis, H. B., Machover, K., Meissner, P. B., & Wapner, S. (1954). *Personality through perception.* New York: Harper & Row.

Wolcott, J. (1989, June). Rand inquisitor. *Vanity Fair,* pp. 32-38.

Wright, H. F. (1967). *Recording and analyzing child behavior: With ecological data from an American town.* New York: Harper & Row.

Wright, L. (1964, April). *Prediction of factors believed relevant to success in a church-related liberal arts college.* Paper presented at the meetings of the Southeastern Psychological Association, Gatlinburg, TN.

Wrightsman, L. S. (1964a). Measurement of philosophies of human nature. *Psychological Reports, 14,* 743-751.

Wrightsman, L. S. (1964b). Parental attitudes and behaviors as determinants of children's responses to the threat of nuclear war. *Vita Humana, 7,* 178-185.

Wrightsman, L. S. (1964c). Some subtle factors affecting students' evaluations of teachers. *S.P.A.T.E. Journal, 3,* 42-51.

Wrightsman, L. S. (1964d). Tender- and tough-minded interpretations of government policies. *American Behavioral Scientist, 7*(8), 7-8.

Wrightsman, L. S. (1965, September). *Attitudinal and personality correlates of presidential voting preferences.* Paper presented at the meetings of the American Psychological Association, Chicago.

Wrightsman, L. S. (1966). Personality and attitudinal correlates of trusting and trustworthy behaviors in a two-person game. *Journal of Personality and Social Psychology, 4,* 328-332.

Wrightsman, L. S. (1972). *Social psychology in the seventies.* Pacific Grove, CA: Brooks/Cole.

Wrightsman, L. S. (1977). *Social psychology* (2nd ed.). Pacific Grove, CA: Brooks/Cole.

Wrightsman, L. S. (1991). Interpersonal trust and attitudes toward human nature. In J. P. Robinson, P. R. Shaver, & L. S. Wrightsman (Eds.), *Measures of personality and social psychological attitudes* (pp. 373-412). San Diego: Academic Press.

Wrightsman, L. S., Baxter, G. W., Jr., Nelson, R. H., & Bilsky, L. (1969, April). *Effects of information about the other player and other player's game behavior upon cooperation in a mixed-motive game.* Paper presented at the meetings of the Western Psychological Association, Long Beach, CA.

Wrightsman, L. S., Bruininks, R., Lucker, W. G., & Anderson, W. H. (1972). Effect of subjects' training and college class and other's strategy upon cooperative behavior in a Prisoner's Dilemma. In L. S. Wrightsman, J. O'Connor, & N. Baker (Eds.), *Cooperation and competition: Readings in mixed-motive games* (pp. 126-140). Pacific Grove, CA: Brooks/Cole.

Wrightsman, L. S., & Cook, S. W. (1965, April). *Factor analysis and attitude change.* Paper presented at meetings of the Southeastern Psychological Association, Atlanta.

Wrightsman, L. S., Davis, D. W., Lucker, W. G., Bruininks, R., Evans, J., Wilde, R., Paulson, D., & Clark, G. (1967, May). *Effects of other person's race and strategy upon cooperative behavior in a Prisoner's Dilemma game.* Paper presented at meetings of the Midwestern Psychological Association, Chicago.

Wrightsman, L. S., Nelson, R. H., & Taranto, M. (1968). *The construction and validation of a scale to measure children's school morale.* Unpublished manuscript, George Peabody College for Teachers.

Wrightsman, L. S., & Noble, F. C. (1965). Reactions to the president's assassination and changes in philosophies of human nature. *Psychological Reports, 16,* 159-162.

Wrightsman, L. S., O'Connor, J., & Baker, N. J. (Eds.). (1972). *Cooperation and competition: Readings on mixed-motive games.* Pacific Grove, CA: Brooks/Cole.

Wrightsman, L. S., Richard, W. C., & Noble, F. C. (1966). Attitudes and attitude change in guidance institute participants. *Counselor and Educator Supervision, 5,* 212-220.

Wrightsman, L. S., & Satterfield, C. H. (1967, July). *Additional norms and standardization of the Philosophies of Human Nature—1967 revision.* Unpublished manuscript, George Peabody College for Teachers.

Wrightsman, L. S., Weir, J. A., & Brusewitz, K. K. (1991, May). *Consistency in beliefs about human nature.* Paper presented at meetings of the Midwestern Psychological Association, Chicago.

Wrightsman, L. S., Wrightsman, S., & Cook, S. W. (1964, November). *Test-retest reliability coefficients for 39 measures of personality, attitude, and response set.* Unpublished manuscript, George Peabody College for Teachers.

Wylie, R. C. (1957). Some relationships between defensiveness and self-concept discrepancies. *Journal of Personality, 25,* 600-616.

Wylie, R. C. (1961). *The self-concept: A critical survey of pertinent research literature.* Lincoln: University of Nebraska Press.

Yeargan, C. (1973). *A study of the effects of inner-city student teaching upon philosophies of human nature scores.* Unpublished manuscript, George Peabody College for Teachers.

Young, C. E., & Wrightsman, L. S. (1968, April). *The construction and validation of a scale to measure three factors in the philosophies of human nature of children.* Paper presented at the meetings of the Southeastern Psychological Association, Roanoke, VA.

Young, J. R. (1970). *The effects of laboratory training on self-concept, philosophies of human nature, and perceptions of group behavior.* Unpublished doctoral dissertation, George Peabody College for Teachers, Department of Special Education.

Zamyatin, E. (1972). *We* (M. Ginsburg, Trans.). New York: Viking.

Zdep, S. M., & Marco, G. L., (1969). Commentary on Kerlinger's structural theory of social attitudes. *Psychological Reports, 25,* 731-738.

Zelen, S. L. (1954). Acceptance and acceptability: An examination of social reciprocity. *Journal of Consulting Psychology, 18,* 316.

Zimmer, H. (1956). Motivational factors in dyadic interaction. *Journal of Personality, 24,* 251-261.

Zuckerman, M., Baer, M., & Monashkin, I. (1956). Acceptance of self, parents, and people in patients and normals. *Journal of Clinical Psychology, 53,* 315-320.

Name Index

Aaron, D., 279
Abramowitz, S. I., 76
Adkins, M. M., 118
Adorno, T. W., 217
Agger, R. E., 145
Ajzen, I., 198
Aldrich, J. H., 129
Ali, Muhammad, 60, 61
Allan, M., 136
Allport, G. W., 7, 17, 30, 61, 73, 75, 101, 198
Alter, J., 12
Altman, B. E., 254, 256
Anderson, J. P., 51
Anderson, R. L., 124, 127
Anderson, W. H., 193
Antiphon, 24
Argyris, C., 282, 284, 285, 288, 289
Aristotle, 30
Ashcraft, C. W., 133, 161, 177, 178, 179
Atyas, J., 275
Avila, D. C., 173

Bach, R., 13
Baer, M., 53
Bailey, D. E., 92, 141
Bailey, D., 49
Baker, J. R., 8, 9
Baker, N., 154, 155, 156, 188, 189, 224
Baldwin, A. L., 50

Baldwin, J., 119
Ballantyne, R. M., 8
Bannister, D., 36
Bar-Tal, D., 47
Barber, T. X., 204
Barefoot, J., 171, 172
Barker, R. G., 208
Barry, J., 158
Barton, A. H., 241
Batson, C. D., 13
Baumhart, R. C., 55
Baxter, G. W., Jr., 86, 87, 193, 194, 195, 196, 211, 212, 213, 240, 241, 243, 250, 251
Bayless, J. A., 117, 241, 250, 251
Beach, L. R., 242
Beattie, M., 77, 261
Bell, P. A., 158
Bellugi, U., 53
Bennis, W. G., 291
Berger, E. M., 53
Berger, P., 282, 284
Bettelheim, B., 47, 290
Bieri, J., 178, 179
Bilsky, L., 193, 194
Bird, C., 211
Birmingham, S., 281
Blake, R., 52
Blake, William, 240
Bliven, N., 275
Block, J., 227

351

Subject Index

About the Authors

Jonatha Atyas, now Jonatha Gibaud, received her PhD in clinical psychology from George Peabody College in 1977. She has been in independent practice of psychology in Nashville since that time, and is also a supervising psychologist at Vanderbilt University Psychological and Counseling Center. She specializes in marital therapy and relationship counseling, and is also active in promoting educational enrichment, and environmental awareness programs for young people.

Norma J. Baker, PhD, is Professor of Psychology at Belmont College, Nashville, TN, and served as Chair of the Department of Behavioral Science from 1975 to 1981. She earned her master's degree from the Southern Baptist Theological Seminary in Louisville, KY, and her doctorate in social psychology from George Peabody College for Teachers in Nashville. She served as president of the Middle Tennessee Psychological Association from 1988-1989, and is a member of Division 2, Teaching of Psychology, of the American Psychological Association. Her current research interests are in the area of death education, with particular attention to the topic of grief. She contributed a chapter on the nature of social change to Lawrence Wrightsman's *Social Psychology in the Seventies* (1st ed., 1972), and is co-editor (with Lawrence Wrightsman and John O'Connor) of *Cooperation and Competition: Readings in Mixed-Motive Games* (1971).

George W. Baxter, Jr., is a retired United Methodist Minister and Professor Emeritus, King College, Bristol, Tennessee. His research interests include altruism and helping with emphasis on children's altruism, attitudes toward amnesty, values and moral behavior, and age differences in attitudes toward human nature, among others. He was elected a Fellow in the Society for the Scientific Study of Religion and was honored with the Algernon Sydney Sullivan Award. He has published chapters and articles in scholarly books and journals.

Robert N. Claxton, PhD, is currently employed in the human resources development area, specializing in performance evaluation and associated supervisor and management training. He has a BS from Florida State University (1962), and earned both his master's degree (1971) and his doctorate (1974) from George Peabody College for Teachers. His research interests and publications are in the areas of attitude-behavior relationship, human organ donor motivation (paper presented at International Conference of Psychology and Medicine, Swansea, Wales in 1979), training and counseling programs for unskilled workers and prisoners, educational staff development and training, program evaluation, management and supervisory training, personnel research, performance evaluation, and other human resources development programs and consulting. He is a member of the American Psychological Association and of the Society for the Psychological Study of Social Issues.

Lois Stack studied with Lawrence S. Wrightsman at George Peabody College with special interests in children's development of trust. As a member of the Research Department of Hutchings Psychiatric Center in Syracruse, New York, for 12 years, she published articles in the areas of mental health and research methodology. In 1985, she became Associate Professor in a master's degree program for registered nurses at the State University of New York Health Science Center at Syracruse. There she developed and taught a new research curriculum, sponsoring many student theses related to health psychology and health care. She retired in 1988.

Lawrence S. Wrightsman, PhD, is Professor of Psychology at the University of Kansas, where he served as department chairperson from 1976 to 1981. For the academic year 1981-1982 he was Intra-University Visiting Professor at the University of Kansas School of Law. He received a BA and an MA from Southern Methodist University and a PhD degree from the University of Minnesota, where he specialized in social psychology and psychometrics. The author or editor of 15 books and numerous journal articles, he has also served as President of the Society for the

Psychological Study of Social Issues (SPSSI) and the Society of Personality and Social Psychology (Division 8 of the American Psychological Association). In 1989 he delivered the first G. Stanley Hall Lecture on the topic of psychology and the law at the American Psychological Association convention. He is one of the editors, along with John P. Robinson and Phillip Shaver, of the recently published handbook titled *Measures of Personality and Social Psychological Attitudes.*

Carl E. Young, PhD, works for Green Spring Mental Health Services, a managed care company, and is the state Clinical Director for Maine and Rhode Island. He was a full-time faculty member at Peabody College (Vanderbilt University), Johns Hopkins Department of Psychiatry and Behavioral Sciences, and the Pennsylvania State University (University Park). He did research on natural care-giving in rural areas and directed an NIMH-funded doctoral program in mental health planning and administration. He had a full-time private practice in California for five years—more recently with family courts (custody issues), law firms (developmental issues and economics), and churches (pastor-congregation conflicts).